MW01480262

and with awe how this goal was sought and achieved by a distant island nation in the face of competition by the sprawling and avaricious United States. Read and savour this book to understand the Anglo-American past in the Pacific and what it means for today and tomorrow."

KENNETH J. HAGAN, Professor and Museum Director Emeritus,
US Naval Academy Captain, US Naval Reserve (Ret.)

"In this book, Professor Barry Gough has told the enthralling story of how the Royal Navy created, developed, and sustained its Pacific station, which became the largest in the British Empire during the nineteenth century. These far-sighted actions not only developed the Esquimalt naval base but they also secured the settlement of British Columbia in the face of threats from Russian territorial expansion, American Manifest Destiny, encroachment, gold prospectors from California, and Fenian filibusterers. This book is a stimulating product of Gough's fifty years of work as an historian deeply involved in British and Canadian naval traditions."

WILLIAM S. DUDLEY, PhD,
former Director, US Naval Historical Center

"*Britannia's Navy* updates and enhances a classic that shaped the study of imperial maritime peripheries. The new edition develops the role of the British captains and admirals who commanded the station and the critical relationship they had with London policy makers at the Admiralty, the Foreign and Colonial Offices, which shaped local policies and their relation with Britain's global economic and strategic position. These relationships depended on an ever improving system of global communications that linked the centre and Imperial periphery, by steamship, telegraph cable and finally wireless. At the same time the presence of the fleet and the development of support facilities, including the vital dry dock, enabled British Columbia to support a modern, efficient British fleet, and the growth of oceanic going commercial steam shipping. The synergy of strategic and commercial interests within the Imperial system, and the security the Navy provided for local communities shaped by the ocean, did much to promote regional economic development. By 1900 the North West Coast was a fully integrated link in the British global system. The Royal Navy played a critical role in the development of British Columbia, from securing the borders with the United States to promoting economic activity, and has left an indelible legacy on Canada's west coast."

ANDREW LAMBERT,
Professor of Naval History, King's College, London

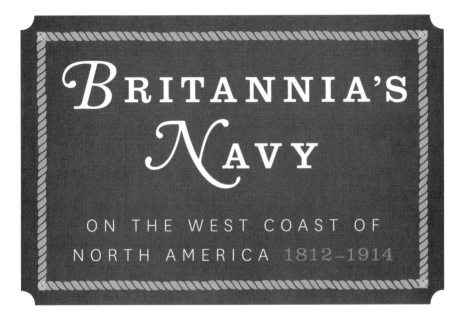

BRITANNIA'S NAVY

ON THE WEST COAST OF NORTH AMERICA 1812–1914

BARRY GOUGH

foreword by

ADMIRAL (Ret'd) JOHN ANDERSON

VICTORIA · VANCOUVER · CALGARY

Heritage House Publishing Company Ltd.
heritagehouse.ca

LIBRARY AND ARCHIVES CANADA CATALOGUING IN PUBLICATION

Gough, Barry M., 1938– [The Royal Navy and the Northwest Coast of North America, 1810–1914]
Britannia's Navy on the West Coast of North America, 1812–1914 / Barry M. Gough.

Revision of: The Royal Navy and the Northwest Coast of North America, 1810-1914 : a study of British maritime ascendancy / [by] Barry M. Gough. — Vancouver, University of British Columbia Press, [1971] Includes bibliographical references and index.

Issued in print and electronic formats.
ISBN 978-1-77203-109-6 (bound).—ISBN 978-1-77203-110-2 (epub).— ISBN 978-1-77203-111-9 (pdf)

1. Great Britain. Royal Navy. 2. Northwest Coast of North America—History. I. Title. II. Title: Royal Navy and the Northwest Coast of North America, 1810–1914

F851.G6 2016   979.5   C2015-908103-3   C2015-908104-1

Edited by Audrey McClellan
Proofread by Karla Decker
Cover and interior book design by Jacqui Thomas
Cover illustrations, front: HMS *Plumper* in Port Harvey, Johnstone Strait, by E.P. Bedwell, 1862. Heritage House Collection; and *back:* The light cruiser *Rainbow,* of the Royal Canadian Navy, lies in Esquimalt Harbour during a snowy January 1911. Acquired for training purposes, she was pressed into action in 1914 and went in search of the German warship *Leipzig,* failing to make contact. Photo courtesy of CFB Esquimalt Naval & Military Museum.
Maps by University of British Columbia Press

The interior of this book was produced on 100% post-consumer recycled paper, processed chlorine free and printed with vegetable-based inks.

We acknowledge the financial support of the Government of Canada through the Canada Book Fund and the Canada Council for the Arts, and the Province of British Columbia through the British Columbia Arts Council and the Book Publishing Tax Credit.

20 19 18 17 16 1 2 3 4 5

Printed in Canada

To P.W.B.

Contents

$\mathcal{L}$IST OF ABBREVIATIONS

Adm. Admiralty or Admiralty Records in TNA

BCA British Columbia Archives, Victoria, BC

Bod. L. Bodleian Library, Oxford

BL British Library Manuscripts (formerly in the British Museum), London

BT Board of Trade Records in TNA

Cab. Cabinet Papers in TNA

CDC Colonial Defence Committee

CMS Church Missionary Society or Church Missionary Society Records, University of Birmingham

CO Colonial Office or Colonial Office Records in TNA

FO Foreign Office or Foreign Office Records in TNA

HBC Hudson's Bay Company

HBCA Hudson's Bay Company Archives, Winnipeg, Manitoba

HM Her/His Majesty

HMCS Her/His Majesty's Canadian Ship

HMS Her/His Majesty's Ship

HMSO His/Her Majesty's Stationery Office

HO Hydrographer's Office, Taunton, Somerset

KCB/CB Knight Commander or Companion of the Order of the Bath

LAC Library and Archives Canada, Ottawa, Ontario

MMBC Maritime Museum of British Columbia, Victoria, BC

NL Naval Library, Ministry of Defence, Royal Naval Museum, Portsmouth, England

NMM National Maritime Museum, Greenwich (now part of Royal Museums Greenwich)

PRO Public Records Office

RCS Royal Commonwealth Society Collections, Cambridge University Library, Cambridge

RE Royal Engineers

RM Royal Marines

RMLI Royal Marine Light Infantry

RN Royal Navy

TNA The National Archives, Kew, Surrey

USN United States Navy

USS United States Ship

WO War Office or War Office Records in TNA

WRO Warwickshire Record Office, Warwick

12n26 In a bibliographic note, refers to, in this example, note 26 on page 12

$\mathcal{F}$OREWORD

Over fifty years ago, as a young passenger on a CPR "Princess" ferry en route to Victoria from Vancouver, I had my first glimpse of what we know today as the Gulf Islands. For a young boy from the Interior of British Columbia, these islands were intriguing. Even more interesting was the way the ferry found its way and, as we neared Victoria, wove rapidly through a narrow channel with lots of rocks on both sides.

In the golden anniversary year of the Royal Canadian Navy, I began my seagoing naval training on the west coast in the Prestonian Class frigate HMCS *New Glasgow*, based out of HMC Dockyard in Esquimalt, BC. Intensive at-sea training in coastal navigation introduced me to many of these islands and the channels and straits that ran between them. Island names, lighthouse locations, channel names and anchorages became second nature. We cadets had little time to question how these names came to be used. Nor did we spend much time wondering why the Dockyard was where it was and how it had developed. There was a tiny maritime museum on Signal Hill, just off Esquimalt Road, but any free time we had was spent adventuring into Victoria, sleeping, or polishing our boots for the following morning's parade.

In the late 1970s, as the commanding officer of the destroyer HMCS *Restigouche*, my exposure to these shores in fair and foul weather was intense. Operational requirements often took us to the inside passages on the east coast of Vancouver Island, in any and all conditions: day, night, fog, and rain, at speeds varying from a comfortable 12 to 15 knots to a sphincter-tightening 20 to 25 knots. Winds and tides were taken into account, but they were rarely limiting to movement. Operational readiness was our raison d'être.

Always busy, I spent little time wondering about how Esquimalt came into existence as a naval base. Nor was the question of early, pre–Royal Canadian Navy, naval activity on the west coast a curiosity. Fortunately for us, Barry Gough, early in his academic career, in satisfaction of his Ph.D. degree at Kings College University of London, did examine these questions and the much broader issue of the significant influence of the British Navy in the formation of the province of British Columbia. This led to the original version of this book being published by UBC Press in 1971.

For those with an interest in the enabling role of sea power in a nation's interests and objectives, this updated version of the original book is a must-read. Barry Gough illustrates how many of the factors national governments struggle with today were present long ago. This includes international relations, government priorities, internal tensions between different departments of government, lack of financial resources, personalities of the key leaders involved in decision making (all men in the nineteenth and early twentieth century), the use of the British Navy in support of government objectives, the role played by key naval leaders and the impact of maritime technological development.

As the author moves us through the decades of the nineteenth century, we are treated to many instances of how the Royal Navy was used to further British interests. As he tells us, it "is best described as achieving peace for the purpose of profit." As the story develops, the harbour we now know as Esquimalt emerges as an important geographic hub for the British Navy. It offered sanctuary from the winter storms, an opportunity to refresh water and wood for the ships, a chance for ships' companies to get ashore to hunt and fish. Eventually coal and vittles were available, and as the nearby Hudson's Bay post of Victoria developed into a thriving town, the sailors could enjoy a real "run ashore." All very nice, but most significantly the Navy based there became the main British agency supporting the colonial government, hydrographic surveying and cross-cultural relations.

In updating the original book, Barry Gough has returned to the foundation of his lifelong passion for researching, teaching and writing about the historical influences on the development of North America westward from the Great Lakes. His writings have been published extensively. When first published in 1971, the original edition of this book—Barry Gough's first major published work—carved out a new slice of our then long-neglected history. He now presents an even stronger argument for the importance of sea power in British Columbia's early political, social, economic and cultural development. The content of this new book from this eminent Canadian historian and author firmly establishes the link from the nineteenth-century maritime history of my province to the beginning days of the Royal Canadian Navy—my navy.

—JOHN ANDERSON, ADMIRAL (RET'D), SIDNEY, BC

$\mathcal{P}$REFACE

Although not the first masters of global power projection, for the laurels on that account go to Portugal and Spain, with the Dutch and French also exhibiting worldwide reach, the British soon became influential on every ocean and every sea—and in the Pacific Ocean, the focus of our study. The process had begun with the "swing to the east" to that vast oceanic world lying between the Cape of Good Hope and Cape Horn, the scene of British commercial and military interests in the age of captains James Cook and George Vancouver, and it continued after Trafalgar and the defeat of Napoleon at Waterloo. The eighteenth-century voyages of the British won for that nation a primacy of influence in the Pacific. Then came the long years between 1815 and 1914 that saw British merchant shipping and British warships extending their influence on every sea. As Mistress of the Seas, Britain merely had to send warships to "show the flag" and investigate rumours of trouble or counter the threats of rivals. All the same, many were the challengers to this primacy, and after the Napoleonic Wars and the War of 1812, and throughout the years to 1914, some new and surprising aspirants entered the field.

Sir William Thomson, Lord Kelvin, the great master of practical science of the nineteenth century, once said that the circumnavigation of the globe under sail marked a notable advance in human progress because it used the natural forces of the elements on a vast scale to serve human ends. Indeed, the trade winds conferred many benefits, and sailing round the world was common by the nineteenth century. Completing that global circuit required getting round Cape Horn, which posed the greatest challenge to ships and sailors. Passage was made in unavoidably high latitudes, where storms were frequent, fog and snow were common, and making observations for longitude and latitude were complicated as the sun was obscured for long periods. By dint of grim experience, mariners learned that when shaping a course from Rio de Janeiro to Valparaiso, in order to deal with the perennial prevalence of strong westerlies, a starboard tack would have to be taken into high southern latitudes and well south of the Horn before gradually hauling northward and squaring the yards for a passage north to the Chilean port— taking perhaps 55 days. In the reverse direction, 39 days might be required, sometimes passing within sight of Cape Horn itself. By the 1840s the Royal Navy had mastered these passages—and discovered that rounding the Horn was always best in winter. After the Panama Canal was opened in 1914, the Horn was almost forgotten, but for the nineteenth century it was the great challenge for ships and sailors, witnessing the rise and fall of sea powers and the making and unravelling of empires, and even today "the Cape Horn breed" are spoken of with greatest reverence.

As the diligent students of ocean voyages collected from ships' logs all the statistical data on the best passages, they made the road past the Horn easier. The heroes in this line of work are Alexander George Findlay and particularly Matthew Fontaine Maury, USN, founder of marine meteorology. *Maury's Sailing Directions*, 1851, indicated passages that would shorten voyages by several days. He had collected observations on wind, weather, temperature of sea and air, atmospheric pressure and other items of interest. Gathered together, they gave the greatest benefit to mariners, and sailing the Great Circle route between British Columbia and Asia came into its own in the nineteenth century. As for barometric pressure, Captain Robert FitzRoy of brig HMS *Beagle*, in which Darwin sailed, was first to recommend the use of the barometer to forecast changes in weather, the amount and rate of change being important.

Beyond Cape Horn, on the Pacific shores of South America, the Admiralty chart was incomplete and the Spanish charts only recently released, and in 1831 FitzRoy had been sent, succeeding Captain Phillip Parker King, to work the waters north to the Galapagos. The results of these surveys meant that from Rio south to the Horn, then north to the Galapagos, ships, naval and merchant, had charts that favoured safe navigation and promoted trade. Thus did opportunities for British merchants open in Latin America and in the islands of the Pacific.

The sea road to the Northwest Coast lay via the Hawaiian Islands, and after Cook's visit to Nootka Sound and Alaska in 1778, many British and Boston merchant ships came this way in search of Native partners in the sea-otter trade, the otter's pelt being the first commodity exported from the Northwest Coast to China. Fur traders and explorers approached the Northwest Coast overland in the face of geographical complexities. At the same time, the manufactures of the Industrial Revolution—muskets, balls and powder, traps and spear tips, hooks and awls—were subverting Native economies and changing irrevocably a way of life. It was the conjunction of these forces during the War of 1812 that brought the future of this area into question.

The rivalry between Imperial Spain and Great Britain over Nootka, resolved by the Nootka Convention in 1790, was essentially about rights of trade and navigation. It marked the flood tide of Spanish ambitions in those latitudes. The War of 1812 brought the United States into the imperial sweepstakes. In the long course of events that followed, the United States became the principal sea power in the Pacific, but all the while there were other contenders in addition to the British—the French, the Japanese and the Russians. What happened on the Northwest Coast, and particularly in British Columbia, was part of a much greater drama.

This book links parts of the globe that were half a world apart from one another. It will always be a matter of wonder how a cluster of off-shore islands adjacent to the continent of Europe came to be the greatest exponent of globalization in the nineteenth century and the most formidable commercial and armed power at sea. One of the central themes of this book is how the British exercised their naval power economically and with effect to obtain their twin purposes, the pursuit of power and the pursuit of profit, in equal measure. This is not a study in drum and bugle history. Rather, it is a story of responding to the needs of the day as they arose. It will be seen that the British never had a grand design to their expansive tendencies. They had no theory of imperialism or of empire. Above all they wanted peace for the purpose of profit, and they fought for stable governments in distant places, and stable places for their investments. They promoted free trade and freedom of the seas—interchangeable ambitions or requirements. That free trade benefitted all nations was an understandable feature of British thinking: the view was that what was good for Britain was good for the rest of the world. The British fought the slave trade and abolished slavery in the British Empire. And, not least, they sought to establish the rule of law on the new frontiers of their influence.

The role of fur traders has dominated early western Canadian and American history. Less well known is the role of the Admiralty, the Foreign and Colonial Offices, and the ships, officers and men of the Royal Navy in "showing the flag" and exercising that form of influence known as gunboat diplomacy out on the western flank of the Americas. British intentions were to promote peace for the benefit of commerce and to avoid territorial additions to an already large imperial estate. But foreign rivals did not always permit such a quiet scenario. In the face of aggressive Russians coming south out of the fog banks of the Alaskan coast, and land-hungry Americans pressing into the Columbia and Willamette River valleys, the British Foreign Office was able, against the odds, to secure the boundaries of the area now known as British Columbia. All this was an exercise in sea power. Just as Britain, during the Nootka Crisis, forced Spain by raising a dominant naval force known in British chronicles as "the Spanish armament," so did it threaten to use naval force to secure British Columbia's northern and southern boundaries—and preserve the whole vast cordilleran area for the British Empire. Why, we might wonder, did they ever bother?

We now know that the British acted with great reluctance in this territorial acquisition. The British nation was "a nation of shopkeepers," as Napoleon said. Commercial expansion remained the goal, whether in the days of mercantile regulation or in the era of free trade that came at mid-century. It mattered little to the British if they added yet another acre to their real estate. They had acquired the Cape of Good Hope to keep out the French, New South Wales as a penal settlement, and various places such as Malta and the Falkland Islands as bases of resupply and security. They otherwise preferred trade to dominion.

But in all things, the British linked profit and power—a reciprocal combination. They made their fortunes from trade, manufacturing and others forms of commerce, including shipping, banking and insurance. They got their security by exercise of their power, and in this last they had two guardians of the *Pax Britannica*—regiments and men-of-war. The British had mastered the art of flexible response. Their fantastic ability to deploy force on a global scale, even in the age of sail, is a fact that boggles the mind nowadays. The British could dominate the seven seas as they wished. But at the same time the War Office sought no more islets or coasts where a battery had to be mounted and garrisoned. Colonial outposts needed to be defended, often by expensive fortifications. The Admiralty was prepared to "show the flag" as required, but on no condition were naval brigades to be sent ashore and into difficult and intractable circumstances. These were features of the "little England" era.

If territorial expansion occurred, however, and the Union Jack was run up on a flagstaff with London's approval, then an entirely different scenario opened to view. "What we have we hold," said the queen, Victoria, and thus it was that once sovereignty was secured on Vancouver Island (and its dependencies, including the mainland), naval power was exercised more forcefully, almost as a God-given right. Given the remoteness of British Columbia—its splendid isolation until the Canadian Pacific Railway arrived at Pacific tidewater in 1885, and the settler migration overland, especially from Ontario, commenced—this was a trading frontier. The history of British Columbia is the history of transportation and thus of communications. The Navy provided the first network and the first web of unity, ably backing up the governors and their agents. It stood strongly against the forces of American Manifest Destiny. This was the gift of British sea power, the protector of profit and power—and the enforcer of law and order.

And what of the officers and men? As a rule, the admirals and captains of Royal Navy ships sailing to the Pacific, as to other distant stations, were of high professional competence. They breathed the spirit of Nelson. They were proud of their service. A self-selecting class, their admission into the Navy and their advancement depended on their reputation, skills in seamanship, and adherence to discipline and the requirements of the service. All the admirals mentioned in this book "knew the ropes," had gone aloft in high winds as midshipmen or cadets, had worked their way up the ladder by application, zeal and good luck. Seniority was the thing, and advancement was often achieved by "walking in dead men's shoes." However, some had been on half pay for years, and professional competence in these persons sagged terribly. Rear-Admiral David Price, "on the beach" for 22 years, finally got his flag, which he wore, or flew, in HMS *President*. When the pressure of war came upon him, he shot himself and died—an episode in the disastrous fight against the Russians at Petropavlovsk, Kamchatka Peninsula, that is told in chapter 5. Price was an exception. Most admirals were excellent and courageous commanders: Sir George Seymour, masterful in deploying ships from an overstretched squadron in the mid-1840s, when tensions seemed to exist everywhere—Tahiti, Hawaii, Alta California and Oregon; Fairfax Moresby and the Honourable Joseph Denman, forthright in promoting British interests; Robert Lambert Baynes, a true strategic visionary who, almost as the godfather of the piece, saw the necessity of Esquimalt as an anchor of British sea power tied to commercial and colonial prospects; and, perhaps the last, Andrew Kennedy Bickford, who in frustration told the Lords of the Admiralty that the ships supplied to him were ludicrously small in number to counter the rise of the United States Navy, and who received a rebuke for his unmistakably correct appreciation of the affairs of the North Pacific world at the close of the nineteenth century and the beginning of the twentieth.

As for the captains, some stand out by their deeds or their opinions. Very poor marks go to Captain the Honourable John Gordon of the *America*, who preferred to profit from the conveyance of specie (a legal arrangement with Mexican authorities, mind) and did so when only the smallest of margins existed in naval units against French and United States rivals. Among the many Royal Navy captains who merit abundant praise are the Honourable Thomas Baillie, who in his sloop kept a long watch in the Columbia River during the heated crisis over Oregon; George Courtenay, who revealed Esquimalt's merits; Geoffrey Phipps Hornby, who was in the hot seat during the San Juan Island "Pig War" crisis; and Commander Mist, who in his gunvessel did important work for the *Pax Britannica* on difficult and distant shores. As amphibious diplomats dealing with problems of murder and piracy, or anti-smuggling and liquor trade suppression, some officers stand out. Some were high-handed: Nicholas Turnour of the *Clio*, who shelled Fort Rupert, or Anthony Denny of the gunboat *Forward*, on the police beat. Others were of higher vision and were less interventionist: James Prevost and George Henry Richards come immediately to mind.

Winston Churchill was once asked if he had said that the traditions of the Navy were rum, sodomy and the lash, and he answered that, no, he had not said that but wished he had. Throughout the age, the sailors, or bluejackets, and the marines (later Royal Marines) were true to their calling and station. Working under close supervision, devilishly demanding rules and regulations, and often situations of deprivation (for the ocean passages under sail were long), they showed pride in their work and shared in the glory of being in the world's premier navy. Of course, they got drunk ashore, brawled and made nuisances of themselves, and sometimes they deserted to the nearest American territory, particularly if gold-rush mania was raging. Sodomy was punishable by death. The lash continued as punishment in the fleet and has never been repealed. It was a tough world, and could not be endured by today's youth. Their parents would not tolerate it. The social fabric of Britannia—the officers and men—existed in a time and in circumstances that enabled global reach in the well-built and well-provisioned ships of the Navy. British supremacy at sea was extended to the coasts of the Americas and to British Columbia's waters in the age of fighting sail.

As rifled guns, steam propulsion, iron hulls, armoured vessels, mines, torpedoes and eventually the submarine and naval aviation appeared, the Senior Service made the shift to modern mechanized warfare, so that by 1914, the end of our epoch in this book, British sea power was as vitally important as it had been in the age of Nelson, but the distribution and deployment of ships on distant stations answered more directly to London. For most of the century it was the individual officer who assessed the nature of the situation facing him, tried to imagine what their Lordships would find acceptable in the circumstances, and then conducted the quarterdeck diplomacy or gunboat action to preserve British and colonial interests. Only when problems arose in the form of murder or piracy did they intervene; otherwise, they left the local villages and peoples alone. This was the unstated British maxim. Throughout the Pacific world, the *Pax Britannica* was being extended, and the sight of a sloop of war or a gunboat brought an age of transformation to the coasts and ocean world that lay beyond Cape Horn.

In the management of their vast imperial estate, the British had to address the concerns raised by powerful domestic segments of British society. None was more important than those who fought for the abolition of the slave trade and the abolition of slavery in the Empire. With victory won, "the saints" turned their attention to a new challenge: the humanitarian lobby sought protection for aboriginal peoples in the British Empire, and it had a powerful and effective committee of the House of Commons on this subject in 1837. As noted, the British were reluctant imperialists. The Colonial Office wanted no further territories to administer. "Rule Britannia" was exercised around the world in support of British trade but never more forcefully than in support of British sovereignty ashore. The consolidation of power in places of sovereign control overseas unavoidably brought the British into often-anguished relations with aboriginal peoples. South Africa and New Zealand are the most dramatic examples, and long frontier wars were fought in each. British Columbia does not bear direct comparison, but as will be seen in chapter 8, all the horrors of cross-cultural violence were exhibited here. The standards of exercising control were different then than now, and the wonder of it all is that, given the militant capabilities of the various First Nation tribes, there were not more violent episodes than are outlined here. In matters of the murder of whites or of Native piracy against settlers, the Crown was obliged to intervene here as elsewhere in the Empire. In that era, as in ours, thoughtful minds turned on questions of whether the punishment met the crime and if justice had been tempered by mercy. It will always be a matter of regret that in the processes of globalization, Indigenous peoples and cultures were transformed and, on occasion, eradicated; languages disappeared; Native domains were curtailed or eliminated; "savage wars of peace" occurred.

The process of history is like an ever-flowing stream, and the historian has the advantage of being able to look back in time, to a certain event (or series of events) that show the interface of societies and technologies. Those of us who have written colonial and imperial histories, explored the interaction of settler societies and Indigenous peoples, and examined some of the violent and coercive encounters, are invariably saddened by what the documents have revealed all too clearly to us. I hope in this book I have given the reader an indication of the grinding circumstances that led to such unhappy events. One can only express regret at the ultimate results and some hope that in peace and reconciliation, wrongs of the past can be rectified. All the same, it is clear that authorities of the nineteenth century acted on different principles than do those of the current day. The trick for the historian is to make sure that those past voices are not silenced, no matter how reprehensible they may be in our own times.

Fifty years ago I began research into a topic that in due course became a ruling passion for me in the historian's line of work. Originally a study of the influence of sea power upon history in a specific quarter of the world, the Northwest Coast of North America, it grew into a fascination with yesteryear's ships and the sailors of the world's then pre-eminent navy, Great Britain's Royal Navy. From the perspective of London, the Northwest Coast was surely the world's farthest shore—out of sight and out of mind. Globalization, the course of human affairs, ended remoteness. The west coast of North America became a flashpoint in international rivalries, from the crucial years of the late eighteenth century right through to the outbreak of the First World War. Against a dramatic backdrop of international rivalry for the control of the lands from California north to Alaska and for the possession of Hawaii, British Columbia was secured to the British Crown by two means—the commercial activities of fur traders overland from Canada and Hudson Bay, and, of greater significance, the British government's use of the naval means of propping up British trade and territorial claims in the area.

The essence of this book appeared in 1971 as *The Royal Navy and the Northwest Coast of North America, 1810–1914: A Study of British Maritime Ascendancy.* It was the inaugural title of the University of British Columbia Press (now UBC Press). This work appears here in revised form, with additional information on settler–First Nations conflict and accommodation based on another book of mine, published by UBC Press in 1984, *Gunboat Frontier: British Maritime Authority and Northwest Coast Indians, 1846–1890.* That book examined the dimensions and the dilemmas of the *Pax Britannica* when it came to the extension of law in the face of Native resistance. In those works, as in this, I owe abundant thanks to archivists and librarians in the United Kingdom, the United States and Canada for help in locating documents that were often difficult to find. An inventory of persons who have guided this book and helped in various ways will be found in the Acknowledgements, but here I wish to extend thanks to Heritage House, and especially to Rodger Touchie, Lara Kordic and Leslie Kenny, for bringing this book to fruition, and I thank Audrey McClellan, my esteemed editor, for excellent work. I alone am responsible for errors and omissions.

—BARRY M. GOUGH, Trafalgar Day 2015

INTRODUCTION

From offshore, a bold flank of hills and mountains could be seen rising in the distance, the shades of grey, green and slate tantalizing to the eye. Snow-capped crags and volcanoes stood as silent witnesses, or sentinels, to the earth's violent eruptions of yesteryear. Closer to the shore, islands and passages presented themselves as if the very stuff of legend and even historical enchantment. Indeed, this had been, in European circles, a subject of much speculation, a theatre of geographical possibilities faced by the early explorers who came by sea and later by land. By the end of the eighteenth century, all that had been laid to rest: the geographic generalities had been set down, if a little boldly. Once inshore, mariners faced a maze of rock and water, with straits, sounds and inlets leading to destinations that could only be imagined. Some of the islands were the world's largest, others mere islets. And as if this labyrinth were not complicated enough, tides and currents, fogs and mirages added to the dangers and to the mystery of this world of rock and water.

That lengthy arc of mountainous and forested land bordering the northeastern quarter of the Pacific Ocean was known to eighteenth-century European navigators as the Northwest Coast of North America. No more accurate geographical name exists today for the Pacific littoral, which runs from Cape Mendocino on the upper California coast to about where the Aleutian archipelago extends from southwestern Alaska. Everywhere the coast is rugged, but more especially so south of Cape Flattery, where good harbours are rare and, in the days of sail, the Columbia River mouth provided a hazardous entrance to the broad and fertile lands of the rich

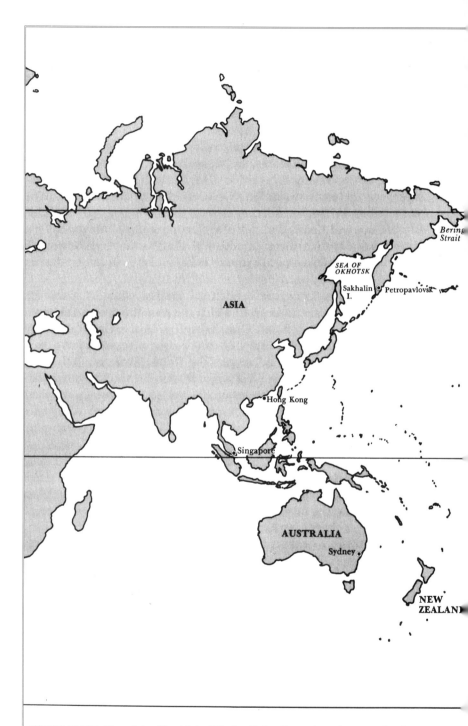

Bering
Strait

SEA OF
OKHOTSK

Sakhalin
I.

Petropavlovsk

ASIA

Hong Kong

Singapore

AUSTRALIA

Sydney

NEW
ZEALAND

CIRCLE 66¼° N.

Sitka

NORTH
AMERICA

London

Esquimalt

San Francisco

Guaymas
Mazatlan
olulu   Tepic
aiian Is.   San Blas
Acapulco

Panama

EQUATOR 0°   Galapagos Is.

Guayaquil

Marquesas Is.
y Is.   Callao   SOUTH
ahiti   AMERICA
Is.
Pitcairn Is.   Rio de Janeiro

Valparaiso
Juan Fernandez Is.

Falkland Is.

500   0   500 1000   Miles

Oregon plain. At Cape Flattery, the welcome waters of Juan de Fuca Strait reach inland and then south into Puget Sound and north into the Strait of Georgia and beyond, where constricted narrows divide Vancouver Island from the mainland. North of Vancouver Island, and stretching to the north and west, the coast is characterized by certain large islands including Haida Gwaii (formerly the Queen Charlotte Islands) and the Alexander Archipelago of southeast Alaska. The entrance to Cook Inlet, where Anchorage, Alaska, now stands, may serve arbitrarily as the northern extremity of the Northwest Coast of North America.

When sailing the coast of this irregular and mountainous landscape, Captain George Vancouver and others remarked that they found it heavily treed with conifers. In their coastal passages these mariners experienced heavy rains in the north and thick fogs everywhere, depending on the season. They were sailing largely uncharted seas. Fish and wildlife were abundant in numerous places along the shore, such as Nootka Sound on Vancouver Island. Whales, sea otters and other sea mammals were in plentiful numbers. The mariners also found Indigenous tribes whose distinctive cultures were based on both the land and the sea. In the late eighteenth century it seemed to observers such as Captain Vancouver that the Native populations were small in number and possibly diminished on account of disease or pestilence. In the mid-nineteenth century the Native villages seemed larger, though the prevalence of diseases, notably smallpox and syphilis, and high rates of consumption of alcoholic beverages, as well as instances of prostitution, gave solemn and unwelcome warning of demographic crises that lay ahead.

Situated some eighteen thousand miles from Europe by the shortest sea lane via Cape Horn, the Northwest Coast was a remote quarter of the globe in the late eighteenth century. Yet the steady expansion of European nations by sea, and of the United States, primarily by land, were to end this isolation.

Typically, one of His Majesty's ships sailing from Portsmouth for assignment on the Pacific station would steer for the Canaries, where fruit and wines were taken on board, as well as water. Then a course would be shaped for Rio de Janeiro, a Portuguese and later Brazilian port, where the British had provisioning contracts despite tetchy difficulties with officialdom. Then it was south toward the Falkland Islands and round Cape Horn (assuming the route via Magellan Strait was not taken—this became more common when steam navigation was introduced). Even before William Bligh's time, the Cape was the dread of mariners. Viewers of *Master and Commander: The Far Side of the World*, the film of 2003, will see actual footage taken in these seas, as experienced by a replica of Captain James Cook's *Endeavour.* "It used to be a saying in the old Navy," the midshipman John Moresby recounted in 1844, "that no ship could round the Horn against the fierce September gales, but we did it after a slant to 60 degrees south, battered and torn till not a rag of spare canvas was left. We youngsters, shivering in the night watches under the icy draught from the main-trysail, did easily believe that we saw the wind devils in actual shape grinning at us from between the bitts or over the guns. At last the wind we wanted came, and plenty of it—for the Horn never gives by halves—and with every sail standing to its utmost, we fled into the quieter waters of the great Pacific."[1]

Beginning with the War of 1812, and for more than a century thereafter, successive British governments were remarkably consistent in pursuing policies designed to protect British commercial interests and territorial claims in what is now the Canadian province of British Columbia. The result is an example of how the official mind of British statecraft, or imperialism, functioned.

The instrument used in implementing these policies was the Royal Navy. Throughout the period 1810–1914, Britain developed and maintained an empire and seaborne trade by means of naval supremacy, carefully nurtured European alliances, skillful deployment of small military forces throughout the globe, and financial strength based on foreign trade.

The British became masters of the ocean, a position they achieved through a combination of shipbuilding, navigation, surveying and rigid rules of seamanship and officer management at sea. The Navy had been steeled by centuries of warfare at sea. What made the conquest of distant oceanic space possible was not just stout ships and jolly tars but also the defeat of scurvy, that grey peril of the seas, and other nutritional deficiencies that could lead to adverse mental and physical effects, including night-blindness, loss of concentration, and mental apathy. By the late eighteenth century the battle was won by providing food and water as required, and observing medical rules and regulations that called for an allowance of lime juice to be issued to every officer and man as a preventive against scurvy, starting on the 14th day after beginning the salt-meat diet. The ship's company was well fed on salt-beef one day and salt-pork the next, but fresh provisions were obtained whenever and wherever possible, and exercise ashore was important.

Being well provisioned with water for these long legs of Pacific voyaging, where a ship might be upward of 80 days at sea between ports, was essential. The old distilling apparatus that Sir Richard Hawkins had used to turn salt water into something "wholesome and sweet" had been set aside in the nineteenth century in favour of water tanks, and so the mariners depended on the limited quantity the tanks could carry or what a chance squall might furnish. The ship's company of HMS *America* suffered grievously from want of water, and British seamen died for lack of it. Sailing from Callao, and still 800 miles from the next destination, the allowance of water was reduced to half a pint. Sailors mixed vinegar with sea water with deadly effect. Of the death of one of his mates, young midshipman John Moresby recalled, "I shall never forget the funeral and the feeling of wrath and sorrow which filled our hearts as the sullen plunge was heard, and the white hammock, quivering as it sank, vanished from our sight. The whole thing was such an unnecessary, clumsy cruelty, as it seemed to us."[2]

Ample supplies of beer and rum, duly controlled, aided good health at sea. Naval officers attended to the health of the seamen with the greatest of care, helped by surgeons who observed all the rules based on lessons that had been learned in the previous century. When Commodore Anson had sailed the Pacific in the 1740s, he lost more than half his men, but there was absolutely no repetition of this sort of thing. Admiral Sir Cyprian Bridge, at Esquimalt in 1855, remarked that in all the time he had voyaged the Pacific, only two deaths were attributable to scurvy, and he noted that the French Marine, not observing the same medical practice, suffered badly in comparison.[3] In those long voyages under sail in the Pacific Ocean, storms in the higher latitudes often placed great strain on the ship's company, but by dint of experience the Royal Navy conquered this oceanic space.

The Spanish and Portuguese empires in Latin America had been built on grand scales, but they were prone to administrative difficulties, illicit trade and the perils of international affairs. Napoleon's invasion of the Iberian Peninsula brought on revolutions in Latin America; wars of independence ensued, and the map of Central and South America was radically transformed. To British naval officers, the quarrels among factions offered only bewilderment, for not only were wars being waged for home rule; they were also being waged to determine who would rule.

British commerce in the Americas made steady gains in the late eighteenth and early nineteenth centuries. Such activity required protection from interference and piracy. The presence of a British man-of-war lying in the roadstead near a trading port was always a salutary sight to British merchants and commission agents. Warships wearing the White Ensign were a constant reminder of British policy, a multi-headed one that included protecting commerce, guarding British life and fostering peace for the purpose of profit. To a certain degree, the pursuit of those objectives meant preventing Portugal or Spain from reasserting their old dominance. By trade and by the fleet, the British became the powerful traders and bankers in these waters. This favoured the nationalists. As Simon Bolivar, famed liberator, put it, "Only England, mistress of the seas, can protect us against the united force of European reaction."[4] An additional, but by no means minor, duty of the Navy on the east coast of South America was suppressing the slave trade, a work carried on by forceful effect in Brazil when, at last, under renewed threat of British naval intervention, that nation finally abolished the pernicious and inhuman trade.[5]

The eastern Pacific, bordering the Americas and stretching westward from Cape Horn to about where the International Date Line arbitrarily bisects the world, was the largest of the Royal Navy's "foreign stations." This vast precinct was dotted by islands and flanked by coasts. "The Pacific is a desert of waters—we seem to have sailed out of the inhabited world, & the *Grampus* to have become the Frankenstein of the Ocean. A few boatswain birds hooted us as we sailed along." So wrote Captain Sir Henry Byam Martin of the frigate *Grampus*. He marvelled at the fact that days would pass before land would be seen or another sail encountered.[6] Despite such distances, the Pacific commanded a recognized priority in British naval expenditure, even in times of general retrenchment in naval spending. British imperial interests, commercial and political, continued to shift slowly but perceptibly to eastern seas after the Napoleonic Wars, as industrial developments at home fed new markets abroad and British governments reluctantly found themselves acquiring new commitments and territories as a last resort to forestall foreign aggrandizements. Yet the means at the disposal of the commander-in-chief on the Pacific station were limited to a handful of frigates, eight or nine sloops and sometimes a ship-of-the-line. The gradual introduction of steam power after mid-century increased the effectiveness of naval units by reducing the long passages from place to place during which uncertain winds might delay for weeks a sailing ship's arrival where she was most needed. All the same, before submarine cables and wireless, communications were only as fast as the ships themselves. By the nature of their work, ships on the Pacific station never acted as a tactical unit but were necessarily dispersed throughout the ocean at critical points where "sloop diplomacy" was being exercised. More often than not, several critical situations existed at any one time. In 1846, Oregon, California and Tahiti all tested Britain's naval resources beyond Cape Horn. With true understanding, a secretary of the Admiralty could refer to these places as wasps' nests.

In such difficult circumstances, much depended on the wisdom of the admiral and his captains, and most showed a high degree of professional competence and dedication. They were masters at deploying ships and using individual units to gather intelligence. Generally speaking, commanding officers of individual ships carried out their duties in conscientious fashion and with punctilio. On the Northwest Coast they faced problems as difficult as those anywhere in the Pacific or elsewhere, and they proved to be dexterous consuls, trade commissioners, justices of the peace and policemen.

The period under our review constituted the last phase of competition for empire in North America, in which the remaining contestants seeking control of the Northwest Coast were Russia, the United States and Britain. Russia lacked a navy of any consequence; thus, she lacked means of compulsion or influence. The Tsar's Ukase of 1821 was the last attempt to consolidate Alaska as a domain for the Russian America Company. Russia's influence gradually waned, and after establishing close relations with the United States during the Crimean War and the American Civil War, she sold Alaska in 1867 to what had been one of her principal rivals a half century before.

The position of the United States was somewhat similar to that of Russia. Her limited naval power until late in the nineteenth century gave Britain a distinct military and diplomatic advantage on the Northwest Coast. But the flow of settlers across the North American continent into the agricultural lands of Old Oregon near the Columbia River in the early 1840s constituted a force that not even the combined strength of the Hudson's Bay Company and the Royal Navy could withstand so long as the area remained—by Anglo-American agreement—a "no-man's land."

Those great fur lords, the North West Company and, after 1821, the Hudson's Bay Company, had won primacy on the whole Pacific cordillera, fighting off various contenders until the fatal division of the area between Britain and the United States by the Oregon Treaty in 1846. While the British lost the agricultural lands near the Columbia River, the opposition manifested there by the Hudson's Bay Company to the United States probably compelled the Americans to press south to take the Mexican province of Alta California. British opposition to the United States also checked American expansion northward from the Columbia River and ports above Puget Sound, with Vancouver Island and the 49th parallel becoming the line of last defence for British territory stretching northward to Alaska. For various reasons, the Hudson's Bay Company had started its consolidation north of what became the boundary line. Commercial motivations bulked larger than diplomatic realities in this process.

After 1846, of necessity, the British Colonial Office embarked on a policy of encouraging settlement by British subjects on Vancouver Island, using the Hudson's Bay Company as the instrument of territorial control and the Royal Navy as the means of protection. These were difficult times to establish settlement in so remote a quarter. The California gold rush relieved the British position briefly by attracting Americans to San Francisco and the banks of the Sacramento. Developments in the goldfields of the Queen Charlotte Islands, the Fraser River and the Cariboo lured the Americans back again and forced Britain to reassert her influence. These "turbulent frontiers" were incorporated into a colonial sphere in which Victoria on Vancouver Island was the regional metropolis. This further consolidation of the area as part of the British Empire was a means of defending the fledgling colony of British Columbia against internal disorders as well as against American expansion.

Meanwhile, the United States, with growing ambitions of Manifest Destiny, was considering ways to buttress her newly won empire on the Pacific coast; eventually railways were built with this strategic objective in mind. As one American historian has explained, a Pacific railway was seen as providing "the necessary protection against Britain's sea power by enabling us to protect our western coasts without resorting to great expenditure for a navy. The shadow of the British lion lay across the path of American thinking."[7]

By the 1860s, certain Canadians were thinking in terms remarkably similar to those of the advocates of railways in the United States. These Canadians had their own notion of manifest destiny that was allied with, and not opposed to, British expansion and imperial consolidation. As a means of transporting troops, they argued, a Canadian railway to the Pacific would complement and assist British naval protection on that ocean. It would also open up British Columbia and the prairies and foothills of the Canadian West to settlement and thereby preserve an enlarged British North America from what some US citizens thought was their natural destiny. But not until 1871 did British Columbia join the Canadian Confederation; and only in 1886, after many delays, did the Canadian Pacific Railway commence its transcontinental service. In the meantime, American railroads and telegraphs had reached the Pacific, the population growth in the American Far West had accelerated, and American maritime activity and aspirations in the Pacific were in the ascendant. During this era of Anglo-American tensions, the burdens of responsibility for the defence of the British colonies on the Northwest Coast remained with the Pacific squadron, an important counterweight to American aspirations. As the century advanced, so did the Navy consolidate its "anchor of empire" at Esquimalt on Vancouver Island, key to the naval protection of British Columbia and British interests in the eastern Pacific.

Canada benefitted from this progression. In the British North American scheme of empire then evolving, a naval base on the Northwest Coast became a necessity for the squadron, initially during the Oregon crisis, and later as British commitments increased in the North Pacific— especially on Vancouver Island and in British Columbia. From the first attempts to provide a naval depot and hospital facilities at Esquimalt during the Crimean War, the value of this port increased until it became, in strategic terms, Britain's principal harbour in the eastern Pacific. It never developed into a naval establishment of the size of Halifax, Simon's Bay or Hong Kong, but it was sufficient to serve the needs of the squadron.

The proximity of Esquimalt to US shores troubled some members of the Admiralty, who argued that the place was indefensible given its remote location and the inadequate size and scattered deployment of the Pacific fleet. Some considered it a liability rather than an asset. Yet it was never totally abandoned, as certain strategic requirements had to be met and, consequently, minimum standards of defence against enemy cruiser raids were maintained during the latter part of the nineteenth century. After the redistribution of the British fleet overseas in 1906, Esquimalt's importance declined further, to the point where it served only a few small armoured cruisers.

Technological changes were crucial in making sea power more effective in the latter part of the nineteenth century. Steam replaced sail as the chief motive power. Armoured steel hulls mounting revolutionary new guns superseded wooden ships with their old 32-pounders. Then came the communications revolution. The transcontinental railway, telegraph, wireless telegraphy, the trans-Pacific cable, a trans-Pacific steamship line and the Panama Canal all exercised far-reaching effects on British strategy. Esquimalt, Hong Kong and Sydney were brought much closer to London.

In these new circumstances, Britain expected the dominions to assume greater responsibility for their own local defences. But Canadian politicians and statesmen, whose national strategy was based essentially on railways, were unwilling and unable, partially because of French Canada, to support schemes for the defence of the British Empire; they created only a small army and militia and, after 1910, a diminutive navy. As the world hurtled toward the catastrophe of 1914 and war with Imperial Germany and the Central Powers, Canadian statesmen and politicians were content to let the defence of Canada rest on British supremacy at sea while it lasted, and on the necessary diplomatic posture of good relations with the United States.

$\mathcal{P}$ROLOGUE

In 1776 the redoubtable captain James Cook of the Royal Navy sailed from England on his third and final voyage of Pacific exploration with instructions to search for the western opening of a northwest passage across North America. During the course of his voyage he visited the Hawaiian Islands, which he called the Sandwich Islands, and then sailed to the North American coast, making a landfall on the gale-lashed coast of what is now Oregon on March 7, 1778. He was on the far side of the world. For almost a month, Captain Cook's men traded in private fashion with the Mowachaht and Muchalaht of Nootka Sound and took away with them some sea-otter skins, thinking they might need the furs as clothing in the Arctic conditions they were to face that same summer. To their surprise and delight, they found that sea-otter fur was "the ermine of Asia," and that these could fetch high prices with eager Canton merchants. After Captain Cook's death, followed by publication of the account of his voyage in 1784, international interest in the maritime fur trade soared.

Meanwhile, the continental trade came to be dominated by independent explorer-traders in a Montreal-based group known as the North West Company—the Nor'westers—although in none of the various forms in which it existed did this company ever receive a charter. Fired by unmatched commercial zeal, they engaged in bitter rivalry with the chartered Hudson's Bay Company and also competed with the American fur-trading interests of John Jacob Astor, America's first tycoon.[1]

By 1793, Boston merchant mariners had gained mastery of the maritime fur trade on the Northwest Coast, partly because they were free of certain monopolistic restrictions that continually hampered the North West Company, which lacked any charter rights. The Nor'westers could not ship sea-otter pelts to markets in China without subterfuge, because other companies—notably the East India Company and, to a lesser extent, the South Sea Company—already had obtained charter rights for the China trade. The ports of Canton and Macao, the principal markets for sea-otter pelts, were essentially barred to North West Company ships, while Americans could enter them freely. The Nor'westers were driven to such stratagems as the use of merchantmen from Boston to transport their cargoes to the China ports. An additional benefit of no less importance to the Americans lay in the fact that their government was not at war at this time, while Britain was at war with France after 1793.[2]

Despite many obstacles, the Nor'westers continued their exploration of new areas. In 1793 a young Scot, Alexander Mackenzie, based at Fort Chipewyan, Lake Athabasca, and using an advance base on the Peace River, reached the Pacific at Dean Channel after completing the first overland crossing of the continent north of Mexico. On the advice of local Natives, he did not proceed further downstream on the River Tacoutche Tesse, which he believed to be the Columbia (it was the Fraser), and passed overland to Dean Channel. By his epic crossing, Canada had staked a transcontinental claim in advance of the United States. Mackenzie's *Voyages from Montreal*, published in 1801, displayed his imperial vision. The upper river was a line of communication to the Pacific "pointed out by nature," and he imagined that in addition to its becoming a vector linking the Atlantic with the Pacific, the whole tied together by posts, it would become a commercial success and a place for civilized occupation. It was this startling declaration of western Canadian empire that led Thomas Jefferson, the new president of the United States, to bring forth his pet project of sending west an army expedition, a corps of discovery, to link the newly acquired Louisiana Territory with the fabled River of the West, now known to be the Columbia River. The expedition of captains Lewis and Clark found no easy passage through the garden, as imagined, but they reached the open Pacific in late 1805 and wintered at Fort Clatsop, beginning their return journey in March 1806. In this we see raw beginnings of the rivalry between the Canadians and the Americans for control of the Columbia country. In London there may have been official indifference;

in the United States capital, alarm bells had been set off—and Jefferson, who despised the British for their imperialistic ways, decided to counter with his own scheme of empire, even if he imagined that what was established beyond the Rockies was an independent republic in obvious alliance with his own government.

Nor'westers Simon Fraser and David Thompson, trading and exploring west of the Rocky Mountains, followed Mackenzie. These explorations led to the birth of the so-called Columbian enterprise. This bold but difficult plan called for a transcontinental overland trading route proceeding westward from Fort William on Lake Superior. Furs would be freighted across the Rocky Mountains at Athabasca Pass and down the rivers to the Pacific. There ships could unload supplies and take on furs for Asian markets. In the winter of 1807–1808, a Company servant described ambitious plans to "form a general establishment for the trade of that country on the Columbia River, which receives and conducts to the Ocean all the waters that rise West of the Mountains." He claimed that the Columbian enterprise would generate markets for British manufacturers. But the rub was that in order to achieve this, official British assistance would be necessary to control a "vast country and population made dependent on the British Empire."[3]

No sooner had the Nor'westers put their bold scheme into effect in the spring of 1810, shortly after the partnership had put up a handful of posts west of the Continental Divide, than the Company's Montreal agents began to worry when they heard rumours of American expeditions fitting out at New York and Boston for the Columbia River, undoubtedly financed by John Jacob Astor. If such expeditions were successful, the Americans would achieve complete control of the rich fur preserve that extended from the banks of the Columbia into the vast hinterland. Almost immediately the Montreal partners proposed to their London associates that the British government assist the traders in establishing, "either from the interior of the North West Country or by Sea," a permanent North West Company post on the Columbia, this to be achieved with the cooperation of the East India Company, which held a monopoly of the China trade.[4] A representation was made to the government of the day. The Nor'westers accompanied their proposal with a warning that American control of the trading region, coupled with the advantage of the prior claims of discovery by the Lewis and Clark expedition, could mean eventual United States sovereignty over the Columbia territory. The urgent appeal for help from Montreal produced no effect when it was presented on April 2, 1810, to the secretary of state for foreign affairs, the Marquis of Wellesley. It bore the signature of the Committee of British Merchants Interested in the Trade and Fisheries of His Majesty's North American Colonies. Immediately following this appeal, a second was made; it too was unsuccessful.

In London, Simon McGillivray prepared for a trade war with the Americans. The most influential Nor'wester at the centre of empire, he was well aware of John Jacob Astor's plan to monopolize the Pacific fur trade. McGillivray already knew that Astor was a powerful trader in the area to the south and west of the Great Lakes. He probably knew that since 1800 Astor had been engaged in trade from New York to the Orient, and that he had sent captains on voyages to the Northwest Coast, California, Sitka and Canton after 1809. It needed little imagination to see two commercial empires in conflict.

McGillivray, knowing the strength of his traders and their excellent organization, believed that the American rivals could be defeated by competition. Accordingly, the North West Company rejected Astor's offer of a one-third interest in his trans-Pacific and transcontinental trading enterprise.[5] In June 1810, Astor, deciding to act alone, formed the Pacific Fur Company as a subsidiary of the American Fur Company. He organized two expeditions, one from New York to reach Oregon by sea and the other from St. Louis to cross by land. Astor's ship, the *Tonquin*, rounded Cape Horn and arrived at the mouth of the Columbia on March 22, 1811. There her crew constructed a fort and marine depot on the south bank, seven miles from the sea. They called it Astoria. It was the beginning of American empire on the far Pacific shore. The *Tonquin* sailed north in eager search of Native people to trade with for sea-otter skins, then disappeared into history in some Vancouver Island location, most likely Clayoquot: her captain blew her up to keep her cargo out of the hands of Natives who had swarmed her decks and invested the hold. This terrible tragedy to officers, men and all involved forms the great marine disaster of the era. This was a nail in Astor's coffin.[6]

Meantime, on November 10, 1810, McGillivray complained bitterly to the secretary for war and the colonies, the Earl of Liverpool, that since the

American expedition had already sailed from New York, it was almost too late to protect the "Columbia country" from falling into American hands, but there might still be time. Because the American vessel would call at various ports along the South American coast, a ship of the Royal Navy could possibly reach the Columbia before the Americans.[7] McGillivray argued that if a British warship sailed immediately to the Northwest Coast to take formal possession and establish a settlement, British rights would be secure. He also recommended that the North West Company send an expedition overland to meet the vessel and build a post under naval protection. He contended that, unless the Company gained naval support, it would be unable to undertake the Columbia project, and the country and trade would fall into American hands. But, for the third time, the government failed to act.

Astor's ship arrived in March 1811. That remarkable fur-trading and exploring genius, the dogged David Thompson, and his fellow Nor'westers reached it overland four months later, on July 15. They did so after exploring and surveying the river and its tributaries as a possible trade route. It was unfortunate for the Nor'westers that Thompson spent so much time surveying, as this probably delayed his reaching the mouth of the Columbia before the Americans.[8] In fairness to Thompson, the geography was complicated, and he wanted to complete his work with methodical precision. He opened the main lines of travel to the traders, and his journals provide our first written history of the immense and breathtaking Columbia country. But as McGillivray feared, the Americans had won the race to the Columbia River mouth. They had established their beachhead of empire at Astoria. And so closed the first phase of Anglo-American rivalry in the Far West.

one

$\mathcal{W}$AR COMES TO THE
COLUMBIA COUNTRY

Nelson was dead. Immortality had enshrined him as a result of his brilliant crushing of the combined French and Spanish fleets at Trafalgar. Napoleon held sway in Europe, though mauled by an ill-judged attack on Moscow. The French soon regained strength at sea. All the same, British mastery of the oceans stood in his way. "So I, had I remained in Egypt, should probably have founded an empire like Alexander," said Napoleon. He was received on board HMS *Bellerophon* and taken into custody, his eventual destination one of lonely exile on St. Helena in the South Atlantic. He complained acidly to Captain Frederick Maitland of the British man-of-war: "Had it not been for you English, I should have been Emperor of the East; but whenever there is water to float a ship we are sure to find you in the way." In the words of the distinguished American historian Alfred Thayer Mahan, "those far-distant, storm-beaten ships upon which the Grand Army never looked, stood between it and the dominion of the world."[1]

After Trafalgar the British had not rested on their oars. Caught in the jaws of fate, Britain raised a mighty navy for the final act to defeat Napoleon, and, in doing so, impressed seamen of British nationality who were found, on inspection, among the crews of United States naval vessels. President James Madison, backed by votes in the Senate and House

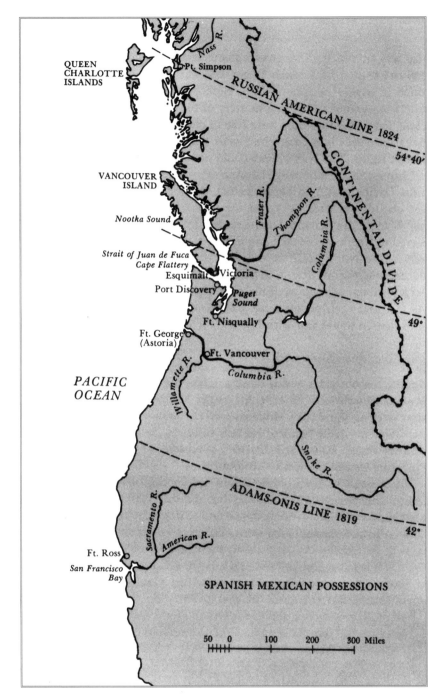

Northwest Coast of North America, 1818–1846

of Representatives, proclaimed a state of war with Great Britain and the British Empire on June 19, 1812. In his message, Madison referred to the renewal of warfare by Native people "on one of our extensive frontiers." He charged the British and the Canadians for this state of affairs. From this particular American point of view, the war would be fought to end the "Indian menace." There was talk of taking Canada by mere marching. While the Americans planned their land campaign, the British made a pre-emptive move, took Michilimackinac on Lake Michigan and forced the surrender of Detroit, following on with a bloody campaign into western Ohio. They were joined in common cause by Tecumseh and his pan-Native alliance. Meantime, the United States bolstered its naval forces on lakes Ontario and Erie; the British, in more makeshift fashion, did likewise. In September 1813 the US Navy scored a resounding victory over Commodore Robert Barclay's British squadron on Lake Erie, and then the tide of American sea power flowed north past Detroit into Lake Huron and beyond. Upper Canada's existence lay in jeopardy, while naval, militia and even fur-trader resources stemmed the tide. The North West Company, self-interested patriots, raised various militia regiments and took the war to the enemy in the upper Michigan peninsula: indeed, they defended imperial interests as far west as Prairie du Chien on the upper Mississippi. At the same time, British generals and agents assured Tecumseh and his alliance that after the war their claims for a Native homeland in the interior would be honoured. That promise they could not keep, leading to charges of treachery on the British side.

At stake, too, were issues of truly transcontinental scale. The war introduced a new factor in the rivalry between the Nor'westers and the Astorians. Late that year, North West Company agents in Montreal again urged their London partners to press the British government for convoy support of a Company supply ship bound for the Columbia River via Cape Horn. The outbreak of war in that year ended the British ministry's indifference to the pleas of the North West Company; the Lords Commissioners of the Admiralty discussed the proposed mission with Nor'westers Donald McTavish and John Macdonald of Garth. They then dispatched the frigate *Phoebe*, with 36 guns and under the command of Captain James Hillyar, to accompany the fur-trading company vessel *Isaac Todd* to the Columbia River and then clear the coast of hostile vessels. The *Isaac Todd*, 20 guns, bearing letters-of-marque that would give her licence to capture enemy merchant shipping, was the first vessel of the Company's Columbian enterprise. With the North West Company partners McTavish and Macdonald on board, the *Isaac Todd* sailed from Portsmouth with her escort, the *Phoebe*, on March 25, 1813, under secret orders to seize Astoria and then form a British settlement at the mouth of the Columbia River.[2] Now, at last, Canadian fur-trading zeal was being backed by British sea power and state policy.

Meantime, an auxiliary expedition set out overland from Canada for the Columbia. Led by the veteran trader John George McTavish, the bold party of a hundred men intended to make the transcontinental crossing so as to meet up with the supply ship and naval escort sometime between May and August 1813. McTavish carried with him an important letter from the British government stating that the *Isaac Todd* was "accompanied by a frigate, to take and destroy everything that is American on the N.W. Coast."[3]

On June 10, 1813, the *Phoebe* led the *Isaac Todd* into the neutral port of Rio de Janeiro.[4] There, the commander-in-chief of the South American station, Nova Scotia-born Rear-Admiral Sir Manley Dixon, learned that Hillyar had experienced great difficulty with the crew of the *Isaac Todd*. Seven of the crew deserted on account of her unseaworthy condition; they had no desire to try to sail round Cape Horn in that ship.[5] She had proved to be a heavy sailer, in part because she was badly stowed and heavily rigged, and because she carried too many guns on deck. Her condition led Dixon to conclude, woefully, "No alteration, I understand, will make her sail even tolerably."[6]

This was a secret mission, and Rear-Admiral Dixon knew nothing of its object until the ships reached Rio; he was disgusted when McTavish and Macdonald, in ignorance or indifference, "made generally known" that the secret destination of the ships was the Columbia River.[7] This breach of security outraged Dixon. He personified the qualities of duty, obedience and courage. The *Isaac Todd* spelled trouble to his command.

About this time, news reached Dixon that the US frigate *Essex*, rated by the British as a 40-gun ship, was at large in the Pacific, capturing British whalers at will.[8] The admiral concluded that the *Phoebe* alone would not be an equal to the *Essex* should they meet in battle. He therefore designated two sloops under his command, the *Racoon*, 26 guns, and *Cherub*,

18 guns, for this purpose. Both had been destined in the first instance for the South Pacific to protect the remaining British merchantmen, a service which could be most effectively accomplished by sinking or taking the *Essex*.[9] After considerable pondering, the commander-in-chief, with seamanlike precaution, ordered a squadron consisting of the *Phoebe*, *Racoon* and *Cherub* to convoy the *Isaac Todd* to the Pacific, thus providing a greater margin of safety.[10]

At Rio the crews readied the four vessels for the arduous passage round Cape Horn. Dixon ordered the government stores shipped in the *Isaac Todd* to be transferred to all three of the British men-of-war.[11] He strengthened the complements of the *Racoon* and *Cherub* by a total of 65 men to ensure that the naval vessels would be strong enough to defeat the Americans at the mouth of the Columbia if the *Isaac Todd* fell behind.[12] Further delays followed when two officers left the *Isaac Todd*. Replacements had to be found, and discontented sailors from that ship had to be held in custody.[13] Every effort was made to get under way as soon as possible, but the four ships did not weigh anchor until July 6, 1813.

Four days after leaving Rio, Captain Hillyar opened the secret Admiralty orders conveyed to him by Dixon. "The principal object of the Service on which you are employed," the orders ran, "is to protect and render every assistance in your power to the British traders from Canada, and to destroy, and if possible totally annihilate any settlements which the Americans may have formed either on the Columbia River or on the neighbouring Coasts."[14] Moreover, Hillyar was to give the Nor'westers "every assistance in the formation of any new settlement they may wish to form for carrying on their trade and in destroying any force of the Enemy which you may find in that quarter."[15]

The plan called for the *Phoebe* and the *Isaac Todd* to arrive together at the Columbia after a passage from Rio "without touching anywhere."[16] In the event that the ships were separated or encountered difficulties, they were to rendezvous at the Hawaiian Islands, the best source of supplies. It was felt that to meet there would conceal the mission better than if they were to anchor in a port on the Pacific side of the Americas. As an alternative meeting place, the Island of Juan Fernandez off the Chilean coast was recommended.

Orders from Rear-Admiral Dixon required that one of the two fur-trading partners should be placed aboard the *Phoebe*. With this precaution the *Phoebe* could complete its mission even if the *Isaac Todd* arrived late at the mouth of the Columbia or failed to reach there at all.[17] Accordingly, Macdonald and five Company servants were transferred to the *Phoebe*, and McTavish, the chief Nor'wester, remained in the *Isaac Todd*.[18] Dixon's admirable instructions reminded Captain Hillyar of the original purpose of the *Racoon* and *Cherub*—to protect British merchantmen in the South Pacific—but gave him complete discretion to retain them as long as he thought necessary to accomplish the more important mission entrusted to him by the Admiralty.[19]

Although the mission to the Northwest Coast was supposedly a secret, details of its objective had leaked out even before the *Phoebe* and *Isaac Todd* left England on March 25, 1813. This news reached Rio de Janeiro by mid-June; from there it probably was conveyed overland immediately and, passing through informants, eventually reached the *Essex*.[20]

The *Essex*, pride of Salem, Massachusetts, and a gift from the citizens of that city to the United States Navy, was the first US warship to enter the Pacific and had already been the first beyond the Cape of Good Hope.[21] After modest success against British shipping, mostly whalers, in the South Atlantic, Captain David Porter of the *Essex* decided to venture alone into the Pacific in March 1813 (about the same time the *Phoebe* and *Isaac Todd* left Portsmouth). Porter planned to survive on the prizes he could capture. He provisioned hurriedly at Valparaiso, Chile, and sailed on March 21 for the Galapagos Islands, then the centre of whaling in the Pacific. From April to October 1813 the *Essex* seized 12 of 20 British whalers.[22] Captain Porter then fitted out one of these captured whalers as a privateer to accompany the *Essex* in her search for unarmed, or poorly armed, merchantmen; the *Essex Junior*, as the captured whaler was named, carried 20 light guns and 90 men.

To this point, Porter had demonstrated in every respect fine seamanship and successful adherence to cruiser warfare, *guerre de course*. Like John Paul Jones or Graf von Spee, he was master of that mode of naval warfare, living for the moment but with a plan to do as much damage to the enemy as possible while food, water and good fortune lasted. The US Navy had begun the war disadvantaged. While the British had always regarded the ever-difficult naval question as central to national existence, the Americans came to this late in the game, and the War of 1812 caught them unawares and unprepared. Those ships in commission were excellent and would do gallant service, even though they were few in number and could not prevent the blockade that the British squadrons maintained on the Atlantic seaboard. But their crack frigates, including the *Essex*, fought the type of naval war their commanders chose, and did so with commendable success.

Meanwhile, the British faced fearful difficulties in the passage from Rio to Cape Horn in the dead of the southern winter. During a heavy gale on July 20, 1813, the escorts almost lost sight of the slow-sailing *Isaac Todd*, and the *Racoon* and *Cherub* sustained minor damage as they tried to keep close to her. Two days later the captains met on board the *Phoebe* and decided that in the event of another gale they would be compelled, for reasons of safety, to sail at a distance from the *Isaac Todd*.[23] Only a few days later, on July 29, the ships were north of the Falkland Islands when thick fog settled in and the Company ship fell behind and lost contact. After weathering a heavy storm, the three men-of-war rounded Cape Horn; on September 11 they reached Crusoe's Juan Fernandez, where they hoped to rendezvous with the *Isaac Todd*, but her whereabouts were still unknown. The squadron remained at Juan Fernandez for a week, hoping to sight the *Isaac Todd*. On September 18 the Nor'wester Macdonald and North West Company servants and stores were again transferred, this time from the *Phoebe* to the *Racoon*.[24] The squadron then headed north, with the *Isaac Todd* unaccounted for and perhaps lost.

Near the equator, on October 2, Hillyar learned from a Spanish brig that the *Essex* had taken one hundred distressed seamen to Guayaquil on the coast of Ecuador.[25] It was thought that possibly these men were taken from the *Isaac Todd*. On this intelligence, which must have seemed convincing, Hillyar concluded that the *Isaac Todd* was lost. He then decided to find the enemy. The *Phoebe* and *Cherub* were sent to the South American coast to hunt for the *Essex*, leaving the *Racoon*—now unescorted—to continue to the Columbia River. Because the *Phoebe* had been allocated by the Lords of the Admiralty as escort for a project to which they attached importance, Hillyar's decision to leave the *Racoon* to execute the mission without escort could be justified only by success.[26]

When Porter first learned of the strong British squadron sailing round the Horn, he prepared for battle. He intended to crown his time in the Pacific by something more splendid than catching enemy whalers. On

October 25 he took the *Essex*, *Essex Junior* and three prizes to the salubrious Marquesas Islands, where a refit was carried out. He ran up the Stars and Stripes as an act of possession, later disavowed by the home government. Then on December 14 the *Essex* and *Essex Junior* sailed for Valparaiso, determined to seek combat with the enemy.[27] They reached what they considered to be the neutral port of Valparaiso on February 3, 1814; five days later the British ships *Phoebe* and *Cherub* also entered the port but took up a position of close blockade.

A clash between the rivals seemed inevitable as soon as both forces ventured out of the harbour. As he was stronger, Hillyar wanted to be in a position to prevent the *Essex* and *Essex Junior* from slipping away quietly before he was ready, so he put to sea, accompanied by the *Cherub*. For nearly six weeks, Hillyar's force sailed close to the extreme western point of Valparaiso harbour, a large open bay facing north. The objective was to prevent the faster enemy warships from escaping between him and the point. From his strategic position, Hillyar would have the advantage of a chase to windward in the prevailing south-southwest wind.[28]

Ill fortune now attended Porter, as the engagement he had sought would be fought under circumstances not of his own choosing. On March 28, 1814, in violent winds, the *Essex* parted one cable and began to drag another. Porter had no option but to cut the cable and make sail. He hoped to pass to the windward of the blockading British vessels. He might have done so had not the main topmast of the *Essex* snapped in a heavy squall near the outer point of the bay. This forced Porter to run eastward and to anchor in what has been claimed were "neutral" waters. This neutrality was debatable, since Britain did not recognize Chilean independence and Spain was an ally. Furthermore, no belligerent man-of-war could hope to take advantage of neutral waters indefinitely, as the *Essex* had done.

Hillyar ignored Porter's intent to take refuge in "neutral" waters and considered the *Essex* fair game. His object was to rake the fine enemy frigate if possible, and, if not possible, to reach a range at which his long guns would be effective and her carronades would not. The powerful *Essex* mounted forty 32-pounder carronades and six 12-pounder long guns and had a minimum broadside of 676 pounds. By contrast, the *Phoebe* carried twenty-six 18-pounder long guns, four 9-pounder long guns and fourteen

32-pounder carronades, while the *Cherub* had eighteen 32-pounder carronades, six 18-pounder carronades and two 6-pounder guns, with minimum broadsides of 476 and 248 pounds respectively. These figures explain why Hillyar kept the *Cherub* in close company to the *Phoebe* outside Valparaiso harbour so as not to be placed at a disadvantage in a single-ship engagement with the *Essex*. They also partly explain Hillyar's tactics in defeating the *Essex*.[29] (Readers with knowledge of Second World War naval history will imagine a parallel with the defeat of the *Graf Spee* by forces under the White Ensign.) In the event, the greater gun-range and manoeuvrability of the *Phoebe* soon proved decisive. Hillyar gingerly kept his ships out of range of the *Essex*'s broadside while doing extensive damage aloft to the enemy.[30] Faced with defeat, Porter surrendered, only two and one half hours after action commenced.[31] By this single engagement, the Royal Navy gained command of the sea in the Pacific. The *Essex* was entered on the Admiralty's books and lists but ended her life as a convict ship in Ireland. Porter and his crew were released on good behaviour and arrived in New York to tumultuous acclaim. Meantime, the wisdom of Hillyar's judgement now depended on whether the *Racoon* succeeded in her mission at the Columbia River mouth.

Astoria on the Brink

In sharp contrast to the assistance that the Royal Navy could now give the Nor'westers, American naval support for the Astorians became impossible as the British employed their naval supremacy in an effective blockade of American ports.[32] After Astor pleaded in 1813 for a warship to protect his enterprise, the secretary of the Navy responded by arranging for the frigate *Adams* to go to the North Pacific, but the British blockade prevented her from sailing. Astor then tried to protect the post and carry on the trade as best he could. He secretly chartered the *Forester*, a British vessel under British colours, but by the time she reached the Northwest Coast, British fur traders were already in possession of Astoria. Her captain was forced to trade between California and Kamchatka on the Russian coast near the Kuril Islands.[33] In Hawaii, the commander of HMS *Cherub* became suspicious of the *Forester*'s ownership and detained some of her crew on board the *Cherub*. The *Cherub* also captured the American fur-trading vessel *Charon* and the armed cruiser *Sir Alexander Hammond* in the Sandwich Islands.[34]

Another of Astor's ships, the *Lark*, was allowed by British naval authorities to leave New York in 1813 on the understanding that she was bound only for Sitka with goods and supplies for the Russians.[35] But she ran aground in the Hawaiian Islands and was a total loss. Astor, as one historian observed, "was the victim of bad tactics, bad luck, and bad strategy."[36] Reverses between 1811 and 1815 dashed Astor's hopes of maintaining Astoria as an essential link with the sea; at the same time, the partners of the Pacific Fur Company there became increasingly aware of their insecure position.

In early October 1813, about six months before Captain David Porter surrendered to Captain Hillyar of the *Phoebe* near Valparaiso, John George McTavish, at the head of his party of Nor'westers, brought news overland to the Columbia River that the *Isaac Todd* and a British frigate were bound for the river mouth to destroy the American post. This convinced the Astorians that their position was untenable. Additional and equally alarming news came from the Hawaiian and Marquesas Islands: Wilson P. Hunt, chief agent of the Pacific Fur Company, brought word from Hawaii of the outbreak of war between the two nations.[37] From the Marquesas, on another occasion, he brought information from Captain Porter of the *Essex* that an even larger force than originally expected, consisting of a frigate, two sloops and a merchantman, was bound for the Northwest Coast to conquer Astoria. The disturbing news forwarded by Hunt on this second occasion was "the death warrant of unfortunate Astoria," in the words of the American author Washington Irving.[38]

The Astorians were faced with a choice of selling their establishments, guns and stocks to the Nor'westers or confronting the guns of the Royal Navy and the Company vessel *Isaac Todd*. They signed a bill of sale on October 16, 1813, nine days after the arrival of McTavish's overland party.[39] This purchase would prove to be important during negotiations for peace and even after the war, but for now it signalled that Astor's dream for a new western empire was shattered.

The Perils of the Sloop *Racoon*

Our story now shifts to the sloop-of-war *Racoon*, of about 423 tons burthen, designed to carry 16 carriage guns. Typical of her time, she measured 108 feet 4 inches on the lower deck, and drew 9 feet. For this mission she had had an increase in ship's complement to 130 and now carried 28 guns.

When, on New Year's Day 1813, she "crossed the Line," "Neptune came on board with his wife & train, mustered the Ship's Company, found a great many new faces among us, ordered all hands stranger below, drank a Bottle of Wine with the Captain on the Quarter Deck, ordered his Carriage to drive to the Fore Castle, where he gave his orders to his Barbers &c. to commence shaving &c." A bathing pool was created in the main deck area, and at the end of the day everyone washed up, "all hands about 9 P.M. quite boozy." The first lieutenant, who wrote the above, concluded his day's narrative: "Found myself rather by the head [intoxicated]. Shaped my course for my Cot. Turned in all standing, being more than half seized o'er." So closed the day of crossing the equator in time-honoured tradition.

The *Racoon* had rounded Cape Horn in heavy weather, all the while fighting high seas and cold winds. Cocos was reached October 7, and summer days lay ahead in these latitudes. Captain William Black of the *Racoon* hoped to find the *Isaac Todd* at Cocos, for in his instructions the island had been specified as a place to take on wood and water, if needed. Two days passed at Cocos without sighting the North West Company vessel, so the *Racoon* sailed for Juan Fernandez. Again there was no sign of the *Isaac Todd*, though the enemy was rumoured to be near at hand. Then it was time to make sail for the Columbia. In due course the sloop recrossed the equator, and before long the tempestuous gales of the North Pacific, with heavy wind and rain, made their expected appearance. They were in latitudes where Captain James Cook, in 1778, had faced a series of gales and a long and weary approach to the Northwest Coast of America.

During the exercise of the guns on October 20, a fearful explosion shook the *Racoon*; 21 men were injured.[40] The burns were shocking in their intensity, and among the severely burned were John Macdonald of Garth and the first lieutenant, John Sherrif, whose hands suffered grievous injury. Apparently one of the guns, or at least the powder in the touchhole, misfired; fire leapt to some cartridges hanging above the gun, and a number of powder horns suspended from one of the joists exploded. The gunpowder, damaged by sea water, had become corrupted and thus unstable.

By mid-November, 15 of the ship's company were dead and had already been "committed to the Bowels of the Ocean on which we now exist," wrote one officer. Large whales played and sounded round the ship, while the cruel wind came directly on their intended course, and it seemed to the same officer that the vessel seemed to be running away from its destination. The weather continued very cold, but a new moon was expected to bring more favourable weather. In spite of her condition and reduced crew, preparations were made for "a grand attack" on Astoria, for on board the belief prevailed that the fort was in American hands.[41] About 80 men with marines were to land from three armed boats—the pinnace, cutter and gig—and take the post either by surprise at daybreak or under the ship's fire. If the ship's guns could not be brought to bear on the target, the landing party would "take the fort sword in hand." The weather proved fickle, the shore cloaked in haze. In the evening they saw land at last. The *Racoon* anchored under Cape Meares, just south of Tillamook Bay, and awaited the dawn.

November 30 broke bright and clear with a smooth sea. More generally, from Cape Disappointment south to the opposite shore and Point Adams, outside the entrance to the Columbia, the sea presented itself as a fearful roil of wind and waves. Black sent boats ahead to sound a passage, there being a large bar at the entrance of the river, and to lay down buoys that had been readied for that precise purpose. This task completed, the sloop ran, with a fine following wind and under full canvas, through the marked gap and crossed the bar, and just after noon came to safe and welcome anchor in Baker's Bay within Cape Disappointment. This was a brilliant feat of seamanship, for the Columbia's bar was a graveyard for sailors, and the *Racoon's* ship's company knew boats sent by Captain Thorn of the *Tonquin* in March 1811 had lost eight men. For his approach, Black had ordered no flags to be flown, so that their nationality could be kept secret. A boat party scrambled ashore with casks for water. Wood was available for ship's fires, and timber for spars as required.

Across the river estuary, about six miles distant, the British traders at Astoria, who now controlled the Columbia, lived in continual fear of an American attack. They assumed that the *Essex* was still at large; thus, the arrival of a warship caused understandable excitement and concern on shore. The guns of the fort fired four signal shots by way of welcome; no reply came from the ship that lay far across the river estuary.

Because no colours of the *Racoon* could be seen from the fort, the Nor'westers prepared to abandon the post if the ship proved to be the enemy. At one o'clock in the afternoon, a party set off in a canoe to determine if the man-of-war anchored in Baker's Bay was friend or foe. Four hours later, when the canoe had failed to return, the traders on shore loaded most of their packs, arms and ammunition into barges and canoes to search for a more secure position up the river. However, toward midnight the original investigating party returned to the fort with joyous news that the unknown ship was the *Racoon*. They had gone on board and celebrated her arrival with a large quantity of Tenerife wine, which accounts for their delay in returning with the good news.[42] It was a joyous day all round, and the Nor'westers ashore now had reassurance that the Royal Navy had arrived.

Captain Black was a seasoned officer with 20 years in the Navy, a good deal of fighting experience and a keen sense of responsibility. He had entered the Navy in 1793, at the time the British had gone to war against the French, and then had served in ships on the Jamaica station, where the toast on Thursdays aboard ship was "A Bloody War or a Sickly Season" (and a quick promotion). He had studied history. From the outset he regarded the Northwest Coast, north of Alta California, as Nova Albion—that is, the territory Francis Drake had clamed for Elizabeth Regina in 1579. He discovered to his alarm that the Russians had erected a post, Fort Ross, north of San Francisco Bay, in 1812; in his opinion the Russians were disturbing the British sovereignty of Nova Albion. Black saw the world through the narrow prism of a dedicated naval officer on state business. If he was definite in his views, he was equally tactful and diplomatic. He was of the Nelson mode, determined to fulfill the mission his superiors had entrusted to him.

Next day, Captain Black, in one of his ship's boats, examined the river mouth, using a copy of the remarkable chart drawn from the survey made by Lieutenant W.R. Broughton in 1792 when commanding the *Chatham* brig in Captain George Vancouver's expedition. Broughton, we note, had performed the act of taking possession of that country in the name of King George III. Black planned to approach the post by the southern channel but, sadly, strong winds and tides forbade this. The weather was deplorable, the river estuary a churning mass, so the Nor'westers sent their coastal schooner *Dolly*, and, at last, after all these delays, on December 12, Black, at the head of a landing party, with a midshipman (Mr. Verdier), four marines and four sailors, reached shore below the fort. They were well entertained at the fort. Black donated some Madeira to the dinner festivities, and a pleasant evening ensued. There was much to talk about, as the demands of the voyage surely could be matched by the trials of overland travel. The traders acquired a high regard for Captain Black. The mariners were not so sure about the ferocious-looking fur traders, most of whom were Scots.

On the next morning, December 13, Black is reported to have exclaimed in disgust when he saw the small stockade, with its slim armament, on a slight hill not far from the water, "Is this the fort about which I have heard so much talking? D–n me, but I'd batter it down in two hours with a four pounder!"[43]

Astoria stood on a rising ground overlooking a small, crescent-shaped bay where small ships could unload cargo into waiting boats and canoes that would ferry the goods to the wharf. To the west could be seen breakers on the river bar, rolling in wild confusion. To the east a desolate and varied aspect presented itself, and in the distance a magnificent, darkening forest. The fort itself was a square of 200 yards surrounded by a 15-foot palisade of timbers driven into the ground. Bastions stood at the northeast and southeast corners and were mounted with four- and six-pounders. A sentry platform topped the double gate facing the Columbia. Inside the palisade stood a two-storey governor's house and some other buildings. The local Native people, the Chinook, posed no threat to the traders, and so no close guard need be kept on them. Even so, they were not permitted to stay the night and were obliged to leave at curfew, when the gates were closed. Outside the walls was an enclosure where the Kanakas, or Hawaiians, slept.

Although they were friendly, the Chinook were also frustratingly hard bargainers, as the Nor'westers discovered. They were accustomed to the presence of Europeans. The first to arrive were the Spaniards under Bruno de Hezeta in 1775, and the Americans under Robert Gray, who had explored the Columbia's mouth in 1792. British trader John Meares had been near the river mouth in 1788, and Captain George Vancouver, RN, was there in April 1792, a month after Gray. The Lower Chinook became guardians of the mouth and lower reaches of the Columbia. It was a position they held zealously, personified in the form of the famed one-eyed Lower Chinook chief Comcomly (actually Madsu or "Thunderer"). Visits from trading vessels made the Lower Chinook rich and powerful. However, the introduction of spirituous liquors was a dramatic, hazardous occurrence on the Lower Columbia, and it did violence to Native ways.

The Astorians were heavy-handed in dealing with Native matters upriver, where there was rivalry between the Chinook and the Nez Perce, but at Astoria the Nor'westers, though cautious, advanced their trade and security with little violence. Prevailing opinion among these traders was that a new post ought to be built upriver.

At mid-afternoon on December 13, Black returned to the post in full uniform, with an armed escort. Coming before the assembled partners and employees of the North West Company, he signalled that the Union Jack be raised on the fort's flagstaff. Then, breaking a bottle of Madeira on the staff, he declared in a loud voice that he was taking possession of "this country" in the name of His Britannic Majesty, and that he christened the post Fort George in honour of the king. After the appropriate cheers and salutes of musketry and artillery, there followed a toast to His Majesty and a speech to explain the new state of affairs to the Chinook people and other local Natives.[44] The ceremony of possession clearly confirmed British control at Fort George, and Black's act formally established the North West Company's ownership of the post. He then sent this report overland, as deciphered, to the Admiralty:

> Country and fort I have taken possession of in name and for British Majesty; latter I have named Fort George and left in possession and charge North West Company.
>
> Enemy's party quite broke up; they have no settlement whatever on this river or coast.
>
> Enemy's vessels said on coast and about islands; while provisions last, shall endeavour to destroy them.[45]

A question often posed, and still unanswered for lack of evidence, is why did the Nor'westers purchase the post from the Astorians, as they did on October 16, when the naval force was known to be on its way? According to one person on board the *Racoon*, the purchase was "diametrically opposite to the fundamental laws of Great Britain under the head of assisting an Enemy."[46] He and others in the British warship hoped that an Admiralty Court would show that the *Racoon* had captured the fort and that the value of the seizure would be given to the ship's company. A generally held view, based on much hearsay evidence and without documentary proof, is that Captain Black thought the Nor'westers and Astorians conspired to defraud him and his crew of the prize money.[47] The controversy had both immediate and long-term consequences. Almost certainly, animosity developed between the sailors and fur traders over the objectives and spoils of war. Furthermore, this confused beginning of British control at the Columbia River mouth tended to complicate the British diplomatic position at discussions leading to the Treaty of Ghent in 1814 and afterward.

On board the *Racoon*, the dreaded appearance of scurvy and the lack of sufficient provisions forced Black to sail from the Columbia River much earlier than the fur traders judged to be in their best interests. Wildfowl and salmon delivered to the ship by the Natives and purchased by the North West Company were welcome. But they were insufficient to offset Black's deep concern for the welfare of his ship's company, and he decided to set a course for San Francisco. There he hoped to find additional provisions, after which he would sail in search of American fur-trading vessels known to winter in the Hawaiian Islands. December brought much heavy weather, delaying departure.

At least one Nor'wester thought Black should sail directly for the Hawaiian Islands to capture "the whole nest" of wintering American vessels. It was proposed that the British fur traders buy one captured vessel for the use of the Nor'westers on the Northwest Coast. Black, however, explained that he could not sell them a prize ship unless an Admiralty Court had condemned it, and the nearest court was at the Cape of Good Hope.[48] He added that he intended to destroy any prizes to prevent them from being retaken by the enemy.

Black's conduct won him the praise of his commander-in-chief, Rear-Admiral Dixon, when the latter advised the Lords of the Admiralty: "The service on which the *Racoon* has been employed has been most ably and meritoriously executed by Captain Black; he speaks highly of all his officers and ship's company in several perilous and trying situations."[49] But some Nor'westers at Fort George had a different opinion. The grumbling Nor'wester Alexander Henry the Younger, whose overall views tended toward exaggeration, had this to say of Black and his men:

> Indeed with the exception of Captain Black, the Officers of the *Raccoon* [sic] are not those vigilant, careful, active and fine enterprising fellows, so much talked of and admired by all the World, as

the main prop of Great Britain. The Navy, were all His Majesty's Naval Officers of the same stamp as those we saw here, England would not long have it in her power to boast of her Wooden Walls.[50]

The fur traders at Fort George remained concerned about their security; they were still under the impression that the *Essex* was at large. If they were attacked they would have to stand alone until the *Isaac Todd* arrived. And many must have doubted that she would ever appear. No news had been received of that ship after she had separated from the squadron in late May 1813. She had failed to arrive at the Columbia, and therefore many at Fort George, traders and sailors alike, naturally feared that she had fallen prey to the *Essex*, as rumoured, or otherwise had become a total loss. Yet they continued to hope she would arrive and alleviate the precarious position of the traders, who were further threatened by warlike preparations of the Chinook. In fact, the slow-sailing *Isaac Todd* was then approaching Monterey, Alta California.

At the Columbia the weather continued poorly through December, and between the ship and the fort the river was a turmoil of wind and waves. Black would have left earlier, but somehow he, or his clerk, had placed Lieutenant Broughton's sailing instructions for the river entrance in the copy of Vancouver's *Voyage* that he had given to the fur traders at the fort. He needed to retrieve these instructions, and it took three perilous days and much worry to do so. Once this was accomplished, it was time to make sail at the opportune moment.

At daybreak on December 31, Mr. Stevens, the master, was sent to view the channel and report if he thought the ship could proceed outward bound in safety. He reported back that, yes, the channel appeared safe and clear, so sail was raised and the ship's sailing master shaped the best course to exit the Columbia. Then came the unexpected: a tide, a fresh breeze aft and a heavy sea such that at times the *Racoon* would not answer the helm. The ship was now in peril. "This certainly was another dismal sight, and the Ship in critical situation. The sea breaking over us, the Ship pitching heavy & scarcely making head way presented a perilous aspect and caused the features of many brave men a gloomy appearance, particularly when she struck twice very hard. I believe few in the Ship expected any other than going to Davys locker in a crack. However, the will of providence ordained it otherwise this time," wrote the author of the private journal.[51] The strong ebb tide took control and drove the ship toward the bar. The *Racoon*, when crossing the bar, bounced badly on the bottom, and in the process her false keel was torn away.

In damaged state, and in one of the great acts of seamanship, the *Racoon* somewhat miraculously reached San Francisco Bay—with seven feet of water in her hold. The ship's company, from constant employment at the ship's pumps, was in a state of exhaustion. Captain Black looked to the Spanish authorities for assistance, as might be expected from this distressing state of affairs, but naval stores and assistance at Spain's San Francisco presidio, northern bastion of New Spain, proved inadequate or unobtainable. Spanish authorities exhibited politenesses but were otherwise unhelpful. In these woeful circumstances, Black and his officers had no option but to consider abandoning the *Racoon* and returning to England overland via Mexico. Then providence seemed to intervene. At Monterey, capital of Alta California, the *Isaac Todd* got word of the arrival of the wounded *Racoon*. The merchantman found the *Racoon* at San Francisco Bay and provided stores and many essentials, including physical help. The *Racoon* was hove down on the beach at Ayala Cove, Angel Island, March 13 to 19, and repairs were effected. She was re-rigged and made ready to sail. The resourcefulness of mariners when in distress on distant shores always invites our admiration. Even so, the historian ponders the role of fate and even the agency of synchronicity. One British officer commented that it seemed as if the *Isaac Todd* had been "sent as by the works of our maker."[52]

All hands readied the *Racoon* for sea. The time had come for British tars and Canadian fur traders to say their goodbyes. The two ships parted company and then stood out under full canvas through the Golden Gate. On January 19, 1814, the *Racoon* shaped a course for fair Hawaii on the hunt for American shipping. Black's long cruise to the Pacific ended with his successful return to England. Half of the ship's company had not survived on account of sickness and accident. The 27-year-old lieutenant who had kept his private journal had seen all the perils of the deep except drowning. From Portsmouth to Rio, round the Horn and back, calls at Juan Fernandez and other places, then to the cold and stormy Columbia, then home via Maui and Tahiti, with grog often in short supply—this was the sailor's life, and the absence from home was often the telling thing, though service in the name of King George might be something to boast of in later years. The sloop-of-war *Racoon* had completed one of the most astonishing voyages on record, and Captain Black became a rear-admiral. (There are many similarities in this expedition to that of Jack Aubrey's ship *Surprise*, as portrayed in the movie *Master and Commander: The Far Side of the World*, except that the enemy was American and not the customary and dreaded French, and the whaler-hunting *Essex* was rechristened *Acheron*.) The *Racoon*'s last days were spent as a convicts' hospital ship in Portsmouth.

As for the *Isaac Todd*, her story may be briefly told. She sailed from San Francisco for the dark and dreary Northwest Coast, and arrived at the mouth of the Columbia on April 23, 13 weary months after leaving Portsmouth. Her welcome arrival at the old Astoria (now Fort George), with arms and ammunition, provisions and supplies of all kinds and distinctions, ensured the preservation of British interests at Fort George during wartime. Both objectives of Hillyar's bold decision were achieved: the *Essex* had been captured, and control of the Columbia River mouth rested in British hands. The *Isaac Todd* sailed for Canton and eventually returned home to England with Chinese goods and sea-otter furs.

By the time the *Isaac Todd* reached Fort George, the North West Company had sent the *Columbia* from England, also bound for the Northwest Coast. Again, a ship of the Royal Navy, HMS *Laurel*, provided a welcome convoy, this time only as far as Rio de Janeiro. The *Columbia* arrived at the strongly fortified Fort George in July 1814.[53] Annually thereafter, ships brought supplies and took away furs bound for the China market. Thus had Sir Alexander Mackenzie's dream been realized. The British succeeded in establishing the Columbian enterprise even while the War of 1812 made extensive demands on the Royal Navy in various places on the high seas. Even today the long arm of British sea power, as exercised in those years so long ago, invites our admiration, but of particular attraction is the skill and endurance of sailors and those who were knowledgeable in "the haven-finding art." The age of fighting sail, of which the War of 1812 is highly illustrative, formed one of the most remarkable eras in human history—and provided one of the most dramatic incidents in the annals of the Pacific Ocean and the Northwest Coast. Few others are its equal.

The Quarrel Begins

Now commenced the paper war for the Columbia River country. Given the Anglo-American rivalry to control the Columbia trade between 1810 and 1814, and the immense expense and difficulty involved—to say nothing of the challenges faced—it seems paradoxical that when peace negotiations began at Ghent, the British government showed little concern for the territory west of the Rocky Mountains. Sailors and diplomats do not always see eye to eye. The criminally neglectful silence of the British plenipotentiaries was later explained to the North West Company by Earl Bathurst, the secretary for war and the colonies, on the grounds that "requiring from the Americans any recognition or guarantee of His Majesty's rights thereto, might lead to cast doubts upon a title which was sufficiently strong and incontrovertible."[54] Such was the excuse for what was probably an oversight. It is also an example of diplomatic double-talk. The French liked to call the British "perfidious Albion." They were ever on their guard against British diplomatic double-dealing.

The American plenipotentiaries took an assertive standpoint. At Ghent they argued aggressively that Astoria should be restored to the United States because it had been in American hands before the war. This reflected the policy of the secretary of state, James Monroe, who instructed the delegation to insist on the restoration of the fort. With reference to the British, Monroe noted, "It is not believed that they have any claim to territory on the Pacific Ocean."[55] Ultimately, the Treaty of Ghent, signed December 24, 1814, stipulated a return to the *status quo ante bellum*. Both during and after negotiations, the Nor'westers made repeated appeals to the British government for protection against the Americans. They hoped to safeguard their post on the Columbia, which they claimed had been acquired by purchase.[56] Nevertheless, the Treaty of Ghent failed to make specific reference to the fort at the Columbia River mouth. In fact, the treaty's "only definite achievement," according to one authority, "was the termination of hostilities."[57] Altogether, the treaty was an unsatisfactory agreement and the cause of later disputes between Britain and the United States. But it was the best in the circumstances of the day.

After signing the treaty, the United States government took steps to recover the post on the Northwest Coast. Secretary of State Monroe told the British minister in residence, Anthony St. John Baker, that inasmuch as the British force had taken possession of Astoria during the war, the United States intended to reoccupy the fort without delay.[58] When Monroe asked that a letter be addressed to the British naval commander in the North Pacific ordering the return of the fort to the Americans, Baker replied that he knew very little about the fate of Astoria, although he believed that the post lay in ruins and was unoccupied.[59] Baker suggested that Sir Manley Dixon, commander-in-chief on the South American station and in charge of British warships in the Pacific, would possess authentic information and could communicate with any authorized American agent on the subject. This useful ploy earned the British some needed time.

Immediately Baker wrote to Dixon to warn him of the developments in Washington. He enclosed copies of the correspondence with Monroe and emphasized that Britain did not recognize any American possession on the Pacific coast.[60] Although Baker did learn from the North West Company in Canada that the possession of Astoria was effected by purchase, he failed to press this advantageous position with the American secretary of state.

It is generally believed that only the lack of naval units during 1815 and 1816 prevented the United States from sending a vessel on a mission of restitution to the Northwest Coast.[61] A suggestion in the autumn of 1815 that a naval expedition explore the Northwest Coast won support from President James Madison, but the need for economy caused the proposal to be set aside. The USS *Congress*, which was to sail in mid-1816 for the Pacific, had to be sent to the Gulf of Mexico instead. Something more secretive was now put into operation. On October 4, 1817, the American sloop-of-war *Ontario*, 20 guns, under Captain James Biddle, sailed from New York for the Columbia on an ill-advised secret mission to take possession of Astoria. But when Simon McGillivray of the North West Company learned of this through a breach in security, he immediately informed Sir Charles Bagot, the British chargé d'affaires in Washington.[62] John Quincy Adams, US secretary of state, appeared "considerably embarrassed" when Bagot asked him if the rumour were true. He admitted that the *Ontario* was sent to assert American sovereignty, but not to destroy the trade of the North West Company.[63]

Bagot was not satisfied with the response. Immediately he notified Viscount Castlereagh, the British foreign secretary, that a vessel had been ordered "to the mouth of the Columbia River for the purpose of re-establishing the Settlement of which the United States was dispossessed during the late war."[64] Bagot then advised the Governor General of Canada to send an overland party to warn the Nor'westers on the Pacific coast.[65] Optimistically, he suggested to the foreign secretary that a vessel from England could arrive at the Columbia before the *Ontario*.[66] But nothing was done in response to Bagot's advice.

Further information reached the Admiralty from Commodore Sir James Lucas Yeo, commander-in-chief on the West African Coast, that the Americans possessed a "restless and hostile spirit" toward Britain.[67] He also reported that he learned during his visit to New York that the *Ontario* was sailing for the North Pacific with commissioners on board "to obtain possession of some Island or Territory in that quarter preparatory to their establishing a very extensive commerce in those Seas."[68] The British cabinet considered this explosive situation and sought to avert a renewal of war. The foreign secretary, Castlereagh, knew that the Nor'westers had actually purchased Astoria—and that tied his hands. But the dilemma arose because Captain Black's report indicated that he had claimed that territory as a conquest of war: provision in the Treaty of Ghent to return to the *status quo ante bellum* meant that Britain had to return any conquest of war. The conciliatory foreign secretary clearly was more interested in the stability of international relations than in additions to the British Empire. In order to give the Americans what he referred to generally as "an additional motive to cultivate the arts of peace," he decided to return the post to the Americans provided it was abundantly clear to them that this would neither recognize United States rights nor relinquish British claims to the territory.[69] To implement this generous, albeit shortsighted, policy, he instructed the secretary for war and the colonies, Earl Bathurst, to inform the fur traders of the proposed restitution of Fort George, previously Astoria, to the United States. At the same time, Castlereagh instructed the Admiralty to send a warship to the Northwest Coast to restore the post officially to American commissioners.[70]

The mission was carried out by the *Blossom*, 18 guns—a "ship-sloop" and sister to the *Racoon* and *Cherub*—which was previously engaged in protecting British commerce in ports on the Pacific side of South America during the war between Spain and Chile. She sailed from Valparaiso for the Columbia on July 12, 1818, carrying Colonial Office dispatches to the

Nor'westers authorizing the restitution.[71] By the time she had anchored near Fort George on October 1, the American ship *Ontario* had arrived, made territorial claims for the United States and departed.[72] The British fur traders, unsure whether peace or war existed, had made preparations to defend the post.[73]

The Dispute Unresolved

In official ceremonies that followed, Captain Frederick Hickey of the *Blossom* and James Keith, a British commissioner and the factor in charge of the fort, signed the Instrument of Restoration. Then the British flag was lowered and the flag of the United States was raised. This act, which must have seemed as ridiculous to the participants as it does now, was intended to symbolize American "ownership" of Fort George. But it did not end the confusion. The Nor'westers continued to use the post as their headquarters on the Northwest Coast for many years. It remained the chief depot of the Hudson's Bay Company, which merged with the North West Company in 1821, until 1825, when Fort Vancouver was erected.

The territorial claims made when the USS *Ontario* came to the Columbia in October 1817 convinced the British ministry that differences between the United States and Britain should be resolved to maintain peace. In the negotiations that led to the Anglo-American Convention of 1818, the British proposed an international boundary along the Columbia River and joint occupancy of the land at the river mouth.[74] This, however, was unacceptable to the United States. The parties finally agreed to what has been called a joint occupation of the so-called Oregon Territory—that is the territory lying between Spanish-held Alta California and Russian America, and between the Continental Divide and the Pacific coast. The Anglo-American Convention of 1818 postponed negotiations between Britain and the United States on territorial claims to Oregon. Failure to resolve the dispute at this time confused rival traders, mariners and diplomats for many years and nearly embroiled the two nations in war in 1846.

By 1818, British dominance in the fur trade at the mouth of the Columbia, and thus over the hinterland, had been gained with the aid of the Royal Navy. In particular, and of critical importance, convoy support given the Nor'westers by British warships during the War of 1812, the success of the *Phoebe* and *Cherub* against the *Essex*, and the completion of the missions of the *Racoon* and *Isaac Todd* ensured continuation of British fur-trading interests on the Northwest Coast. Although the contest for the Columbia country ended in Britain's favour in terms of trade, the unwillingness of the war-weary British ministry to obtain recognition from the United States in 1815 and 1818 of British territorial control led to protracted negotiations during the next three decades. The American war did not achieve the aim of annexing Canada, but it did give Americans full jurisdiction over the Native tribes south and west of the Great Lakes within the national boundaries of the United States. The British reneged on their promise to protect the Native nations south of the line, and this sadly prefaced the British withdrawal. Beyond the Mississippi, in time, as Manifest Destiny gathered momentum, settlement projects and missionary societies advanced their interests, and independent fur traders, the mountain men, worked the margins of what became, after 1821, the Hudson's Bay Company's imperium.

Out on the far western margin of the continent, the rivals were exercising sea power and determining the course of history. The "sloop diplomacy" practised during the war set the pattern that would be followed for almost a hundred years in these seas. Antipathies between John Bull and Brother Jonathan, begun in the War of American Independence, were reinforced by the War of 1812. By 1818 the final struggle for territorial control in the farthest west had started in earnest. At the time, no one could imagine that the two countries would quarrel over more than just Oregon, but would also have a spat over the San Juan Archipelago, the Alaska–Yukon Boundary and the Bering Sea pelagic sealing grounds. In the waters beyond Cape Horn, the grand duel was being acted out bit by bit in a great contest of wills, and of threats and counter-threats. It was one in which, on both sides, the quality of ships, their provisioning and repair, and the skills of the officers in command and the sailors under discipline who sailed those distant seas far from home are to this day a matter of wonder and admiration.

$\mathcal{E}$MPIRE OF THE SEAS

At the close of the Napoleonic Wars in 1815, Britain stood unrivalled as a world power. This was due to her naval strength, which developed during the eighteenth century in the long struggle for supremacy and empire with Spain, France and finally the United States. In the words of that astute commentator Admiral Sir Cyprian Bridge, British naval power was "so ubiquitous and all-pervading that, like the atmosphere, we rarely thought of it and rarely remembered its necessity or its existence."[1] British influence rested also on her industrial system, then expanding into a worldwide business organization, stimulated by the increase in overseas trade.[2] Britain held a virtual monopoly of all tropical produce, and her ships—both merchant and naval—were "available for the maintenance of power on and over the seas."[3] Her marked naval superiority, together with well-nurtured European alliances, eliminated the threat of war for the half century beginning with Waterloo and ending with the Crimean War.[4]

The active services of the British fleet in these years were in character distinctly different from its work up to 1815. But in no sense are they less interesting or unimportant to our understanding of sea power. British naval historian William Laird Clowes, in his multi-volume history of the Royal Navy that crowned the age of Queen Victoria, makes clear the importance of these generally quiet years between 1816 and 1856:

63

In the forty years, British admirals fought no great pitched battles with formidable foes; and although the period is that of Algier, Navarin, St. Jean d'Acre, and Sebastopol, it is more especially the period of small wars with uncivilised [*sic*] peoples, of steady, but nearly noiseless, extension of the Empire, and of onerous policing of the ocean. It witnessed the practical extinction of piracy, and of the over-sea slave trade; and, in connection with those subjects . . . the record of many almost forgotten deeds of heroism. It witnessed also many scarcely-remembered exploits which were undertaken in defence of British interests in all parts of the world, and for the protection and advancement of British trade . . . although the period was, upon the whole, one which it is customary to call a time of peace, scarcely a year of it passed without seeing the Navy actively and gallantly engaged in some corner of the world.[5]

He might have added that this was a supreme age for British science and information gathering in an era of globalization and for giving a boost to independent-minded, anti-imperial regimes in Latin America. This was the age of *Pax Britannica*, and it helped to reformulate the world.[6]

In recognition of the expansion of British political influence and maritime enterprise beyond Cape Horn during this period, a separate naval station for the Pacific was created at Valparaiso in 1837. This command evolved from the old South American station and assumed its western duties.[7] The growth of British interest west of Cape Horn paralleled that east of Cape of Good Hope: the Australasian station established in 1859 and the China station founded in 1864 grew out of the old East Indies and China station. The Pacific station headquarters at Valparaiso met the two eastern stations at 170° west longitude.[8] From this new headquarters, men-of-war protected British interests in Central and South America, and they carried treasure from ports as far north as the Gulf of California.[9]

Britain's chief rival in the northeastern Pacific in the years 1818–1843 was the United States, which lacked all territorial advantage until American settlers began trekking into Oregon in 1842.[10] In 1818, both Britain and the United States held Oregon by agreement; both watched Russian expansion in North America with suspicion; both observed Spain's declining power in California with more than casual interest; and both vied for power in the western hemisphere. Both countries sought to resolve several major issues, including the extent to which Russian activity should be allowed to expand on the continent; the question of sovereignty of the Hawaiian Islands; the possible acquisition of Alta California by one of the powers; and their dispute over Oregon.

The Russian Challenge

Russia was the first to challenge Britain's claims to the Northwest Coast, which were recognized by the Nootka agreement with Spain in 1790. Alexander Baranov, the governor of the Russian American Company in North America, had established a settlement at Sitka in 1799. His aim was to develop a great North Pacific empire; to this end he built Fort Ross on Bodega Bay, Alta California, in 1812 as an agricultural and fur-trading centre and a possible defence post. The Russian American Company also maintained a station on the nearby Farallon Islands, and it considered the Hawaiian Islands as a possible focal point of activity.

As long as the Russians did not interfere with British traders in and around Nootka Sound, the steady Russian ascendancy in Alaska received scant attention from the British government. This situation changed, however, when Tsar Nicholas I proclaimed, in his Ukase of 1821, territorial sovereignty for Russia over the lengthy arc extending from Siberia along the coast of North America to 51° north latitude, near the northern tip of Vancouver Island, and dominion over adjacent seas 115 miles from the coast. This declaration ran counter to the claims of Great Britain and the United States, which by their convention of 1818 had established a condominium over the Pacific slope west of the Continental Divide, from 42° north latitude, the northern border of Alta California, to an undetermined point in Alaska.

The Admiralty, experts on gathering naval intelligence, knew that in 1815–1818 the Russian explorer Otto von Kotzebue had greatly extended Russian knowledge of the American continent in and around the sound that bears his name; they knew also that in 1823 the tsar had ordered him on a "scientific mission" to Kamchatka, near the Kurile Islands, and to the Northwest Coast of America to protect the Russian American Company from smuggling carried on by foreign traders. Knowledge of von Kotzebue's mission and of Russian continental and maritime designs as promulgated in the Ukase of 1821 spurred British promoters of Arctic exploration on the one hand, and the Hudson's Bay Company on the other, to consider ways to contain their rival.

It now fell to the Foreign Office to hold the line on Russian pretensions. It could not agree to either the territorial or maritime claims of the tsar. The Hudson's Bay Company—with which the North West Company was now merged—as well as British whaling interests and Sir John Barrow, the influential Admiralty secretary and promoter of Arctic exploration, all objected to the fact that the Russian intrusion, if recognized, would end free navigation on the coast.[11] Accordingly, stiff diplomatic opposition was expressed in London, plans for British exploration in the Arctic were undertaken and Hudson's Bay Company activities in what is now Yukon developed apace.

John Franklin, the explorer, proposed a survey of the shores of the Polar Sea from the mouth of the Mackenzie River westward to the northwest corner of America. The "objects to be attained," he advised Barrow on November 26, 1823, "are important at once to the Naval character and the Commercial interests of Great Britain." The particular advantage would be, he felt, "the preservation of that Country, which is most rich in Animals from the encroachment of Russia and preventing the Establishment of another and at some Period perhaps a hostile Power on any Part of the Northern Continent of America."[12] The Hudson's Bay Company offered assistance to the project in order to prevent a Russian claim to the undiscovered northern coast at the expense of British interests.[13] The Admiralty immediately decided to send two ships under command of Captain William E. Parry to find a northwest passage via Prince Regent Inlet. Franklin was to proceed by way of the Mackenzie River and the shores of the Polar Sea as planned. Captain Frederick William Beechey, meanwhile, received instructions to sail from England to Bering Strait via Cape Horn, extend the geographical knowledge of the northwest coast of Alaska and, at Kotzebue Sound, meet and supply Parry and Franklin should they complete their intended travels from the east. (Of course, the explorations of 1825–1827 did not result in finding a northwest passage.)

The Hudson's Bay Company had its own plans for checking Russian aspirations at the same time. In 1822 the Governor and Committee had already determined to expand Company interests as far north and west of the Fraser River as necessary "to keep the Russians at a distance."[14] Subsequently, the muscular Samuel Black was sent by the Company to explore the waterways parallel to and west of the Mackenzie River and Rocky Mountains, with a view to drawing trade in the Stikine territory away from the Russians on the coast. Thus began for the Company a successful and little-known program to stabilize and push back the north-western frontier of its operations, first on land and, after 1826, on water. So adroit was the Company in its dealings on the upper portion of the coast in the 1820s and 1830s that British warships were not required to uphold national interests.

The British were in a strong bargaining position against Russia, whose maritime claims of 1821 contravened international law and whose trading aspirations could now be contained by the Hudson's Bay Company. At all odds, British trade was to be protected where British claims were legitimate. A convention was signed on February 28, 1825, in which Britain and Russia entered into an agreement that established the southern boundary of Russian America at 54°40' and its eastern limits along Portland Canal to 56° north latitude, and thence by the height of mountains parallel to but no nearer than ten leagues from the coast to the 141st meridian, on which line it would run to the Arctic Ocean. The Russians acknowledged British navigation rights on the coast and on rivers cutting through the Russian *lisière* or coastal strip. The British could also trade at Sitka and on the Russian coast south of Mount St. Elias for a ten-year period.[15] These terms, essentially the same as those of a Russian–American convention of April 17, 1824, stayed Russian progress eastward and southward while at the same time they restored British and American maritime rights.

By diplomacy and trade, therefore, the British had entrenched their own position in northwestern North America, including the coast of that area. They had done so with remarkable ease against a weaker power without resorting to the use of the Navy to make clear their position. The aim of the British was trade—not colonization. But the Monroe Doctrine, announced by the president of the United States in 1823 in an effort to end further European colonization in America, was viewed in London at the time with contempt. It has been argued that the doctrine was aimed at Britain, not Russia.[16] The Foreign Office was nonetheless prepared to uphold British interests on the Northwest Coast in the face of Russian or American rivalry, or both.[17] Foreign Office policy continued to hold that the colonization of the unoccupied portions of America would be open as before.[18]

Peaceful expansion in the face of the Russian challenge was the result of careful and successful development by the Hudson's Bay Company and the fact that differences of opinion between Britain and Russia were resolved amicably. By 1839, American and Russian competition in the fur trade of both the coast and the interior had been eliminated, and the Hudson's Bay Company reigned supreme on the Northwest Coast of North America.

The Hawaiian Islands

In the Hawaiian Islands, international rivalry was less clearly defined and much less easily resolved. British sovereignty had been offered by the Hawaiian monarchy during Captain Vancouver's visits but had been declined by London. Shortly after the War of 1812, France, the United States and Britain began to display interest in the islands because of their strategic location between the potentially rich markets of the Americas and those of Asia.[19] The maritime powers considered them to be the *entrepôt* of the Pacific; their proximity to North America seemed to imply that their destiny would be determined by the nation that controlled the Pacific slope. This explains why, in 1827, the British prime minister, George Canning, refused to enter into an agreement with the United States in which Britain would have "foregone the advantages of an immense indirect intercourse between China and what may be, if we resolve not to yield them up, her boundless establishments on the N.W. Coast of America."[20] Knowing that the East India Company monopoly would expire in 1833, after which trans-Pacific trade would flourish, and wary of American aspirations in the Pacific, Canning would not place in jeopardy the future advantages that would accrue from a commerce linking two hemispheres. To him this represented "the trade of the world most susceptible of rapid augmentation and improvement."[21]

By 1820, Honolulu had become the principal port in the Pacific, and it remained so until San Francisco became an important maritime centre after the California gold discoveries of 1848. Consequently, British men-of-war visited the Hawaiian Islands periodically.

On the long cruises to Hawaii, for reasons of navigation, captains preferred to sail before the southeast trade winds from the major South American ports of Valparaiso and Callao. After reaching the Doldrums, they relied on the northeast trade winds to complete the course to Honolulu. Then, crossing the "horse latitudes," they followed the Japan Current to the Northwest Coast, San Francisco or Monterey. Some of them took on treasure shipments at various Mexican ports for safe conveyance to England before returning to Valparaiso and finally sailing home at the completion of a three- or four-year commission in the Pacific.

These treasure shipments provide a minor but interesting parenthesis to maritime history. The carrying of specie in Royal Navy ships in lawless areas had been authorized "for centuries," but by the nineteenth century was virtually confined to the Pacific coasts of Latin America. Admiralty regulations pertaining to the conveyance of specie seem to have existed early in that century, though it was not until 1819 that a statute formally stated the conditions of the lucrative scheme. The statute was followed by the proclamation of William IV, dated June 8, 1831, that reduced the "freight" from 1.5 to 1 percent. At the completion of the voyage, the freight was divided into four parts: two parts for the ship's commander, one part for the commander-in-chief on the station, and one part for the Greenwich Hospital for Seamen. Thus, in the case of the *Grampus* returning to England in 1848 with one of the largest treasures of the period, amounting to $2,628,900 (Mexican, equivalent to about £107,000), her captain received nearly $13,145, and the Commander-in-Chief, Pacific, and Greenwich Hospital about $6,573 each.[22]

Returning to navigational problems in the Pacific, by the mid-1840s, "steam navigation" and the establishment of bunkering facilities were advanced enough to permit paddle-wheelers to visit the north Pacific coast without following the usual tracks via the Hawaiian Islands. Paddle-wheelers could also reach various Pacific islands more quickly than ships dependent on wind as the sole motive power. At first steam-assisted ships did not appear in great numbers because of problems of maintenance, cost, fuel reliability and radius of action. Even as late as the mid-1850s, when the screw-propeller began to replace the paddle-wheel, the majority of warships depended entirely on the wind or were steam-assisted; thus a clockwise track of British warships was common from the coast of South America to Tahiti, Hawaii, the north Pacific coast and then south to Valparaiso. In the Pacific, the ability of a commander to get his ship under sail as quickly as possible from point to point across vast reaches of water still required great skills in navigation and seamanship.

One of the early visits of the Royal Navy to Honolulu occurred in 1824, when HMS *Blonde*, 46 guns, under Captain Lord George Byron, conveyed home the remains of the Hawaiian royal couple, who died of measles while on a visit to England. A 46-gun frigate was sent—much larger than the sloops of 18 to 26 guns that usually patrolled the seas at this time—which indicates the political importance Canning gave to this mission.[23] The Hawaiians had looked to Britain for security and protection ever since the visit of Captain Vancouver in 1794. The Foreign Office considered the *Blonde*'s presence especially desirable and timely, since both the Russian and American governments were "known to have their eyes upon those islands which may ere long become a very important Station in the trade between the N.W. Coast of America and the China Seas."[24] Fear that the French held superiority at sea in the Pacific was also a factor.

For these reasons, and especially to consolidate their interests in the islands, the British concluded that a naval base should be established if a suitable situation could be found. None was discovered then, and Britain was obliged to rely on irregular visits of warships and the appointment of Captain Richard Charlton as consul in 1824 to guard her interests. She sought to encourage commerce, preserve the islands as a place of refreshment for ships of the Royal Navy and maintain the prevalent Hawaiian disposition "of looking to British Connection in Preference to that of any other Power."[25]

By the 1830s the Hawaiian Islands experienced the growing trade and increasing settlement that Prime Minister Canning had prophesied earlier for the islands and for the littoral of the North Pacific. Often the Hawaiian Islands served as wintering headquarters for sea captains who sought hides and tallow on the coasts of California, whales throughout the North Pacific, and walrus teeth, sandalwood, pearl shell and other commodities among the Pacific islands.[26] Moreover, according to Captain Michael Seymour of HMS *Challenger*, who visited the Hawaiian group in 1834, exotic products such as sugar cane, indigo and ginger could be grown there, as well as enough tobacco to supply all the Northwest Coast, California and Mexico.[27]

Already the islands provided a promising outlet for British manufacturers; each year £50,000 to £60,000 worth of British goods were sold there. Chief among the British trading organizations was the Hudson's Bay Company. In 1834 the Company established a commercial house in Honolulu, where it sold naval stores, hardware and foodstuffs, while salmon and timber were marketed from the Northwest Coast. As it did in San Francisco, the Company also acted for a time as British consular agents in the Hawaiian Islands.

As Britain's political, strategic and commercial interests grew, the government watched with suspicion the increase of American maritime activity in the Hawaiian Islands. The Royal Navy intensified its vigilance over the islands, and the visit of HMS *Actaeon*, 26 guns, in late 1836 helped to re-establish British influence there.[28] As was common in those days, her commander, Captain the Honourable Edward Russell, used coercion to force the Hawaiian king to remake the local laws defining alien property and to recognize the rights of Englishmen.[29]

Some indication of the degree of Anglo-American rivalry in the islands in the late 1830s is illustrated by the attitude of the British admiral in the Pacific in 1837. When the line-of-battle ship USS *North Carolina*, 92 guns, entered the Pacific in that year, followed by three corvettes under the same flag, the implication seemed clear to Rear-Admiral Sir Graham Eden Hamond: "These Yankees are sly dogs," he recorded in his journal, "and I suspect they have some intention of seizing upon the Sandwich Islands."[30] His reaction was natural enough, although he certainly misjudged the Americans on this occasion. Thus, by 1837 an annual visit of a British warship was considered necessary to guard national interests and watch out for covetous rivals.[31]

During 1841, an examination of British policy for Hawaii and other areas in the northeastern Pacific revealed that the ministry was clearly against "the formation of new and distant Colonies," all of which would involve "heavy direct and still heavier indirect expenditure, besides multiplying the liabilities of misunderstanding and collisions with Foreign Powers."[32]

This review of policy occurred when Sir George Simpson, the governor of Hudson's Bay Company territories in North America, indicated that in the course of his travels he would be prepared to compile a secret report for the government on "the Commerce and Navigation of the North Pacific."[33] His proposal was rejected, as the colonial secretary, Lord John Russell, explained, because Britain did not want to colonize the Hawaiian Islands, which were bound to become American anyway.[34]

The colonial secretary's views were shared by Sir John Barrow, a secretary of the Admiralty and usually a promoter of British interests in the North Pacific. Barrow wrote: "Our cruizers [sic] have free access to them, and are readily supplied with anything they can afford, but even in these casual visits they frequently have to contend with the American traders and Missionaries, particularly at the Sandwich Islands; and with the French Catholic Missionaries political as well as religious, at the Society Islands."[35] By stationing troops or ships in these islands, Barrow warned, Britain would only place herself in a "Wasp's Nest," and endless disputes with foreigners and Natives would follow.[36] He reasoned that Britain should also avoid a "Wasp's Nest" on the Northwest Coast, where the United States and Russia had already established themselves: he wanted to avoid a predicament based on territorial claims such as that at Nootka Sound. Barrow would admit only that a port near the Columbia River would be advantageous to British maritime enterprise.[37] The British ministry, whose views were reinforced by Barrow's recommendations, rejected the Simpson proposal on the grounds that Britain did not contemplate "any new acquisitions at present . . . either on the Shores, or among the Islands of the Pacific."[38]

Simpson remained unconvinced. During his travels of 1841 and 1842, he became certain that the Hawaiian Islands, California and Oregon would fall to the Americans unless the British government awakened from what he regarded as its lethargy.[39] In Honolulu and San Francisco, for example, he found British residents critical of their government for not sending enough British warships to protect them. Simpson thought the situation was alarming in view of the "very frequent" visits of American men-of-war and "increasing" calls of French men-of-war.[40] He suggested that naval vessels in the North Pacific could "run across with the Trades" to Honolulu and then back via California, thereby providing British influence in the northeastern Pacific.[41] The Royal Navy, as has been shown, did indeed give consideration to the region at this time, and was in fact using the very passages that Simpson recommended, although less frequently than he wished.

Simpson's reports lent weight to the warnings from naval commanders on station, who said that British influence was weakening. Admittedly, Simpson's expansionist views were inconsistent with the ministry's contention that extending sovereignty was not worth the trouble and costs of administration and protection. Undoubtedly, his dispatches, relayed from the Hudson's Bay Company's London headquarters to Whitehall, increased the ministry's interest in the political futures of Hawaii, California and Oregon.

Although a marked change in British policy occurred in the years 1841 and 1842, it was dictated less by the opinions of Simpson than by the circumstances of international rivalry. French imperial designs on islands in the Pacific, as well as on California, became apparent when the British captain Jenkin Jones reached Alta California in 1841 in the *Curaçoa*, 24 guns, to investigate the semi-official mission of Duflot de Mofras, an emissary landed from the French corvette *Danaide*.[42] Jenkin Jones found that the motives of the French investigation were more than scientific, and concluded that a systematic plan of French expansion throughout the Pacific was in operation.[43] These fears, shared by the commander-in-chief in the Pacific, were fully realized when an expedition under the command of Rear-Admiral Du Petit-Thouars in the frigate *La Reine Blanche*, 60 guns, carrying a large military force, doubled Cape Horn in 1842 and claimed the Marquesas Islands for France.[44] These developments exposed French imperial designs in the Pacific and showed the British position of *laissez-aller* to be obsolete.

In consequence, according to the "new Foreign Office policy" of October 4, 1842, American and French activities in the Hawaiian Islands were to be watched more closely than ever before. This decision was based on two considerations. In terms of commerce, British trade in the region showed substantial increase, exceeding that of the United States and France combined, as Captain Jenkin Jones reported.[45] In terms of strategy, the value of Hawaii as a freely accessible base for the Royal Navy justified more visits by British warships, especially since the Pacific station was to be reinforced by three men-of-war. Appropriately, the Foreign Office adopted an all-inclusive policy with political, commercial and strategic implications. It indicated the government's disinclination to establish "a paramount influence" in the Hawaiian Islands. At the same time, it stated that "no other power should exercise a greater degree of influence than that possessed by Great Britain."[46]

Complications arose when Captain Lord George Paulet of HMS *Carysfort* proclaimed British dominion over the Hawaiian Islands on February 25, 1843. His action was prompted by a desire to prevent the islands from falling to a French force under Du Petit-Thouars, who was thought to be sailing there from Tahiti.[47] This declaration of a British protectorate was unauthorized. Nevertheless, when news of it reached London, the Foreign Office, acting according to the new policy announced in October 1842, justified it on the grounds that the influence of the United States had exceeded that of the British.[48] To add to the confusion, the Commander-in-Chief, Pacific, Rear-Admiral Richard Thomas—who had not yet received instructions to this effect—saluted the Hawaiian ensign on reaching the Islands on July 31, 1843, thereby disavowing Paulet's action of five months earlier. To this day he is remembered as a great friend of the Hawaiian Kingdom.

The solution to this imbroglio was the Anglo-French Treaty of November 28, 1846, signed in London. The two nations agreed "reciprocally to consider the Sandwich Islands as an independent State, and never to take possession neither directly nor under the title of Protectorate, or any other form of any part of the Territory of which they are composed."[49] But failure to include the United States in this act of self-denial meant that Britain could not act unilaterally as American pressures for annexation increased toward the end of the nineteenth century.[50]

Alta California

Like the Hawaiian Islands, Alta, or Upper, California was coveted by several nations. Foreign traders were active in Alta California in defiance of all Spanish laws by the beginning of the nineteenth century. Their mercantile activities continued to expand there after 1821 despite restrictions by the new authority, Mexico.

In 1805 the Russians arrived in Alta California. And in 1812 they founded the agricultural and fur-trading post Fort Ross near Bodega Bay, lying at about 39° north latitude on the coast. They were followed by

American trappers, who crossed the cordillera to the Pacific shores in 1826, and by Boston ships engaged in the hide and tallow trade. A further influx of foreigners occurred in 1829, when the Hudson's Bay Company began sending annual fur brigades to Alta California from Fort Vancouver on the Columbia, which for four years had been the hub of the Company's Pacific maritime trade. The French came to the area by sea.

Foreign interference by the United States, Great Britain, Russia, France and even Prussia was feared by Mexico. The Mexican province, with its good ports and rich lands, promised to be a major prize for one of these powers. As for Great Britain, her presence was sustained by occasional visits from ships of the Royal Navy.

Scientific inquiry as well as international rivalry took HMS *Blossom*, Captain Frederick William Beechey, to San Francisco Bay and Monterey in 1826 and 1827. The *Blossom* was one of several British ships assigned to special service in Pacific and Arctic exploration after the Napoleonic Wars, when the Navy renewed its exploration of the Pacific and its search for a northwest passage from the Atlantic to the Pacific via Arctic waters.[51]

The British attached great importance to these expeditions: as late as 1845, for example, Sir John Franklin's party was still seeking the passage to the west across the northern shores of North America. The Admiralty knew at that time that France and the United States had fleets in the Pacific, which made discovery of a northwest passage strategically important, since the shortest way home for French and American men-of-war would be "through the Polar Sea"—if a sea lane could be discovered.[52] The *Blossom's* voyage to the Pacific and the Bering Sea demonstrated the Admiralty's belief that "knowledge is power." In gathering scientific information and conducting surveys, the voyage was a logical sequel to the voyages of Cook, Vancouver and Broughton.[53]

As mentioned earlier, Beechey carried orders for the *Blossom* to proceed to Ice Cape, Alaska, to meet and supply captains Parry and Franklin, who were searching for a passage along the Arctic coasts. Beechey's orders were to sail from England to the Pacific by way of Cape Horn, verify the existence of some Pacific islands and reach the Bering Strait by July 10, 1826, when it was believed that Arctic waters in this region would be ice-free.[54] When the *Blossom* reached Cape Barrow, pack ice confronted her. Winter was coming, supplies were short and there was danger of being icebound. According to plan, the *Blossom* then sailed to San Francisco. Carpentry stores and medicines were unobtainable on the American side of the Pacific without going too far south; Beechey therefore set a course for Canton via Hawaii. Although he had spent an unsuccessful season in Arctic waters, he did complete extensive surveys of the North Pacific.[55]

The *Blossom* returned to the Arctic in the summer of 1827. She found no sign of Captain Franklin; Parry had returned to England. Beechey continued his surveys and then returned to San Francisco Bay for the winter. For two months he directed an extensive examination of that magnificent landlocked bay, which was published in a chart. He did not hesitate to state in his *Narrative*, published in 1831 by Admiralty authority, that the site possessed all the requirements for "a great naval establishment," and by its advantageous position in the North Pacific promised to become very important.[56] His writings drew world attention to San Francisco Bay, a harbour destined to play a dominant role in United States maritime expansion in the Pacific. Beechey also examined other coastal areas, including the important Mexican port of Mazatlan.

Immediately after Beechey's account appeared in print in 1831, the British Hydrographic Department approved plans for a more detailed inspection of the eastern Pacific.[57] The *Beagle* went to the coast of South America as far north as Ecuador, in keeping with expanding British–South American trade. The barque *Sulphur* and her tender, the cutter *Starling*, went to sections of the Pacific coast from Valparaiso to Alaska in 1836–1839, primarily to examine the mouth of the Columbia River and extend Beechey's earlier surveys of San Francisco Bay, especially the rivers and arms flowing into it, the Farallon Islands off the coast, and the hazardous bar at its entrance.[58] They were asked also to determine the exact longitude of the north Pacific coast, which Captain O.V. Harcourt of HMS *North Star*, 28 guns, believed was about 40' incorrect in Captain Vancouver's charts.

Beechey was the obvious choice to command the mission of the *Sulphur* and *Starling*. In line with common practice, he drafted his own instructions, and these found Admiralty approval. Unfortunately, poor health prevented Beechey from directing the survey. The task was assigned first to Lieutenant Henry Kellett, then passed to Captain Edward Belcher, who had been in the *Blossom* as assistant surveyor.[59]

This survey coincided with the need to examine Russian activity in Alta California. At first, British interest in Russia's Ross colony was casual: "You know they are 'interlopers,' as Master Purchas would say, and have a flourishing settlement there," Beechey informed Captain Beaufort, the hydrographer, on November 1, 1836.[60] Nearly a year later, however, Lieutenant Andrew Hamond of the sloop *Rover*, 18 guns, was in the Mexican port of Mazatlan when he learned from visitors to Alta California of Russian expansion southward from a "grand settlement at Nootka Sound."[61] If this were true, it constituted an obvious challenge to British claims.

Hamond's report of Russian aggrandizement on the north Pacific coast led his father, Rear-Admiral G.E. Hamond, the commander-in-chief, to give instructions that the next ship proceeding to Mexico in 1838 should investigate Ross colony.[62] But HMS *Imogene*, 28 guns, commanded by Captain H.W. Bruce, was unable to visit the Columbia River in 1838 because of pressing matters in the Hawaiian Islands and elsewhere. Consequently, the responsibility fell to Belcher. His description of Fort Ross in 1839, based on information gathered by a "friend," contains no political overtones. However, at the time of the examination, Belcher and the Russian governor were distrustful of each other owing to the "anticipated rupture" between their parent nations in other parts of the world over the Eastern Question.[63] Even as late as 1841 the British remained suspicious of Russian intentions near San Francisco Bay and at Nootka Sound.[64]

Although the Mexicans did not challenge the Russians directly at Fort Ross, they indicated that foreigners south of San Francisco were unwelcome. This became evident in 1840, when officials in Monterey, the capital of the Mexican province of Alta California, imprisoned 40 British and American citizens for subversive activity and deported them to Tepic, in the Guadalajara province of Mexico, some fifteen hundred miles distant. Because no British man-of-war was present at the time, the British vice-consul there, Eustace Barron, called on the United States Navy to act for British as well as American interests.[65] Forceful diplomacy, combined with the visit of the American sloop *St. Louis*, resulted in release of the prisoners and brought to an end what is known as the Graham incident.

To guard against further provocations, Barron and Sir Richard Pakenham, the British minister in Mexico City, sent pleas to London for naval support and an increase in the strength of the Pacific squadron.[66]

These pleas did not go unanswered; the *Curaçoa* was sent to the California ports to ascertain the condition of British subjects. Her commander, Captain Jenkin Jones, carried supplementary orders requiring him to object to arbitrary actions of Mexican officials against British residents and to warn them that they would be held responsible by the British government if a repetition of the Graham incident occurred.[67]

At this stage, the Foreign Office was evidently prepared to rely on naval visits to protect British interests in Alta California. Then an overly zealous American commodore, Thomas Ap Catesby Jones, seized Monterey prematurely in 1842 because he thought the British ship-of-the-line *Dublin*, flagship of Rear-Admiral Richard Thomas, had sailed from Callao to occupy California under a secret Anglo-Mexican treaty. This event prompted Britain to appoint a vice-consul for the region. Thereafter, consular activities and regular calls by British frigates and sloops sufficed to guard British persons and property in Alta California until war broke out between Mexico and the United States in 1846.

The Oregon Country in the Balance

The fate of British trade in the Columbia River country was of greater concern to Britain than trade in California because of the strength of British claims to the area and the presence there of the Hudson's Bay Company. Since 1818, Britain had jointly occupied the territory with the United States. Diplomatic discussion in the mid-1820s failed to resolve the underlying Anglo-American rivalry for possession of the territory, so the modus vivendi was renewed in 1827 for an indefinite period. According to the terms of the agreement, it could end one year after notification was given by either power.

The sovereignty of Old Oregon was still in dispute when the previously mentioned British surveying ships *Sulphur* and *Starling* reached the Northwest Coast in August 1837 and again in the summer of 1839. They were the first British warships to call there in more than two decades, and their activities were extensive. After leaving the Hawaiian Islands for Cook's Straits on July 27, 1837, they arrived at the Russian post of Port Etches on August 26 and took several observations. On September 12, Belcher was at Sitka, where Russian hospitality proved excellent and stores were purchased. Nootka Sound was reached on October 5, and observations again were taken. It was too late in the season to enter the mouth of the Columbia River, so Belcher repaired to San Francisco Bay, where the ships were refitted and the Sacramento River was examined to "the Fork," its then navigable limit about 150 miles upstream. On November 30 he was at Monterey, and later he called at San Blas and Panama. By 1839 he was back again at Honolulu. He visited the Kodiaks and reached Sitka on July 19 of that year and the Columbia River on July 28.[68] Captain Belcher had several assignments to complete, one of these involving a discreet examination of Oregon, as his hydrographic instructions noted:

> Political circumstances have invested the Columbia river with so much importance that it will be well to devote some time to its bar and channels of approach, as well as to its inner anchorages and shores; but you must be exceedingly careful not to interfere in any manner with the subjects of the United States who live on its banks; neither admitting nor contesting their claims, respecting which there is a distinct understanding between the two Governments, and if necessary you will find some prudent pretext for desisting from the survey, rather than risk any collision or even remonstrance.[69]

All these undertakings were designed to facilitate the production of new charts that were becoming essential as increased trade brought British vessels into contact with the coasts of the Americas from Chile to the Columbia.[70] No other instructions of a political nature were given at this time, but presumably Belcher was to keep an eye on Russian and American activities from Monterey north to Sitka.

Many years later, at a meeting of the Royal Geographical Society, Belcher disclosed that he had been instructed in 1838 by the British government and the Commander-in-Chief, Pacific, to make a confidential report on Oregon.[71] If this indeed were the case, and there is no reason to doubt Belcher, two developments probably explain why a mission was sent. First, the British government knew that William Slacum, a United States Navy lieutenant masquerading as a private individual, had visited the Columbia River in December 1836. Both Chief Factor McLoughlin at Fort Vancouver, who bluntly described Slacum as "an agent of the American government, come to see what we are doing," and the Commander-in-

Chief, Pacific, were well aware that the United States was casting longing eyes on Oregon.[72] Second, in the United States Senate, a bill had been introduced for the military occupation of Oregon from 42° north latitude to 54° 40' north latitude, the ending of Anglo-American condominium and the promotion of settlement.[73] Whether or not Belcher actually received instructions remains obscure. If he did, probably the Admiralty, in conjunction with the Foreign Office, must have realized that a survey of the Columbia's mouth by the *Sulphur* and *Starling* offered Belcher an opportunity to report on the state of British interests in Oregon and the influx of Americans.

Their examination of the intricate entrances to the river revealed a new navigable channel, which Hudson's Bay Company officials deemed inferior to the commonly used northern one. As seemed to be the fate of most British warships that ventured into the river in those days, both vessels met with mishap: touching ground was an occupational hazard of surveying ships. In damaged condition, the *Starling* was forced to navigate one hundred miles of confined waterway upstream to Fort Vancouver, where Belcher began his political investigation, and the ships' companies made repairs to the vessels.[74]

Belcher had firebrand tendencies (unusual in British naval officers), and he ignored the Anglo-American joint occupation agreement as explained in his instructions, assuming that the territory was British. He reported to the commander-in-chief in an elated manner: "The Americans do not possess an atom of land on the Columbia!"[75] Although he was received hospitably at Fort Vancouver, in accordance with orders from the Company headquarters in London, Belcher was highly critical of the inability of a British "possession" to supply British warships with provisions.[76] He appears to have received the same kind of welcome and help given other travellers and settlers, but he attacked his hosts for harbouring American missionaries, whom he thought to be representatives of the United States government.

The visit of the *Sulphur* and *Starling* to Oregon, and Belcher's subsequent indictment of the operations of the Company, brought divergent reactions from Company officials in London. On the one hand, they rejected Belcher's charges as false. On the other hand, they were grateful that the British government had awakened at last to the danger faced by the Company's interests on the Pacific slope, these interests being especially valuable because they were linked to British enterprises in other areas of the Pacific.[77]

It seems certain that Belcher criticized the Company unduly. With little knowledge of problems facing the fur trade, he evidently judged the Company mainly on patriotic grounds. Moreover, he was unaware of "the obvious course of events . . . the passing of European Population to the NW Coast of America and to its ultimate consequences in the Trade of the Pacific and of China," as Lord Ellenborough, the First Lord of the Admiralty, so aptly analyzed the situation in 1846.[78] This would account for Belcher's later explanation in 1859 that he was perplexed by Britain's loss of Oregon in 1846 because, during his visit in 1839, the British flag flew over old Fort Astoria while not a single American was on the Columbia. Oregon was lost, Belcher claimed, by the lack of "prudence" exercised by the government and the "overzealous desire" of Dr. John McLoughlin, the director at Fort Vancouver, in introducing American missionaries into the Willamette Valley.[79]

His official report had one lasting effect. It initiated suspicion of the Company's role west of the Rocky Mountains, particularly regarding the reception of American settlers at Fort Vancouver. The British government, however, was not prepared to resist American claims and had no alternative strategy except hard words or, unacceptably, war. In the years between the visit of the *Sulphur* and *Starling* in 1839 and peaceful agreement with the Americans in mid-1846, the ministry surely must have known that as long as the Hudson's Bay Company remained primarily a commercial organization and the lack of British settlement in Oregon continued, the westward flow of American landseekers could end the chances of British dominion over the banks of the Columbia. The government clearly was more concerned with trade than territory, a fact which a close examination of the Oregon Treaty of 1846 reveals. Its terms guaranteed Hudson's Bay Company rights of trade even without territory.

British Policy Hardens

British policy for the area of the northeastern Pacific in 1818–1843 may be summed up as fundamentally reserved and adaptive in nature. Before 1840, when international rivalry there was in its formative stages, Britain generally regarded the moves of Russia, France and the United States with rather casual interest. Thereafter, whether she wished to or not, as she sought to avoid "wasps' nests," she found herself inextricably drawn into contests for Oregon and Hawaii, and, to a lesser degree, for Alta California. Behind this change in policy was the desire to reject American dominance in the western hemisphere, curtail Russian aggrandizement in North America, and check French imperialistic moves in the Pacific Islands in the 1840s. Although the British government was unwilling to support the Hudson's Bay Company's proposal of 1841 for British expansion to prevent competing nations from extending influence in Hawaii, Oregon and Alta California, the government did show that it would not allow any existing British commercial and strategic advantages to go unprotected, especially in the neutral Hawaiian Islands.

Of course, no rival could ignore British naval supremacy, which provided the means for Britain to extend her influence in the northeastern Pacific during the peaceful period between 1818 and 1843. The primacy of the Royal Navy also prevented threats of intervention by Russia, France or the United States as Latin American countries were winning their independence; the Royal Navy constituted the agency under which these countries could throw off the last vestiges of Spanish domination.[80] However, supremacy of the Royal Navy did not preclude possible alliances of rivals so as to undermine British dominance.

The actual number of visits of British men-of-war seems few during this time, with perhaps only eight calling on the north Pacific coast excluding Mexico, and at least twice that number at the Hawaiian Islands.[81] Even so, these visits sufficed to protect British political and commercial interests. At the approach of the mid-century, ships of the Royal Navy appeared with greater frequency, which indicated the growing importance of these seas to Britain. Time and again after 1815, Britain let slip many an opportunity to obtain the Hawaiian Islands and Alta California. Trade, not territory, was the overriding ambition. And already the British were fighting to end the trans-Atlantic slave trade, waging distant wars in Afghanistan, and fighting vicious conflicts in that place of reluctant empire, South Africa. The quagmires of empire seemed never ending.

Throughout the years 1818–1843, Britain found herself drawn into disputes as a result of political and commercial advances by Russian,

French and American competitors in the Hawaiian Islands, Oregon and California. It bears remembering that Britain did not seek to expand her empire with additions of questionable value, places expensive to defend and troublesome to govern. But she could not isolate herself from the contest, because she feared Russian, French and American aspirations and was forced to protect Hudson's Bay Company interests.

Britain was not alone in exploring the western flanks of the Americas and the islands of the Pacific. In 1838 Charles Wilkes, USN, as commander of the United States Exploring Expedition, began a four-year exploration approved by Congress consisting of six vessels. Hawaii, the Columbia River, the Strait of Georgia and Puget Sound were but a few of the places examined. Wilkes spelled out the future importance of the harbours of Puget Sound. He went even further, proclaiming that Oregon and Alta California were destined to be the basis of a powerful maritime state, with Puget Sound and San Francisco the keys to this prodigious prospect of sea empire. One of Wilkes's vessels, the *Peacock*, laid her bones on the Columbia's treacherous bar, and this event deflected United States official and private attention north to Puget Sound.[82] Until such time as the mouth of the Columbia River could be improved by dredging and proper navigational aids, the ports of Puget Sound took on enhanced meaning in the fast-developing quarrel over Old Oregon.

three

$\mathcal{M}$AN-OF-WAR DIPLOMACY IN THE OREGON CRISIS

The Anglo-American Convention of 1818, which was renewed in 1827, recognized the historic claims of both Britain and the United States to Oregon but did not provide for any means to settle the dispute over sovereignty by arbitration. War would be the alternative should diplomacy fail.

The territory in dispute in 1844–1846 lay west of the Continental Divide between the northern boundary of California (42°N) and the southern extremity of Russian America (54° 40'N). Britain and the United States each claimed this region by virtue of exploration, discovery and trade.[1] Each nation realized that a solution to the Oregon question probably would be found in an equitable division of the country. Apart from the often exaggerated vote-getting election slogan of the Democratic Party in America—"Fifty-four Forty or Fight"—that swept James K. Polk into the presidency in 1844, each nation eventually saw the advisability of compromise. Essentially, therefore, the issue was how to divide Oregon between the two claimants. In other words, should the boundary extend along the 49th parallel from the ridge of the Rocky Mountains to the sea, as the United States insisted? Or should it follow the Columbia River from where its course intersects the 49th parallel to the Pacific, as Great Britain initially contended?

If war were to be avoided, as each party wished, it was necessary to limit the area in contention to that which extended west and north of the Columbia River to the 49th parallel, including the southern tip of Vancouver Island. Within this territory were three geographical regions of importance to fur trade, settlement and maritime development. The nucleus of British commerce on the Northwest Coast was Fort Vancouver, situated about one hundred miles inland near the head of navigation on the Columbia River. Fort Vancouver was built on the north bank of the river in 1825, as officials of the Hudson's Bay Company realized that the Columbia might become the international boundary. Nearly opposite Fort Vancouver, the Willamette River joined the Columbia after draining the Willamette Valley. The Columbia River basin may have been rich in furs and lands for settlement, but it was not readily accessible to shipping owing to dangerous, shifting shoals at the river's mouth.

The second area of contention was Puget Sound, reaching southward from Juan de Fuca Strait. In addition to providing fine anchorages, this body of water offered possibilities of great maritime expansion for the nation that could control its shores. It also furnished, from the north, a more sheltered and safe approach to the Columbia country than that via the Columbia's estuary. Ships could anchor near Fort Nisqually, at the head of the sound, and from there travellers and traders could reach Fort Vancouver by going through the Nisqually and Cowlitz river valleys.

The third district of importance, especially to the British, embraced the southern tip of Vancouver Island. This area had several fine harbours readily accessible to ships, and there was arable land nearby. For these reasons, the Hudson's Bay Company, whose maritime operations on the coast and in the Pacific were hindered by the difficult navigation of the Columbia River up to Fort Vancouver, built Fort Victoria in 1843. The Island was also almost certain to be in British territory after an agreement was reached with the Americans.[2] Vancouver Island was therefore the focal point of British concern and the last line of defence against American expansion in Oregon.

Throughout Oregon, the Hudson's Bay Company held a British commercial monopoly. The Company successfully destroyed competition by American and Russian traders on the Northwest Coast in the 1820s and 1830s. However, it was unable to halt the flow of American settlers who came overland by way of the Oregon Trail after 1842, and settlement spelled the end of the fur trade in the Columbia River basin in more ways than just the destruction of habitat for fur-bearing animals. Although the implications of the influx of Americans received scant attention in discussions between the British and American governments to reach a compromise over the Oregon boundary, it must be remembered that Britain could not have controlled an area populated by Americans. In retrospect, the only feasible method of permanent defence that Britain could have employed in this region was British settlement. This view is supported by reports from British naval and military officers, submitted in 1845 and 1846, which described American settlements on the south bank of the Columbia River and in the Willamette Valley. The British ministry knew that Company interests, at least south of the Columbia, would have to be sacrificed for the preservation of peaceful Anglo-American relations.

The Company understandably opposed a surrender of the Columbia River basin and Puget Sound, and warned the Foreign Office accordingly. It felt that the British would lose a valuable field of commerce and, more important, that the Americans would gain the upper reaches of the region, giving them "the command of the North Pacific and in a certain degree that of the China Sea, objects of the greatest commercial & political importance to Gt. Britain."[3] The Company also fully realized that New England commercial and shipping interests sought these ports.[4] It appeared to Dr. John McLoughlin, director of the Company's Western Department, that the United States Navy also hoped to develop a base on Puget Sound.[5] The British government was caught between the appeals of the Hudson's Bay Company for support and the demands of the American government for "All Oregon."

Naval Support for the Hudson's Bay Company

While diplomatic developments ran their course, the Royal Navy protected British interests on the Northwest Coast. The first mention of plans to support the British position in Oregon was contained in instructions to the Commander-in-Chief, Pacific, written in late 1842, which ordered a warship "to the coasts of the Territory of the Columbia River, the Straits of San Juan de Fuca [sic] and Gulf of Georgia."[6] Why no ship carried out this duty remains obscure; most likely the demands of the station were such that no vessel was available for this service. However, the plans were fulfilled late in 1843, when the Foreign Office advised the Admiralty to instruct the British admiral in the Pacific to send a warship to the Northwest Coast to "show the flag" at the main centres of Hudson's Bay Company trade.[7] The task fell to the sloop *Modeste*, 18 guns, Commander the Honourable Thomas Baillie.

HMS *Modeste* entered the Columbia River safely on July 7, 1844; her object was to indicate to the Americans that Britain would not tolerate interference with her trading interests and territorial claims in Oregon. Baillie rightly believed that his mission could best be achieved by taking the *Modeste* upstream to Fort Vancouver. Aided by a Company pilot, he navigated the treacherous waters as far as the post, where he learned that most of the 2,000 settlers—of whom only 450 were British—lived south of the Columbia and that only a few lived north of the river. His report strengthened the view of the British government that only the territory south of the river should be relinquished to the United States.[8]

After a three-week stay at Fort Vancouver, Baillie sailed downstream for the river mouth, where the *Modeste* (as the *Racoon* had done three decades before) grounded on the notorious bar and narrowly escaped disaster. After repairs were effected at nearby Baker's Bay, he exited the river safely and pointed the *Modeste* to the north and Fort Victoria. But the harbours of Vancouver Island's southern tip were as yet uncharted, and Baillie chose instead to run in to Captain Vancouver's old anchorage, Port Discovery, across Juan de Fuca Strait from Fort Victoria. After receiving provisions from the Company off the entrance to Victoria harbour, the *Modeste* sailed for Port Simpson, the main trading centre on the north coast, near the northern extremity of British claims. There, a further examination of her hull revealed more extensive damage than had been disclosed at Baker's Bay, but successful repairs eliminated the possibility that she might have to return to England.[9]

Having completed her mission, the *Modeste* sailed for the Hawaiian Islands. Her visit to the disputed district was significant in that it marked the first of a series of visits by the Royal Navy to show the Americans, and, indeed, the Hudson's Bay Company, that Britain intended to protect her interests in Oregon, notwithstanding Lord Aberdeen's conciliatory foreign policy.

This was the first use of "gunboat diplomacy" in the Oregon crisis, and it coincided with the formation of plans in London to reinforce the defences of British North America. In the event of war with the United States, the critical areas of operation would be the Atlantic seaboard, the St. Lawrence River, and Lakes Ontario and Erie. In preparing for hostilities, the Admiralty and the War Office were reminded of the experiences of the War of 1812. During that war, waterways were essential to communications, and sea power on the lakes played a decisive role. Consequently, in 1845, the Royal Navy sent Captain F.R. "Bloody" Boxer to examine American military establishments on the Great Lakes. This officer advised the Admiralty that Britain's defence of Canada and the "exposed frontiers of Canada West" depended on maintaining "the command of the navigation of the lakes."[10] He suggested methods, later largely implemented, to increase British maritime strength on the Great Lakes and to convey troops there. His reports and those of other investigators reflected the need for increased military preparations during the gravest foreign crisis to face Britain since the War of 1812.

Sending infantry supported by artillery to the remote Northwest Coast posed all sorts of problems in the event of military operations there. Soldiers would have to be transported overland from Canada or sent by sea. Sustaining them on the spot would pose logistical nightmares. Even so, Baron Metcalfe, the Governor General of Canada, thought that European and native troops from India would bolster the British cause.[11] When the United States Congress passed an Oregon bill to incorporate the territory to 54° 40' in the Union, the British prime minister, Sir Robert Peel, considered secretly sending to Oregon a frigate bearing Royal Marines and a small artillery detachment.[12] But this remained only an idea, as the foreign minister, Lord Aberdeen, wanting no army units involved, contended that the strength of the Royal Navy in the Pacific sufficed to deal with any incident or circumstance arising. Simultaneously, Sir George Simpson, the governor of the Hudson's Bay Company territories in North America, thought that the British position could be strengthened by stationing four warships (two sail and two steam) in the Columbia River with a large body of marines and two thousand Métis and Natives on board.[13] The wildly ambitious proposal of the "Little Emperor," as Simpson was called, did not bear fruit. However, he did convince the Governor and Committee of the Company, the Governor General of Canada, the Duke of Wellington and the Foreign Office that the British should have a military post near Fort Garry, Red River, to counteract American influence in the Canadian Northwest.[14] And finally, "in deference to the earnest entreaties of the Company," the British government sent 346 troops of the 6th Regiment of Foot, the Royal Warwickshires, from Cork to Lower Fort Garry by way of York Factory in Hudson Bay.[15] These soldiers reached their destination September 18, 1846.

As an aid to this expedition, two British officers stationed in Canada were sent to Fort Vancouver "as private travellers." They were to report to London and Montreal on the feasibility of sending troops overland to Oregon in the event of American encroachment on British rights there. They were also asked to gather information on American settlers and, in collaboration with officers of the Royal Navy, to ascertain the possibilities of defending British interests on the Northwest Coast from an American attack. This hasty investigation was promoted by Simpson, who met with Peel and Aberdeen in London on April 3, 1845, and sailed for Montreal three days later with complete authority from the ministry to arrange details of the military reconnaissance of Oregon. Lieutenants Henry J. Warre and Mervin Vavasour were chosen for the undertaking, and Simpson accompanied them from Montreal to Fort Garry.[16]

The first stage of their frontier travels presented so many difficulties that these young British officers immediately advised the secretary of state for war and the colonies, in what was surely a wild imagining, that a route via York Factory would be much better for any cavalry or artillery that might be dispatched to the Canadian Northwest.[17] Warre and Vavasour then began their long journey on horseback across the wide plains and through the difficult passes of the Rockies, accompanied by their guide, Chief Factor Peter Skene Ogden, and seven Company servants. They hoped to reach the Pacific by mid-August, in advance of Lieutenant John Frémont of the United States Army, who was thought to be on a similar mission for the United States.[18]

The hazards they faced soon convinced Warre and Vavasour that Simpson's proposal to send British soldiers overland to Oregon was impracticable, to say the least, and certainly optimistic. Alternatively, they realized that establishing control over the strategic waterways of the area, chiefly the Columbia River and Puget Sound, in order to exclude American warships from the region could defend Oregon best. As for Fort Victoria, they thought it "ill-adapted either as a place of refuge for shipping or as a position of defence."[19] But not so Fort Nisqually, which Vavasour described as having fine harbours, accessible at any season to ships of any size, and therefore the most suitable place for disembarking British troops.[20]

Warre and Vavasour found Cape Disappointment to be the key position in the defence of that part of Oregon. Perhaps with some exaggeration, Simpson had emphasized that British fortification of this headland on the north bank of the Columbia would be advantageous, for enemy warships entering the river would have to "pass so close under the Cape" that shells from a battery "might be dropped almost with certainty" upon their decks.[21] Even so, the merit of Simpson's proposal became evident to Warre and Vavasour when they reached the river entrance. Consequently, they recommended that Chief Factor Ogden buy the land from two American settlers under the pretence that it would be used as a Hudson's Bay Company trading post.

Subsequently, Vavasour submitted plans to his commanding officer in Canada for three batteries of heavy guns at Cape Disappointment, and an additional battery of similar guns at Tongue Point on the south bank of the river.[22] With these fortifications, it was believed the British would be able to control the entrance to the hinterland from the sea. Moreover, as Warre so cogently pointed out, they could control "the whole of the country south of Puget's Sound, there being no other harbour or place of landing between the Columbia River and St. Francisco [sic], where ships of sufficient tonnage to navigate the Pacific could enter or remain at anchor in safety."[23] Nothing came of these plans, for reasons that remain obscure. Probably the British ministry realized that the military defence of Oregon was impracticable. In any event, in a war over Oregon, the decisive theatre would not be the Northwest Coast but the Atlantic seaboard and Great Lakes region. In other words, a war over Oregon was unlikely to take place there.

Meanwhile, what Peel had referred to in September 1844 as "a good deal of preliminary bluster on the part of the Americans" grew in intensity.[24] By early March 1845 the prime minister, although unable to persuade Aberdeen of the merits of sending a secret task force from Britain round the Horn to the Columbia, convinced him that a British warship should appear on the Northwest Coast from time to time, and that the flagship of the Commander-in-Chief, Pacific, should also call there. Subsequently, the Foreign Office advised the Admiralty that "Rear Admiral Sir George Seymour should himself visit that Coast at an early period in the *Collingwood*, 80 guns, with a view to giving a feeling of security to our own Settlers in the Country, and to let the Americans see clearly that H.M.'s Govt, are alive to their proceedings, and prepared, in case of necessity to oppose them."[25] With these words the British ministry gave its first indication of being ready to use the Royal Navy to oppose the American "bluster."[26] The change of policy prompted Aberdeen to write to the British minister in Washington: "At all events, whatever may be the course of the American Govt., the time is come when we must endeavour to be prepared for every contingency."[27]

Defence Preparations

The British ministry could be assured that Rear-Admiral Sir George Seymour would employ warships to their best effect in support of British policy. Seymour was an outstanding officer whose forcefulness and ability made him the choice of Lord Haddington, the First Lord of the Admiralty, and Sir Robert Peel as Commander-in-Chief, Pacific, a position to which he was appointed in May 1844. Seymour knew a good deal about the Northwest Coast. Before he sailed for the Pacific on September 7, 1844, he had read Vancouver's *Voyages*, Robert Greenhow's *Memoir on the North West Coast of North America* and the secretary of the Navy's report to Congress in November 1843 on American activities in the Pacific. He had also studied the events leading to joint occupation of Oregon, examined charts of the Columbia, discussed the importance of the region with Sir John Barrow at the Admiralty and visited Hudson's Bay House in London. He was anxious that the ships under his command should do everything within Foreign Office instructions to keep Oregon and California out of American hands, and to save as many South Pacific islands as possible from falling under French control.[28]

But the Commander-in-Chief, Pacific, acted under the handicap that plagued his predecessors and successors until the advent of the telegraph and wireless telegraphy. Several months must elapse before a reply to his most urgent message could reach him from the Admiralty. At the time of the Oregon crisis, dispatches from London reached him by a circuitous route, via Jamaica and Colón by monthly steam packet, then across the Isthmus of Panama by mule or horse, and on to Callao, the port for Lima, and eventually Valparaiso by Pacific Steam Navigation Company ships. This took 55 days, considerably shorter than the 120 days previously required on the route around Cape Horn, but still a long time. There was no certainty that a reply would reach the Admiral immediately, however, for he might be absent from port at the time. Furthermore, sending ships from point to point in the vast eastern Pacific was time-consuming. The passage from Valparaiso to Hawaii was at least 60 days, and from Hawaii to the Northwest Coast a further 21 days under the best conditions. In view of these limitations, the responsibility placed on the flag officer as an interpreter of British diplomacy was great indeed. He had to assess the validity of old intelligence in relation to his latest instructions and make the best possible disposition of his forces under the circumstances. Similarly, captains under his command frequently were required to exercise judgement concerning their actions and movements.

Seymour was at Lima, Peru, on July 6 when he received orders to sail for Oregon. He had to decide whether to sail first for Tahiti, where he hoped to forestall the French, who were planning to establish a protectorate, or to sail directly for the North Pacific. He decided to wait at Lima for news of events in London and Washington. On July 14 he read a Liverpool paper reporting that no action on the Oregon issue could occur for some time, no matter how arrogant President Polk might be.[29] He therefore decided to sail for Tahiti and then for Honolulu, where he could obtain further intelligence on the state of the Oregon question.

Seymour knew, in setting a course for Tahiti in the *Collingwood*, that the British frigate *America*, 50 guns, Captain the Honourable John Gordon, was bound directly from England to the North Pacific because of the Oregon crisis and would soon be in Juan de Fuca Strait.[30] Seymour realized that the *America* could not cross the bar of the Columbia, because she drew more than 15 feet of water. Therefore, she would have to take up her station in the less hazardous, albeit less influential, position at Port Discovery, near the entrance to Puget Sound. From there a party could go by water and land to Fort Vancouver. Seymour believed that this would suffice to show the British in Oregon that their government was "well inclined to afford them protection."[31]

Rear-Admiral Sir George Francis Seymour, Commander-in-Chief, Pacific, during the Oregon, California, Hawaiian and Tahitian difficulties, was a man of superb tact and ardent disposition. He deployed naval units to the Columbia River and Juan de Fuca Strait to shore up Hudson's Bay Company and British interests at the time of the Oregon crisis. He had once sailed in the *Victory* under Nelson in the Mediterranean, later becoming a Lord of the Admiralty. CFB ESQUIMALT NAVAL & MILITARY MUSEUM

When Chief Factor John McLoughlin at Fort Vancouver received news that the *America* was on the way, he complained to the governor of the Hudson's Bay Company in London that a frigate would be absolutely no use to the Company in Oregon; instead a smaller vessel that could ascend the river to Fort Vancouver was required.[32] McLoughlin's complaint was legitimate, but he did not know that Seymour intended to send the sloop *Modeste* back to the coast of Oregon and to Fort Vancouver, if necessary, to strengthen the British position.

The *America* did not reach Juan de Fuca Strait until August 28, 1845, owing to calms and contrary winds. The crew had suffered greatly from being on strict water rations during the long and hot course crossing the equator. Captain Gordon of the *America* was the brother of the Earl of

Aberdeen, the foreign secretary, and one of his officers was Lieutenant William Peel, son of the prime minister and an able officer in his own right.[33] The presence in the ship of two persons with such prominent connections caused at least one official, Thomas Larkin, the United States consul in Monterey, Alta California, to ponder the purpose of the *America's* visit to the Pacific Northwest.[34]

From the *America's* anchorage in Port Discovery, Lieutenant Peel sailed by launch to Fort Victoria. He had two purposes. His first assignment was to deliver a letter given to Gordon in England and addressed to the officer-in-charge of the fort, explaining that the principal object of the *America's* visit was to assure Company authorities that the British government would oppose American encroachments in the Columbia River basin. The second purpose, to speed this intelligence-gathering mission, was to request the use in Puget Sound of the Company steamer *Beaver*.[35] The *Beaver* was then away trading so the request could not be granted; consequently, Peel and his party were forced to take the frigate's launch to the head of the sound and then travel overland to Fort Vancouver.[36]

Peel had been ordered by Captain Gordon—and may even have been selected by Seymour—to report on the settlements on the banks of the Columbia and Willamette Rivers.[37] His two reports are well known and reveal the judgement that distinguished him as an officer. In the first, addressed to his captain, he gave details on the territory investigated.[38] In the second letter, to Richard Pakenham, the British minister in Washington conducting talks with the United States government on Oregon, he expressed agreement with Gordon's belief that Vancouver Island must be retained by Britain if the 49th parallel became the demarcation line. Gordon's contention was based on the fact that the northern channel around Vancouver Island was unnavigable for sailing ships, and thus Britain would lack access to the inland passages from Juan de Fuca Strait to latitude 51° north latitude.[39] Peel noted that the Island commanded Juan de Fuca Strait, possessed a good harbour and had been selected by the Hudson's Bay Company as the eventual hub of trading activities on the Northwest Coast. In his description of growing settlements between the Willamette and Sacramento Valleys, he foretold the inevitable American control of the port of San Francisco, which would give the United States a decided maritime superiority in the Pacific.[40]

Peel's report reached the Admiralty with vital dispatches from Gordon and McLoughlin on February 10, 1846. On the same day, copies were sent to the Foreign Office. It is not known if this intelligence had any influence on the British ministry or the discussions then taking place in Washington. Undoubtedly it added greatly to British information on the Oregon country at a critical stage in negotiations with the United States.

Before the *America* sailed from Fort Victoria for Honolulu on October 1, 1845, Captain Gordon and other officers enjoyed the hospitality of Roderick Finlayson, officer-in-charge at Fort Victoria.[41] "Capt. Gordon," wrote that great raconteur, Finlayson, "was a great deer-stalker. We met a band of deer and had a chase after them on horseback. The deer ran for a thicket into which the horses with their riders could not penetrate and of course no deer were had." Finlayson tried to mollify the disappointed Gordon. "I said to him I was very sorry we had missed the deer etc., and also remarked how beautiful the country looked." Gordon replied that he would not exchange "one acre of the barren hills of Scotland for all he saw around him."[42] What especially disgusted Gordon was that the salmon were caught by baits or nets, and not by the alluring fly as in his beloved Scotland. "What a country," he is reported to have exclaimed, "where the salmon will not take to the fly."[43] The writer and fisherman Roderick Haig-Brown liked to comment that on his Scottish moors, the old captain would have been a fine fellow and a generous host; out in the colonies, by contrast, and in command of a man-of-war, he proved a sticky and disgruntled old character. This is probably a fair assessment. Not all the naval officers on the coast shared Gordon's negative reactions. Finlayson stated that several who visited Fort Victoria earnestly desired to be sent on a mission of conquest, claiming "that they could take the whole of the Columbia country in 24 hours."[44] Gordon's apathy with regard to British and Company interests in Oregon was also noticed by James Douglas, then chief factor at Fort Vancouver, who now had good reason to wonder to what degree the promised naval protection would be made available should circumstances require it.[45] Gordon evidently saw no reason to prolong his visit to Juan de Fuca Strait or to visit Nootka Sound, and by October 1 the *America* had cleared Cape Flattery, bound for Honolulu and the ports on the west coast of Mexico.

About a week later the *Modeste*, Commander Baillie, returned to Juan de Fuca Strait to continue protection of the Hudson's Bay Company.[46] The obvious reason for her reappearance lay in the fact that she was more manoeuvrable and had a shallower draft than the *America*. She therefore could enter the Columbia to support the British position, if required. Rear-Admiral Seymour knew that the Hudson's Bay Company would require assistance to maintain law and order, especially in view of the great tide of immigration then flowing into Oregon. He had already informed the Admiralty that he was willing to stop the Americans if circumstances required drastic action, despite his inability to send even small ships such as the *Modeste* into the Columbia without some degree of hazard.[47]

At Fort Nisqually, Commander Baillie found Hudson's Bay Company officials most anxious for him to take his ship into the Columbia. James Douglas, for one, told him of McLoughlin's warning to Gordon that unless the government took "active measures," they would lose Oregon.[48] Under these pressures, Baillie sailed for the river mouth and eventually brought the *Modeste* to anchor off Fort Vancouver on November 30, 1845, the passage having taken almost a month owing to difficult winds and currents in the river.

What were the reactions at Fort Vancouver to the reappearance of the British sloop? Warre and Vavasour considered the arrival of a British warship extremely timely, as it encouraged British subjects to support their rights. Moreover, it discouraged Americans from taking the law into their own hands; and it gave protection to Hudson's Bay Company property.[49] In other words, they believed that the presence of the *Modeste* achieved the desired effect: American immigrants who had arrived recently were acting peaceably. McLoughlin, who wrote that the ship's presence "has both a moral and political effect and shows that our government is ready to protect us," held a similar view.[50] The importance of stationing a British warship at Fort Vancouver is best revealed by the fact that the *Modeste* remained until May 1847. She was indeed indispensable to British authority in the Lower Columbia.

The Oregon crisis was on Seymour's mind continually, even while he attended to affairs in Tahiti. On August 19, 1845, he ordered Captain John Duntze of the frigate *Fisgard*, 42 guns, to prepare to sail with the paddle-wheel steamer *Cormorant*, 6 guns, to Puget Sound during the spring of 1846 if the United States and Great Britain did not soon come to an agreement.

With this possibility in mind, Seymour also considered a plan "to push our Steamers" right into the Columbia. There they would be beyond any gun batteries that the Americans might have built on Cape Disappointment.[51] The *Cormorant* and *Salamander*, 6 guns, both paddle-wheel sloops, were the only steamers then available to Seymour. There seems to have been not more than two steamers on the station until about 1857, when some screw-frigates and corvettes became available.

The conscientious Seymour's worries were somewhat allayed when he reached Honolulu in the *Collingwood* in September 1845. He believed that news of the British flagship's presence at Honolulu, news hub of the Pacific, would eventually reach Oregon and convince Americans there that Britain attached great importance to her interests on the Northwest Coast.[52] At Honolulu he met his American counterpart, Commodore John F. Sloat. The air was charged with mutual suspicion. All the same, each expressed hope that the two home governments could reach a peaceful agreement on the definition of the Oregon boundary. Seymour was especially concerned for the fate of Alta California after his conversation with Sloat.[53] At this time, Sloat told him that if the Oregon question were not settled, it would be entirely the fault of the American government.[54]

When Seymour returned to Valparaiso on February 15, 1846, he learned that Sloat's squadron was being reinforced from the East Indies station by the ship-of-the-line *Columbus* and the frigate *Constitution*. This information substantiated his fears that the United States Navy was soon to act against either the British in Oregon or the Mexicans in Alta California—or perhaps both. Therefore, he hastened north to Callao with the brig *Spy*, 6 guns, to await dispatches from London and New York. There he learned of President Polk's "arrogant declaration" of December 2, 1845, to the United States Congress.[55] Polk had reasserted the Monroe Doctrine, called for an end to the joint occupation of Oregon and proposed that federal jurisdiction be extended to that territory. Such expansionist views could hardly fail to provoke a war, Seymour believed.[56] "To provide for war taking place," he sent the *Cormorant* north, along with a supply of coal in the chartered merchant ship *Rosalind*; made arrangements for the provisioning and deployment of the squadron in case of war; and issued instructions for part of the squadron expected at Valparaiso—particularly the frigate *Grampus*, 50 guns, on her way from England.[57]

Before the *Collingwood* left Callao for the North Pacific to meet the growing crisis, Seymour penned a lengthy report to the Admiralty, informing their Lordships of the situation and appealing for additional naval support. In essence, he expressed concern over the inadequacy of his squadron for guarding British interests in the vast Pacific. At a time when the possibility of war with the United States and France was rising, he had only 15 ships under his command: one ship-of-the-line, two frigates, ten sloops, one brig and one storeship.[58] The inferiority of the squadron was substantiated in his "Account of Foreign Naval Force at present employed in the Pacific," which accompanied his letter to the Admiralty. This listed the French naval vessels at 16 (two frigates, nine sloops and five smaller ships) and the American vessels at 11 (one ship-of-the-line, two frigates, five sloops and two schooners, with an additional frigate, the *Congress*, expected). Clearly, the British would be at a disadvantage in the Pacific if France and the United States joined forces in a war.

To counteract the growth of rival sea power in the Pacific, especially American influence in Oregon, Seymour boldly appealed to the Admiralty for two ships-of-the-line for duty in Puget Sound. He also requested an arsenal or port for his squadron, as well as a naval-stores depot somewhere between the Northwest Coast and New Zealand. Seymour realized, however, that enlarging his squadron would not overcome the limits of the role that the Royal Navy could play in supporting the British position in the Pacific Northwest. As he admitted to the Admiralty, the rapid increase of American settlers would suffice to give them control of the Lower Columbia without the aid of the United States government. Unless a British military force opposed them—and Seymour was reluctant to send naval brigades a great distance from their ships—the Royal Navy could do very little beyond the areas accessible to ships.[59] This was a fact the Americans knew well.[60]

Nevertheless, he sought to strengthen his case for an increase in the number of British men-of-war in the Pacific by sending a private letter to his friend the Earl of Ellenborough, the First Lord of the Admiralty. Seymour could not ignore the deteriorating situation in Oregon, even though some of his acquaintances at the Admiralty considered Polk's address to Congress "mere blustering." It was essential, as he explained to Ellenborough, that "a force commensurate with the superiority of our Navy over that of all other Nations should be sent to these seas."[61]

These words achieved their desired effect. The Admiralty supported Seymour's urgent demands and informed the foreign secretary on June 6, 1846, that it was necessary to increase the Pacific squadron to give it "a decided preponderance" over that of the United States.[62]

The decision was made with some reluctance. Their Lordships feared that strengthening the force in the Pacific would weaken the Royal Navy in home waters, for the French had 16 or 17 ships-of-the-line in commission.[63] Fear of French intentions arose two years earlier, in 1844, when the Prince de Joinville published his famous *Note sur l'ètat des forces navales de la France*, in which he contended that French steam-power could transport thirty thousand French troops across the English Channel at night. This pamphlet touched off a stormy debate in England on national defence, in which alarmists such as Lord Palmerston, influential statesman, foreign secretary and later prime minister, had warned that steam had "bridged the channel."[64] Thereafter, the Admiralty kept a sharp eye on the strength of the French at sea.

These developments prompted the Lords of the Admiralty to explain to the Foreign Office that the Royal Navy was placed in an awkward position by the possibility of a French invasion of England and a war with the United States over Oregon. Henry Corry, the secretary of the Admiralty, explained the gravity of the situation in these words:

> My Lords consider that it would be inconsistent with the character this country has hitherto borne as a Predominant Naval Power, and with that degree of prudent precaution which under the most flattering circumstances of amity with France we ought still to observe, were we to exhibit our Naval Force at home as inferior to that of France, and this too at a period when there are unsettled differences with America, which may unfortunately terminate in war.[65]

But if an increase in force for the Pacific were authorized by the Foreign Office, more ships would have to be commissioned for protection at home, a difficult matter owing to the shortage of seamen.[66]

The reply of the foreign secretary, Lord Aberdeen, to the recommendations of the Admiralty indicated that war with the United States seemed then to be unlikely. He disagreed with Seymour's proposal for strengthening the Pacific squadron on the "supposed probability of war with the

United States or with France, or with both countries."[67] Although Aberdeen could see the wisdom in a small increase in the force for the Mexican coast to protect British merchants and trade—especially as war between the United States and Mexico appeared imminent—in his opinion the Oregon question provided no threat to British interests. In fact, owing to diplomatic developments, Seymour's fears were now believed to be unfounded.[68]

Aberdeen's confident answer regarding the state of Anglo-American relations can be explained by the fact that Britain gained the upper hand in her diplomatic dealings with the United States by June 1846. In these negotiations she was able to use her supremacy at sea as a threat. The British cabinet, like Seymour, was outraged by Polk's statement, mentioned earlier, to the United States Congress on December 2, 1845. Certainly, Peel decided that the time had come for action when on January 6, 1846, he informed a friend, "We shall not reciprocate blustering with Polk but shall quietly make an increase in Naval and Military and Ordnance Estimates."[69]

From January to June, Ellenborough at the Admiralty repeatedly urged the prime minister to further increase the estimates to prevent the Royal Navy in the Pacific and elsewhere from becoming inferior to the American force.[70] Concessions were made to Ellenborough in this regard but finally Peel was forced to state categorically that he could not sanction further demands on the Treasury in time of peace. He concluded his sharp rejoinder to the First Lord by declaring that Britain was far in advance of her American rival in actual preparedness for war.[71] Peel assured his colleague that the United States knew this and would see the advantage of signing a treaty ending the dispute over the Oregon boundary. Nevertheless, Ellenborough, the most belligerent member of the cabinet, remained unconvinced. Eventually, in July 1846, he resigned in objection to the unwillingness of his "timorous Colleagues" to be ready for war.[72]

The Treaty of 1846

The strength of the Royal Navy may well have been inadequate in Ellenborough's view. It is now clear, however, that Britain's superior strength at sea proved to be a decisive factor in precipitating an agreement between the two powers over Oregon. On January 6, 1846, Louis McLane, the American chargé d'affaires in London, met with Aberdeen to discuss the points of dispute. His report of this meeting to officials in Washington warned that the British planned to commission immediately some 30 ships-of-the-line in addition to steamers and other vessels held in reserve.[73] In all likelihood, this alarming news induced the Americans to adopt a less belligerent attitude.[74]

Meanwhile, at the Foreign Office, plans were underway for a carefully calculated diplomatic manoeuvre. The intent was to draw from the American delegate to the negotiations in Washington a proposal that the boundary west of the Rocky Mountains should be the 49th parallel to the middle of the Strait of Georgia, and then the middle of the channel leading to the open Pacific, thereby leaving Britain in full possession of Vancouver Island. Under the threat of British sea power, the Americans accepted these terms, which formed the basis of the Oregon Treaty signed on June 15, 1846. The final partitioning of the continent between Britain and the United States, therefore, was achieved by an adroit combination of British diplomacy and naval primacy.

Throughout the period when the ministry was reaching an accord with the United States government, Rear-Admiral Seymour possessed sufficient strength on the Northwest Coast to protect British interests in the region. After the *Congress*, 54 guns, flagship of Commodore Robert F. Stockton, arrived in the Pacific, Seymour concluded that the Americans were about to take action against the British in Oregon.[75] Consequently, he had carried out his plan, discussed above, of sending the *Fisgard* and the steamer *Cormorant* to join the *Modeste* in those waters. He was confident that they would reach Juan de Fuca Strait before the *Congress*, thus forestalling an American occupation of Oregon.[76]

The difficulty of sending ships into the river mouth handicapped the Navy's support of the Hudson's Bay Company at Fort Vancouver. Ships that drew more than 15 feet could rarely pass over the bar, and most ships at Seymour's disposal had a draught in excess of this. As a result, on April 30, 1846, the *Fisgard* was forced to take up a station at Fort Nisqually, at the very head of Puget Sound, after reaching Juan de Fuca Strait and receiving supplies at Fort Victoria. Her captain, John Duntze, had instructions that emphasized he was to send the *Cormorant* and even, if circumstances warranted, the *Fisgard* into the Columbia in order to "afford British subjects due security."[77] However, the matter continued to disturb Seymour, who noted in his diary on July 19 that his sleep would improve if, somehow, he could put the *Fisgard* into the Columbia River without danger.[78]

By this time, other ships had been sent north to check American influence in Oregon and Alta California.[79] The *Grampus*, 50 guns, was to join the *Talbot*, 26 guns, at Honolulu; the *Juno*, 26 guns, *Frolic*, 16 guns, *Collingwood* and *Spy* were in Californian and Mexican waters.

Seymour also expected the *America* to be in the northeastern Pacific. To his surprise and disgust he learned that she had sailed for England "without orders, with money."[80] In this, Captain Gordon had acceded to the pressure of British merchants on the Mexican coast. They feared a Mexican–American war and thought their funds would be endangered if sent to England in the smaller warship HMS *Daphne*, 18 guns. Gordon evidently thought this was the best means of protecting British interests. The *America* reached the English port of Spithead on August 19, 1846. According to Seymour, Captain Gordon had made an "ill judged decision which might have turned the fate of war with the U.S. against us by taking off the station the only strong ship except the *Collingwood* when he was aware I considered war most probable."[81]

When the *America* reached Portsmouth, a court martial was assembled, "and after due deliberation to the pros and cons," as a junior officer recalled somewhat sarcastically, "our worthy old Chief was doomed to be reprimanded, as indeed if a war with the United States had been brought on, he would have deserved to have been shot. Fortunately for him Polk and Aberdeen made it up somehow."[82] The charge of "leaving his station contrary to orders of his Admiral" was "fully proved," and Gordon was "severely reprimanded."[83] At the court martial, pecuniary gain from the freight monies he received for conveying funds to England was ruled out as a motive. Gordon retained command of the *America* for a brief time and then returned to take advantage of a newly instituted retirement scheme.

As for Seymour, his anxieties ended on August 23 when he learned that Britain and the United States had resolved the Oregon question. With obvious relief that there would be no further need to send warships over the bar of the Columbia, he wrote to the senior naval officer on the Northwest Coast to inform him of the treaty. His frustration with the whole crisis was revealed when he added, "The terms are what I understand our

Government were ready to give two years ago without all the bluster which has since occurred."[84]

The treaty effectively signified the end of the Hudson's Bay Company's territorial—but not commercial—domination in Old Oregon. Important provisions in the agreement allowed the Company to retain full navigation rights south of the 49th parallel and to enjoy access to the ports of Puget Sound.[85] Although it could be argued that, technically, the treaty did not limit the Company's enterprise, the interests of the Hudson's Bay Company in Oregon understandably declined after 1846.[86] American commercial interests would not abide the old chartered company, and it became the whipping boy of American politicians. The British frontier moved north. Before long the new depot at Fort Victoria began to flourish as it took the place of Fort Vancouver, which was, in any event, outliving its usefulness as the hub of Company trade in the Pacific. Indeed, Fort Victoria constituted a more suitable port than Fort Vancouver for an organization whose interests west of the Rockies were becoming increasingly involved in coastal shipping, trade with the Hawaiian Islands, and commerce with London by way of the sea lanes round Cape Horn.

Success of Naval Diplomacy

The crisis over the Oregon territory had begun regular British naval operations on this coast, and the Navy continued to safeguard the property rights of the Hudson's Bay Company in Oregon for three years after the signing of the treaty. Because the terms were variously interpreted in Oregon, the *Modeste* remained at Fort Vancouver until May 3, 1847; she left only after Captain Baillie received information that cleared up all confusion.[87]

Thereafter, Seymour pursued a policy based on the conviction that the security of Company interests in what had become American territory could not depend on the continued presence of one of Her Majesty's ships in the Columbia River. He recommended to his successor that a ship should "show the flag" in Puget Sound in the summer of 1848 as an alternative to a Hudson's Bay Company request for a small force to replace the *Modeste*.[88]

In recognition of the continuing presence of the British at Fort Vancouver, Seymour also advised that ships on station occasionally visit the settlements on the Columbia.[89] British warships were on the Northwest Coast in 1847, 1848 and 1849, but none ventured into the Columbia; the gradual extension of American authority in Oregon Territory coincided with the withdrawal of the Hudson's Bay Company. The Americans were sealing their own westernmost frontier, but at no time during this transfer of influence were British interests endangered.

In review, the Royal Navy played a dual role throughout the Oregon crisis. In the first place, ships on the Northwest Coast acted in various capacities—upholding the interests of the Hudson's Bay Company, maintaining law and order, and acting as deterrents to any possible American filibuster. According to Company officials at Fort Vancouver, the *Modeste's* presence helped prevent a "collision between the inhabitants of British origin, that would have led to most serious difficulties with the parent states."[90] Six ships were stationed on the coast during 1845–1846, and others were ready to act in support of British interests if needed. Hudson's Bay Company officials were accordingly grateful for such overwhelming protection. As Chief Factor James Douglas remarked, the British government had indeed shown "an extraordinary degree of solicitude and taken most active measures for the protection of British rights in this Country."[91]

In the second aspect of its dual role, the very fact of the Royal Navy's predominance in the world—if not always in the Pacific, as Seymour and Ellenborough knew—proved instrumental in keeping the peace.[92] There is little reason to doubt that the Oregon compromise, as two notable scholars of American sea power have shown, "saved the United States from a repetition of disasters" characteristic of the War of 1812.[93] The overall fact of British supremacy at sea, the operations of British warships at points of stress such as Oregon, and artful British diplomacy in European and American affairs enabled Great Britain to accomplish its objectives: to protect colonial territories of her worldwide empire and to provide security for the homeland and for growing seaborne trade. As a result of this strength, Polk's "bluster" proved to be exactly that. An inkling that the Americans were overmatched in naval power, and knew it, is given in a complaining letter sent to the Navy Department by Commodore John D. Sloat, USN, who flew his flag in the frigate *Savannah*. He noted that it seemed useless to ask for reinforcements, as at gathering places such as Mazatlan "it is immaterial what force we have here, they will always send double."[94]

The Foreign Office could be charged with being halfhearted in dealing with the Americans over Oregon. Why did they not get the whole of the territory when the Hudson's Bay Company was dominant there? Because United States diplomacy was effective, the pressures of Manifest Destiny exercised all due influence, land hunger was strong and the Willamette had become a location of "Indian wars" and reprisals. By contrast, the British pursued their well-affirmed policy of minimum intervention. Preferring trade to dominion, they did not seek any further real estate for their already large and widely scattered empire. But the tide of Oregon affairs was drawing London into the vortex, and the British went to Vancouver Island as sovereignty holders not because they wanted to be there but because, by default, they had to be there. This was reluctant empire—an empire in which they would be happily content to let the lords of the northern forest be the imperial masters in any future colony developed on that island.

four

COLONIZING THE PERFECT EDEN

The Oregon Treaty of 1846 gave Britain the essential thing—title to Vancouver Island and to the continental territory north of the 49th parallel, sometimes known as New Caledonia. The treaty underscored a conflict of interest between settlement and fur trade: Americans received the arable lands of the Columbia Basin, the British the less fertile territories of the northern fur-trading domain. The boundary, therefore, was in a very real sense an extension of the interests of the two nations: the United States inherited agricultural lands suitable for settlement, and Britain retained a fur-trading area with a distinct maritime character.

Among the complex questions in need of solution that led the Hudson's Bay Company's Columbia Department to shift its headquarters from Fort Vancouver on the Columbia River to what was called from the outset Fort Victoria on Vancouver Island was the vital one of having a marine base of operations situated so it could service both sail and steam vessels owned or chartered by the Company. The bar to the Columbia was treacherous—a veritable graveyard of ships and sailors. American eyes were cast covetously on Puget Sound. British eyes focused on Vancouver Island. James Douglas, whom we now describe as the fixer in all of these arrangements, had gone to Sitka and to Alta California to enhance HBC trade relationships: the Company was diversifying its trade, and the marine requirements were increasing daily. At his superior's request, Douglas had a look at Vancouver

Island and thought a harbour at the northern end the best. No decision was made on this, and in 1842, the critical year, he examined a harbour near the southern tip of the Island that the local people, the Lekwungen, called *Camosack*, or Camosun as generally spelled by the English settlers, meaning "rush of water." To the west and nearby lay another harbour of a much grander scale, Esquimalt—*Iswhoymalth* is the way Douglas spells it on his 1842 map, meaning "a place gradually shoaling." (Manuel Quimper, sailing on reconnaissance for the King of Spain, had entered this body of water in 1790 and called it Puerto de Cordova.)

Douglas, brought from Fort Nisqually in the *Cadboro* and landed with a party of six at Clover Point, outside of Victoria Harbour, had hiked overland and then gazed upon Camosack. Two sites immediately suggested themselves to him where a stockaded fort, or depot, might be thrown up, but the best (and that chosen) was where shipping could come near to shore and offload or load without the need of intervening boats; the other was disadvantaged in this regard. On his plan, Douglas indicated where the fort ought to be placed. The feature that led Douglas to prefer Camosack to a port at the northern end of the Island was its agricultural prospects, self-sufficiency being essential. Here he discovered plains about six miles square containing valuable land suitable for tillage and pasture. "It was this advantage and distinguishing feature of Camosack, which no other part of the coast possesses, combined with the water privilege on the canal [the Gorge], the security of the harbour and abundance of timber round it, which led me to chase [choose] a site for the establishment at that place, in preference to all others met with on the Island." A location at the north end of the Island would have been closer to the main Native populations, as Douglas had pointed out, but because a marine depot was the essential need, his recommendation was taken up by his superiors, and by force of character Douglas laid out a larger stockade than the grumbling John McLoughlin, his immediate boss at Fort Vancouver, thought was warranted. The place had idyllic features, and Douglas described it to a friend as "the perfect 'Eden,' in the midst of the dreary wilderness of the North west coast, and so different is its general aspect, from the wooded, rugged regions around, that one might be pardoned for supposing it had dropped from the clouds into its present position." It had rich productive soil, verdant fields of clover, grasses and ferns (proofs of fertility), and not a mosquito. Nor, he added, were they likely to "meet with molestation from the natives."[1] In fact, when it came time to build the fort, Native labour was eagerly forthcoming. The climate was agreeable, though there was worry of water shortage in summer.

A Roman Catholic priest, Father Bolduc, had accompanied Douglas from Nisqually, and on Sunday March 18, 1843, mass was celebrated, with twelve hundred members of the local First Nations—Cowichan, Clallam and Saanich—assembled in a modest sanctuary formed by fir branches and a boat's canopy. Bolduc wrote: "It was in the midst of this numerous assembly, that, for the first time, the sacred mysteries were celebrated; may the blood of the Spotless Lamb, fertilize this barren land, and cause it to produce an abundant harvest."[2] The night before, a great comet had passed through, "a luminous streak in the heavens," Douglas called it. It was a propitious sign.

By its very nature, the entrance to Victoria Harbour deterred great commercial activity, for it was narrow, intricate and choked with shoals. In certain winds, as Richard Charles Mayne of the Navy noted, a heavy sea

> sets on the coast, which renders the anchorage outside unsafe, while vessels of burden cannot run inside for shelter at or near high water. Vessels drawing 14 or 15 feet may, under ordinary circumstances, enter at high water, and ships drawing 17 feet have done so, although only at the top of spring-tides. But it is necessary always to take a pilot, and the channel is so confined and tortuous that a long ship has considerable difficulty in getting in. With every care, a large proportion of vessels entering the port run aground . . . I cannot imagine any sensible master of an ocean ship endeavoring to wriggle his vessel into Victoria with the larger and safer harbour of Esquimalt handy.[3]

But any thought of shifting the commercial port from Victoria to Esquimalt was long since past. Property values in Victoria were on the rise, and the town was steadily building. Douglas's choice had determined all, but it may be wondered if he had ended his reconnaissance one harbour too soon.

What sort of man was James Douglas? Many are the descriptions of him, and many critical ones, especially from Americans—they thought him autocratic, which of course he was. He combined business and administrative capabilities in equal measure. He could be violent when aroused. He was a patriot, standing against unbridled democrats. He preferred British law, order and authority. Crown and Company administration, as it developed, suited him perfectly, for he could control it and give it a future with the foresight only he possessed so clearly and abundantly. The times favoured him. He had married the daughter of a Northwest Company trader and a Carrier woman, and almost all the great trading figures of the age that gathered around him at Fort Victoria were similarly connected with the Native tribes, or First Nations. Douglas himself constantly sought a better knowledge of the First Nations. When he founded Fort Victoria in 1843, he could be described, in B.A. McKelvie's words, as

> austere, just, and meticulous in all things; an accomplished business-man and shrewd diplomat, deeply religious and tolerant. He lived behind a mask and it became part of him. It was necessary in order to impress the Natives and overawe the rougher element among the Company's servants that he maintain "face" at all times. He remembered that the old adage was "familiarity breeds contempt," so he maintained a grand aloofness, even among his associates. He was dignified and courteous to all, but he made a confidant of no one. As a result, it was the mask and not the man himself that was presented to the public gaze. He was pictured by writers of his time as being cold, righteous, but unfeeling.[4]

He would brook no opposition and this, combined with his firm convictions, could and did lead him into trouble with the home government—twice in fact: once in 1856, when he pushed for a military expedition to take Puget Sound; and again in 1859, when he proposed a forced landing to oust the Americans from San Juan Island. Of true imperial vision, he bears comparison to Raffles of Singapore and, in the North American context, to Sir Guy Carleton (Lord Dorchester) of Quebec and John McLoughlin, "the father of Oregon."

Colonizing Vancouver Island

The rising tide of human affairs benefitted Douglas, and in the sense that nature abhors a vacuum, he was quick to fill it—and was the logical choice for the Company and then the Crown, though not immediately, to place upon his broad shoulders the many heavy burdens of colonial development. In 1846 the British government, which had learned a key lesson from the quarrel with the United States over Oregon, began systematic agricultural colonization of Vancouver Island to consolidate its control of the remnant of the Oregon Territory left to it by the Oregon Treaty. It did so to halt the advancing tide of American settlement on the far western frontier. Sir James Stephen, the forceful permanent under-secretary of state for the colonies, known to friend and foe alike as "Mr. Mother Country," argued that Vancouver Island should be colonized because of its good harbours, at least one of which would be suitable for a station for the Royal Navy in the Pacific. On strategic grounds, he knew that a British naval base at Vancouver Island would serve as a counterpoise to the American port of San Francisco and thus limit the rise of a rival maritime power in that ocean.[5] He was an empire builder. He had warned against taking California as another "wasp's nest." Now the situation was fundamentally changed. The need was to prop up besieged British authority on this remote frontier.

The burning question was who should undertake the task of taming this wilderness where farmland was at a premium? Certainly not the government itself, because any further drain on the imperial purse would be unacceptable to Parliament.[6] The Hudson's Bay Company had not forgotten the ill success of its Red River Colony and believed settlement of the land to be incompatible with the fur trade—antithetical was the word most commonly bandied about in self-serving fur trade circles. On the other hand, the governor of the Company, Sir John Pelly, determined that to protect the fur trade, no other organization but the Company should conduct the colonization of Vancouver Island.[7] This was an unlikely scenario, and Pelly had to convince the Colonial Office, which ruled over all the colonies from its rickety and unhealthy office at 11 Downing Street.

Earl Grey, the secretary of state for war and the colonies, was well disposed toward the Hudson's Bay Company. When he accepted the position in Lord John Russell's Whig ministry in July 1846, the question of the

"Old Square Toes," giant of British Columbia's commercial development, Governor Sir James Douglas, KCB, was steely minded and firm handed. Americans thought him autocratic, which he was. He wanted to land troops on San Juan Island but was overruled and chastised.
CFB ESQUIMALT NAVAL & MILITARY MUSEUM

future of Vancouver Island was of minor importance in comparison to the challenges that faced the Colonial Office in other parts of the Empire— New Zealand, Australia, the Cape, the Maritime Provinces and Upper and Lower Canada. Grey was committed to both reform in colonial policy and a belief in empire.[8] As a master of compromise, he surmounted objections of "Little Englanders" by replacing "economic restraint" with "political freedom." This fundamental principle, historian E.E. Rich has explained, rested "upon a common heritage of laws, institutions and experience— in effect upon emigration from Great Britain."[9] Like his fellow colonial reformer Edward Gibbon Wakefield, Grey believed that privileged land companies could be used to populate waste areas and relieve overpopulation at home. The Hudson's Bay Company was a staple-trading rather than a land company, but Grey maintained that its large financial resources and experience in governing the Native peoples in western America made it the best-qualified agency for colonizing Vancouver Island.[10] It was a form of empire on the cheap, but with the Navy's protection. The Senior Service was every colony's best insurance policy.

While discussions between the Colonial Office and the Company proceeded, Lieutenant Adam Dundas, RN, cautioned the British government against entrusting the responsibility to the Hudson's Bay Company. Dundas, who returned to England after service in HMS *Modeste* during her lengthy Columbia River visits, discussed the problem with his brother George, a Member of Parliament who shared the view that the best way to colonize Vancouver Island was with Scottish emigrants.[11] He may have been right, but the tide of empire was running against him. At a meeting with Benjamin Hawes, parliamentary under-secretary at the Colonial Office, Lieutenant Dundas described from first-hand knowledge the disadvantages of placing the Island under Company superintendence. These remarks greatly influenced Hawes, who asked Dundas to compose a memorandum on the subject for the Colonial Office.[12] In his memorandum, Dundas stressed that the Company was dominated by a spirit "wholly and totally inapplicable to the nursing of a young Colony," and that the role the Company would play as the colonizing agency at Vancouver Island would be "repugnant" to colonists, who would consequently leave.[13] This was fair warning.

Neither these words nor parliamentary opposition led by William Ewart Gladstone, a former colonial secretary, deflected Grey, who was predisposed to support the Hudson's Bay Company.[14] The proposal of the Dundas brothers for colonizing Vancouver Island with Scottish emigrants was rejected. So, too, were schemes proposed by Mormons from Utah, by British whaling interests, by a joint-stock company of settlers and by a coal-mining and colonization corporation.

In lengthy discussions lasting through 1847 and ending in May 1848, the Colonial Office and the Hudson's Bay Company agreed to terms of the charter of grant.[15] Under these terms the Company agreed to bring British settlers to Vancouver Island: the government made it clear that the Company could gain no "pecuniary profit" and was to apply all proceeds from land and mineral sales to "the colonization and improvement of the Island."[16] The success of the undertaking, according to the Colonial Office, now depended on the Company's ability to inspire sufficient confidence to attract settlers to Vancouver Island.[17]

To provide for naval facilities, the charter stipulated that the Company should reserve lands for which the government would pay a "reasonable price."[18] By this means, the Hudson's Bay Company was also to defray all costs of defence, "except, nevertheless, during the time of hostilities between Great Britain and any foreign European or American power,"[19] a clause which became important during the Crimean War.

Behind all these provisions lay a carefully calculated intention of government to establish a colony for settlement, and not to prolong the fur trade.[20] For this reason the government made provisions for the political management of the colony. Local government, independent of Company interests, was invested first in a governor, and eventually an elected assembly was established. In July 1849 the Colonial Office appointed Richard Blanshard, an English barrister with some colonial and military experience, to the office of Governor of Vancouver Island.[21] Blanshard was chosen because he was not a servant of the Company and thus could function independently of the colonizing agency, or so the Colonial Office hoped. He held degrees from Oxford and Cambridge and had been called to the Bar, was well travelled and was a person of high intelligence and gentlemanly conduct. His father was prominent in London business circles. The appointment would have been an excellent one had not the old fur barons of Fort Victoria frozen him out from the management of the colony. As we will see, Blanshard had legal knowledge and was firm in all his actions. If the Colonial Office had listened to the opponents of monopoly, such as Lieutenant Dundas and Sir James Stephen, an alternative agent of the Crown at Vancouver Island might have been found.[22] But we need to remember the British government intended not to spend a pound, shilling or penny on the project. This son of misfortune, Blanshard, was cast to the winds of fate, and we will take up the tale of his misfortunes later in this chapter.

All the time that the colonial enterprise for Vancouver Island was being debated and decided, the Company still had to defend its interests in the Columbia, and it still needed to issue dividends for stockholders. Although the Company had decided in 1843 to transfer its general headquarters in the northeastern Pacific from Fort Vancouver on the Columbia River to a suitable location on Vancouver Island, and planned to withdraw from Oregon after the Oregon Boundary Treaty, that withdrawal was not, and could not, be easy. Company officials considered it necessary to maintain law and order in Oregon until the United States assumed its rightful duty,[23] and it appeared that the Royal Navy would be needed for this, as it had been during the Oregon crisis. Indeed, the famous massacre at the Whitman mission near Walla Walla in 1847 seemed proof to the Company that a British warship should be stationed in the Columbia. But Rear-Admiral Phipps Hornby, Commander-in-Chief, Pacific, argued with much merit that supporting Company interests in American territory did not come within his jurisdiction.[24] He was content to rely on the presence of the large new frigate *Constance*, 50 guns, in the waters of Juan de Fuca Strait in 1848 to maintain order in the "Columbia Country."[25]

Captain George Courtenay of the *Constance* supported the arguments of the admiral. After his visit to Esquimalt (where his ship anchored in handsome style in lovely Constance Cove on July 25, and remained there for six weeks), he wrote trenchantly of the anomalous position of a monopolistic British commercial concern still acting south of the line as an overlord on United States sovereign soil. He believed that the sooner the Hudson's Bay Company gave up its posts and farms in Oregon and retired within British territory, the sooner an end would come to "their bickerings with the Americans."[26] The commercial advantages of remaining in Oregon would keep the Company there as long as possible and, in his words, would induce it "to cry Wolf" as long as the government in London listened.[27] His objections were partially addressed the year following, in 1849, when the western headquarters of the Company were transferred to Fort Victoria. The Company, in a phrase, was in political retreat but it was not in commercial retreat, and even after the 1846 treaty it reorganized and regenerated itself to meet new conditions.

The more we learn about Captain Courtenay, the more we understand the Navy's steadying position on colonial affairs then unfolding. Courtenay was not easily led by Company arguments. Socially he was at least a notch above most of the fur trader "lords of the forest" that he met. Like many an officer he had "interest" and had entered into the books on the nomination of the powerful Admiral Lord St. Vincent in the year of Trafalgar, 1805. He had fought through the wars against Napoleon (and was decorated), and he had distinguished himself in West African anti-slavery patrols and been British consul in Haiti. Arriving at Vancouver Island, he made his own assessment of the state of affairs. He quizzed Factor Roderick Finlayson on the burning matters of the day and did not get full answers; he concluded that HBC servants had the greatest reluctance, driven by fear, to provide information. One author, Allan Pritchard, puts it this way: "Courtenay's correspondence and reports make it clear that he considered the concerns of Douglas about American depredations and threats to the company's property and interests on the Columbia to be exaggerated: he thought that the company, 'having for years lorded it over that Country,' was simply failing to adjust to the new realities." Sadly, he did not meet Douglas, and Douglas was defensive on this score, writing vividly, "The ordeal we have endured for the last twelve months has given us a lesson of experience which can never be effaced from our minds." This was true, and that lesson, in turn, shaped the Vancouver Island colonial mindset, which dug in against Americans and American politics. Pritchard draws this outstanding conclusion: "Nothing either in Courtenay's upper-class background or long naval service is likely to have given him special appreciation of the problems of the fur traders, and misunderstanding was increased by the

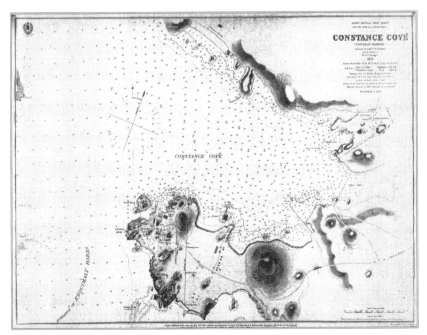

The preferred anchorage of Constance Cove in Esquimalt, British Columbia, as surveyed by HMS *Plumper* in 1858. This chart was published by the Admiralty under the superintendence of Rear-Admiral George Henry Richards. CFB ESQUIMALT NAVAL & MILITARY MUSEUM

lack of communication resulting from Douglas's absence [in Hawaii]. No doubt, however, Courtenay was carrying out higher official policy in recommending resignation and restraint, and avoiding any risk of diplomatic incidents with the American authorities."[28]

In summary, the commander-in-chief did not allow the Navy to overstep its authority by placing a ship in the Columbia River to guard the Company's property in Oregon, but neither did he ignore the need to protect the Vancouver Island settlements and British imperial interests and potential there. Until the visit of the *Constance* in 1848, Company officials complained that the British Admiralty was unconcerned about "the only British territorial possession in these seas: a circumstance which we exceedingly regret, and to which the attention of the British Government ought to be forcibly drawn." Soon these same officials had changed their tune and maintained that a warship should be permanently stationed to guard Fort Victoria, which was "peculiarly exposed to be attacked and plundered by predatory vessels."[29]

The graceful HMS *Constance*, a 50-gun frigate built at Pembroke dock, Wales, shown here under bare poles and facing heavy seas. Designed by the noted naval architect Simonds, she was launched in 1846 and immediately sent to Vancouver Island, entering Constance Cove, the secure anchorage at Esquimalt, named for her. CFB ESQUIMALT NAVAL & MILITARY MUSEUM

The next warship to visit these waters was the frigate *Inconstant*, Captain John Shepherd commanding, in May 1849. The *Inconstant* came under orders to aid and protect Fort Victoria, then menaced by the prospect of an Indian uprising.[30] It was difficult to judge the seriousness of the threat. The long-standing dispute between the Company and several parties of Haida and Tsimshian—who visited Victoria annually to trade pelts for guns, ammunition, liquor and other items—had reached alarming proportions according to authorities. The officer-in-charge at the post, Roderick Finlayson, wanted to defuse the situation, but he urged Captain Shepherd to refrain from issuing any ammunition while the ship lay in port; he sought to prevent further military stores from finding their way into Haida and Tsimshian hands.[31] This was unwarranted advice. The previous year, almost the whole ship's company from the *Constance*—250 sailors and Royal Marines—paraded outside the stockade in a display of arms as a warning to nearly one thousand Natives.[32] The situation had not altered since that time. In spite of his concern, Finlayson worried about an Indian war, and he wanted no coercive measures taken by the Navy; he contended that an Indian war would be "extremely impolitic" at a time when British emigrants were expected to settle on Vancouver Island.[33] He seemed to think the war scenario was unlikely, but he did like the cozy support the Navy provided by its mere presence.

In contrast, fears of an attack were well founded, according to Captain Shepherd, who believed and reported that the colony could not survive for long unless a detachment of troops came out from England. Admiral Hornby had a similar view.[34] When this suggestion reached London, and eventually Hudson's Bay House, the Company opposed undertaking the costs of defence, arguing that one object of the Company was to civilize the Native people, which could be achieved best by conciliatory measures without the use of troops.[35] Admittedly, however, the Company realized that periodic calls by British warships would assist in keeping Natives and Americans alike in awe of British sovereignty on Vancouver Island.[36] The Company thanked the Admiralty for directing the Commander-in-Chief, Pacific, to send ships to the Northwest Coast.[37] The government failed to press its demands for reimbursement on the Company, and the matter of defence languished until another crisis arose.

Blanshard Arrives as First Governor

Fresh from a long passage under sail from Callao, then under steam when the welcome, quiet waters of Juan de Fuca Strait had been entered, the full ship-rigged paddle-wheeler *Driver*, classified as a sloop and mounting 6 guns, cast anchor at Ogden Point, the entrance to Victoria harbour. The date was March 9, 1850, and it was evening. Snow covered the ground. A messenger, possibly a lieutenant, and boat crew rowed through the entrance and communicated with the sleepy settlement. The *Driver* drew 15 feet and, accordingly, Commander Johnston chose to seek local knowledge before entering the passage leading to the fort. He went ashore the next day, and, when he met with James Douglas, discovered that the chief factor was surprised to learn of the governor's arrival. Douglas said that a house for His Excellency had begun to be built, but that he would have to lodge Blanshard in his own house when the governor left the *Driver*. That same day Mr. McNiven of the HBC piloted the vessel under steam right into Victoria Harbour.[38]

Douglas faced this perhaps unwelcome development with the taciturnity that was his characteristic personal trait. This was just another incremental passage in the affairs of the British Empire on the Northwest Coast of America. Why should he express any delight at the arrival of a viceregal authority? But he would play by the new rules.

The next day, March 11, one of immense importance in Canada's history, His Excellency Richard Blanshard landed, under a salute of 17 guns from the *Driver* and the same given in reply from the fort, to read his commission and proclamation as governor and commander-in-chief in and over Vancouver's Island and its dependencies. Blanshard heralded formal empire, one of global proportions. When he read his commission, the common law of England became effective. He was the first duly commissioned representative of the Crown.

The greeting he received was official but cool, bordering on suspicion. Blanshard was 32, and Dr. W.F. Tolmie, who met him at Fort Nisqually, described him as "a tall, thin person with a pale countenance—is a great smoker, a great sportsman—a protectionist in politics and a latitudinarian in religious matters. His manner is quiet, rather abstracted, tho' free from hauteur, or pomposity; he does not converse much."[39] For the first few weeks the governor stayed aboard the *Driver*, then in the fort, and later still

One of the early, powerful steamers, HMS *Driver*, a paddle-wheeler seen here off Cronstadt in the Baltic. She had the imperial duty of delivering His Excellency Richard Blanshard, Governor of Vancouver Island, to Victoria in March 1850, signalling the beginning of British colonial administration. CFB ESQUIMALT NAVAL & MILITARY MUSEUM

in a small house and office built outside the stockade. Each of these three steps brought less congeniality.

Blanshard took things in hand immediately and set out to solve several problems. At the outset he understood the ongoing process whereby the Company was establishing its base of coastal operations at Fort Victoria, and that involved removal of materials and livestock, as well as horses and oxen, from Fort Nisqually on Puget Sound. Soon after his arrival, and at his request, the *Driver* conveyed 86 cattle and 830 sheep from Nisqually to Victoria. It was an unusual cargo for a naval vessel, but elsewhere in naval history there are examples of the service giving a needed hand to strengthen British interests ashore.[40] The proximity of the American frontier was obvious, but Blanshard, we surmise, had no need for close relationships there. When the American army commandant at Steilacoom on Puget Sound requested permission to come to the colony and apprehend two army deserters, Blanshard politely declined on the grounds that no reciprocal arrangement existed. With regard to the more pressing matters of colonial security and the protection of British lives and shipping, Blanshard brought all his imperial instincts to bear. He knew that visits by HM ships were occasional or periodic. To meet the regular defence needs of the colony, and taking up the views of Captain Shepherd, he advised the colonial secretary that regular troops, preferably marines, would suffice for the colony's security; mobility of force was what was required. He thought two units of troops would be enough. In this he took the advice of Captain Walter Colquhoun Grant, formerly in the Scots Greys, and the colony's first independent settler.[41] One unit would be stationed at Fort Rupert, a mining settlement on the north Island, and the other at Esquimalt, established on a cantonment formed on the plains near that harbour, the origins of the Macaulay Point military establishment. He recommended an officer of the Royal Engineers be sent to recommend advantageous sites for the required barracks and establishment.[42]

The governor possessed the imperial mindset, and he knew about imperial defence from travels in the West Indies, British Honduras, and the Punjab, where he attached himself to a unit of the British Indian Army during the Sikh war. In his broad thinking and familiarity with the law, he was ahead of his time in this outpost of empire, which was unsettling to the old fur traders. Blanshard differed from wary Company officials, who, undoubtedly fearing London's interference, did not believe a regular military force was necessary for protection, even though they realized that American encroachments on British territory were possible.[43] Because the government again failed to take a stand on the matter, British warships on the coast remained the only means of coercion at the governor's disposal. Blanshard was no fool, and it is surprising that somehow the generality of opinion is that he was not up to the task. But who could stand up to the power of the Company, its minions and James Douglas?

First Gunboat Actions

Blanshard's suggestion that military force be sent to Vancouver Island was driven, in part, by an incident that occurred at Fort Rupert. The HBC had purchased Native title to the land near the fort in order to develop a coal mine, and one of the local Native bands, the Nahwitti, had gathered to form a new village nearby and join in the commercial exploitation of the coal resources. There were many tensions. In 1850, for example, some Nahwitti men murdered three British sailors, deserters from the merchant ship *Norman Morison*, which was trading in the area. Blanshard requisitioned the corvette *Daedalus*, 19 guns, Captain George Wellesley, to investigate. On its arrival at Fort Rupert, a boat was lowered, manned with young lieutenants and midshipmen, as well as armed sailors and marines, and deployed ashore to arrest the criminals, though they were unsuccessful.[44]

At that time, no Royal Navy ship had been authorized to remain on the Northwest Coast as a guardship, so when the *Daedalus* sailed from Vancouver Island for San Francisco in search of provisions, the governor was alarmed that the murderers of the British seamen remained at large. It was in response to this incident that Blanshard proposed having two companies of regular troops stationed on Vancouver Island. Simultaneously, he decried the fact that ships of the Royal Navy, which came "at rare intervals, and for short calls," were the colony's sole safeguard.[45]

The Company could see no merit in Blanshard's belief that only the presence of an overwhelming force, in the form of either a warship permanently stationed at Vancouver Island or sufficient troops, could impose the authority of the Crown.[46] Yet it admitted that a British warship could help Company officials deal with the Native problem. Like Blanshard, the governor of the Company urged Grey to request that warships pay more frequent and longer visits to the colony. In response to the Colonial Office suggestion that the Company undertake permanent measures of defence instead of relying on occasional visits by ships of the Royal Navy, the Company explained that its posts were adequately defended by Métis in its employ, a view which suggests the Company was little interested in encouraging settlement at a distance from its forts.[47] As a result, full responsibility for colonial defence beyond the Company stockades rested with the Navy. It is small wonder that settlement did not prosper.

Meanwhile, under the guidance of Chief Factor James Douglas, the Company sought reconciliation with the Nahwitti. Douglas considered Blanshard's desire to hold the whole tribe responsible for the murders "as unpolitick as unjust," a policy that might possibly lead to an Indian war of disastrous proportions.[48] He exaggerated the case, for a pan-Native alliance was impossible given different tribal interests and instincts.

When the Commander-in-Chief, Pacific, Rear-Admiral Fairfax Moresby, learned from Captain Wellesley of the *Daedalus* that the Nahwitti had evidently flouted British authority, he determined to put an end to the problem by taking the matter out of the hands of the Company.[49] He made a visit to Esquimalt in his flagship, the frigate *Portland*, 50 guns, accompanied by the sloop *Daphne*, 18 guns, Commander E. Fanshawe. Moresby, we might note, was a powerful figure in the nineteenth-century Royal Navy. As a captain he had brokered difficult anti-piracy arrangements with various Muslim peoples in the Arabian Gulf, significant to establishing a Britannic peace there and on the east coast of Africa. He was, equally, a zealous anti-slavery advocate and a powerful force in the fight against slave traders. He much resembled the *Pax Britannica* in person, and he was a diligent proponent of law and order. He had excellent diplomatic skills and was a conscientious practitioner of British policy—that peace had to be maintained for the protection of British interests. He had high credit at the Admiralty.[50] So what followed was not an aberration in British policy of that time but rather an extension: the long arm of British authority was being exercised on distant Vancouver Island. Moresby's appointment reflected the Admiralty's view that a "hands-on" naval diplomat was needed to deal with the difficulties at Vancouver Island.

After conferring with Blanshard and Douglas at Fort Victoria, Rear-Admiral Moresby dispatched the *Daphne*, bearing the governor, to Fort Rupert to exact rigorous justice. Moresby shared Blanshard's view that the whole tribe was to be punished unless the guilty few surrendered. When the murderers were not given up by the tribe, the *Daphne* "stormed and burned" the camp, forcing the tribe to seek refuge in the forest.[51] In this action, two of the Nahwitti were killed and some sailors wounded. The Navy's use of "forest diplomacy" did not bring the murderers to justice, but a pathetic event followed: the attack on the village so terrified the tribe that they executed the guilty themselves to bring peace, and delivered the corpses to Fort Rupert.

The episode was described by Dr. John Helmcken, there as justice of the peace, as "the miserable affair." It ended in much finger pointing, which has been continued by historians to this day. Would Douglas have acted differently than the forthright Blanshard? All indications are that he would have done exactly the same. At that time, cross-cultural encounters of a violent sort were all too common on the Empire's frontiers. The case sparked a departmental review and led to an examination of the rules of intervention in such cases—and suggested lines of conduct for naval officers. In 1853 the Law Officers of the Crown, on referral, advised the Foreign Office of the extent to which ships' commanders could exact redress from Natives "in cases where the wrongs done by them to British Subjects extend to the loss of life by unprovoked and deliberate murder." The guidance specified that if naval commanders should *actually witness* murder of British subjects, redress could be exacted from the chief of the tribe to which the offender belonged. Without witness, extreme forbearance was to be used before resorting to force.[52] The rules of engagement had been established, and the laws of war set down. In time, constables and

123

Rear-Admiral Fairfax Moresby, Commander-in-Chief, Pacific, 1850–1853, disliked the overbearing influence of the Hudson's Bay Company in colonial affairs. Greatly admired by William Wilberforce, champion against slavery, Moresby had served on anti-slavery patrol on the East African coast with distinction. One of the giants of the *Pax Britannica*, he had two sons in the Navy. One of them—John Moresby of the *Thetis*—rose to admiral and was author of the delightful memoir *Two Admirals*. CFB ESQUIMALT NAVAL & MILITARY MUSEUM

other police would be present, and interpreters would be appointed to help with the taking of evidence, or to serve as intermediaries. Actions by ship commanders would carry the backing of colonial authority and imperial law. "Quarterdeck diplomacy," so called, bore the imprint of the officer commanding given the circumstances of the case.

As these new rules of intervention were set, the old order established by the Hudson's Bay Company was being swept away, and some of the Company factors and officers seem to have been the last to realize that new masters were now in charge of colonial affairs. For a time the old order had the new one placed upon it. The lines of distinction were blurred. It was the Company that could not carry the day in the long run, but there seems always to be sympathy for the Company and its "servants" as those who were best able to bring justice to the cultural interface. Perhaps this is the right view. But the tide of change was inexorable: the HBC could not continue its time-honoured imperium of *lex talionis*—an eye for an eye and a tooth for a tooth.

All this lay ahead. The Company was restrictive in its sale of lands, and that it had managed the control of agricultural spaces to its own benefit brought much hostile comment from Blanshard, officers of the Navy, and Rear-Admiral Moresby. The admiral was particularly glaring in his comments, passed through to the ministry in London: the Company, he charged, was dominated by an illiberal spirit quite unsuitable for the free and liberal reception of an immigrant community.[53] As for the colony's first governor, that figure of misfortune, Blanshard, he found his position untenable in a colony where Company interests were dominant and problems of Island settlement were largely ignored. He understandably suffered from mental strain and perhaps melancholia. Upon learning that the Colonial Office had accepted his tendered resignation, and without regret, he sailed from Vancouver Island in HMS *Daphne* on September 1, 1851.

Douglas Becomes Governor

James Douglas, appointed to succeed Blanshard as governor, and characterized by a commanding presence and bold policies, was able to maintain order on the coast through the combined influence of the Company and the Navy. He was already the agent of the Hudson's Bay Company in the new colony. Now, at the age of 48, he added to his duties what he later described as a "responsible and disagreeable office," solely to please the Governor and Committee of the Hudson's Bay Company.[54] Douglas's interests at this stage were "unmistakably those of the Company, of the fur trade, and of Victoria as a port and depot, rather than the broader aspects of settling the whole Island."[55] It must be added, however, that Douglas—in both aspects of his role, as colonial governor and as Company official—remained dedicated to strengthening British interests on the Northwest Coast.[56] In this regard, his outlook coincided with that of Earl Grey. The secretary of state for the colonies wanted no additional problems to arrive on his desk. He left Douglas alone.

Rear-Admiral Moresby had no quarrel with Douglas, whose experience, intelligence and vigour had earned him rapid promotion in the Company. All the same, he objected to the Company's reluctance to support colonization.[57] He found during his visit in 1851 that the difficulties faced by colonists wishing to obtain land, for example, were "incompatible with the free and liberal reception of an Emigrant Community."[58] This charge, as well as others, reinforced those of Blanshard. The commander-in-chief's report on the state of the colony proved to be only one of several that exposed the domination of the Company and its unwillingness to encourage colonization.[59]

These charges did not go unanswered by the Company, which asserted that everything was being done "for the colonization and improvement of the Island, which it is no less their interest than their duty to promote."[60] It is evident, however, that the Company was unwilling to invest in an unproductive colony. The California gold rush drained labour from the Pacific Northwest, the fur trade was in decline and the colony lacked colonists. "God's will be done," Douglas wrote despairingly to Sir George Simpson, the governor of the Company in North America, in March 1854. "I have done everything in my power to give it an existence in defiance of the adverse circumstances of the times, which have caused me so much trouble and anxiety."[61]

Nor did the future look any brighter: continental expansion by the Americans since 1845 threatened to absorb British possessions on the Northwest Coast.[62] Douglas, especially, was well aware of the threats to the colony from the United States, which assumed a military form in 1859 with the occupation of the disputed San Juan Island. Unlike Blanshard, who thought that the Hudson's Bay Company was reneging on its obligations as a colonizing agency, Governor Douglas blamed the British government for the ill success of the colony. The government was apathetic, Douglas noted, about Vancouver Island, "the only British possession of the west coast of America and a most favourable point commercially and politically for counterbalancing the rapidly growing influence of the United States in this part of the world." Unless the British government ended its indifference, Douglas believed, all the efforts of the Company to develop settlements and check American peaceful penetration were doomed.[63]

One method of countering any attempted filibuster from the American shore, Douglas contended, was not to station troops that would be difficult to transport to the decisive quarter, but rather to put in place an armed government or naval steamer. Such a vessel could sail with ease through intricate, tide-bound waters to the place of need.[64] In Douglas's scheme lies the origin of a proposal implemented at Vancouver Island during the Crimean War.

Douglas was not alone in recognizing American aspirations for continental dominion at a time when British interests in the whole of the western hemisphere were endangered. The British minister in Washington, Sir John Crampton, complained in early 1853 to the foreign minister, Lord Clarendon, that the Monroe Doctrine appeared to be developing into a United States law for the Americas, made without the due consent of nations.[65] Indeed, Britain's awareness of American power in the New World changed her statecraft toward the United States in 1853.[66] British policy was committed to Vancouver Island, which Douglas in his ignorance did not realize. Similar concern was felt for the endangered position of Britain's other North American possessions, as well as her sphere of influence in the Caribbean and her communications across the Isthmus of Panama. The latter were endangered by American desires to dominate the route from the Atlantic seaboard to California.

In short, United States pretensions to continental dominion at midcentury alarmed the British government. Continued reassertions of the Monroe Doctrine ended what Douglas believed to be indifference on the part of the British ministry.[67] The revised policy aimed at the peaceful containment of American expansion; it met with success in British North America in general and in Vancouver Island in particular. This change of attitude around 1853 marked a turning point in the history of Britain's interest in the Northwest Coast. After this time, Britain relied largely on the Royal Navy to prevent American expansion on the coast.

The Royal Navy and the Island Resources

From the beginning of regular operations in the North Pacific in the 1830s, British warships faced two major handicaps. First, they depended on strategic commodities such as spars, timbers and coal that came invariably from distant Europe. Second, they did not have an adequate naval base anywhere in the Pacific, although storeships were positioned on the South American coast at Valparaiso in 1843 and at Callao in 1847. Gradually it became apparent to naval officers that the natural resources of Vancouver Island offered solutions to their problems, provided the Admiralty and the Hudson's Bay Company could agree to their use.

During the sailing-ship era, timbers for shipbuilding ranked high in strategic value. With insufficient forests at home, the search for this essential staple continued; sources were found in the Baltic and North America. John Meares, the first to profit in the spar trade of the Northwest Coast, wrote with little exaggeration in 1791 that the fine stands of timber on that coast would be sufficient for the needs of "all the navies of Europe."[68] The Hudson's Bay Company entered this trade in the 1830s and sold timber suitable for a variety of purposes—masts, spars, piles and deals—in various Pacific ports, notably Honolulu.[69]

But the Royal Navy did not fully recognize the value of Pacific Northwest timber until the Oregon crisis brought British warships frequently to the region. In 1845 the captain of HMS *America* was instructed to report on timbers "fit for the Navy."[70] He procured at Port Discovery, which was the actual centre of Douglas fir distribution, as many spars as the shored-up decks of the *America* could carry. The Commander-in-Chief, Pacific, Rear-Admiral Seymour, an expert on naval stores,[71] preferred the spars that the *America* brought from the Northwest Coast to those cut from a softer species of wood near Monterey, California. The former were fashioned for the masts of the flagship *Collingwood*.[72] Seymour was so impressed by the quality of these timbers that he ordered a shipment of spars sent from Vancouver Island to Portsmouth dockyard for testing.[73] The tests showed that the fir of Vancouver Island was superior to that from

Riga in the Baltic, then considered by the Admiralty to make the best spars in the world.[74] As a result of Seymour's initiative, the Admiralty had gained a new source of spars.

Although the value of this resource was unquestioned, one problem remained: how were they to transport these bulky, heavy materials some eighteen thousand miles by way of Cape Horn to England, at a price competitive with spars from the Baltic and the Maritime colonies? The example of the unfortunate Captain E. Swinton of London and his agent, Captain William Brotchie, shows the difficulties involved. Swinton proposed in 1844 to supply the Admiralty with spars from the Northwest Coast suitable for topmasts. Three years after his proposal, their Lordships agreed to receive some 80 spars for trial.[75] Swinton then sent the merchant ship *Albion* to Juan de Fuca Strait to fill the contract. Brotchie, her supercargo, and a victim of new US Revenue zeal, chose to cut spars near New Dungeness on the American side of the strait. There, in April 1850, the ship was seized by United States customs officials for cutting spars on United States soil without permission.[76]

Undeterred, Brotchie next sailed in HMS *Daedalus* for the north end of Vancouver Island, reported to be another suitable source of spars.[77] He was plagued by financial problems resulting from the confiscation of the *Albion* and was unable to convince the Hudson's Bay Company to enter into the spar trade with him. Brotchie never made the venture a success, although he did send several shipments of spars to England after 1852.[78]

Not until 1855, when the Crimean War led to a great increase in construction of ships and dockyard facilities, did the Admiralty turn to the Northwest Coast as a formal source of supply for spars.[79] But it should not be forgotten that during the preceding and following decades, many warships sailed from Vancouver Island bearing new spars of sturdy quality, sometimes stowing them for the later use of other ships on the Pacific station. Generally speaking, the timber problem had been solved for British warships employed in this vast ocean at a time when sail remained the chief means of motive power.

The Importance of Coal

Even more important to a navy increasingly dependent on steam was the necessity of finding a ready and cheap source of coal.[80] The Admiralty was generally opposed to the introduction of steam in the late 1820s and 1830s. In 1836 the senior naval officer in the Pacific pressed the Admiralty to attach a steamer to the Pacific squadron. He argued that such a vessel would be invaluable in those seas where, because of calms and trade winds, passages were "more precarious, and uncertain" than in any other quarter of the world.[81] Alexander Forbes, a promoter of British expansion in California and the Pacific, also believed that the Pacific squadron, supplemented by one or more steamers, would be better able to protect British interests and encourage British trade in Pacific America.[82]

By the 1840s their Lordships were obliged to recognize, if reluctantly, the strategic advantages of ships that were able to manoeuvre independently of the wind. In 1846 steamers played only an auxiliary role to sailing ships, as indicated by the fact that the paddle-wheel sloop *Cormorant*, Captain George T. Gordon, proceeded to the Northwest Coast during the Oregon crisis partly to tow sailing vessels in the straits. In the confined waters separating Vancouver Island from the mainland, where strong tides are prevalent, the great advantages of steam propulsion were clear.[83]

Eventually, the success of the screw-propeller removed the objection to the paddle-wheelers with their limited broadsides. At the same time, the gradual introduction of engines of higher pressure increased the efficiency of auxiliary power. As a result of this revolutionary technological advance, by the mid-1850s almost all new ships were equipped with steam power of some sort. British naval operations during the Crimean War—especially at Petropavlovsk in the northwestern Pacific—revealed the full advantages of steam for all warships. Although sail was employed in the Pacific on some warships until just before the First World War, steam became increasingly prevalent after 1843, when the Admiralty ordered the first steamer, the paddle-wheel sloop *Salamander*, to the Pacific.

A steam vessel was "endowed with a constant and voracious appetite for coal."[84] Hence the commander of the *Salamander* was under strict instructions to economize on the use of this costly commodity.[85] Some idea of the expense involved in supplying a steamer is shown in the case of the transport *Rosalind*, chartered at £250 per month to deliver coal to Fort Victoria for the use of the steamer *Cormorant* during the Oregon crisis. If a local supply could be delivered to the Navy at a price competitive with English coal, the fuel problem would be solved.

The rapid growth of steam navigation in the Pacific after 1840 led the Hudson's Bay Company to develop mines off the northeast coast of Vancouver Island: one important consumer of Company coal was the Pacific Mail Steamship Company, which began a service between Panama and the coast of Oregon in 1848 with three paddle-wheel steamers of one thousand tons burthen.[86]

At the time of the Oregon crisis, the Hudson's Bay Company began a serious investigation of surface outcroppings of coal reported by Indigenous people in 1835 at Beaver Harbour.[87] This coal was already being used by the Company steamer *Beaver*, but the Company investigated and hoped to develop the mine commercially in order to supply the Pacific squadron and other users of coal on a regular basis. The efforts of the Company to promote this trade coincided with investigations and trials by ships of the Royal Navy to determine if the Vancouver Island coal deposits would meet the needs of the squadron.[88] An examination in 1846 of the *Cormorant* by Commander George T. Gordon—whom Rear-Admiral Seymour considered one of the best steam officers in the Navy—revealed abundant quantities at Beaver Harbour of a quality "at least equal to the best Scotch coal."[89] The significance of this was clear to Seymour. The deposits, he informed the Admiralty, would add greatly to "the future value of the British Possessions on the North West Coast and contribute the means to extend their commerce, and to facilitate their defence, as California and the Neighbouring Countries become of more consequence, and acquire additional Population."[90] Very wisely, he recommended that these mines be reserved for the public interest, or, in other words, that the Crown should regulate the exploitation of the coal deposits.

As with spars sent from Vancouver Island, samples of coal were tested in England. The Museum of Practical Geology in London reported to the Admiralty that the coal was suitable for steam propulsion.[91] In fact, the samples were so promising that at one stage the Admiralty planned to send a steamship and sloop from England with a scientific officer and equipment to test the fuel more fully.[92] This expensive plan was not carried out, probably because subsequent reports by naval officers proved sufficient to convince the Admiralty of the quality of Vancouver Island coal.

Before the Hudson's Bay Company received the charter of grant for Vancouver Island, word of extensive coal deposits on the Island bolstered the British government's conviction that the Island should be in proper hands for the development of this resource.[93] Samuel Cunard, pioneer of trans-Atlantic steam navigation, urged the Admiralty in 1848 to reserve the mines for the Crown,[94] which would prevent private interests from staking claims and prohibit American steamship interests in the Pacific from entering into contracts with the Hudson's Bay Company for the coal. The Admiralty accepted this recommendation and advised the Colonial Office accordingly.[95]

The coal deposits became an important consideration in discussions between the Colonial Office and the Hudson's Bay Company on the terms of the charter of grant. To ensure that coal mining would aid the public welfare at Vancouver Island, the Colonial Office asked the Company to modify and accept an agreement similar to that already concluded between the government and Henry Wise, a proprietor on the Island of Labuan, a British naval outpost in the South China Sea. Under this agreement, Wise paid a lease and royalties and agreed to supply coal to the Royal Navy at the pit's mouth for 11 shillings per ton.[96] The Hudson's Bay Company explained glibly that it did not seek financial gain in colonizing Vancouver Island, and that all profits from coal mining would be spent in promoting the good of the colony. It refused to accept revised terms such as those relating to Labuan Island.[97] The statement of good intent evidently satisfied the British government. Ultimately the two parties agreed to a royalty of two shillings and six pence per ton, of which the Company would get 10 percent, the rest going to the development of the colony. Unfortunately for the Navy, the fuel remained expensive, and this often prohibited its use.

Meanwhile, Captain Courtenay of the *Constance* had been dispatched to the Northwest Coast to report on the state of British interests there and to evaluate, on the basis of what evidence he could gather, the coal deposits at Beaver Harbour. When the *Constance* reached Esquimalt on July 25, 1848, Courtenay sent to Hudson's Bay Company officials at Fort Vancouver and Fort Victoria copies of Cunard's recommendation to the Admiralty, along with a request for information on prices of Vancouver Island coal delivered both on the spot and at South American ports.[98]

Courtenay never went to Beaver Harbour. After examining some coal samples obtained by the *Cormorant* in 1846, he tried by various means to strengthen British claims to the resources. First, he urged James Douglas

to instruct subordinate Hudson's Bay Company officials to "keep a vigilant lookout" over the coalfields and to evict any persons found settling near the mines.[99] Second, he had a hut erected on the site of the deposit to constitute a "claim," as was customary, and he had a proclamation posted in the Queen's name to warn intruders against mining or settlement.[100] Courtenay's gesture had no legal basis, or so Douglas and Rear-Admiral Hornby thought.[101] Erection of the hut was more a symbolic act than anything else. It merely reinforced locally what the British government was emphasizing in its dealings with the Company—that is, that the coal was to benefit British public interests such as the colony and the Navy rather than private interests. Such tensions that existed between Company and Navy were bound to increase by Courtenay's actions, for the fur lords probably saw them as meddling in their commercial affairs.

By mid-1849 the mines at Beaver Harbour were in production, and nearby Fort Rupert had been built to protect the settlement from Native

Before the introduction of oil-fuelled engines, the Navy ran on coal. The work of the coaling party was always one of danger and difficulty, though the task was often completed with much satisfaction, as this photo attests.   PHOTO COURTESY SHERRI ROBINSON

attack.[102] Gradually the coal trade developed as steam navigation in the Pacific increased. When the paddle-wheeler *Driver* visited in 1850, her commander reported no less than twelve hundred tons of coal lying on the beach, collected by Native labour. The place was booming. He found an establishment of 40 Company servants, including eight Scottish miners.[103] British naval commanders sometimes complained of finding shale in the coal, but the Company gradually found a means of quality control. In 1852 the Company began work on promising outcroppings at Nanaimo, closer to Fort Victoria.[104] This coal proved superior to that from the mines at Beaver Harbour, which were abandoned subsequently. Bituminous coal from Nanaimo was adequate for low-pressure boilers but gave way to Welsh anthracite when high-pressure steam engines were introduced after the 1860s.

Paradoxically, although good coal was available at Vancouver Island, the Royal Navy in the Pacific was forced to rely heavily on coal from Britain that was purchased on the Chilean coast and shipped as ballast on the outward passage in vessels making the return voyage laden with the potent fertilizer guano. Coal was cheap at Valparaiso and other ports.[105] In any case, it was less expensive than that from the Northwest Coast. "Eventually Vancouver Island promises a plentiful supply," Rear-Admiral Hornby advised his successor in 1851, "but owing to the difficulty and uncertainty of working the Mines, and the exorbitant price of 50s per Ton demanded by the Hudson's Bay Company, it is not desirable to look to that quarter at present."[106]

From time to time, however, Her Majesty's ships did purchase coal from the Company, as in the case of the paddle-wheel sloop *Virago*, in 1853, and to a greater degree during the Crimean War. Although this coal was exorbitant in price, its availability made any steamer visiting the remote Northwest Coast virtually independent of supplies from other parts of the Pacific station or England.[107] As for the Company, its coal trade represented one encouraging element in an otherwise depressed economy at Vancouver Island.

The possibility that the Island might satisfy the Navy's requirements of certain naval stores increased in 1850 with a report that the Hudson's Bay Company had discovered the nettle hemp plant growing in profusion.[108] Specimens of rope made from this fibre were sent to London and were found to bear strains in excess of Admiralty standards. It was argued in 1851 that the discovery of hemp might have almost as great an effect on the prosperity of the colony as the coal mines.[109] But the Admiralty did not enter into a contract with the Company to receive a supply of hemp, as far as can be determined. Nor did the Company develop the industry on a commercial basis. As with spars and coals, the promising hemp resource was not exploited by the Admiralty, whose supplies from other quarters were adequate.

Esquimalt as a Future Naval Base

During the Oregon crisis, the need for a naval station on the north Pacific coast became apparent to the Commander-in-Chief, Pacific, Rear-Admiral Seymour, and to the First Lord of the Admiralty, the Earl of Ellenborough, who advocated that Britain should seize San Francisco Bay for that purpose. No action took place because Ellenborough's warlike suggestion was inconsistent with British policy.[110]

Commanders-in-chief received instructions to be on the lookout for a suitable situation, especially an island off the coast of Central America, preferably on a possible inter-oceanic route, in view of the projected Panama Canal. Officers commanding British warships examined several positions, even that old whalers' haunt, the Galapagos. They found their true answer at Esquimalt, an easily accessible and safe harbour adjacent to Victoria on Vancouver Island. It was, as the forward-thinking Governor Blanshard advised Earl Grey in 1850, "the only Harbour in the Southern part of the Island worthy of notice, as it is of large extent, has good anchorage, is easy of access at all times, and in all weather is well watered and in many places the water is of sufficient depth to allow ships anchoring along the shore."[111] True, it was far from any possible site for a trans-Isthmian canal. But it had unique strategic value because it could halt American encroachment on British soil on the Northwest Coast.

The Navy's interest in Esquimalt derived from the Oregon crisis. The possibility that, in the event of war with the United States in 1846, many British warships would be sent to Juan de Fuca Strait led Rear-Admiral Seymour to dispatch the barque *Herald*, 26 guns, Captain Henry Kellett, and the brig *Pandora*, 6 guns, Lieutenant James Wood, to examine the intricate island waterways from Cape Flattery through Juan de Fuca Strait to and including Puget Sound and Haro Strait. The southern tip of Vancouver Island, which had not been surveyed in the days of Vancouver and Broughton, was of particular interest because of the increase in shipping, and expansion of Hudson's Bay Company trade. Kellett directed the examination of Victoria, Sooke and other harbours. Wood surveyed Esquimalt Harbour, aided by naval instructor Robert Inskip and midshipmen from the frigate *Fisgard*.[112] In 1846 the *Herald* and *Pandora* also charted Hood Canal, Puget Sound and Haro Strait. In late summer 1846 the *Pandora* examined the Gulf of Georgia. Detailed reports on the First Nations of Juan de Fuca Strait were sent to London. The findings of these and other surveys were published in Admiralty charts in 1847–1849.[113]

The first published Admiralty chart of Juan de Fuca Strait was the greatest navigational guide to mariners, one of immense value, that provided base material for later additions. Commander Wood wrote detailed directions for the Strait area, and this became, in effect, the first chapter of a British Columbia Pilot, or sailing directions. This information constituted a valuable addition to the Navy's knowledge of Vancouver Island, for it permitted commanders in daylight and clear visibility to enter the straits without undue fear of obstacles to navigation. It was now certain that ships-of-the-line could enter Esquimalt with ease.[114]

Surveys were the harbingers of commerce, and the work of Wood and Kellett gave the greater gift to maritime prospects. With lighthouses and buoys, these waters were becoming safer for mariners. The marine toll lessened, but human error occurred all the same. And until tide and current tables were compiled, many problems could still beset shipping, as was the case with HMS *Hecate*, which nearly came to grief in fog when she drifted onto the rocks inside Tatoosh Island.

For the moment, the Strait of Georgia and eastern Vancouver Island were not surveyed by the Navy. There were two reasons for this: first, steam was required for getting safely in and out of Rosario Strait, the easternmost passage to the Strait of Georgia; and second, all shipping going to Fort Rupert and Beaver Harbour went by the long outside route under sail. When, as we will see, there was a naval expedition to Cowichan Bay in 1853, the beginning of coal mining at Nanaimo at about the same time and, most significantly, the commencement of gold fever for the Fraser River, all this changed. But for the moment the surveying priorities were for the west coast of Vancouver Island—Klaskino, Klaskish, Nuchatlitz, Esperanza and Nootka Sound, with further work at Quatsino and Nasparti.

By mid-century, the assets of Esquimalt and Vancouver Island had been recognized by naval commanders and Company officials alike. Among the former was Lieutenant (later Commander) James Wood of the *Pandora*, who saw in Vancouver Island, with its colony and naval base, a place to restore British prestige in the North Pacific.[115] Rear-Admiral Moresby, the first commander-in-chief to visit the Northwest Coast, also appreciated the possibilities of developing a naval depot at Esquimalt when he called there in 1851. Consequently, he recommended that the colonial government reserve the harbour and its shores for the Crown. In Moresby's view, Esquimalt was the only place where an establishment meeting the essential criteria for a depot for Her Majesty's ships could be formed.[116]

Hudson's Bay Company officials expressed similar views. The Company agent at San Francisco, for example, had political reasons for writing to his superiors in London in 1849 that the sooner the British government established a naval depot on the Island the better.[117] He reasoned that such a base—together with one in the Hawaiian Islands—would counterbalance the great influence Americans were exercising in the Pacific through possession of California and its ports.[118] James Douglas also knew that the Royal Navy could provide protection against American expansionists who acquired the banks of the Columbia in 1846 and who would undoubtedly turn their attention to Vancouver Island—the only part of "British Oregon" that he believed could be colonized.[119]

With this in mind, Douglas wrote to Hudson's Bay Company headquarters that the harbours of the southern tip of the Island offered several splendid sites for a secure naval base where ships of the Royal Navy could provision and refit. Not only did Vancouver Island contain ports preferable to any in Pacific America, but it also possessed coal deposits that ships could take advantage of, as well as "the finest spars in the world for the trouble of dragging them from the forests."[120] In a concluding remark that reveals Douglas as a man with considerable foresight, he noted: "The colony and naval depot would be a material benefit to each other, the one producing and the other consuming the products of the land."[121]

Clearly, Esquimalt, with its accessibility to spars and coal, water and provisions, would be an asset to the Royal Navy in the entire Pacific as a base and also as a position of strategic importance to British interests in the North Pacific. How these qualities caused Esquimalt to evolve into a naval station during the 1850s and 1860s will be discussed later.[122]

Changing Status of Vancouver Island

Developments at Vancouver Island in the seven years following the resolution of the Oregon boundary question in 1846 were not at first encouraging for several reasons. First attempts at colonization did not meet with success. The plans of the British government for settlement failed because the Colonial Office selected a staple-trading company as a colonizing agency rather than a land company. It should be added, however, that the Hudson's Bay Company was only partly to blame for this state of affairs; it might have fulfilled its obligation better if arable lands at low prices had been abundant.

Earl Grey's faith in the Company's ability to colonize the land proved ill-founded. The faltering progress of the Colony of Vancouver Island showed, in large measure, that frontier communities of settlement do not grow quickly, if at all, under the dominance of a monopoly. Thus, by 1852 only 300 persons lived at Fort Victoria and 150 at Fort Nanaimo—and most of these were Company servants. In fact, only 435 emigrants had been sent out by this time; 11 had purchased land, and another 19 had applied for land.[123] In short, the prospects of the colony appeared bleak because the Hudson's Bay Company had not effectively promoted settlement.

More auspicious was the growing association of the Royal Navy with Vancouver Island during the period between 1846 and 1852 when Commanders-in-Chief, Pacific, assigned at least one ship annually to visit the Northwest Coast in support of British interests. These ships undertook a variety of tasks encouraging to the eventual settlement and economic development of the Island. They transported foodstuffs for the Company to aid settlers, punished unruly Natives and kept Americans in awe of British power during this unsettled period in Anglo-American relations.

When warships came to Vancouver Island for these purposes, spars, coal and hemp were tested to determine their suitability for naval require-ments. A safe harbour, Esquimalt, was found. Adjacent waters were charted to facilitate the coastal trade upon which the life and progress of the colony mainly depended. Thus, as Douglas had predicted, the Royal Navy and Vancouver Island experienced mutual benefits. Both Victoria and Esquimalt owed their pre-eminence to Douglas, and this pair of ports formed together a mighty but still infant seat of maritime development, ship repair and construction, provisioning and victualling, recreation, and medical facilities and personnel. In the late 1840s and through to the 1850s the whole was in a rude state: the roads were rough, infrastructure poor, and social conditions appalling. Drinking water was in short supply; there were no sewers and often no septic tanks. Boardwalks and ramshackle bridges and footpaths were the order of the day. The HBC cared little for the civic order and the civic infrastructure, but in 1862 the incorporation of Victoria brought municipal government, one of the earliest representa-tive bodies in all of what became western Canada.

By 1853 there were indications of an approaching end to the combined efforts of the Hudson's Bay Company and the Royal Navy at Vancouver

Island. The climax came in 1858 when the charter of grant held by the Company was not renewed.

The informal partnership of fur traders and sailors on the Northwest Coast, which began with the expedition of the Royal Navy's *Racoon* to the mouth of the Columbia River in 1813 in support of the North West Company, lasted throughout the Oregon crisis and the early years of the Colony of Vancouver Island. After that the Royal Navy was chiefly responsible for protection of the seaboard colony, which was moving toward self-government and provincial status in Canada. One after another, some of the Navy's greatest ships made their way to the distant Pacific. On December 12, 1852, the razéed frigate *Trincomalee* reached Valparaiso, fresh from Portsmouth. Her commander, Captain Wallace Houstoun, was an outstanding officer. An excellent seaman, with surveying and scientific skills, he took a firm but friendly position in regards to his occasionally unruly crew. "Trinco," as she was affectionately known, had been built in Bombay of teak, and was a strong ship. She sailed to Esquimalt on imperial duties, to guard against possible American filibustering at the time of a gold rush in Haida Gwaii. She saw all the major ports of call, and even voyaged north under instructions to support the relief ships *Enterprise* and *Investigator,* which had been sent to find Sir John Franklin and his lost ships. Much time was passed pleasantly in Honolulu, and she joined Rear-Admiral Henry W. Bruce's flagship, the *Monarch*, for an intended renewed attack on Petropavlovsk, Kamchatka, during the Crimean War. The story of her career has been well told by Andrew Lambert, and it is noteworthy that this frigate survived the decades, became the sea-cadet training ship *Foudroyant* (she was in Portsmouth when I boarded her on a tour of inspection with Rear-Admiral P.W. Brock in about 1970), and today she is to be found, beautifully restored, in Hartlepool, where she presents to the modern onlooker an authentic glimpse of naval life in the age of sail. There never could be enough frigates. Nelson famously declared: "Was I to die this moment, 'Want of Frigates' would be found stamped on my heart."[124] And all praise and honour are due to those, such as the HMS Trincomalee Trust, who have kept the memory green and the record accurate about a ship and a chapter in the age of fighting sail whose magic and majesty still spark our imagination and invite our gratitude.

five

ᘜAR WITH RUSSIA IN THE PACIFIC

In March 1854, Britain and France entered the Crimean War, largely to curtail Russian ambitions and to protect the British corridor to India and the Far East, and French spheres of influence in the Near East.[1] From the outset the Allies had command of the sea, and they took the naval war to the enemy in inshore waters: the Allied navies clashed with the Russian enemy in four locales—the Black Sea, where the Crimea became the major battleground; the Baltic Sea; the White Sea; and the North Pacific Ocean. The North Pacific was far from being the decisive theatre of action, naval or otherwise, but the activities of the Royal Navy there spurred the development of a naval depot and hospital at Esquimalt and safeguarded British interests along the Pacific coast of North America from the dangers of a threatened Russian–American alliance. As will be seen, the chief operations of the Pacific squadron consisted of an attack, which failed ignominiously, on the Russian outpost of Petropavlovsk, on the Kamchatka Peninsula; a brief occupation of the by-then-deserted post the following year; a search for elusive Russian warships on Asian and American shores, which demonstrated the weakness of the Russian navy's position in the Pacific; and visits by the Royal Navy to Esquimalt for coal, medical services , ship repairs, provisions and naval stores.

Owing to its remoteness from the Baltic and the Black Sea, where the final outcome of the conflict was decided, the North Pacific has

GUN EMPLACEMENTS
1854

Ⓐ 5 guns
Ⓑ 11 guns
Ⓒ 3 guns
Ⓓ 5 guns
Ⓔ 5 guns
Ⓕ 9 guns

N

FORTE

Ⓔ

Gorge
Seamen
Marines

Ⓕ
Magazine

VIRAGO

Attack of
4 Sept. 1854

TOWN

HARBOUR
5

PRESIDENT

7   4½

Saddle battery

OBLIGADO   Ⓓ   AURORA

6   DVINA

5   SPIT

Ⓑ

PT. SCHAKOFF   Ⓐ

EURYDICE fired at Point battery
4 Sept. 1854

EURYDICE

FORTE, PIQUE & PRESIDENT
shelled batteries 31 Aug. 1854

AVATCHA BAY

Sea of
Okhotsk

KAMCHATKA

Amur R.

Avatcha Bay

SAKHALIN I.

PACIFIC
OCEAN

PRESIDENT's marines landed
by VIRAGO to spike original
3-gun battery

Ⓒ

Soundings in fathoms

100   0   200   400   600   Yards

Allied attack on Petropavlovsk, 1834

This map is reprinted with permission of the original publisher from *The Royal Navy on the Northwest Coast of North America, 1810–1914* by Barry Gough © University of British Columbia Press 1971. All rights reserved by the publisher.

been overlooked as an area of the Crimean War.[2] The failure of the Allies against the Russians in battle at Petropavlovsk in 1854 was not well reported at the time, and the fiasco described in this chapter resulted in little more than a demonstration of why an assault force should not land in the face of superior enemy numbers defending a strong position. Little has been written on the Petropavlovsk affair in the Pacific theatre of the war, and no previously published account has been based on the very detailed Admiralty sources.[3]

The Deepening Crisis

As Russia expanded her interests in Siberia and the North Pacific during the mid-nineteenth century, she sought to foster settlements and trading posts on her eastern shores. By fortifying centres such as Ayan on the Sea of Okhotsk and Petropavlovsk on the Kamchatka Peninsula, which lay only a few miles from the Kurile Islands, she hoped to strengthen her fur trade in North America, exploit the rich whaling grounds of the North Pacific and enter into commerce with China and Japan.

On the very eve of the war, Russia gained *de facto* control of the Amur River, a highway of destiny—a waterway leading eastward from Siberia to the Sea of Japan. The Chinese supposedly held the river mouth, but Russian naval explorations from 1849 to 1855 revealed that Chinese gunboats did not defend the Amur, as one mistaken Russian admiral had maintained.[4] Consequently, Russia extended her influence down that river to its mouth and along the adjacent shores of Eastern Asia with impunity. From their explorations and surveys near Sakhalin, the Russians learned that the Amur could be entered from the sea by two passages, either from the north or from the south entrance to the Gulf of Amur (or Tartary). However, the Allied commanders were under the impression from the findings of La Pérouse and Broughton that it was impossible to enter the river's shallow mouth.[5] Subsequent events revealed that British naval officers, much to their embarrassment, were ill informed about the mouth of the Amur.[6] The matter was no longer of academic interest; it was of strategic importance.

A dominant motive for Russian eastward expansion at this time was fear of British aggrandizement in the North Pacific, especially along Asian shores.[7] Although Britain had no such plan, the Governor General of

Eastern Siberia, General Nikolai Muraviev, was suspicious of English intentions. He believed that Britain wanted to become the dominant power in that ocean, and he favoured a Russian–American alliance to check British maritime ascendancy.[8]

Moreover, Muraviev knew that Russian ports on Sakhalin and the Kurile Islands would be easy prey to hostile British warships; Russian naval vessels depended on these islands for supplies. Through Muraviev's initiative, a thousand men, chiefly infantry and field artillery, were sent down the Amur from the Transbaikal Provinces, along with stores for Russian warships.[9] By the spring of 1854, a third of the force and General Muraviev himself joined the 50-man garrison at Petropavlovsk. There, unbeknown to the British or French, they completed extensive preparations to defend the post, which had become the Russian bastion of the North Pacific, against a possible Allied naval attack.

The situation was markedly different on the Northwest Coast of North America, where British and Russian fur-trading organizations understood each other's problems and even did business with one another while the parent nations fought. Indeed, the British and Russian companies entered into an agreement in 1839 that formed the basis of an understanding that lasted until Russia sold Alaska to the United States in 1867.[10] The terms of the 1839 agreement assigned to the Hudson's Bay Company almost total control of the maritime fur trade as far north as Cape Spencer, increased the Company's influence in the Stikine Territory beyond the *lisière* or coastal strip, and gave the Company other commercial advantages. For the Russians it guaranteed a steady supply of land-otter skins and foodstuffs from the British traders. Finally, because war between the respective nations seemed possible in 1839, the agreement specified that in the event of such a conflict, the Russian American Company would guarantee the peaceful removal of their British counterparts from the *lisière* for up to three months after learning of war.[11]

When war loomed early in 1854, Russian American Company officials pressed for a further agreement with the Hudson's Bay Company for a proclamation of agreed neutrality over the whole Northwest Coast in time of war.[12] Here was a company-to-company arrangement. When the matter was referred to the Foreign Office, the British government consented to the proposal because territorial acquisitions had been renounced as a war aim.

In keeping with this policy, instructions were sent at once to commanders of British warships in the Pacific, advising that hostile acts were not to be committed in the Tsar's American dominions.[13] But the fine point of distinction consisted in the fact that neutrality was to be "territorial only."[14] During war, Russian warships and merchantmen on the high seas were liable to capture, and the coasts and posts of Russian America were subject to blockade.

This "quarantine" of the area in time of war was unquestionably beneficial to the commercial interests of both nations. But in excluding Russian America as an object of war, the British government may have acted too hastily. By August 1854 the possibility of a Russian–American alliance had led Palmerston at the Home Office to suggest to the Earl of Clarendon, the foreign secretary, that the "nominal possession" of the area might "forestall the Bargain between Nicholas and the Yankees."[15] Moreover, at least one imperially minded Canadian favoured seizing the territory as an addition to British North America of strategic and commercial importance.[16] In any event, the Anglo-Russian pact on neutrality of the Northwest Coast did not help Russia overcome her major disadvantage in the North Pacific as elsewhere during the Crimean War—that is, her inferiority to the Allies at sea. The British squadron in the Pacific could have damaged Sitka and other Russian settlements. But the British government had no intention of upsetting trading relations between the Russian American Company and the Hudson's Bay Company. Neither did it seek territorial expansion there. For these reasons, the government adopted essentially a passive policy for the northeastern Pacific.[17]

On February 24, 1854, nearly a month before the Allies declared war on Russia, the Admiralty acted on the advice of the Foreign Office and instructed commanders-in-chief on the foreign stations to cooperate with their French counterparts against Russia in the event of war.[18] So inevitable did hostilities appear that their Lordships also sent orders to the commander-in-chief on the China station to plan operations against Russia.[19] And British and French admirals in the Pacific needed to know only that war had been declared before moving against the enemy.[20] The paddle-wheel sloop *Virago* was sent to Panama to await such news from England.

Outbreak of War

On May 7, 1854, the *Virago* brought to Callao dispatches for Rear-Admiral David Price, Commander-in-Chief, Pacific, informing him that Britain and France had joined forces against Russia on March 28. A state of war existed. Price was 64, and he had not been at sea for 22 years. He had waited patiently on the Navy List until such time as his name rose to the preferred place where, if selected by the Lords of the Admiralty, he could fly his new flag in command of a squadron or fleet. Price, however, did not act with any apparent haste. Two days after receiving this news, along with certain instructions, he issued a general memorandum to his squadron indicating the part it should play in the conflict:

> In carrying out these instructions the Rear Admiral desires to record his opinion that there will be much to be done upon this Station by the Squadron under his Orders, and that Great Britain has a right to expect from it a proper account of the Russian Frigates that are known to be on the Station as well as the numerous Privateers that it is known will be [there].

To these words, Price added his hope that men on the station would show such bravery in action as to "render them not only superior to their Enemy but inferior to none in the World."[21]

Price's primary aim was to clear the seas of Russian shipping. He knew that the enemy frigates would avoid their stronger opponents and probably seek refuge in harbours on the coast of Siberia. So he proceeded, rather slowly, to gather his force at successive points—Callao, Nuku Hiva (the French Pacific naval headquarters in the Marquesas Islands) and Honolulu—before sailing for the northwestern Pacific.[22] By the time the combined squadron reached the Hawaiian Islands on July 17, it consisted of the *President*, 50 guns; *Amphitrite*, 24 guns; and *Virago*, 6 guns; and the *Forte*, 60 guns; *Artemise*, 30 guns; *Eurydice*, 22 guns; and *Obligado*, 18 guns, the last four of these belonging to France.

The arrival of the Allied squadron did much to strengthen British and French influence in the Hawaiian Islands, although this was not the purpose of the call. Since 1846 the two governments had upheld a policy of independence for the Hawaiian kingdom. On this occasion, Rear-Admiral Price and his counterpart, Rear-Admiral Fevrier-Despointes, stressed to Kamehameha III that Hawaiian sovereignty was of utmost importance in view of American pressures to annex the islands.[23] The growing Russian–American *rapprochement* increased the strategic importance of the islands. If Sakhalin remained in Russian hands and Hawaii were under American control, British and French power in the North Pacific would be reduced correspondingly.[24] The auspicious appearance of eight warships,[25] the largest squadron yet seen there, certainly added weight to the concerted pressure of the French and British admirals.[26] This display of naval power, reinforced by simultaneous diplomatic activity in Washington by Britain and France, delayed—if but for a few decades—the American annexation of Hawaii.

At Honolulu, a further indication that Russia and the United States might be acting in concert reached Price in the form of news that San Francisco merchants were fitting out American privateers to aid the Russians in the Pacific. He decided therefore to dispatch the *Amphitrite* and *Artemise* to the California coast to protect allied trade; in order to keep this mission secret, the two vessels remained with the squadron until three days after its departure from the Hawaiian Islands.

The Allies at Petropavlovsk

Rear-Admiral Price learned also at Honolulu from a Hudson's Bay Company agent that two Russian warships—later discovered to be the *Aurora*, 44 guns, and *Dvina*, 12 guns—were bound for Petropavlovsk on the Kamchatka Peninsula.[27] He had known earlier of the existence of these ships, for the *Aurora* arrived at Callao in mid-April to find four British and French warships awaiting news of the declaration of war.[28] Yet Price did not sail from Callao to pursue the Russian ships until 10 days after receiving this information. Probably he was reluctant to engage the enemy, a view that is substantiated by strange events preceding the attack on Petropavlovsk.

In point of fact, Price had little to fear from his enemy at sea; the ships of the Russian imperial navy certainly were not the equal of the British and French in the Pacific from the point of view of numbers, condition or armament. The only Russian ships of note in the Pacific were the frigate *Diana*, 50 guns, and the *Aurora*, the few others being corvettes and brigs. Russian commanders realized their inferiority, as shown by the fact that Russian vessels sought the protection of the mouth of the Amur River and of harbours on the Asian coast such as Ayan, Petropavlovsk and De Castries Bay.[29]

Even though the Allies acquired command of the sea in the Pacific at the very outset of the war, they were unable to engage the enemy at sea. As will be shown, success eluded them because the superior geographical knowledge possessed by Russian captains enabled them to evade Allied warships, which searched the North Pacific in vain.[30] Frustration was the order of the day.

The *Aurora* and *Dvina* found safety in the most important of the Russian havens, Petropavlovsk. The town lay seven miles inland from the entrance to, and on the eastern shore of, Avatcha Bay on the Pacific side of the Kamchatka Peninsula.[31] A long, narrow, mountainous peninsula pointing southward guarded the town on the west; between this and the shore lay "a clear and deep narrow entrance" leading to an inner harbour, at the head of which was the town.[32] Close behind a sandspit, which extended west-northwest from the mainland toward the peninsula, lay the *Aurora* and *Dvina*—protected in this position from being hulled near the waterline.

On arrival, August 29, 1854, the Allies found the defences of Petropavlovsk stronger than expected, but not particularly formidable.[33] The outer defences of primary importance consisted of three batteries: a 5-gun battery at the extremity of the peninsula, an 11-gun battery on

The action against Russian emplacements at Petropavlovsk, Kamchatka, in 1854: units of the French and British navies bombard the shore. The *Virago* can be seen to the left, the only vessel with steam power. The landing parties were severely repulsed with high casualties.
GOUGH COLLECTION

147

the opposite shore, and a 3-gun battery farther out on the same side.[34] The broadsides of the Russian ships also faced the harbour entrance and approaches. According to one estimate, a total of 800 Russians and 52 guns defended the town.[35]

But events were to show that outward appearances were deceiving. These words of Commander F.W. Beechey, written after his visit there in 1827, were prophetic: "Should the North Pacific ever be the scene of active naval operations, Petropaulovski must doubtless become of immense importance. At present it may be said to be unfortified, but a very few guns judiciously placed would effectually protect its entrance."[36]

Debacle at Petropavlovsk

The strength of the squadron assembled seemed to indicate that the Allies could make themselves masters of Petropavlovsk with little trouble: there were three frigates (the British flagship *President*, Captain Richard Burridge; the *Pique*, 40 guns, Captain Sir Frederick W. Nicolson, Bart.; and the *Forte*, flagship of Rear-Admiral Fevrier-Despointes), plus a corvette (the *Eurydice*) and a brig (the *Obligado*). The squadron's handicap was that it possessed but one steamer, the *Virago*. Although she was weak in armament, she proved invaluable in the operations because her 120-horsepower engines gave her the manoeuvrability that the other vessels lacked in those confined waters during the lengthy calms that prevailed. In total, six vessels were assembled, painted black on the exterior of their gun decks to conceal their armament, mounting 190 guns, and carrying some 2,000 men. Despite the strength of this force, it was evident throughout the engagement that followed that the lack of steam power in five of the ships placed them at a distinct disadvantage in exchanges with shore batteries. Indeed, manoeuvrability proved to be as important as armament, a development that underlined the potentialities of steam as a motive power.[37]

During the afternoon of August 29, 1854, Rear-Admiral Price reconnoitered Avatcha Bay in the *Virago* to determine the strength of the Russian fortifications; he concluded that the outer defences, already mentioned, were of no great strength. At last the bombardment began. The guns of the *Virago* opened up on the enemy's saddle battery; other ships may have joined in. Ships firing against forts was always a dubious matter, invariably favouring the forts, but not in this instance. The time for an amphibious assault had come, and later that day, on board the flagship *President*, plans were made for an attack the next morning, but even then uncertainty reigned. The extent of these plans is not known, and one source claims, perhaps in excess, that none were made: "No decided opinion was given as to the strength or size of it (Petropavlovsk) or even the capability of attacking it, consequently, no plan for the morrow was made."[38]

A strange turn of events now overtook the squadron, one previously unheard of in British naval annals. In the early afternoon of August 30, just as the *Virago* was towing the *Forte*, *Pique* and *President* into position, Price shot himself through the lungs and died three hours later. Captain Burridge in the flagship at first thought this was an accident, but later concluded that the act was a result of "intense mental anxiety."[39] Undoubtedly, at the climax of his professional life, Price was unprepared for war and unequal to the task.[40] The clerk's assistant in the *Pique* gives the best available evidence in support of this view in a comment: "Throughout the whole voyage [from Callao] he had evidently shown great weakness in allowing everybody to sway him as they willed; consequently when he was expected to show forth in the purest and truest light, his nerves gave way under the responsibility . . . and by this act of his . . . threw the Squadron into a state such as is unparalleled in English naval history."[41]

The responsibility for implementing the plan against the batteries now devolved upon Fevrier-Despointes. When the Russians ashore heard that the British admiral had committed suicide, they refused to believe it and, wanting to claim credit for the death, insisted that a shell fired from a well-aimed Russian artillery piece belonging to the shore batteries had killed him.[42]

During the early-morning calms of the following day, the *Virago* — engines barely equal to the task—placed the *President*, *Forte* and *Pique* before the batteries near the harbour mouth. In order to take the three-gun battery on the east, which, "from its raking position, was expected to give some annoyance," a party of marines and seamen were landed from the *Virago*; they captured and spiked the guns.[43] But when a body of Russians disembarked from the *Aurora* to counterattack—their number being two hundred according to one claim[44]—the Allied party withdrew and re-embarked safely under cover of fire from the *Virago*.

At this juncture in this trial-and-error campaign it became clear that a battery near the landward end of the spit on the eastern shore would have to be silenced, as it was directly in line with the Allied ships, the Russian ships behind the spit, and the town. Then the Allies could get their vessels closer to shore and bring their guns to bear on the Russian ships and the town. Fresh afternoon breezes permitted the *President* and the *Forte* to close on the battery, whereupon all four Allied ships fired at and silenced the emplacement. Then they withdrew for the night out of range from other batteries—suffering some damage during the process.[45] This brought to a conclusion what might be called a prelude to defeat.

Three days of correspondence and discussion followed in the Allied ships. The French admiral, worried by the damage the *Forte* had sustained, showed reluctance to press the attack, contending that it was impossible for the Allies to make themselves masters of Petropavlovsk without great loss of life, defended as it was by such apparently formidable batteries.[46] He advocated, as a better alternative, that the squadron should cruise to intercept a Russian squadron consisting of the frigate *Diana* and two consorts. In his view, this was preferable to making a landing, which would risk weakening the Allied force and rendering it inferior to Russian warships at sea. Like Fevrier-Despointes, Captain Nicolson, the senior British officer, was mentally unprepared for the responsibilities thrust upon him by Price's death.[47] In his reply to his superior he did not fully reveal his anxieties, but stated simply that he hoped the Allies would meet the Russian squadron somewhere in the North Pacific.[48]

Subsequent questions from Fevrier-Despointes demanding categorical answers forced Nicolson to oppose the views of the French admiral. Nicolson knew and admitted that casualties were unavoidable, but he had reason to believe that if the batteries were attacked from the rear, as some Americans there had advised him, success would be certain.[49] The fall of the batteries, capture of the Russian ships and destruction of the defences would make the place unfit as a retreat for the expected Russian frigates. His most conclusive remark emphasized that unless further attempts were made, the national honours of England and France would be compromised.[50] It seems certain that if Nicolson had not exerted pressure on Fevrier-Despointes in this fashion, the Allied ships would have withdrawn, bringing the encounter to an early, albeit unsuccessful, conclusion.

But after receiving additional intelligence respecting some batteries not visible from the Allied warships, and after further consultations with

Nicolson and other officers, both French and British, the French admiral agreed to simultaneous attacks on the saddle battery and the round fort near the gorge—the latter being the most northerly position of Russian defence along the shore. In short, the frontal attack was abandoned for one from the rear.

On September 4, 350 men from each nation were in readiness in the *Virago*. On one side of the steamer lay the *Forte*; on the other the boats for the disembarkation. The *President* was in tow.[51] As the ships drew near the northern half of the peninsula, the Russian guns opened fire with success, doing damage to the riggings of the *Forte* and *President*. The *President* engaged the saddle battery at six hundred yards before silencing it, while the *Forte* put the round fort out of action, thereby allowing marines and seamen to land. The assault plan called for marines, assisted by seamen from the *Forte* and *Eurydice*, to ascend the steep hill that guarded the town on the west.[52] Simultaneously, seamen from the *Pique*, *President* and *Virago* were to move by the road to the left of the hill, clear the gorge and thereby open the way for a direct advance on the town.

This overall plan was doomed from the outset, largely because the landing party had neither special training nor opportunity to rehearse the operation. On the left, the seamen met with little success against the Russian battery firing grapeshot down the gorge. On the right, the marines suffered heavy losses in consequence of enemy fire from superior positions along the ridge and on both sides of the saddle. Captain C.R. Parker, RM, was killed; his subalterns were wounded; the men fell back; and when all attempts to rally them failed, they fled in utter disorder to boats on the beach, several being killed by musketry during the embarkation. The guns of the *Forte*, *Obligado* and *Virago* covered the retreating force as best they could, and when all the men were on board, the ships moved out into the bay.[53] The Allies had been repulsed decisively.

The attack from the rear thus was as much a failure as the frontal assault. Because the Russian ships in the harbour were the most important object, the attempt to take the town seems to have been inconsistent with the original plan.[54] This is borne out by the views of Rear-Admiral H.W. Bruce, Price's successor, who after consulting with British, Russian and American witnesses concluded that the marines and seamen were evidently "landed to *spare the ships*; where had the party been at their guns, and in the proper place . . . their enemy was prepared to yield." Bruce informed the First Lord of the Admiralty, Sir Charles Wood, "As far as I have heard the land attack was a badly managed business . . . not only was the attack wrongly made but badly executed."[55] In London there was much despair.

The Allies paid a heavy toll for poor reconnaissance, faulty planning and bad execution. Of the 700 landed, there were 209 casualties: 26 French and 26 British killed or missing, 78 French and 79 British wounded.[56] Nevertheless, the chaplain of the *President*, the Reverend Thomas Holme, overstated the case when he described the battle as "a most bloody defeat" and "a tragedy perhaps more horrible than has ever happened in the British Navy."[57] Holme probably had never before witnessed a battle. The confusion of the whole train of events, plus the heavy casualties, led him to an exaggerated conclusion. The publication of Holme's account has done little to dispel the generally held views of terrible carnage. Admittedly, the

Commander-in-Chief, Pacific, Rear-Admiral Henry William Bruce (1854–57), veteran of many naval campaigns, had been a midshipman at Trafalgar and flew his flag in HMS *Monarch*, 82 guns.
CFB ESQUIMALT NAVAL & MILITARY MUSEUM

events at Petropavlovsk were a fiasco, but there was no wholesale slaughter as in the Charge of the Light Brigade.[58]

Nonetheless, news of the repulse was not well received in London, and inaccurate reports found their way into the British press. When the official account reached the Admiralty, their Lordships voiced their displeasure in a dispatch sent to Captain Nicolson. This informed him that the defeat was "of a nature which ought to impress upon the officers of H.M. Ships that the utmost discretion is necessary in undertaking expeditions on shore and detaching Seamen and Marines from their ships in the neighbourhood of fortified positions of the Enemy, with imperfect knowledge of the Nature of the Country and the force expected to be encountered."[59] The reprimand failed to recognize that the shortage of steam-assisted vessels in the Pacific prohibited the Allies from "wheeling around in small circles" and delivering successive broadsides against the shore batteries, as was done in the successful operations at Odessa on the Black Sea.[60]

Owing to the number of wounded and the lateness of the season, it was necessary to postpone further assault on Petropavlovsk until the following spring, when the harbour ice had broken up. The squadron sailed September 7. Outside Avatcha Bay, they sighted two sails in the distance. The *President* and *Virago* gave chase and captured the *Anadis*, a Russian government schooner, and the *Sitka*, 10 guns, a Russian American Company vessel bound for Petropavlovsk with army officers, gunpowder and provisions. The Russian prisoners told Nicolson—and he had every reason to believe them—that the enemy at Petropavlovsk was indeed stronger than the Allies had been led to expect.[61] After this, the warships and the prize *Sitka* sailed for the Northwest Coast of America, some three thousand miles away.[62]

The *President*, *Pique* and *Virago* reached the welcome confines of Esquimalt on October 3. Their crews repaired sails and running gear, blacked down rigging, painted hulls, and cut and stowed spars and firewood. The ships received a large, but insufficient, quantity of provisions from farms close to Esquimalt. Coal was brought from nearby Nanaimo, and water from adjacent lakes and streams. Although much-needed hospital facilities were not available, the value of Esquimalt as a place of repair and refreshment was clearly evident.

War Scare at Vancouver Island

Arrival of the squadron eliminated the danger of a Russian attack from Sitka or Petropavlovsk. This had worried Victoria residents, especially James Douglas, the governor of Vancouver Island. When unofficial news of war reached Victoria in mid-June, the gravity of the situation led him to draft hurried plans for defence.[63] As wise as these plans were, they won little support in London or the colony. His proposal for a regular military force of five hundred men, along with pieces of ordnance, brought a terse rejoinder from the War Office that the Commander-in-Chief, Pacific, had received instructions to send warships frequently to the colony.[64] Nor did Douglas get much support from the Legislative Council of Vancouver Island. This body rejected a militia scheme proposed by the governor,[65] although arrangements were made to charter and arm the Hudson's Bay Company steamer *Otter*, at the expense of the imperial government, to serve as a guardship until Britain made adequate provisions against an attack by Russian warships or privateers.[66]

Douglas had been especially alarmed by rumours that a Russian frigate had sailed from San Francisco to shell Victoria. But Commodore Charles Frederick in HMS *Amphitrite* at San Francisco advised the Admiralty on November 13, 1854, that no such vessel had been sighted at either place. Because Vancouver Island was considered neutral territory, he was certain that the governor's fears were unfounded.[67]

Still, British possessions on the coast were liable to blockade by Russian vessels, and on this basis Douglas's apprehension was justified; the neutrality agreement in no way guaranteed the protection of Vancouver Island from blockade or from interception of supply ships from England by the Russian warships and privateers thought to be at large in the Pacific.[68] Only the presence of British men-of-war could allay the fears of the colonists.

Naval Searches and Blockades

After remaining 13 days at Esquimalt, the squadron sailed on October 16 for San Francisco Bay, evidently in search of hospital facilities and more provisions. Within this bay, the British vessels anchored at Sausalito, the favourite watering place, where they found Her Majesty's Discovery Ship *Plover*, from Arctic discoveries.[69] The *Amphitrite*, flagship of Commodore Frederick, arrived from Hawaii to join the other British vessels. Frederick then transferred his broad pendant to the *President* and sailed in her for Valparaiso to meet the incoming Commander-in-Chief, Pacific, Rear-Admiral Bruce.[70]

Bruce's predecessor Price had embarrassed the service, the nation, his shipmates and probably his family. Mental illness may have been a factor in his death, but more likely it was the result of want of courage in a leader unused to combat and afraid of failure. His death closed an era of promotion by "walking in dead men's shoes." As his replacement, the Lords of the Admiralty sent to the Pacific an admiral who knew a great deal about command. He was a proven leader of ships and in ship-handling, and was zealous in all he did. He had won laurels in the anti-slavery crusade in West Africa and had been in command of a bold action at the Lagos lagoons, seizing from an African pirate king a slave-traders' nest. "I cannot withhold the expression of my regret for the very severe loss which has attended this achievement," he wrote to the Admiralty by way of explanation, "but in which I trust their Lordships will feel that the dignity of England has been asserted and the honour of the flag gloriously sustained." Bruce won the applause of their Lordships, and his action set the new standard of intervention in West Africa in protection of British interests. In larger measure, the guiding force in British policy, Lord Palmerston, gave this affirmation: that "trade cannot flourish without security," and that "cudgels, sabres or carbines would be needed to keep ill-disposed persons from exerting violence that rendered trade insecure and prevented its operation."[71] Bruce embodied the new model admiral of *Pax Britannica*.

As soon as Bruce reached Valparaiso by packet from Panama on February 5, 1855, he began deploying ships under his command to fulfill his object: defeat of the Russians at Petropavlovsk. Vast sailing distances in the Pacific made supplying the squadron a difficult matter, so the *Rattlesnake* was used as a storeship at Honolulu.[72] Warships received provisions and naval stores from her before making the final leg of the voyage to Petropavlovsk. Bruce planned for the squadron to sail to Esquimalt after the attack on the Russian post. He knew that hospital facilities, coal, and fresh meats and vegetables would probably be needed, so he sent a request to Governor Douglas asking that these be ready for the following July.[73] There was a surprise in store for him.

Douglas, who was also still the agent for the Western Department of the Hudson's Bay Company, had always shown a willingness to do business with the Royal Navy for the twofold reason that the warships brought business for the Company and gave the colony protection during their calls. Something more permanent would be agreeable. Thus, he lost little time in informing Bruce that a thousand tons of coal had been ordered from the Nanaimo mines, and that two thousand sheep and as many head of cattle as possible would be purchased from the Puget's Sound Agricultural Company post, Fort Nisqually. In order to ensure that supplies would always be on hand for British warships, Douglas advised Bruce that he considered it a "proper and necessary step" to appoint a commissary for the squadron.[74] Finally, he explained that hospital buildings would be available to receive the sick and wounded of the fleet. In this way the governor—at once businessman and public servant—prepared to meet the squadron's needs after what was expected to be another assault of major proportions at Petropavlovsk. He was not without the wiles to exploit the imperial connection for the benefit of the Company and the Colony. And we return to this story of affirming London's support below.

Prior to the 1854 fiasco, the Admiralty thought the British force of seven vessels "unnecessarily large" and, in consequence, Price had assigned four of the seven ships intended for use against the enemy to other duties on the station.[75] But in 1855 the Admiralty reinforced the Pacific squadron. A ship-of-the-line, the *Monarch*, 84 guns, was ordered to the Pacific because of fears of a Russian–American alliance and a possible American seizure of the Hawaiian Islands; the frigate *President* remained on the station; and the screw-corvette *Brisk*, 16 guns, was sent to replace the less powerful paddle-wheel sloop *Virago*.[76] In addition, the Admiralty ordered two vessels from the China station—the screw-corvette *Encounter*, 14 guns, and the paddle-wheel sloop *Barracouta*, 6 guns, to rendezvous with ships from the Pacific station prior to the attempt on Petropavlovsk.[77] They were intended to supply more steam propulsion to the Pacific squadron and thus overcome the disadvantage from which the Allies suffered in 1854. The *Encounter* and *Barracouta* arrived at the rendezvous on April 14, 1855, "full of coal and with a large supply of ammunition."[78]

The formidable squadron of 12 British and French vessels approached the coast of Kamchatka on May 30, 1855, with every expectation of finding the Russians firmly entrenched at Petropavlovsk.[79] But when the fog cleared two days later, Bruce reconnoitered Avatcha Bay in the steamer *Barracouta* and found to his amazement that the Russians had vanished.[80] It was reported that one of the few American traders, who were now the sole inhabitants of the post, said to Bruce: "I guess ye're rather late, Admiral."[81]

An explanation for the Russian evacuation was given by Captain Martinov, the aide-de-camp to the governor general of Eastern Siberia, who appeared from the hinterland to exchange prisoners with the Allies.[82] Evidently officials in St. Petersburg believed that Petropavlovsk could not withstand another attack by Allied warships unless the frigate *Diana*, 50 guns, arrived to strengthen the position. Accordingly, orders were sent to the effect that, should the Russian ship not appear, Petropavlovsk was to be abandoned and an escape made in the *Aurora*, *Dvina* and other available vessels. In fact, the *Diana* was wrecked off Japan in January 1855. Thus the Russians, some 470 in number, cut their way through the ice in the harbour, sailed from Petropavlovsk and hurried to safety in De Castries Bay and subsequently in the Amur River.[83]

All Bruce could do was conduct a thorough examination of Avatcha Bay: only a deserted and dismantled bark was found in a nearby harbour. He then ordered the destruction of the gun emplacements and garrison buildings at Petropavlovsk.[84]

There was, then, no engagement with the enemy: taking the post without a shot being fired was the direct result of Allied supremacy at sea. The capture of the Russian post demonstrated the inadequacy of Russian naval power, a decided advantage to Britain and France throughout the war in other seas as well.

Bruce was determined to seek out the Russians on Asian shores, so he now sent ships to several points: the *Encounter* to the mouth of the Amur, before returning to the China station; and the *Barracouta* and *Pique*, and later the *Amphitrite*, to scrutinize the north entrance to Tartar Strait and the port of Ayan. These vessels discovered that the enemy had withdrawn from Ayan, removed the guns and levelled the batteries.[85] The British destroyed a half-built Russian American Company vessel there, then left to search for the north entrance to the Amur. But heavy weather and strong currents made this impossible.

At this juncture, a squadron of British and French ships from the China Seas under the command of Commodore Charles Elliot assumed the duty of finding the Russian vessels on the Asian coast. This allowed the *Pique* and *Barracouta* to sail for Hong Kong, and the *Amphitrite* for the Northwest Coast of America. In his search for the Russian ships, Elliot was at first successful, finding them in De Castries Bay. In the belief that he would need reinforcements, he withdrew and returned with more ships only to find that the Russians had again escaped, this time into the mouth of the Amur.[86] The increasingly frustrated Lords of the Admiralty vented their disappointment on Elliot and his commander-in-chief.[87] Once more the Russians, as a result of their superior geographical knowledge, had made British naval commanders look foolish.

In the meantime, the Commander-in-Chief, Pacific, believed that he might find the elusive Russian vessels at Sitka, the major depot of the Russian American Company on the eastern shores of the Pacific. He sailed thence on June 30 in the flagship *President*, leaving behind the *Amphitrite* and *Trincomalee*, the latter to exchange prisoners with the Russians and to await the *Monarch* before sailing with her to Sitka to join the *President*, *Brisk* and *Dido*. Eventually, the French vessels *Forte*, the flagship of Rear-Admiral Fourichon,[88] and the *Obligado*, *Alceste* and *Eurydice* joined the British off Cape Edgecumbe, Krusov Island, on the west side of Sitka Sound.

The search on North American shores proved as unrewarding as that on the Asian coast, for neither in the harbour of Sitka, which was visited July 13, nor in nearby channels and inlets were Russian warships found.[89] With completion of their duties on the coast of Russian America, the Allied ships dispersed on July 17, after the arrival of the *Monarch* and *Trincomalee* from Petropavlovsk. The French vessels sailed for San Francisco, while the British made for Esquimalt or San Francisco.[90]

Why all the ships in the British squadron did not go directly to Vancouver Island seems clear. San Francisco, a centre of maritime interests in the Pacific, was a frequent port of call for Russian ships. It was a place to be watched for American naval and privateering activity in view of rumours of an alliance between Russia and the United States.[91] Consequently, the British and French warships periodically exchanged the duty of keeping under close surveillance Russian merchant ships, which dared not set to sea from this port for fear of capture. They also watched American shipping. Occasionally, Rear-Admiral Bruce received unsubstantiated accounts of Russian warships and American privateers at large in the Pacific. This confirmed his decision to assign Allied warships to watch Sitka as well as San Francisco during the final phase of the conflict.[92]

The Treaty of Paris, March 30, 1856, brought the Crimean War to a conclusion. The treaty terms were largely consistent with the recognized reasons for the entry of the Allies into the war. The life of the Ottoman Empire was prolonged, and Russian aspirations in the Near East were curtailed.[93] The treaty contained no reference to Russian expansion in the Pacific, which caused the British government to watch its former enemy with growing suspicion in the postwar period. In fact, British warships were dispatched to the northwestern Pacific in 1857 and 1858 to investigate Russian activities and trade at the mouth of the Amur River—which China recognized in 1858 as a Russian possession. Subsequently, reports to the Admiralty indicated that the Russian presence on Asian shores was permanent.[94]

Lessons of the War

In drawing conclusions about the naval aspects of the war with Russia in the Pacific, it should be noted first that nothing approaching a general fleet action occurred, not even a notable duel, because the Russian force was no match for the Allied navies and it sought safety in waters largely unknown to the Allies. Second—on the technical side—the war witnessed the introduction on a modest scale of steam propulsion for fighting ships and the use of shell as a general ship weapon. The effectiveness of shellfire revealed itself in engagements with shore defences, and the first experiments with armour were made.[95] Third—on the human side—the debacle at Petropavlovsk, like operations in the Baltic and Black Seas, revealed the need for younger senior officers as well as for greater thoroughness in preparing for war. Fourth, as a result of exaggerating the importance of coastal operations, the Admiralty decided to construct large numbers of gunboats and shallow-draught vessels.

From the point of view of naval strategy in the Pacific, perhaps the most important lesson revealed at Petropavlovsk was the value of steam power over sail. Sail was virtually useless in such inshore, or littoral, actions. Accordingly, the transition from sail to steam was accelerated. Sir Charles Wood, the First Lord, comparing the British with the French Navy in 1857, remarked that in the future, sailing vessels ought to be almost "left out of consideration."[96] In the following year he went even further when he said, "Sailing vessels, though useful in time of peace, would never be employed again during war."[97] However, neither the current financial resources nor the engineering capacity of Britain permitted a complete and immediate turnover. Nor could sails be dispensed with entirely on the Pacific station, where long passages under canvas were necessary and supplies of coal unreliable. Coal was expensive, the wind was free. Even as late as 1893, the Constructor for the Admiralty, Sir William White, was insisting that sail power in cruisers was still a necessity, vital for England's readiness at sea.[98] For this reason, sail training for officers and men continued and was only phased out in the early twentieth century.

The Crimean conflict also revealed, as the historian and maritime strategist Sir Julian Corbett noted generally, "how impotent [sea power] is of itself to decide a war against great continental states, how tedious is the pressure of naval action unless it be nicely coordinated with military and diplomatic pressure."[99] But there were explanations for the disappointing performance of the Royal Navy, including "the inefficient condition of the fleet, its indifferent leadership, and the antiquated state of its supply organization."[100] Quick successes were impossible under these circumstances.

The outmoded system of supplying the Royal Navy was improved after the Crimean War. In the course of this conflict, as we have seen, the first concentration of British warships occurred in the North Pacific. Five warships, including the first line-of-battle ship to visit the place, the *Monarch*, called at Esquimalt in 1855 for refit and refreshment. Although the value of Esquimalt became increasingly apparent during the war—particularly as a point of supply for the Pacific squadron—it was not until the British Columbia gold rush of 1858 and the Anglo-American dispute over the San Juan boundary in 1859 that the presence of British warships led to establishment of a provisional, and eventually permanent, stores depot there.

On the other hand, as an immediate and unexpected result of this war, the Navy came into possession at Esquimalt of the beginnings of a store establishment in three buildings known locally as "the Crimea Huts."[101] It will be recalled that in February 1855, Rear-Admiral Bruce requested that Governor Douglas build a temporary structure to serve as a hospital to receive casualties that might result from a second attack on Petropavlovsk. But Bruce failed to give exact instructions as to what was required, and so the governor proceeded, through no fault of his own, to erect what he thought would be adequate structures. When the matter of reimbursement arose, the Admiralty owed nearly £1,000 to the Colony of Vancouver Island. Bruce was justifiably distressed that a "temporary" structure should cost so much, because it was no longer of use as a hospital.[102] Douglas went so far as to suggest that a storekeeper be appointed. Bruce was obviously annoyed, but the governor knew how to extract the imperial benefit, and the Admiralty did not disappoint.

Bruce, an advocate of a naval base at Esquimalt, was prepared to recommend the retention of the buildings for hospital purposes if a store and provisions depot were formed there.[103] For his part, Douglas urged the Colonial Office to press the Admiralty for the amount outstanding.[104] The dispute continued into 1857, when the Admiralty paid not only the cost of the Crimea Huts but also considerable interest and maintenance charges.

These three buildings—known as the Crimea huts—were constructed on Governor Douglas's instructions as a hospital to receive wounded and convalescents expected from 1855 actions against the Russians at Petropavlovsk, Kamchatka. However, they became a political football as to the exorbitant costs expended. Douglas won; the Admiralty demurred. Situated on Duntze Head, Esquimalt, they rank among the earliest of buildings of the nascent naval base.

CFB ESQUIMALT NAVAL & MILITARY MUSEUM

One of the buildings became headquarters for Captain Richards and his fellow officers and clerks undertaking the coastal survey.

Thus, as a byproduct of war, the Pacific squadron found itself with a shore establishment at Esquimalt, the first of its kind in the eastern Pacific. This outcome came in a curious fashion, perhaps typical of the calamities and unexpected occurrences that the squadron experienced during the Crimean War. The Navy's operations were less than satisfactory in all the theatres of war. Yet Allied superiority at sea contributed substantially to the final result, which was the defeat of Russia. As for the ill-starred Rear-Admiral David Price, his suicide was covered up at the outset so that the lower deck would not see in his action an example of cowardice in the face of battle.[105] He had been 22 years a rear-admiral, but when the challenge of command was eventually offered him he proved unfit for the task, and he withered in the face of a battle that he knew or imagined he could not win. His is the only known case of a British flag officer committing suicide. He was an example to all in the Admiralty and in the Senior Service that the old system of appointments of flag officers had to come to an end. Mind you, on shore the War Office and the British Army were not free from the abundant criticism that came their way as a result of the appalling communications, ditherings and miscalculations of Lords Lucan and Cardigan that led to the ill-fated Charge of the Light Brigade. Not least in importance, this war demonstrated that Russia was soon to express a muscular presence on the Pacific. By possession of the Amur, the Empire of the Tsars now had a foothold on the Pacific hard by the Chinese Empire and near to Imperial Japan.

six

GOLD-RUSH CRISES

The British Empire expanded chiefly as the incidental result of activities carried on by British traders, merchants, soldiers, sailors and colonial governors rather than from conscious government designs to acquire and consolidate territory beyond Britain's shores. Except for Vancouver Island—proclaimed a colony in 1849—this was certainly true of British territory on the Northwest Coast of North America at the middle of the nineteenth century. The colony was a fief of the Hudson's Bay Company, and the "mainland" was held by a trade monopoly. Settlers were few; the largest populations were Indigenous. In Britain and throughout the Empire, the distant possession of Vancouver Island was little known and little heeded until successive gold discoveries in the 1850s and 1860s, each followed by a flood of adventurous and sometimes lawless miners, transformed this peaceful scene. Officials in Whitehall, colonial authorities in the wilderness and naval officers on the coast took steps to protect British soil from being seized by thousands of Americans coming from California and Oregon.

During these turbulent years, the Royal Navy supported the colonial government's actions to enforce law and order, and implemented decisions of the British government designed to guard against American encroachment. The commanders-in-chief on the Pacific station and senior naval officers at Esquimalt employed such force as was required or available to protect territorial claims, uphold law and report on developments in the goldfields. In short, throughout this era the Navy was a major instrument of British policy for colonial territory on the Northwest Coast, a region whose primary attraction had evolved from furs to settlement, and then to gold. Without naval support, local civil authorities would have been powerless.

Haida Gwaii / The Queen Charlotte Islands

Early in August 1850, Governor Blanshard of Vancouver Island notified his superiors in London that some Haida people had discovered gold on Haida Gwaii (at that time, the Queen Charlotte Islands).[1] These islands were not unknown, for they had been truly profitable haunts for maritime fur traders, and in 1787, Captain George Dixon, sailing in the vessel *Queen Charlotte*, named them for his ship. Dixon and his men had done their share in hunting the sea otter to near extinction. Other merchant traders had followed and completed the terrible work. Now gold was the allure. The governor also advised London that the Hudson's Bay Company planned to send an expedition to barter with the Haida for the precious metal.[2] Blanshard's successor, the ever-vigilant James Douglas, backed by fellow Hudson's Bay Company officials, urged the British government in 1851 to exclude ships of American registry from the islands. These efforts, under the guise of protecting British sovereignty, were clearly designed to make the Company masters of the goldfields and keep interlopers from Company domains. The pattern was easily recognized in Whitehall. The secretary of state for war and the colonies, Earl Grey, who was dissatisfied with the Company's efforts to colonize Vancouver Island, would not agree to extend its charter of grant to the islands.[3] For the moment the matter rested there.

In early 1852, Governor Douglas learned to his consternation that four vessels carrying some 550 adventurers plus their crews had sailed for Gold (Mitchell) Harbour. He believed that the history of American expansion in the previous two decades supported amply his contention that the lawless "floating population of California" would operate with a virtually free hand in the goldfields unless the authority of the Crown were strengthened by a show of British power. He thus made two requests for aid: one to the Commander-in-Chief, Pacific, Rear-Admiral Fairfax Moresby; the other to the Colonial Office.[4]

After the Oregon Treaty of 1846, the British government, taking no chances, pursued policies designed to protect "British Oregon" from irregular

HMS *Thetis*, a handsome 36-gun frigate, Captain Augustus L. Kuper, sailed to Gold Harbour in the Queen Charlotte Islands (Haida Gwaii) and elsewhere during her round of duties on the Pacific Station, 1851–53. HERITAGE HOUSE COLLECTION

settlement by Americans. Now, when the governor's alarming statement reached London—pointing out that Americans intended to colonize and establish an independent government in the Queen Charlotte Islands "until by force or fraud they become annexed to the United States"—the government acted quickly.[5] Douglas was appointed lieutenant-governor of the islands, and the Foreign Office instructed the Admiralty to have Rear-Admiral Moresby station a vessel there permanently—a guardship— to protect British territory against "marauders without title." Further, the British minister in Washington was directed to ask the United States government to restrain its expansive citizens.[6] In this threefold action the British government showed a clear determination to check anything resembling an American filibuster. These islands were not to fall to Manifest Destiny.

The Navy had anticipated the governor's needs. By the time Admiralty instructions reached Moresby, he had already dispatched the frigate *Thetis*, 38 guns, Captain Augustus L. Kuper, from Callao to the Northwest Coast.[7] This was an interim measure, for in response to the governor's request for a steam vessel—of more use in the numerous bays and confined waters of the islands of Haida Gwaii than a sailing ship such as the *Thetis*—Moresby intended to send the paddle-wheel sloop *Virago*, 6 guns, Commander James C. Prevost, after her refit at Valparaiso.[8] The flagship *Portland* was also available if required for service on the Northwest Coast. And Kuper possessed instructions to request the use of the Hudson's Bay Company steamer *Beaver*, if needed.[9] The commander-in-chief was confident that these measures would be adequate to deal with the Americans. He was right. The *Thetis* and *Virago* sufficed to meet the emergency.

The big frigate *Thetis* made sail first for Fort Rupert, then for the Queen Charlottes, tacking back and forth through foggy and gale-tossed Goletas Channel before reaching open water and the 130-mile passage across to Dixon Entrance and Queen Charlotte Sound. Three days later they sighted the islands, and young gunnery lieutenant John Moresby provides us with commentary. With the help of an HBC pilot they found the inlet, Mitchell, and entered the narrow channel, "with pine and cedar clad mountains rising 1,000 feet above our mastheads on either side, whilst underneath the lead found no bottom at 70 fathoms." At the head of the inlet a waterfall came from a mountain gorge, and the ship was secured with hawsers to trees on either side. "It was a wild scene in itself, and its strangeness was increased by a flotilla of large Indian canoes—graceful in the extreme, and manned by the finest-looking natives we had yet seen. They were perfectly naked, well built and muscular, with skins that under the paint and fish-oil were almost white. Some of the girls were really pretty. They spoke little, even to each other, and expressed no astonishment at the unwonted sights before them, but were eager to barter their furs and gold specimens for any rubbish we could spare." They were from the Skidegate peoples, "now recognized as the finest and most advanced in the arts of any on the northwest coast." The ship's band provided entertainment. The carved posts of the fronts of the massive lodges, bold and imaginative, attracted the attention of the observers. Ashore the vegetation was so thick as to make walking almost impossible, but a shore expedition found its way inland to idyllic mountain lakes, then returned to ship. At the lakes, Moresby said, it seemed as if the observers were suspended in space—"we floated between the two azures of water and sky."[10] Such was, and is, the enchantment of these islands. Captain Kuper named the lakes Moresby Lakes for the young officer. Moresby Island is named for

John Moresby's equally famous father, Rear-Admiral Fairfax Moresby, then Commander-in-Chief, Pacific.[11]

Throughout the summer of 1852, Captain Kuper issued declarations of British sovereignty there. However, he did not prohibit about a dozen American merchantmen from visiting mining districts, as Douglas wished him to do.[12] Because of the presence of the *Thetis*, her replacement after January 1853, the *Virago*, and still later HMS *Trincomalee*, a small sailing frigate mounting 26 guns, no attempts were made to overthrow British authority.[13] The zealous Captain James C. Prevost further deterred lawlessness by posting a notice warning Americans against selling goods or visiting the islands for mining without licence.[14] How effective this vain notice was can only be imagined. On the other hand, the warning was necessary only briefly, as the rich output of these islands dwindled within a few months. Before long the miners transferred their attentions to new Eldorados on the mainland.[15]

Fraser River Gold Fever

On the eve of the Fraser River gold rush, an unrelated event forced the British to pay attention to boundaries and passages between southern Vancouver Island and the American shore. In 1856, the United States government took the initiative and appointed a commission to settle the business of the channel separating the two jurisdictions. The Oregon Treaty specified a line along the 49th parallel to "the centre of the Gulf of Georgia, and thence southward, through the channel which separates the continent from Vancouver Island, to the Straits of Juan de Fuca." Vancouver's ships had used the easternmost passage, Rosario Strait, as had some Spanish vessels, and the Hudson's Bay Company had tended to use the same channel. But here was the problem: no hydrographical survey had been made before the ink on the treaty was dry—a pity, for it would have saved much aggravation, and the results might have advantaged the British claim. Now it was too late. The British would have to make do. They appointed their own commissioner for the purpose—Captain Prevost, in the screw-corvette *Satellite*, 22 guns. But he was not a surveyor of the seas, and a specialist in surveying was needed to survey the disputed waters and then continue the work in Vancouver Island and mainland British Columbia waters. This led to the selection of Captain George Henry Richards, and he sailed for

167

Vancouver in the small steam-sloop, barque-rigged *Plumper,* a vessel lightly armed and very rotten in some particulars. With only 60 horsepower, she was a poor choice for surveying the San Juan Islands (and many other inner waters where rushing currents were strong). She might have been fine on the West Africa coast chasing slavers, but in such inshore waters to which she was destined, where she could only make six knots under power, she proved a disappointment and, as will be noted, soon needed to be replaced. (There is more on this survey later in the chapter.)

Soon after Richards' arrival, in late 1857 and early 1858, news of fabulous gold strikes on the Fraser spread quickly around the world. No statements are more exaggerated than those of gold miners, as the senior naval officer at Esquimalt, Captain Prevost, was well aware.[16] He knew that many reports from the diggings were of doubtful credibility, but he informed the commander-in-chief on the Pacific station, Rear-Admiral Robert Lambert Baynes, that the existence of a great abundance of gold on the Fraser River was beyond doubt.[17] To prove his point he sent a sample of gold to the Admiralty. He foresaw that lawlessness, misery and bloodshed would be the consequences of the impending mass movement of prospectors into an area that lacked all means of subsistence.[18]

The dangers inherent in an avalanche of alien miners into an unsettled area that was controlled by the Hudson's Bay Company were also abundantly clear to James Douglas, both as the governor of Vancouver Island and as an official of the Company. Douglas, who was long an opponent of American expansion in the Pacific Northwest, could see that British authority would be confronted with an American challenge based on numbers. Hence, in late December 1857, he used provisional regulations to establish Crown control over mining rights in the Fraser and Thompson districts of New Caledonia, an area that he did not actually govern.[19] The promulgation of laws by a central figure appears to have been the opposite of what happened on the California mining frontier, where miners made their own laws and exacted their own justice. By asserting the power of the Crown, Douglas sought to restrain the influx of foreigners into British territory, and in this, generally, he had the support of his superiors in London.

From the outset it was his intention to stabilize the frontier. To strengthen his position, Douglas requested that the British government place a naval or military force at his disposal.[20] He then stressed to the

Commander-in-Chief, Pacific, that the only solution to the impending crisis of unrestricted entry of twenty to thirty thousand foreigners into the unpoliced gold districts lay in maintaining the governor's authority with sufficient naval force.[21] Douglas knew that the two British warships then designated for coastal duties—the heavy corvette *Satellite* and the screw surveying vessel *Plumper*, 12 guns—would assist if required, but he was anxious that nothing should interfere with their survey of the disputed San Juan Archipelago for the Boundary Commission. Nevertheless, he soon had to ask the senior naval officer that the *Satellite* take up a station in the south arm of the Fraser River to enforce Douglas's proclamation forbidding mining on the mainland by unlicensed persons.[22] This was a crafty move on the governor's part, for there the corvette would strengthen the hand of the chief of customs against American vessels openly violating "the British frontier."[517]

The Navy now came to the governor's aid to uphold civil authority in this unorganized territory. Captain Prevost, in the *Satellite*, chose to meet Douglas at Point Roberts—the nearest American encampment to the mouth of the Fraser River—as a show of British power. Next he sent a launch with a guard of six Royal Marines to aid customs authorities at Fort Langley, 30 miles up the river.[24] Finally, in conformity with the governor's request, he positioned the *Satellite* at the mouth of the Fraser, where she remained for most of the summer. By this time it was patently clear to the anxious and responsible Prevost that he would require support, especially since the boundary in nearby waters was an issue of contention between the British and American governments.

Prevost went with Douglas to the goldfields. At the conclusion of this inspection tour, on June 7, 1858, Prevost again advised Baynes, this time in more emphatic terms, that a naval force was necessary to maintain British rights, law and authority, and to support the governor in his difficult position.[25] Although most miners were law-abiding, Prevost warned that this might not continue when twenty thousand persons known to be en route from San Francisco arrived. Already at Hill's Bar, a miner's profit averaged 60 dollars a day; when the river fell during the summer, further discoveries and increased yields were likely. The bustle on the riverbanks seemed to indicate that "the whole country" was "rich in gold," richer even than California.[26] Lesser men than Prevost and Douglas might have

The lower deck personnel as well as officers found hunting excitement ashore or in shallow waters. Shown here are trophy items collected from southern voyages. PHOTO COURTESY SHERRI ROBINSON

given up their responsibilities and joined the throng. For such, the Navy enforced the rules against desertion, and permissions for shore leave were closely watched.

To reach the goldfields, two routes were common. One was from Whatcom (Bellingham) in the adjoining Washington Territory overland to the Fraser. Many Americans went this way to avoid licensing officials at the British port of Victoria and in the river mouth. The trail was hazardous. Generally speaking, adventurers "found that geographic conditions are stronger than patriotic leanings, and a navigable river is a better highway than a rude mountain trail."[27] For this reason, many turned back to try the easier route: by stern-wheeler, boat, raft or canoe up the Fraser River as far as possible and the rest of the way on foot.

For most miners who came from California by sea, Victoria was the halfway house, the stepping stone to the Fraser. Overnight a tent city grew up around the Hudson's Bay Company post. The population rose from 500— before the *Commodore*, the first vessel from San Francisco, arrived with 450 miners on April 25, 1858—to some 6,000 by late July. People arrived in swarms, in all kinds of crafts. They brought their own money, printing presses, businesses, mining methods and squabbles. But the mere presence of the Royal Navy in the harbours of Victoria and Esquimalt constituted a psychological force sufficient to quell lawlessness and disorder ashore.[28] The rush of miners and merchants into Esquimalt, the Navy's principal anchorage in the North Pacific, especially concerned the senior naval officer there. Speculation meant that the Admiralty would be forced to purchase properties for any future naval establishment at astronomical prices.[29]

Maintaining Order

The problems of maintaining authority at Vancouver Island were minor compared to those on the banks of the Fraser. The governor's method of controlling the population was by issuing licences, a disagreeable matter for all concerned. In addition to paying for the costs of administration and police, the licences enabled the government to check on the numbers in the goldfields and established the supremacy of the Crown from the time the miners entered the Fraser. The licences were five dollars a year, without regard to the nationality of the licensee. Thus any American claims of discrimination on grounds of citizenship were unfounded.

Because the Fraser River had many entrances, the job of the Navy was difficult. Off the mouth of the south arm, officers and men of the *Satellite* boarded vessels to preserve territorial rights by issuing licences to the miners.[30] On one typical occasion a launch, cutter and gig—all well-manned and armed—halted the American stern-wheeler *Surprise* and compelled miners on board to buy licences. Many American vessels, however, navigated other channels unnoticed. To minimize this practice, Prevost recommended that the governor's proclamation be posted on all steamers carrying passengers from Victoria to the Fraser River, and that all passengers sailing in those vessels should have mining licences.[31] Moreover—in order to stop evaders of the regulations—he proposed that a small vessel should be stationed below Annacis Island, where the north arm enters the main stream of the river. If this proved insufficient, a gun battery mounted on the south bank of the river would halt riverboats that failed to heed warnings of British revenue agents or, as they were later called, gold commissioners.[32]

Other measures designed to eliminate the illegal entry of miners into the mining districts were added. The Company steamer *Otter* kept watch on the route of passenger ships between Victoria and the river mouth. In early August, when the river was at its lowest and the rush was at its peak, the *Plumper* joined the force in the river. To check illegal entries via the overland route from Whatcom, the *Satellite*'s launch, and later the colonial government guardship *Recovery*, under Prevost's orders, were stationed at Fort Langley, some 30 miles from the river mouth. In all, four tax-collecting vessels were operating in addition to auxiliary boats enforcing regulations as miners moved up the Fraser River to the goldfields beyond Fort Hope.

While the two naval vessels were busy on the coast, the British government, in late June 1858 (and on the basis of recently received news), gave serious attention to the growing crisis on the mainland. If British authority were to be upheld, an adequate "show of force" must be put in place. For this reason, Rear-Admiral Baynes at Valparaiso received instructions, dated June 28, 1858, to proceed in the *Ganges*, or send a senior officer, to Vancouver Island to determine the adequacy of the naval force.[33] Apparently, Baynes had no knowledge of the degree of gold excitement when he wrote to Governor Douglas on June 25, 1858, that because of the pressing needs of the station and the shortage of vessels, only the *Satellite* and *Plumper* were available for guarding the river and Victoria. When further alarms reached London from Douglas, the Admiralty instructed Baynes in concise terms that upholding British sovereignty during the Fraser River gold rush was the most pressing duty of ships on the Pacific station. It was essential, the Lords of the Admiralty instructed, for the commander-in-chief to give the governor of Vancouver Island all the support he required.[34]

However, help for Douglas was not yet in sight. The arrival of the corvette *Calypso*, 18 guns, Captain Frederick Montresor, at Esquimalt in mid-August left Baynes unable to meet Douglas's plea for more warships.[35] The *Calypso* lacked steam power; she was thus useless for service in the intricate mouth of the Fraser.[36]

When Douglas asked Montresor to send a marine detachment in support of his intended excursion to the goldfields, Montresor declined the prospect. His instructions did not give him discretionary powers, and he felt compelled to leave Esquimalt on August 25, having completed his mission of supplying the *Satellite* and *Plumper*. The *Calypso*'s orders left little leeway. She was required to reach Hawaii by early October, remain there during the period the whaling vessels called, and keep watch that Mormons rumoured to be coming from Utah did not try to seize Hawaii.[37] The governor's appeal to Montresor was not unanswered, however; Captain Prevost of the *Satellite* was able to send a substitute force instead.

Prevost correctly predicted a mass inrush from California. Up to June 15, 1858, more than ten thousand adventurers started out from San Francisco.[38] During the six-week period ending July 1, for example, some 19 steamers, 9 sailing vessels and 14 deck-boats carried six thousand hopeful argonauts into British territory.[39] Moreover, the "tide of immigration" continued to roll on with no promise of ending,[40] which led one contemporary to remark, "Never, perhaps, was there so large an immigration in so short a space of time into so small a place."[41] Small wonder that Douglas and Prevost feared lawlessness in the face of this overwhelming migration of toughened diggers.

Under these pressures, Prevost abandoned the boundary survey to give full attention to safeguarding British interests on the mainland. In late August he sent a bodyguard for the governor during the latter's investigation of the mining camps. But he was handicapped by desertions. The *Satellite* had a complement of 260 men. By the end of August 1858, at least 20 men had fled to the goldfields, and 30 were patrolling the river mouth in small vessels.[42] Therefore, he was able to supply a force only of sufficient size to afford the governor security on his second mission to the Fraser. This contingent consisted of Lieutenant Howard S. Jones, RM, and 20 marines, with Lieutenant-Colonel J.S. Hawkins, RE, and 15 sappers and miners.[43] By the time they reached Fort Hope, the dispute between some miners and incensed Natives had been settled.[44] The fracas revealed that a large number of regular military rather than naval troops should be stationed in the region for the preservation of life, order and British prestige.[45] On September 26, 1858, Douglas and his marine guard, now two less because of desertions, returned to Victoria.

But this was not the last naval sortie into a wilderness that naval officers justifiably contended was becoming more and more the responsibility of the War Office. As already mentioned, the *Satellite* and *Plumper* were under instructions since early July to maintain order among "adventurers resorting to the gold fields."[46] If the need arose, Governor Douglas planned to make further calls on the Royal Navy to reinforce his declared policy that "all claims and interests" would be "rendered subordinate to the great object of peopling and opening up the new country, and consolidating it as an integral part of the British Empire."[47]

Meanwhile, the Admiralty ordered reinforcements for the Pacific station to meet the emergency. Initially, Sir John Pakington, the First Lord, ordered the *Argus*, a paddle-wheel sloop of six guns, be sent. But at the urgent insistence of Sir Edward Bulwer Lytton, the secretary of state for the colonies, he was forced to dispatch a larger vessel, a steam-frigate. Pakington firmly believed that Baynes would reach Vancouver Island before "*any* fresh ship" could do so, but he succumbed to Lytton's pressure and sent Captain Geoffrey Phipps Hornby from London across Asia to Hong Kong to assume command of the screw-frigate *Tribune*, 31 guns, a ship that had seen much action in what the British called the Second China War. The ship's company had seen much action in riverine small-boat work.[48] Phipps Hornby was a great organizer and a clear thinker, and once the frigate was refitted and provisions arranged, she shipped no fewer than 164 marines for the new mainland colony of British Columbia. This was in keeping with Pakington's instructions that the Commander-in-Chief, China and East Indies, was to dispatch the *Tribune* to Esquimalt "with as many supernumerary Marines as she can carry and he can spare."[49] The corvettes, the *Pylades*, 21 guns, and the *Amethyst*, 26 guns, were to follow as soon as their services in the Far East were no longer required. The *Tribune*, having called at Yokohama, arrived at Esquimalt February 13, 1859, where she found the screw-corvette *Satellite* under Prevost.

Transferring these ships from China waters to the Northwest Coast constituted the quickest method of reinforcement that the Admiralty could adopt.[50] The Navy had been adept at making a rapid response, deploying units as required. The intelligence-gathering capabilities were finely tuned. All the same, in these days before the advent of the telegraph and fast cruisers, sending orders across Asia to dispatch ships across four thousand miles of the North Pacific was a matter of three or four months. Another mode of reinforcement took even longer. The two gunboats *Forward* and *Grappler*, specially fitted out for service in the new colony, sailed from England in August 1859, escorted by the screw-frigate *Termagant*, 25 guns; they did not reach Esquimalt until July 12, 1860, almost a year later.[51] Thus, while Douglas's requisitions continued to reach Whitehall, the secretary of state for the colonies could only issue reassuring reports to the anxious governor that more ships were on their way.[52]

Of the many warships sent in response to the Fraser River gold rush, the first to come to the support of Prevost and Douglas was the flagship *Ganges*, 84 guns, with Rear-Admiral Baynes on board.[53] Baynes had intended to sail from Callao in the paddle-wheel sloop *Vixen*, 6 guns, a more useful vessel under the circumstances than the line-of-battle ship *Ganges*, but a defect in *Vixen*'s hull prevented her use, so the long passage under sail was completed. Upon her welcome arrival at Esquimalt on October 17, 1858, Baynes immediately offered his cooperation to the delighted Douglas. The fact that Admiralty instructions to Baynes emphasized the great importance of securing the newly established colony of British Columbia—"no part of his station was more important than B.C."—reveals the level of the British government's anxiety for their endangered territory.[54] Douglas was understandably pleased that more resources for maintaining law and order were now at his disposal.

Ironically, by the time Baynes and the *Ganges* reached Juan de Fuca Strait, the miners had begun their exodus to California. They preferred the more comfortable climate of San Francisco to a bleak winter in flimsy tents

Rear-Admiral Sir Robert Lambert Baynes, Commander-in-Chief, Pacific, during the Fraser River and San Juan Island crises, was knighted for his forbearance and firm direction so as to avoid war with the United States. A geopolitical visionary, he was the chief architect of the design to make Esquimalt into a prominent strategic anchor of the British Empire in the eastern Pacific. In this, he found a willing partner in Governor Douglas. CFB ESQUIMALT NAVAL & MILITARY MUSEUM

on the Fraser's frozen banks. The miners were followed by merchants, who left their makeshift shanties in Victoria as business declined.[55] This development prompted Baynes to report to the Admiralty that although he had been sent to the scene as a result of pressures exerted on the British government by the governor of Vancouver Island, everything was now peaceful.[56] Indeed, the gold rush continued to decline.

Creation of British Columbia as a Colony

At the same time that the Admiralty dispatched additional ships and men to the Northwest Coast, the Colonial Office and Parliament consolidated the British hold on New Caledonia—that vast area west of the Rockies that Queen Victoria significantly now named "British Columbia." By an

Act of Parliament dated August 2, 1858, the colony on the Pacific came into being.[57] Lytton as secretary of state for the colonies thought it would be strange indeed if the imperial government were obliged to contribute to the upkeep of the colony, "which has been actually forced into existence through the sample supplies of gold afforded by the country it occupies."[58] British Columbia, he believed, was unique in the Empire: in its gold it yielded an immediate source of prosperity, which many of the early colonial settlements lacked.[59] He was adamant, therefore, that the colony should pay its own way, for the free-trade principle on which mid-Victorian imperial policy was based left scant room for additional levies on the British taxpayer. However, the mother country was to continue to contribute the "protection of her navy, and in time of emergency, of her troops."[60] The action of Parliament in creating the colony took the control of British Columbia out of Hudson's Bay Company hands immediately, as Lytton intended; Douglas was appointed governor providing he sever his Company connections. The gold rush thus led to creation of a new colony in which British free-trade practices would have further scope.

The first governor of Britain's newest colony was installed in office at New Fort Langley, a place chosen as the seat of government on account of its strategic position on the Lower Fraser between the sea and the gold region. Douglas proceeded to Fort Langley via Point Roberts in the *Satellite*, which the commander-in-chief provided so that His Excellency could disembark near the river mouth with "the customary honors, salutes, etc." Baynes believed this display would be beneficial to the governor's authority in the infant colony.[61] The governor, accompanied by Rear-Admiral Baynes and various civic officials and naval officers, transferred to the screw-steamer *Otter* at Point Roberts for passage into the entry to the Fraser River, where he and his suite shifted to the venerable paddle-wheeler *Beaver*. The two vessels proceeded upstream to New Fort Langley. The guns of the *Beaver* put up a salute, the mountains opposite giving back the echoes. It was terrible weather for such a propitious day, and apparently, once the British flag was raised it could be seen not floating over the main gate but dripping in soggy salute. The party went indoors, a hundred crammed into the main room. There Douglas assumed the office of Governor of British Columbia. The date was November 19, 1858.[62] This was a crowning moment for him. The officials and dignitaries feasted that evening, and the next day members departed by various means. Douglas, in the *Beaver*, was loudly cheered in splendid style. As he departed and made his way back to Victoria, he remained concerned about having adequate naval and military power to fulfill the duties of his office. Baynes did not disappoint him.

Douglas and Baynes were trying to imagine the future, and their careers and reputations were on the line. They forged a partnership in crisis management. The matter of sufficient force to meet the expected rush during the spring of 1859 arose before the departure of the flagship *Ganges* for duties on other parts of the station. On December 22, 1858, Baynes informed Douglas of his reluctance to sail from Esquimalt unless he were assured, first, that the governor did not fear an outbreak of violence; second, that Douglas knew that the *Satellite* and the *Plumper*, both powerful steam vessels, were at his disposal (on request to the senior naval officer), and were sufficient to meet any emergency; and third, that he did not consider the Admiral's presence necessary for "the preservation of that good order" that Douglas had "so happily established in both colonies."[63]

HMS *Ganges*, famed teak-hulled vessel built in Bombay by the Wadia Brothers, East India Company, was flagship of Rear-Admiral Sir Robert Lambert Baynes, and was the first ship-of-the-line to enter Esquimalt Harbour. Here in this crowded scene she is seen, with sails backed, at target practice for a shore bombardment. GOUGH COLLECTION

Obviously, Baynes did not wish to be chastened by the Admiralty a second time for ignoring British interests on the Northwest Coast. For the moment, Douglas thought that the *Tribune* and *Pylades*, expected from China, would be adequate for assisting the colonial government. But Baynes disagreed, claiming that even more warships should be on hand during the spring when a great influx of gold-seekers would arrive.[64] He himself promised to return in the *Ganges* when circumstances permitted, and he was clearly willing to provide additional ships should conditions warrant. As a result of Baynes's advice, Douglas recognized the importance of having a "respectable" naval force to face the large immigration expected in the spring.[65] In Baynes, the governor had found a powerful ally.

Indeed, in January 1859 an incident occurred at Hill's Bar, a camp on the Fraser's icy banks near Yale where rowdy California miners had chosen to winter. Douglas received reports that the notorious vagabond Ned McGowan had broken out of prison at Yale and was conspiring to overthrow British authority. Quickly, he called on the senior naval officer at Esquimalt for support. Prevost sent the *Plumper* to the Lower Fraser River with all the marines and seamen available from the *Satellite*—a total of 47 men together with a 12-pounder (Light) Brass Howitzer field-piece—a tidy and strong show of force. When the Admiralty received a copy of this letter, they advised the Colonial Office that a *military*, not a *naval*, force should aid the civil power, because the use of seamen and marines on shore made Her Majesty's ships "inefficient for the general Service of the Station."[66] Prevost did what was best in the circumstances, but his action did not endear him to the Admiralty: Their Lordships always disliked sending men and equipment ashore on expeditions regarded as of doubtful necessity. What might have been vital on the frontier often seemed inconsequential at the centre of empire. Prevost's other difficulty was that over one hundred men had deserted from the *Satellite* for the goldfields, weakening the ship's company considerably.

For other than shallow-draught stern-wheelers, navigation of the Fraser in winter was next to impossible, and the *Plumper*, whose speed under steam in flat seas was six knots, could not move farther up the river than Langley, just below MacMillan Island. In the event, the *Plumper* had gone farther up the river than most had expected.[67] From there her commander, Captain Richards, was forced to dispatch the young and rising Lieutenant Richard

Charles Mayne by canoe to communicate with officials upstream at Fort Yale.[68] Because of the transportation problems of the expedition, Mayne's objective was to find the acting lieutenant-governor, Colonel Richard C. Moody, RE, and explain that reinforcements would have to wait in the *Plumper* until the stern-wheeler *Enterprise* returned to Fort Langley to convey the force to the critical area.[69] Shortly after the two men met, Moody anxiously directed Mayne to carry secret instructions to Fort Hope, 20 miles downstream, to order up 25 Royal Engineers. After that, Mayne continued 65 miles downstream in the *Enterprise* to bring up the force waiting in the *Plumper* at Fort Langley.[70] Then the stern-wheeler returned to the head of navigation bearing 21 small-arms men and 7 marines from the *Plumper*, plus the marines and field-piece party from the *Satellite*— 77 men in all.[71] When he reached Hope, Mayne found instructions from Colonel Moody to advance with the seven marines and leave the bluejackets at Hope. Ironically, by the time the force arrived at Yale, the situation was under control; McGowan and other desperados had been arrested by the local constabulary.

"Ned McGowan's War" was a true farce, but the resolute manner in which the threat was faced and extinguished showed that Douglas would not tolerate lawlessness in the new colony. Timely supporting action by the Navy brought about full restoration of order and patently demonstrated the Douglas rule that "laws cannot be disregarded with impunity, & that while the intention exists to maintain them, the power to carry out that intention is not wanting."[72]

By mid-February 1859, the *Tribune* and *Pylades* reached Esquimalt from the Far East, freeing the *Satellite* and *Plumper* to resume their duties with the Boundary Commission.[73] The *Tribune* brought an extra 164 "supernumerary" Royal Marines from China to aid the civil power in British Columbia.[74] Of these, 139 officers and men were set to the task of clearing the site of the new colonial capital, New Westminster. The interfering Douglas overstepped the mark when he proclaimed that these men would receive double pay and a free grant of land after six years' service. Previously, the ships' companies of the *Satellite* and *Plumper* received three months' double pay, and Douglas assumed that the new men would receive double pay as well. Baynes and the Admiralty opposed this, however, even though it could prevent desertions to the goldfields, for they feared that it would set a precedent for all ships visiting the new colony.[75] Much to Douglas's embarrassment, double pay was not awarded. On the recommendation of the Colonial and War Offices, the Admiralty ordered the marines—in short supply in other parts of the Empire—to withdraw from work that had little to do with protecting British interests.[76]

Arrival of the ships from Asian waters brought new impetus to the social affairs of the Colony of Vancouver Island. And it was time for a party. Lieutenant Charles W. Wilson of the Royal Engineers, under date March 15, 1859, tells the following:

> We gave a ball to the fair ladies here; two of the men of war the *Satellite* & *Plumper* with ourselves, determined to join together & give a grand ball to the ladies of Vancouver Island. I was appointed one of the ball committee with some others & we set our heads together to do the best we could in this part of the world. The first thing was to find a place large enough for the occasion & the only house we could find was the market place, a most dismal-looking place, enough to drive all thoughts of dancing out of ones head, however we got all the flags we could from the ships & turned in 30 or 40 sailors, & in a short time a fairy palace of flags was erected, so that not a particle of the building was visible; we then rigged up some large chandeliers & sconces of bayonets and ramrods wreathed with evergreens which when lighted up produced a regular blaze of light & made it quite a fairy scene. We also got up a large supper room in the same style & managed to provide a first-rate supper. Everybody came to the ball from the governor downwards nearly 200 in all & we kept the dancing up with great spirit till ½ 3 in the morning. Everybody was quite delighted with it & it goes by the name of "the Party" par excellence; no body says ball in this part of the world, it is always party. The ladies were very nicely dressed, & some of them danced very well, though they would look much better if they would only learn to wear their crinoline properly.[77]

The spring of 1859 failed to bring the great swarm of prospectors expected by civil and naval authorities.[78] Doubtless the gold yields were insufficient to attract miners. Perhaps, also, the restrictive practices of the governor—as enforced by the gold commissioners and supported by the Navy and the military forces—proved too stifling. The British adventurer Radcliffe Quine, for example, claimed that fifteen thousand persons "left for a freer and better government."[79] Admittedly, democratic government did not mark this first period of British Columbia's colonial history. But in view of the transplanted American population numbering in the thousands, the autocratic power exercised by Governor Douglas in 1858 and 1859 proved wise. He was supported by the "hanging judge," Matthew Begbie, who was said by one historian, with exaggeration, to have "trained an unruly public into habitual reverence for the law."[574]

The majority of miners returned to the motherlode country of California; others were drawn from the Fraser River by reports of new findings in Idaho and Montana. But the remote British territory on the North Pacific still continued to attract some gold-seekers, and in August 1859, for the second time in the decade, the Queen Charlotte Islands became a centre of attention. Again, Douglas requested that a British warship visit the mining camp of a prospecting expedition,[81] all the while hoping that the *Forward* and *Grappler*, two gunboats he knew had been sent specifically to aid the colonial government, would soon reach Vancouver Island and be available for service. Actually, the *Pylades* was at hand to assist the governor, but there was no need for this vessel to go to the islands because the miners returned to Victoria sooner than expected, and empty handed.[82]

Gold-seekers were drawn to the Cariboo Country, where large nuggets were unearthed in the summer of 1860. Among those who hurried into the upper reaches of the Fraser, especially along the Quesnel, were sailors from Her Majesty's ships at Esquimalt and marines from the guard at San Juan Island. They left their posts for what they thought would be more lucrative occupation. Hopes of higher wages and of striking it rich certainly added to the seamen's innate desire for a change, which Nelson said would induce them to desert from heaven to hell. Desertions from merchant ships were commonplace: the British merchantman *New Briton* in Esquimalt lost all her crew to the Cariboo goldfields.[83]

On July 30 that same year, far from the Cariboo, the *Satellite* sailed for home. She had been in Vancouver Island and coastal waters since before the Fraser River gold rush, taking part in the Boundary Commission, patrolling the south arm of the Fraser River in a show of British power, and carrying the first governor of British Columbia to his installation. Richard Charles Mayne took special notice: "She had been nearly four years in commission, three of which had been spent at this place. Her departure could scarcely fail to remind us of the change that had taken place since she had entered Esquimalt Harbour three years back. It was the first time its waters had ever been disturbed by a steamship of such a size; and now, as she steamed out from the changed and busy port, homeward bound, she gave back the hearty cheers of two of Her Majesty's frigates, two sloops, and as many gunboats."[84]

Captain Richards's Great Survey

All the time the gold mania was in process, the Navy kept to its other duties, which were, on the face of things, mainly constabulary in nature. To make more effective this policing power, and to provide for the commercial benefit of the colonies upon which the future of the imperial estate on this coast depended, the marine survey continued unabated. Captain George Henry Richards has already been introduced in respect of this. He was an aquatic globetrotter.[85] He had been to the Pacific in HMS *Sulphur*, taken an active part in the Chinese war of 1839–42 and boosted his reputation as a seagoing fighter. He surveyed the southeast coast of South America and was promoted to commander for gallantry in storming the forts in the River Parana. He surveyed New Zealand waters during the Maori Wars and then went to the high Arctic to search for Captain Sir John Franklin. He was a man of tremendous physical strength, and although he apparently suffered a hand injury, perhaps in the Parana affair, he made one of the most extraordinary sledging journeys on record when searching for Franklin. But his monument lies in the waters and shores of British Columbia, where he directed the massive survey under tremendous pressure, with the aggressive Americans then searching out the goldfields of the Fraser and Cariboo, and the United States Army landing intemperately on the disputed San Juan Islands. Surveying was the harbinger of commerce, and at the time that Richards was in these waters, the challenges to promote change were mighty, the colonies largely out of the mainstream of world commerce and affairs. It must be kept in mind that during these years, the Hudson's Bay Company was losing its monopolistic dominance, San Francisco and Sitka were the main ports of call in western North

America, a canal across Panama was only a dream, a Canadian transcontinental railway likewise, and no docking facilities existed at the nascent naval base of Esquimalt. And if this were not enough, a great squabble had developed between the Colony of Vancouver Island and the Colony of British Columbia as to primacy in trade and commercial futures.

Richards was like the expert in intricate navigation of Joseph Conrad's *The Shadow Line*: "His brain must have been a perfect warehouse of reefs, positions, bearings, images of headlands, shapes of obscure posts, aspects of innumerable islands, desert and otherwise." He compiled an immense dossier on southern British Columbia waters called "Report of Captain Richards on the Harbours of Vancouver's Island and British Columbia, 23 October 1858." Richards submitted this to Governor James Douglas, and the whole was reprinted, with supplementary correspondence, in the Parliamentary Papers, Part II for 1858, which dealt with British Columbia and Vancouver Island. Richards recommended that if Vancouver Island was not to be part of British Columbia, the site of a seaport for British Columbia could be just above Annacis Island, 10 miles below Fort Langley on the Fraser River. This was what sparked the battle royal between Victoria and what became New Westminster as to primacy for commercial growth. The saga can be traced in the press and Colonial Office records.

During the 1860 survey season, Richards surveyed Haro Strait, Burrard Inlet, Nanaimo, Johnstone Strait, Nootka and others. Rain, and northern winds that brought thick fog to Johnstone Strait, hindered the work, and by late September it was always wise for the survey boats and crews to be back in pleasant Esquimalt. "Wild-fowl also began to make their appearance in large quantities from the northward, reminding us unpleasantly of the near approach of winter," wrote Lieutenant Mayne, who served with Richards. "We were not sorry, therefore, to receive orders to move southwards."[86] The work was long and arduous, and there always existed the possibility of an attack by local Natives.[87]

In the 1861 and 1862 survey seasons, the work continued in different locales—pressing north to the new mission station of Metlakatla, for instance, and to Fort Rupert, Vancouver Island, then in sad decline. Mrs. Richards had joined her husband, courtesy of an agreement with the Admiralty, and their first son was named Vancouver, after the explorer (not the city, which was not yet founded). Mr. and Mrs. Daniel Pender's first son, also born on Vancouver Island, was named Esquimalt. As for place names, Richards followed the injunction of Admiral Francis Beaufort, a former hydrographer, that Native names were to be kept wherever possible, and the application of politicians and statesmen was to be kept in line. Richards also encouraged the continuance of Spanish place names on this coast. But some places did not have Native or Spanish names that could be called up, and accordingly we find Thormanby Islands, in Malaspina Strait, named after the racehorse who won the 1860 Derby; Merry Island, named for the owner, J.C. Merry; Buccaneer Bay, a faltering contestant in the Derby; and Tattenham Ledge, named for that well-known turn in the course where horses head round the corner, then down the straight for the winning post.

Richards' private journal reminds us of the clear-headed nature of the commander, which explains how he was able to be a great leader of men, direct a team of commissioned and non-commissioned subordinates, and keep up morale, prevent desertion and maintain strict discipline afloat and on shore.

In 1862 it was time for Richards to say goodbye. He received the thanks of many civic organizations, none stronger than that from New Westminster, where the municipal council thanked him for "portraying the Navigation of the Fraser River in its true colours. His survey had shown to the world "an incontrovertible proof of the great capacity of that Noble stream for Commercial purposes." Richards had brought the *Hecate* (which replaced the *Plumper* in 1861) right up to the wharves, thereby dispelling many misapprehensions that had been circulated about how a ship of her size (900 tons burthen) could navigate to that port. "The value of your Services to this Colony can not be too highly appreciated; the Accurate Surveys of our Coast will be invaluable to unborn generations of Mariners; and Commerce will ever owe you a debt of gratitude." To this friend of British Columbia were extended best wishes for continued prosperity and success and grateful thanks.[88] Richards kept private his own views, as this entry for November 1, 1862, reveals: "The Town of NWr has increased somewhat, but there are not the same unerring signs of prosperity as at Victoria. A miserable contracted jealous feeling pervades all classes, military included, and a wretched kind of repining that they cannot alter their geographical position, a desire to quarrel with everyone who comes from

Victoria, or says a word in its favour." The contrast between the two places was great, he observed, and he noted that the miners coming south for the winter got on the first ferry bound for Victoria. He added wryly, "The misfortune of New Westminster is that Vancouver I[slan]d with its beautiful harbours and pleasant resting places exists."[89]

From New Westminster, Richards took the *Hecate* to Roche Harbor, San Juan Island, "to visit, victual and pay the Marine Detachment." The camp was prettily situated and in excellent order, the detachment consisting of 70 men. Then it was to Esquimalt and four days at anchor before steaming into Victoria Harbour to fire a salute and assist in celebrating the coming of age of the Prince of Wales. Governor Douglas gave a great dinner, well attended: "I have rarely attended a more rowdy affair," Richards noted. There was a brief call to Nanaimo to take on coal, and then it was time for a return to Esquimalt, where new orders from Admiral Washington, the hydrographer, directed that Daniel Pender would continue the surveying work—Edward Bedwell, second master and ship's artist, declining the opportunity, to Richards' displeasure. Then came December 22 and the final departure for home. Edward Blunden, in a whaler, who saw the *Hecate* disappear from view just beyond Race Rocks, recounted that not a dry eye existed among his boat's crew. Richards was much loved and so was the ship's company. The bonds among the sailors had been strengthened by all the work accomplished together. Master John Gowlland, who watched the proceedings from the deck of the *Hecate*, wrote with much sentiment and mixed, charged emotions: "We steamed away round Race Rocks—passed Cape Flattery in the afternoon and at dusk the shores of the old Island faded gradually from our view with the approaching nightfall until we lost sight of it all together, maybe for years and maybe forever !!—Good bye old Vancouver—& to tomorrow our voyage to dear old England—Homeward Bound !!!"

In later years, Richards became a pillar of the scientific world, a Fellow of the Royal Society and a Fellow of the Royal Geographical Society. Like many a great hydrographer, he went into the private world of commerce— in his case helping lay down submarine cables across the North Atlantic. In his time he sailed the seven seas and knew all about triangulation, lunars, chronometers and how to regulate them, the drawing of draft plans and the engraving of charts, and how knowledge was best disseminated in the

Victorian world. He had the capacity, too, to keep his political superiors on their toes and to be careful what they said about the workaday world of plumbing the depths of the oceans and shoals, and of finding reefs and rocks that posed hazards to shipping. The account he gives of how the *Plumper* ended up on the south side of Juan de Fuca Strait rather than on the north shore, where Richards thought he was, is a testament to the fact that these were (and are) dangerous waters, with tricky tides and currents, prone to storms and blanketing fog. As Richards was reminded, he inhabited the natural world, with all its wonders, surprises and difficulties. Such is the life of the mariner. He was recalled to London to become hydrographer and served in that capacity until 1874. He was the guiding force for the *Challenger* expedition that sailed in 1872 to complete, in four years, the great undersea exploration of British science in the Pacific, thereby realizing a precious dream of Richards. Thirty-six engraved charts published by the Admiralty, and the Vancouver Island Pilot, are his legacy in British Columbia waters.

When Richards sailed from Esquimalt for home in *Hecate*, he left one of his understudies, Master Daniel Pender, in charge. Pender was placed in command of the *Beaver*, hired from the Hudson's Bay Company.[90] He surveyed the channels between the north end of Vancouver Island and the northern boundary of British Columbia on the coast, in 54°40' north latitude, and surveyed the harbour at the entrance to Skidegate Channel in Haida Gwaii, as well as several useful anchorages on the mainland. Pender also surveyed the bar at the entrance of the Fraser River, updating particulars of the changes that had occurred in the channel. As for Master Blunden, he served as second-in-command to Pender, but in 1865, after many years' service in the Navy, deserted—presumably for the goldfields.

Events in the Stikine Territory

Discoveries of gold in the far northern Stikine region during the years 1861 and 1862 involved the Navy directly. Access to the goldfields was mainly by the Stikine River, which coursed through the Russian–American panhandle at about 57° north.[91] But both Russian and British officials on the coast remained confused as to the terms of the 1825 Anglo-Russian convention that, in fact, allowed British subjects free navigation through the panhandle to the British hinterland.[92]

In order to prevent any misunderstanding with Russia concerning British rights to navigate the Stikine River, the Commander-in-Chief, Pacific, Rear-Admiral Sir Thomas Maitland, dispatched the paddle-wheel sloop *Devastation*, 6 guns, Commander John W. Pike, to Sitka so that her captain could discuss the matter with Russian authorities.[93] Pike found the governor of the Russian American Company grateful for the concern shown by the Royal Navy.[94] Evidently the Russians planned to station at least one vessel at the mouth of the river to supply food and clothing at "moderate" prices to distressed miners as they retreated from the goldfields with the beginning of winter.[95]

The *Devastation* then steamed from Sitka to the mouth of the Stikine River, where Pike received requests from numerous persons for protection. At one settlement, Port Highfield, he found that Europeans were saved from outraged Natives by reports that a British warship would "surely visit Stikeen during the season."[96] When the Russian American Company steamer *Alexander* arrived with provisions and clothing for the destitute miners, Pike, who was uncertain of British rights of navigation in the Stikine Territory, relinquished control over the Natives to the Russian naval officer in command of the *Alexander*. Then the *Devastation* sailed for Vancouver Island carrying 44 refugees from a wilderness soon to be transferred to the administration of the governor of British Columbia.[97]

By July 1863, this new maritime frontier was included within the boundaries of British Columbia. For the Navy, the most important consequence of the Stikine rush was that it increased by seven hundred miles the extent of coast to be protected by the Royal Navy. Rear-Admiral Maitland also explained that he had suggested to the governor that proclamations be issued warning British subjects against travelling in canoes from Victoria to the Stikine River unless accompanied by armed coasting vessels or steamers. While the *Devastation* patrolled the north coast, and the paddle-sloop *Hecate*, Captain George Henry Richards, surveyed the northern part of Vancouver Island and "kept the Indians in awe," the *Grappler* and *Forward* guarded Nanaimo and Victoria. Farther north there was an urgent need for a powerful ship with good sea-keeping abilities, and this necessitated the presence of yet another vessel in the waters as far north as the Stikine.[98] This vessel was the screw-sloop *Cameleon*, 17 guns, Commander Edward Hardinge, sent by Maitland in the spring of 1863 to protect British subjects expected on the north coast during the mining season.[99] Here, as in the Queen Charlottes and Fraser River gold rushes, the Royal Navy provided the policing.

Use of Naval Personnel Inland

During the 1850s and 1860s, officials used naval personnel at inland points as well as on the coast. The Fraser River gold rush revealed the necessity of this, though the issue was not confined to this period or to the Pacific station. It became a subject of lively debate in 1867 and 1868 when a dispute arose over the use of sailors on shore at a distance from their ships. At Grouse Creek in the Cariboo, the presence of Governor Frederick Seymour—the successor to Douglas—and two naval captains was sufficient to halt a quarrel between rival gold-mining companies. But no sooner did the party leave the district than the wrangle began again.

The governor then asked the commander-in-chief, Rear-Admiral the Honourable George F. Hastings, what aid would be available in the event of a rebellion, explaining that he doubted "whether Her Majesty's Possessions on this Coast are to expect more than the moral support of Her Majesty's Forces in case of difficulty, internal trouble and possible rebellion. Such I believe is not the case on the other side of the Rocky Mountains."[100] Seymour seemed to ignore the fact that seamen might have to be dispatched some seven hundred miles inland, which was contrary to Admiralty instructions that officers and men were not to be employed at a distance from their ships. Thus Hastings rightly could promise cooperation only if vessels or their boats could be deployed.[101]

The need for a force never arose, but the question reached London. On the one hand, the secretary of state for the colonies, the Duke of Buckingham and Chandos, held that in "event of riot threatening life and property," available forces should be sent, providing the safety of the ships could be maintained.[102] On the other hand, the Lords of the Admiralty—who had the final say in this case—were willing to supply what they termed "local aid." They would not sanction sending officers and men a distance from their vessels for fear of "rendering the ships inefficient."[103] This was a stern defence of the Pacific station standing order of 1865, which stipulated that the Navy would act where ships could sail.[104]

Stretching their legs ashore after having sailed thousands of miles at sea, about 80 naval ratings with rifles, preceded by marines and flanked by a midshipman or two, the leading seaman wearing a cutlass, swing up the old Esquimalt Road. CFB ESQUIMALT NAVAL & MILITARY MUSEUM

The Navy was an effective instrument of Britain's policy for upholding British sovereignty on the Northwest Coast during the turbulent gold-rush years in the Queen Charlotte Islands, lower Fraser River country and the Stikine territory. During each successive rush of adventurers into these three unorganized frontiers, British warships were on hand to enforce law and order.

Undoubtedly, Governor Douglas played a significant role during these years. His importance should neither be ignored nor overestimated. Without the various means at his disposal to enforce the authority of the Crown—for example, the Royal Engineers, the gold commissioners, a very stern judge, and the men and ships of the Royal Navy—he would have been virtually powerless, and without doubt historians would have given him considerably less attention.[105] Douglas was resourceful, but essentially it was the assistance that the imperial government was able to provide that proved decisive in maintaining British presence on the Northwest Coast during the gold-rush years. In particular, the Navy reached the scene of each crisis before the establishment of colonial jurisdiction in that region.[106] In each case, the commander-in-chief or the captains of warships took action that strengthened British control over territories that became integral parts of what was known after 1866 as Her Majesty's Crown Colony of British Columbia and its Dependencies.

$\mathcal{P}$IG WAR ON THE
SAN JUAN ISLANDS

San Juan Island, which dominates the channel between the southern tip of Vancouver Island and the mainland, lay on the route of the adventurers bound from Victoria to the Fraser River goldfields. As the surgeon of the British warship *Plumper* wrote in October 1859, it was "the Military Key to British Columbia." He noted somewhat acidly that while the British were "diplomatizing, the Yankees landed 600 soldiers & took possession of it: had the councils of Govr. Douglas prevailed we should have turned them out of it for we have enough force here just now to have eaten them."[1] This episode in international history has all the ingredients for an operetta by Gilbert and Sullivan or Rudolf Friml, for its plot is dramatic as well as comic, and in the end the quarrel was resolved by a third power, supposedly neutral.

Evidently, San Juan was strategically important to the British.[2] Furthermore, the Royal Navy predominated in nearby waters. One wonders now—as the angry inhabitants of Victoria did then—why forces were not embarked from British warships to oust the Americans. The answer is that British policy in the mid-Victorian years was characterized by restraint. Britain was secure at home and abroad. She sought no self-aggrandizement. Naval commanders on foreign stations during this period frequently served as interpreters of the policy of "minimum intervention." They had to

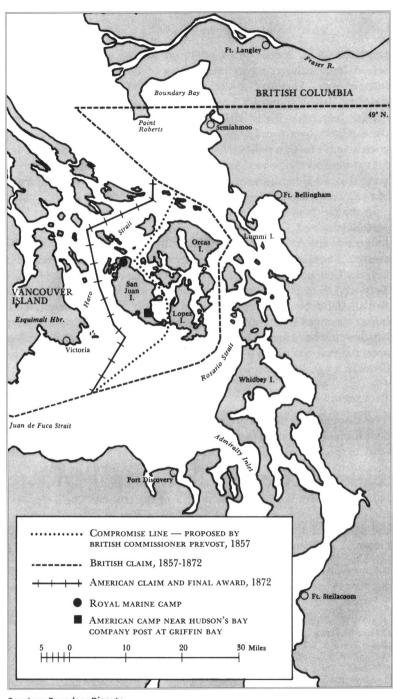

San Juan Boundary Dispute

This map is reprinted with permission of the original publisher from *The Royal Navy on the NW Coast of North America, 1810–1914* by Barry Gough © University of British Columbia Press 1971. All rights reserved by the publisher.

decide how and when to employ force in guarding British commercial and territorial interests. Sometimes, as in the San Juan crisis, British citizens at the scene of contention considered these officers overly cautious. But their actions conformed to their government's foreign policy. No officer dared to intervene where powerful nations had claims to the same territory unless British rights were in grave danger; if he did so without cause, he would face the censorship of Parliament, the Foreign Office, the Admiralty and the British public.

In the San Juan crisis, it is to the credit of Rear-Admiral Robert Lambert Baynes and Captain Geoffrey Phipps Hornby that their sound judgement and patience prevailed, and that an Anglo-American war was averted. The same cannot be said of either Brigadier-General W.S. Harney, the commander-in-chief of the United States Army in the Oregon Territory, or James Douglas, the governor of Vancouver Island and British Columbia. Douglas advocated strongly that the American filibuster contrived by Harney should be met with a like measure, a tactic that would have brought a clash of arms. Fortunately, no local incident occurred that was explosive enough to embroil Britain and the United States in a war over a few islands of little value.[3]

Dispute in the Making

The dispute over San Juan Island's sovereignty arose from a vague definition of the boundary separating Vancouver Island from the mainland, as specified in the hastily formulated Oregon Treaty of 1846. That agreement called for a demarcation between territories of Britain and the United States west of the Rocky Mountains along "the forty-ninth parallel of north latitude to the middle of the channel which separates the continent from Vancouver's Island; and thence southerly through the middle of the said channel, and of Fuca's Straits to the Pacific Ocean." There was no difficulty in determining the land boundary: but what constituted "the middle of the channel"?

Signatories to the treaty did not know there was more than one principal channel leading southward into Juan de Fuca Strait. In fact, there were two channels. The first and most easterly channel, called Rosario or Vancouver Strait, had been explored in 1792 when Captain George Vancouver visited the Northwest Coast. On that occasion he sent Lieutenant Broughton in the *Chatham* to make a cursory survey of the myriad islands that bar an easy passage from Juan de Fuca Strait to the Strait of Georgia.[4] The second and most westerly passage ran through the eight-mile-wide Canal de Haro, now termed Haro Strait, dividing San Juan Island from Vancouver Island. Haro Strait provided the most direct route for Hudson's Bay Company steamers bound from Fort Victoria to the coal mines at Nanaimo in the 1850s. But this passage had been relatively unknown when the Oregon Treaty of 1846 was signed.

After 1846, Royal Navy steamer-driven vessels such as the *Cormorant* and *Driver* followed the eastern channel as shown on Captain Vancouver's charts. Indeed, when it became clear by 1852 that a dispute existed as to what formed "the middle of the channel," British naval commanders continued to take the eastern channel through Rosario Strait, hoping that this would give added weight to the importance Captain Vancouver had attached to that waterway.[5] Lieutenant Charles Wilkes, USN, had drawn maps of the strait in 1841.

Between Haro Strait and Rosario Strait lie three main islands—San Juan, Orcas and Lopez. Only the westernmost, San Juan, need be of concern here. On that island the Hudson's Bay Company established a fishing station in 1850 and a sheep farm three years later. Their reasons were both political and commercial, but principally the Company wanted to settle the island to strengthen British claims.[6] In 1854 the Americans countered by including San Juan and adjacent islands within Whatcom County, Washington Territory—an act that led the Foreign Office to advise the Admiralty to send a naval force to "show the flag" in the disputed straits.[7]

The war then on the verge of breaking out was all about taxes and who had the right to tax. Tax collectors are relentless and unforgiving. Isaac Eby was Collector of Customs for Washington Territory in 1854, and he travelled to the islands to collect taxes. At one stage he threatened to seize Hudson's Bay Company property for taxes. Douglas, not to be outdone, appointed John Griffin of the Company as justice of the peace, with instructions to arrest any person who might disturb the Queen's peace. The Victoria-based customs collector, James Sangster, was landed by the British to uphold their claim. Each side was claiming the islands according to their varied interpretation of the boundary. Griffin tried to arrest one Henry Webber, Inspector of Customs for the United States, but this attempt was foiled. Webber exited the scene temporarily the next day, and a year later left altogether in fear of a Haida raid from northern waters. The US revenue cutter *Jefferson Davis* arrived on the scene, and Douglas protested its being stationed in the San Juans, in what he regarded as British inshore waters. Then the sheriff of newly constituted Whatcom County attempted to levy taxes on British property. An armed sheriff, Ellis Barnes, actually arrived with an armed party demanding payment of taxes, $80. The Hudson's Bay Company refused: 34 breeding rams were taken away by the sheriff. The Company filed a claim for damages amounting to $15,000, and so the tax problems mounted, while the boundary commissioners tried to settle the matter. On these idyllic islands, the tax assessors came and went, and all the while the tempers did not abate. Such was the state of affairs before the pig was shot.

After Rear-Admiral H.W. Bruce visited the Northwest Coast in 1855, he drew his own conclusions. To London he reported "a serious difficulty" developing over the ownership of San Juan "owing to the grasping spirit and habits of the neighbouring Americans."[8] All the same, he was confident that the frigate *President*, due at Vancouver Island late that same year, would strengthen the hand of Governor Douglas, described as "a man of clear views, ability and decision of character."[9] Bruce, perhaps forewarned about Douglas, received a caution from the First Lord of the Admiralty to avoid an incident with the Americans—not because of the real estate in question but because of the great anxiety in England over the possibility of war with the United States, partly due to American support of Russia in the Crimean War.[10] Bruce was also instructed, on February 16, 1856, to draw all his ships north to Central America and Vancouver Island as a show of security to British interests in the face of American filibusters.[11]

The year 1856 passed without incident; a crisis in Anglo-American relations was avoided by the establishment of a mixed commission of two to rectify the ill-defined boundary. In response to Foreign Office suggestions that a naval officer be appointed British boundary commissioner and that a ship—a steamer if possible—be stationed at Vancouver Island to "give weight" to the British case, the Admiralty selected Captain James C. Prevost, familiar with those waters from his service in the *Virago*, and they assigned to him the powerful *Satellite* for the task at Vancouver Island. Prevost reached Esquimalt in June 1857.[12] He was joined later by the chief surveyor and astronomer on the British side, Captain George H. Richards, in HMS *Plumper*.

From June to October 1857, discussions between Prevost and his American counterpart, Archibald Campbell, revealed differences of opinion as to a matter of procedure. The British wanted merely to establish the water boundary, but the Americans intended to define the entire boundary between British and American lands west of the Rockies.[13] It was finally agreed that the land boundary should be surveyed, and 65 Royal Engineers were sent from England in the summer of 1858 for the purpose.[14] Meanwhile, the *Satellite* and *Plumper* continued to survey the waterways.

On the maritime-boundary question, the views of the two commissioners were irreconcilable: Prevost, acting on instruction from the Foreign Office, contended that the line should run through Rosario Strait; Campbell argued in favour of Haro Strait.[15] The British commissioner's argument rested on considerations of navigation and trade. As he explained in a letter to the Admiralty, Rosario Strait provided the best passage for sailing ships, and control of it was essential to the rapidly growing trade in Nanaimo coal, which was carried almost exclusively in sailing vessels. With Rosario Strait in American hands, ships would coal at Bellingham Bay on the American mainland rather than sail through the difficult Haro Strait to Nanaimo.[16]

These points reveal Prevost's ignorance of a clause in the Oregon Treaty that guaranteed to both parties freedom of navigation in the straits south of the 49th parallel. But even if he had been aware of this clause, Prevost might not have emphasized it. He rested his case on "natural law rather than artificial legislation," an argument made popular by the Swiss jurist Vattel.[17]

Prevost did recognize that if San Juan were in American hands, Britain's main outposts on the North Pacific, namely Victoria and Esquimalt, would be imperilled because of the island's proximity to the southern tip of Vancouver Island. Later this danger caused admirals on the Pacific station considerable anxiety. Prevost stated the danger clearly to the Foreign Office when he wrote: "As the value of Vancouver's Island to us as a Naval Station and perhaps a terminus of a great railroad scheme becomes generally known, the [British] possession of San Juan as a wall of defence to its peaceful occupation will be equally appreciated."[18]

In other words, the defence of Esquimalt would be facilitated by British ownership of San Juan Island. The Americans seemed equally aware of San Juan Island's strategic value. The United States Board of Engineers concluded: "By establishing a military and naval station at Griffin Bay, on the southeastern shore of San Juan Island, we shall be able to overlook those inner waters equally with Great Britain from Esquimalt harbour, and thus counterbalance the preponderance she is seeking to establish."[19]

The Admiralty, however, generally did not support Prevost's appeals to check the steady but peaceful American penetration of San Juan.[20] Their Lordships' primary concern was free navigation of the straits, although they acknowledged that ownership of San Juan Island would be advantageous.[21] A year later, when British policy and claims came under review, the Admiralty did not deviate from this stand.[22]

By December 1858 the survey of the maze of waterways had been completed by the *Plumper*, with the *Satellite* acting in an auxiliary capacity. A report submitted by Captain Richards of the *Plumper* gave added weight to the Foreign Office opinion that Britain's claims to San Juan were just.[23] Nevertheless, the Foreign Office was anxious for compromise with the Americans and did not insist that the international boundary should be drawn down the middle of Rosario Strait.[24] Essentially the question became one of deciding on which side of San Juan Island the boundary should run. But within a few months, the dispute entered a more hazardous stage.

The Provocative Pig

How war nearly erupted between Britain and the United States over the shooting of a Hudson's Bay Company pig on San Juan is a colourful and often exaggerated tale.[25] According to the British view, the guilty party was Lyman A. Cutler, an American "squatter" on the Company's land. Evidently, the provocative pig made several profitable forays into Cutler's potato patch. The last occurred on June 15, 1859, when the irritated farmer shot the pig. Immediately, Cutler realized his blunder and offered $10 compensation to Hudson's Bay Company officials. A war of words followed between Cutler and Justice of the Peace Griffin, and in the end Cutler took to the security of the woods.

The shooting heightened attention over which nation possessed sovereignty. The tax collectors' war was about to be succeeded by something more treacherous. Already American officials had attempted to collect taxes from the Company for landing thirteen hundred sheep without observing United States revenue laws, but this attempt was thwarted by Douglas.[26] To many American settlers, however, the killing of the "British" pig appeared to be a justifiable retaliation. In the mistaken belief that Cutler had been mistreated by British authorities, the incensed settlers petitioned military authorities in Oregon for assistance.[27] The matter was getting dangerously out of hand.

As a result, on July 18, 1859, Brigadier-General W.S. Harney at Fort Vancouver ordered a 60-man infantry detachment to proceed from Fort Bellingham to protect Americans on San Juan from the indignities and insults the British authorities had recently offered them. On July 27, Captain George Pickett, D Company, Ninth Infantry Battalion, arrived on the steamer USS *Massachusetts* and landed with 461 men on the south end of the island, opposite Griffin Bay. This was on and near the best agricultural land on the island, farmed by the Hudson's Bay Company. The landing place lay close to the Company's dock. The American soldiers took up positions with instructions to oppose any interference by colonial officials of Vancouver Island.[28] From the *Massachusetts* were landed a number of guns, including eight 32-pounders, one 6-pounder, and five mounted howitzers, and Pickett deployed this artillery on hills overlooking the beach, training the guns on the guns of the British squadron.

Harney's action was based on two erroneous assumptions. First, he believed that the Royal Navy was implicated in the insult by the use of a British naval vessel to transmit a Hudson's Bay Company official to the island to seize Cutler.[29] On this, Harney was misinformed. As Baynes later stated to the Admiralty, no ship of the Royal Navy was in the region at the time of the incident.[30] In reality, the vessel was the *Beaver*, and it was "purely accidental" that A.G. Dallas, president of the Board of Management of the Company's Western Department, was on San Juan.[31] Secondly, Harney assumed that San Juan Island was "as important to the Pacific States as Cuba is to those of the Atlantic."[32] The second assumption was probably decisive for Harney. Very likely he intended to gain San Juan for an American naval base, which he believed would provide a counterpoise to Britain's base at Esquimalt.[33] Whatever the pretext, Harney's unwarranted and unauthorized conduct, resulting as it did from anti-British and expansionist tendencies,[34] brought embarrassment to the American government and caused his recall.[35]

It is ironic that prior to the so-called pig battle and Harney's rash acts, the British government had informed Washington of its hope that "local collisions" could be avoided.[36] But the British government erred in making no attempt to rescind or modify instructions relayed to Governor Douglas by the Colonial Office.[37] These instructions gave Douglas a formal sanction for his own view that the Americans were intruders on San Juan, which he always considered a dependency of the Colony of Vancouver Island. Further, Douglas found encouragement in his instructions for believing that Americans should be warned against claiming sovereignty. The governor's conduct in this crisis has been questioned by his most eminent biographer.[38] In Douglas's defence, it must be stated that his policy was in keeping with Foreign Office instructions to maintain British rights on San Juan. Douglas, who dealt firmly with Americans earlier during the Fraser River gold rush, intended to do much the same on the disputed island.

Well within the terms of his Foreign Office instructions, the governor sent a magistrate and justice of the peace, Major John de Courcy, to

The handsome screw-frigate HMS *Tribune* arrived from China in February 1859 to shore up the British defence during the dispute over the San Jan Islands. Phipps Hornby, the senior Royal Navy captain, refused Governor Douglas's demands that forces be landed at San Juan Island. She was again on Pacific Station 1864–65, and grounded on the treacherous Sandheads, Fraser River, and was obliged to be lightened of all guns and stores before floating. CFB ESQUIMALT NAVAL & MILITARY MUSEUM

enforce law and order on "the British island." On July 27, 1859, after arriving from Victoria in the *Satellite*, de Courcy read his commission under a British flag at Griffin Bay.[39] At this stage, both the Americans and the British realized the dangers of the situation and acted with due caution.

To support the magistrate with force, Douglas, who had no soldiers at his disposal, turned to the Royal Navy; for once, the governor did not have to wait for warships to arrive. His pleas for British warships during the British Columbia gold rush in 1858 had resulted in the arrival of the frigate *Tribune* and the corvette *Pylades* from the China and East Indies station. The flagship *Ganges* was expected at Vancouver Island during early August 1859 to protect British interests at the height of the gold-rush season. Consequently, the question of assuring sufficient ships to deal with the San Juan emergency never arose as it did in other crises on the Northwest Coast.

By sending the *Tribune* to Griffin Bay, where the Americans had made camp, Douglas planned to prevent further American landings on the British "dependency."[40] It was his intention, at this stage, to use the *Tribune* against the American soldiers on shore only if they were erecting fortifications or making further landings.[41] At the same time, he intended to have the British magistrate accomplish the eviction of the Americans on shore. In short, Douglas anticipated that the Americans would withdraw when faced with British law backed up by the *Tribune*.[42]

But when the governor learned that the Americans (now some 100 to 150 in number) were making preparations to oppose the British with arms, he requested that another warship be sent to the scene from Esquimalt. As a result, Captain Michael de Courcy, the senior officer at Esquimalt and cousin of the British magistrate, dispatched the *Satellite* to join the *Tribune*, and on August 1 the *Satellite*, hitherto engaged in the Boundary Commission, was placed under orders of Captain Hornby of the *Tribune*.[43] Such overwhelming superiority of naval force at San Juan, Douglas thought, surely would prevent the Americans from resisting the British magistrate by arms or otherwise.[44]

Because the crisis seemed certain now to intensify, the Legislative Council of Vancouver Island met the same day, August 1, and decided that Colonel J.S. Hawkins, RE, should be sent to London with information for the British cabinet on the state of affairs. In the hope that a ship could reach San Francisco by August 5, when the packet for Panama was scheduled to leave, the *Pylades* left Victoria with Hawkins aboard. Headwinds outside Cape Flattery proved too strong for her steam engines, capable of 350 horsepower, and her commander concluded that she would be unable to reach her destination in time. Therefore, he turned back toward Vancouver Island, where he thought his ship might be more useful in protecting the colony if the erratic Americans attacked.[45] Hawkins reached London by other means.

At the same meeting on August 1, the Legislative Council resolved to withdraw the British magistrate from San Juan and reverse the decision to land troops, as it was clear that a joint occupation could only result in bloodshed.[46] These wise policies can be attributed to Captain Michael de Courcy, the senior naval officer, who overruled the more bellicose Douglas.[47] Despite the prudence of the Council, Douglas maintained firmly the belief that force should be met with force. His convictions were based on his long awareness of American advancement into the Pacific Northwest prior to the Oregon Treaty, and his belief that Britain and the Hudson's Bay Company were about to lose further domains.[48]

At San Juan, meanwhile, the presence of the Royal Navy did not result in an American withdrawal.[49] On August 2, the *Plumper* brought 46 Royal Marines and 15 Royal Engineers from the Fraser River to increase the military force available if a landing proved necessary.[50] As long as the British remained in their ships and the Americans occupied San Juan, American *de facto* control of the island was ensured. Nevertheless, Captain George Pickett, in charge of the American detachment, was justifiably alarmed when he saw the *Tribune, Satellite* and *Plumper* lying in Griffin Bay in "a menacing attitude"; he reported that the British warships were of such overwhelming strength that his troops would be a mere "mouthful for them."[51] This led Brigadier-General Harney, who was still in command, to write immediately to San Francisco, the headquarters of the United States Pacific squadron, for naval support.

"Tut, tut, no, no, the damned fools"

The preservation of peace in this tense situation can be attributed largely to the actions of Captain Geoffrey Phipps Hornby of the *Tribune*, son of Admiral Sir Thomas Phipps Hornby, who was Commander-in-Chief, Pacific, from 1847 to 1850. Captain Hornby was one of the most respected

Sir Geoffrey Phipps Hornby, son of an admiral and himself later a First Sea Lord, was of stern and unrelenting character and was not to be pressured by Governor Douglas during the San Juan Island crisis. He arrived at Esquimalt on February 13, 1859, in HMS *Tribune*, fresh from China, to bolster British capabilities. CFB ESQUIMALT NAVAL & MILITARY MUSEUM

sailors in the Royal Navy. His discretion during the San Juan crisis won him the praise of his commander-in-chief and of the Admiralty. He believed that neither British nor American troops should occupy the island, and he rightly held that the British could afford to be forbearing in view of their superior naval strength. Thus his objective was to place on the Americans the responsibility for any rupture that might occur in the already endangered Anglo-American relations. Because Pickett refused to withdraw his force at Hornby's demand, Hornby told him that the American government would be responsible for subsequent developments, and that British marines and engineers would be landed if "the honor or the interests of England" were in jeopardy.[52]

Pickett's force was strengthened greatly on August 1 by the arrival of 120 United States troops in the armed transport *Massachusetts*.[53] At this difficult moment, Hornby and Prevost were on the island, searching for Pickett to discuss joint occupation.[54] David Boyle, the first lieutenant, was left in charge of the *Tribune*. He had been in command for an hour when the *Massachusetts* anchored near the *Tribune* and prepared to disembark soldiers. Boyle informed the captain of the troopship that the British intended to prevent troop landings. The Americans ignored this warning, ordered the boats to be lowered and proceeded with the disembarkation. Just as Boyle was about to beat to quarters, the *Plumper* brought instructions cancelling the governor's orders to prevent any more landings of American troops.[55] An incident that might have led to war was avoided by only a few minutes.

Four days later, on August 5, the *Ganges*, the flagship of Rear-Admiral Baynes, Commander-in-Chief, Pacific, reached Esquimalt. Baynes, who had no previous knowledge of the crisis, had arrived to coincide with the height of the gold-rush season. Upon learning of the "pig war" and of the governor's warlike plans, he is reported—perhaps with some exaggeration— to have said, "Tut, tut, no, no, the damned fools."[56] At once he realized that a collision of forces had been avoided only through the sound judgement and restraint of Hornby, for the implementation of the governor's original policy would have resulted in war.[57] Although Douglas evidently was ignorant of a larger consequence of his policy—war between rival maritime powers—Baynes saw the crisis in its true perspective, and his reaction was justified.

The admiral had two reasons for rejecting the governor's plans. First, the orders to Hornby of August 2 would have meant a clash of arms in which the British would have been forced to evict the Americans from the island and hold it against attack.[58] Second, the landing of British forces was not required, for British claims to the island were in no way invalidated by the absence of British troops there, nor were British citizens in any way endangered.[59] Baynes's logic testifies to his admirable ability to view the petty squabble in perspective, for at stake here was the preservation of peaceful Anglo-American relations.

Douglas tried to cast aside the admiral's criticism by turning on Hornby and blaming him for inactivity. Douglas believed that if Hornby had disembarked troops, further American landings and fortifications would have been prevented. Indeed, although Douglas claimed that he had been forced to agree with what he termed derisively a "passive and retrograde" policy as urged by the naval officers at the meeting of the Legislative Council, he had ordered Hornby to participate in a joint occupation.[60] Surely this indicates the governor's failure to foresee the consequence of the action he expected Hornby to pursue. In general, Douglas's point of view won little, if any, support from naval or army officers, including Colonel R.C. Moody, the officer commanding the Royal Engineers in British Columbia. Moody praised Hornby for not following orders given in Douglas's "very clever letter," which would have placed the responsibilities for landing troops squarely on Hornby's shoulders.[61]

While Baynes pursued his policy of forbearance, the Americans continued to land troops, to the increasing disadvantage of the British. Within a week of the admiral's arrival, between 200 and 300 were in possession of San Juan—further proof to Baynes that the *Ganges* should not return to England as expected but remain instead to strengthen the British position.[62] Another week saw the balance of power shift to the Americans in terms of actual soldiers available. The Americans had 400 men, 6 field-pieces and 100 to 150 civilians on the island, plus 400 artillery men at Fort Steilacoom on Puget Sound. By comparison, circumstances were unfavourable to the British because of insufficient military force, isolation of Vancouver Island from other parts of the Empire, dependence of the colony on American routes for mail and supplies, and numerical predominance of Americans in the colonies of Vancouver Island and British Columbia. All of these factors, as Baynes perceived, were certain indications of the folly of going to war.[63] But war would have been equally foolish for the Americans. As the secretary of state for the colonies, the Duke of Newcastle, later explained to Governor Douglas, the superiority of British sea power on the Northwest Coast at the same time made clear to the Americans the wisdom of Britain taking "the moderate course of remonstrance instead of violent measures."[64]

As a result of the crisis, the British government made speedy preparations to reinforce the Pacific station. Stationing a garrison of several hundred soldiers at Vancouver Island would not have appealed either to Parliament or the British public at a time when colonial garrisons were being reduced, so the more popular and less permanent measure of dispatching ships-of-war was taken. On the suggestion of the foreign secretary, Lord John Russell, the first-class screw-frigate *Topaze*, 51 guns, and the screw-corvette *Clio*, 22 guns, were sent to join the five warships already on the Northwest

Coast.[65] The Foreign Office further recommended, in instructions dated October 3, 1859, that the *Ganges* should remain at Vancouver Island until ordered to return to England.[66]

Sending additional ships to foreign stations such as the Pacific in time of need prevented the reductions in Treasury estimates sought by the Chancellor of the Exchequer, Gladstone. During this crisis, the First Lord of the Admiralty, the Duke of Somerset, bemoaned the fact that the introduction of steam power had not resulted in the anticipated reduction of vessels on distant stations: "At present time there is an unusual, and I hope, never to be repeated demand upon our naval force; from Vancouver's isle to the river Plate from the West Indies to China the Admiralty is called upon by Secretaries of State to send ships of war."[67] A few days later he wrote to Gladstone on the same subject:

> If there were any certainty as to the demands which would be made on the Admiralty for naval force, we should be relieved of much embarrassment, but the calls are always sudden & unforeseen. The other day for instance two vessels, a frigate & corvette were directed to be sent to Vancouver's isle and an eighty gun ship, which we had ordered home was detained there by the Admiral (very properly under the circumstances). This however makes a difference of above 1000 men: and I do not see how the Admiralty can be prepared for such contingencies. The undeniable fact is that we are doing or endeavouring to do much more than our force is sufficient for.[68]

It is little wonder that the First Lord of the Admiralty felt pleased that the world was not larger, for there seemed to be no "limit to the service of the fleets."[69]

The Pacific squadron was then composed of 13 ships (one ship-of-the-line, three frigates, eight corvettes and one paddle-wheel sloop).[70] But during the period from 1845 to 1865, the number of ships varied from 9 to 16 according to the needs of the day and the units available to the Admiralty. Extra ships were sent to the Pacific as needed to deal with crises on the Northwest Coast, especially the Oregon dispute, the Fraser River gold rush and the San Juan problem. While the British government sought no additions to its mid-Victorian empire, at the same time it was reluctant to allow any possession or territory to which it had claims to pass to a rival nation. The best means of enforcing this policy was to send ships of the Royal Navy, although the drain on the Treasury often proved to be an embarrassment to a ministry that preached economy.[71]

Another outcome of the San Juan incident was that the American secretary of state assured the British minister in Washington, Lord Lyons, of the peaceful intentions of the United States government. The intemperate Harney was recalled, and General Winfield Scott was sent to the Pacific Northwest by the War Department in the prestigious capacity of commander-in-chief of the United States Army. Scott possessed instructions to effect a joint military occupation until the nations agreed on a definite boundary; when he reached Puget Sound, he proposed such an occupation by a force of 100 men from each nation. This proposal was agreeable to Douglas but not to Baynes, who favoured a joint civil occupation, thereby "placing matters exactly as they were previous to General Harney's unjustifiable act."[72] Ultimately, the American proposal was accepted by the British government as it did not compromise rights and it prevented war.[73]

A further dispute between Baynes and Douglas developed when the governor received Colonial Office instructions to requisition from Baynes a Royal Marine detachment for the military occupation of the portion of San Juan Island assigned to the British by the Anglo-American agreement. Baynes, who clearly lacked confidence in Douglas, asked for a copy of the document, evidently to verify the request from the British government. Affronted, Douglas refused on the grounds that because he was the Queen's representative, his instructions could not be delegated.[74] In this situation of mutual distrust, the British government sided with Baynes.[75] The petty squabble ended when the commander-in-chief received instructions from the Admiralty and Foreign Office to send a captain and 100 marines to the island to participate in the joint occupation while the sovereignty of San Juan remained undetermined.[76]

Subsequently, Baynes ordered Captain George Bazalgette, RMLI, in charge of the marines, to set up camp at Garrison Bay near Roche Harbour on the island's north end, and on March 21, 1860, the detachment landed from the *Satellite*.[77] For 12 years the marines maintained their vigil at "English Camp," Garrison Bay, some 10 miles northwest of the "American Camp" at Griffin Bay. Throughout this period, British warships visited San Juan occasionally, but after the *Pylades* returned to Esquimalt on December 7, 1859, the use of warships as a "show of force" at the island was suspended.

In retrospect, Baynes's policy of non-intervention appears to have been the correct one. At the time, however, not only Douglas, but the colonial legislature and the Victoria press thought otherwise. On August 17, 1859, for example, the *British Colonist* carried an editorial asking "Why were not troops landed at San Juan?" Five days earlier, the Speaker of the Legislature asked the same question: "Why all this expense and show, if for a parade? . . . Instead of fighting, Her Majesty's Captains take to diplomacy."[78]

Admiral Baynes and Captain Hornby were well aware of the reasons for not intervening. Throughout the crisis, the Navy remained "perfectly passive" and "forbearing" to a degree to which Baynes feared the Admiralty might not approve.[79] But he justified his policy on the "almost certainty" of a clash of arms in a very remote quarter of the world. In his opinion, providing the British flag was not compromised, the interests of Britain and the Pacific colonies were served best by reducing the chances of war.

The commander-in-chief's successful strategy won the wholehearted approval of the Admiralty. In fact, the First Lord of the Admiralty, the Duke of Somerset, commended Baynes in glowing terms. He informed him that the members of the British ministry often talked of the "good sense and prudence" that Baynes displayed during the crisis caused by the "intemperate proceedings" of General Harney, which would have resulted in serious complications if Baynes had not "met them by calm remonstrance and dignified but conciliatory language."[80] Shortly thereafter, Baynes was knighted for his outstanding services to Great Britain.[81]

Treaty of Washington, 1871

The Treaty of Washington of 1871 finally resolved many long-standing Anglo-American difficulties.[82] In discussions leading to the treaty, the Americans rejected compromise, for in such a solution, Great Britain probably would have received San Juan Island. Negotiators for the United States, therefore, insisted that the arbitrator, Kaiser Wilhelm I, Emperor of Germany, should decide which channel—Haro or Rosario—was most in accordance with the terms of the 1846 agreement. American insistence upon this point ended any British hope for an equitable division of the archipelago, and the issue thus rested upon the strength of the claims of the rival nations.

Of the two cases presented to the kaiser, the British was obviously the weaker for two reasons.[83] In the first place, hydrographic data showed that Haro Strait was the main channel. In the second place, historical evidence revealed that in discussions preceding the Oregon Treaty, Lord Aberdeen, the foreign secretary, had merely wanted to preserve for Britain Vancouver Island, and not the adjacent islands.[84] An additional point was that in the course of negotiations, the British, acting on Captain Prevost's recommendation, had proposed the middle channel as a compromise position, thereby weakening their own case. Not surprisingly, therefore, the kaiser, in his award of October 21, 1872, named Haro Strait as "most in accordance with the true interpretation of the Treaty."[85] The entire San Juan archipelago thus became American territory; accordingly, the Foreign Office quickly instructed the senior naval officer at Esquimalt to withdraw the British garrison. This was accomplished by the British warships *Scout* and *Peterel* on November 25, 1872, an event which brought to an end the 12-year joint occupation of the island. And so ended the one-shot war that caused such tensions and so much aggravation.

To citizens of the new Canadian province of British Columbia and, indeed, to many Canadians on the eastern side of the Rockies, the kaiser's award appeared as a betrayal of Canadian interests on the Northwest Coast, much like the Oregon Treaty.[86] That London seemed indifferent is reflected in an editorial in *The Times*—often described as "cut the painter" advice—which told Canada to assume responsibility for her own affairs, the days of apprenticeship being over. Viscount Milton, who had written an early history of the dispute, thought it "unjust and impolitic on the part of the Mother Country to virtually sacrifice the independence and power of her colonies at the same time that she is urging self-reliance and independence upon them."[87] Most Canadian politicians held similar views.

Sir John A. Macdonald, as prime minister of Canada and a member of the British delegation at discussions leading up to the Treaty of Washington, believed that even if the island were awarded to the Americans, as long as England remained "mistress of the seas" she could still "seize upon the island and hold it against all comers" should war break out. The United States gained a strategic advantage from the possession of San Juan Island, for if batteries were mounted to command Haro Strait, the passage of British warships through that channel could be prevented. Macdonald noted with dismay this state of affairs, but he too understood that British Columbia was dependent on the British squadron in the Pacific for protection. "Whenever she ceases to have the naval supremacy the whole coast will be at the mercy of the American fleet."[88] Macdonald had touched on a matter that was assuming greater significance in view of the growth of American hemispheric interests: the security of Canada depended in large measure on peaceful Anglo-American relations.

Britain lost San Juan Island, but she did not lose the peace. The overall security of her worldly interests demanded forbearance in certain instances. Self-assertion and interference were not her objectives. Certainly she possessed naval power at Vancouver Island sufficient "to have eaten" the American soldiers on San Juan, as the surgeon of the *Plumper* remarked, but a belligerent course of action was inconsistent with London's policy.

Showing the flag was an expensive proposition: the protracted quarrel over San Juan Island revealed again the necessity of maintaining a large British naval force in the Pacific. During the period from 1859 to 1866, no fewer than 12, and sometimes as many as 16, warships were on the Pacific station.[89] As a result of gold-rush crises, problems with hostile Natives, growth of trade and the San Juan dispute, the Commander-in-Chief, Pacific, was forced increasingly to spend more time in northern waters.

eight

$\int$ END A GUNBOAT!

In the cabin of a man-of-war riding at anchor in Valparaiso, Chile, Rear-Admiral Sir Thomas Phipps Hornby, surveying the various papers that lay before him, wrote to the secretary of the Admiralty a brief warning about the unsettled state of race relations at Vancouver Island and its dependencies. Of a distinguished family, son of a vicar and of a daughter directly related to the 12th Earl of Derby, he had been one of Nelson's junior officers in the *Victory*, Nelson's flagship, during the blockade of Toulon in 1804. Now, having been promoted to commander and then captain, he had advanced in seniority on the *Navy List* by "walking in dead men's shoes," and at last had been made rear-admiral in 1846. The next year he had been given the favourable Pacific command in succession to Sir George Seymour, and he flew or "wore," as they used to say, his flag in the old *Asia*, 84 guns. Sixty-two years old, he accepted the appointment with reluctance, but it did allow him to take his son, Geoffrey T. Phipps Hornby, with him as his flag lieutenant to give him a chance of promotion.[1] He also took to Valparaiso his wife, three daughters and another son, and built a new admiral's residence ashore.[2] Finding the steam side-wheeler *Driver* much preferable to the *Asia* for matters of mobility and the gathering of news from junior officers, Rear-Admiral Phipps Hornby had shifted his flag. Now, with all this naval intelligence to sort out, and with priorities to set, he was commenting on affairs of state thousands of sea miles away.

From various reports of ships' captains who had called at Esquimalt and visited Juan de Fuca Strait, he had learned some undeniable facts; the salient one was that the locale was in possession of various Native tribes or nations of considerable martial ability.

Three-quarters of a century previous, Captain Cook had described how the original inhabitants at Nootka had the highest regard for the resources in their possession, and though there had been no altercation with the Royal Navy down to Phipps Hornby's time, the worry persisted that the coming of traders, coal miners, settlers and prospectors for gold would heighten tensions and cause endless difficulties. British statesmen and admirals were well aware of the violent history of the westward course of empire in the United States, and they made every attempt to ensure there was no such repetition on British soil. The Colonial Office kept a close watch on these matters.

Captains James Wood, Henry Kellett and others, especially and most recently Captain John Shepherd of the frigate *Inconstant*, had, in their reports of proceedings, advised the admiral on the northern state of affairs. The Hudson's Bay Company was withdrawing its establishments from Oregon and concentrating its commercial efforts north of the new boundary. It was on the basis of this intelligence, and information from Company officers, that Phipps Hornby formed his summary conclusion. He wrote to London: "As regards the Colonization of the Island, if such is the Company's object, it is anticipated that much resistance would be offered by the Indians, the tribes to the northward being described as numerous, well armed, brave and warlike, and Captain Shepherd's opinion is, that no colony could be established upon it, without being in its infancy rendered safe against the Indians, by the presence of a strong detachment of troops." He added, in closing, "I shall continue as heretofore occasionally to detach one of the Ships of my Squadron to Vancouver's Island for the due protection and support of the Hudson Bay Company's servants, particularly in the spring of next year during the removal of their establishments from United States Territory."[3]

Here was the beginning of a new naval task: sending warships to provide protection to the Company and to the colony. Recently, the admiral had learned that coal miners had gone to Fort Rupert, and as he had intimated, it was to the northward that the greatest challenge might be faced.

The newly appointed governor, Richard Blanshard, had not yet arrived on the scene, and when he did, he took precisely the same line of reasoning as Captain Shepherd: troops were needed. As described in chapter 4, Fort Rupert became the first flashpoint in cross-cultural relations, and as the influence of colonization and governmental authority expanded on that maritime frontier, so, too, did the authorities find themselves in often-intractable problems. The episodes at Fort Rupert and the village of Newitty were the inaugural ones in the use of "gunboats." Right through to 1890, British warships were deployed on such duties—on the west coast of Vancouver Island, at Cowichan, in islands of the Strait of Georgia, at the mouths of the Skeena and Nass Rivers, at Metlakatla and even in Alaska (at the request of US authorities).[4] The Admiralty and Colonial Office papers are replete with accounts of the use of gunboats and the perplexing dilemmas presented to authorities in the face of expanding frontiers of settlement, law and order—and Native responses. We have forgotten many of these sad episodes in cross-cultural violence.

From the perspective of our own times, the use of coercive force against First Nations brings feelings of dismay and revulsion. The use of such force signifies a breakdown in peaceful relations, as it is invariably used in response to circumstances that seem beyond remedy. Often, violence begets violence. The end results—and the legacies—leave deep resentments in societies where the oral tradition is living history. Some of the episodes from the era being examined here continue to resurface with much righteous indignation on the part of historians who are attracted to the subject but who have little understanding of the history of law. There is always a regrettable tendency to see the past through present-day glasses and to judge accordingly. Force was the fuel of empire, and gratuitous aggravations led to Queen Victoria's little wars on frontiers as different as New Zealand, Cape Colony, Natal and Tasmania. The extension of British dominions by conquest or cession was to be avoided, yet the process went on. As early as the 1830s, colonial secretaries, such as the high-minded Lord Glenelg, lamented that it was the circumstances on the frontier that invariably led to war. He thought official uses of violence unforgivable, but as he said, with some regret, from these encounters developed "the laws of war."[5]

In his time, the House of Commons had struck a powerful select committee on aboriginal affairs in the Empire "to consider what measures ought to be adopted with regard to the native inhabitants of countries when British settlements are made, and to the neighbouring tribes in order to secure to them the due observance of justice and the protection of their rights, to promote the spread of civilization among them, and to lead them to the peaceful and voluntary reception of the Christian religion."[6] This reflected the official mind of imperialism. In 1852 the Third Earl Grey, who oversaw the founding of the Vancouver Island colony, thought that the extermination of "less-civilized" people could be averted by the "enforcement of order." This combined mission of civilization and Christianity was "a high and noble object well worthy of considerable sacrifice on the part of the British peoples."[7] Grey argued that the mother country had to provide assistance to the colonies, for if colonists were left to their own devices in the face of actions by aboriginals, their use of violence would be unchecked. In other words, constitutional law was seen as the means of preventing abuses on the frontier. The Colonial Office and the Admiralty discussed various episodes, and matters were often referred to the Law Officers of the Crown for advice on the rules of engagement. In the background, too, were the volunteer associations—the Aborigines' Protection Society and the Church Missionary Society. They saw themselves as self-appointed guardians of aboriginal peoples and made it a matter of concern to keep a watch on the affairs of the frontier. They often were a thorn in the flesh of the Colonial Office.[8]

The Navy as Constable

"Send a gunboat!" was an age-old call familiar to all flag officers afloat. In this Victorian age, however, the workaday occupation of the Navy was a constabulary one. Ships of the Royal Navy, like regiments posted on frontiers, were guardians of empire. By mid-century, and in every way, steam spurred on the imperial purpose, on the high seas and in inshore waters, estuaries and rivers. Vessels totally dependent on sail were at the mercy of winds and tides. Shallow-draft gunboats could be used in rivers if the depth of the channel sufficed, or armed parties in smaller boats could be sent in on their constabulary duties where larger vessels could not travel. In navigable waters, steamers could act independently of the natural forces, assuming their engines were strong enough and a fuel supply was at hand. In the mid-1840s, sloops having steam as auxiliary power had come into service.

HMS *Plumper*, on the coast as a surveying vessel under the command of Captain Richards, was one such—a pre-gunboat. Unsuitable for many tasks on account of inadequate engine power, she was relieved, in 1861, by the more powerful and commodious paddle-wheel sloop *Hecate*, a formidable persuader on the coast until she sailed for home in December 1862.

It bears remembering that it was the difficulties of waging a naval campaign in inshore waters during the Crimean War that led the Admiralty to conclude that, in future, all vessels laid down for the Navy would have steam power as an auxiliary mode of propulsion. The Northwest Coast still required ships with sailing rigs, for in many cases the distances were vast, but for inshore, riverine and coastal work—and in the interests of speed— steam engines were the essential requirement. The same war had also led to all sorts of smaller vessels being laid down for inshore waters, and thus was born the classic "gunboat," though the term is often used as a figure of speech.

Wooden gunboats such as the *Forward* and *Grappler*—whose very names signified advance and aggression—represented the new industrial age. Costing £10,000 each, they had been fitted out for urgent service in British Columbia to counter Native "threats" and check the possibility

One of the first two gunboats sent to the British Columbia coast, HMS *Forward*, like her sister ship *Grappler*, was one of the "cheap and nasties"—economical to build and to man but lacking sufficient steam power to deal with the currents on that coast, though useful in certain inshore conditions.
CFB ESQUIMALT NAVAL & MILITARY MUSEUM

of American aggrandizement. They measured 106 feet in length and had a draft (when barnacles and seaweed did not increase it) of 6 feet 6 inches. They had reciprocating engines of 60 nominal horsepower (206 to 233 hp actually developed) driving screw-propellers that gave a service speed of 7.5 knots. They had a fore-and-aft rig that gave adequate speed under sail in suitable winds. They were designed to carry a 68-pound gun on the forecastle, a 32-pound gun aft, and two 24-pound howitzers amidships (the weight being the projectile fired). With a complement of 36 to 40 officers and men, they were a cheap and effective show of power in British Columbia waters and had long lives.

The second evolution of gunboat design included the handy gunboat *Boxer*, equipped with larger engines that turned twin propellers (in British Columbia waters 1869 to 1875). Yet another supplement in power, and with still larger engines and bigger hull, was the elegant gunvessel *Sparrowhawk*. This vessel completed two commissions in these seas, 1865 to 1868 under Commander Porcher, and 1868 to 1872 under Commander Mist. The

The powerful gun vessel HMS *Sparrowhawk*, the instrument of authority that extended the *Pax Britannica* into all the distant marine margins of the British Columbia coast, and even southeastern Alaska, where such a vessel could steam in safety. In her first commission on the Northwest Coast, 1865–1868, she was commanded by Commander Porcher and on her second, 1868–1872, by Commander Mist, who joined her July 1868. CFB ESQUIMALT NAVAL & MILITARY MUSEUM

demanding seas and nautical conditions of the Northwest Coast, including southeast Alaska, necessitated vessels that could keep the seas in all weathers. On occasion, heavily gunned and powered steam-corvettes, such as the *Clio*, and steam frigates, such as the *Sutlej*, undertook gunboat actions in waters that had been surveyed.[9]

The customary technique of the gunboat commander involved the use of force as the last resort. The young lieutenant commanding would wiggle his vessel into a position where guns could be used. He would parley with the chiefs or headmen. He might take chiefs as hostages. He might employ interpreters and send them with police to shore. He might hire Native informants. As a preliminary show of power, he might fire his guns or shoot off rockets at a chosen target. He might seize property, such as canoes, thereby sealing off avenues of escape. He would set deadlines and demand compliance. In the 1880s, he might even show his new searchlights at night. If offenders were caught or handed over by their tribe, tried and convicted, he might flog them for petty crimes, such as pilfering. Those guilty of more serious crimes would be hanged before the assembled tribe, a portable scaffold being available. However, if a process of escalating pressure failed to bring results, the ultimate arbiter would be used. This might involve destroying villages, fish weirs and canoes, and also killing inhabitants if any remained in the village after the expiry of the warning time. In many cases the smouldering ruins of a village and a scattered tribe were the telling testaments of the process of keeping Natives in awe of British power.

At first glance it might seem as if a gunboat commander was his own agent, acting independently. This was not so. On the coast the Navy did not act independently as policemen. Whatever quarterdeck diplomacy was conducted by commanding officers was invariably backed by official sanction. Here, as elsewhere, the mission of British imperialism was to bring peace, order and good government to the areas of British settlement, and to carry civilization and Christianity to the uttermost extremities of the earth. The security of British commerce and settlement was ensured by skillful diplomacy and military influence, most notably by the Navy. "The true strength of imperialism," the Earl of Carnarvon, Disraeli's colonial secretary, said in 1878, lay in building a powerful and munificent English community and in restoring law, order and liberty in "backward societies," and thereby creating a system "where the light of morality and religion can penetrate into darkest dwelling places." There is much high-sounding rhetoric here, emblematic of the age and the imperial purpose. In the nineteenth century, Britons saw it as their mission to extend their authority to the "savage" and to the "uncivilized." Imperial administrators were married to the concept of law and order or, to use the time-honoured phrase, "peace, order and good government."

From the beginning of the Navy's proceedings in Vancouver Island waters, as recounted in "the miserable affair" that embroiled Governor Blanshard, the Hudson's Bay Company, the Navy and various local Native bands and nations (see chapter 4), there could be no pleasure for naval personnel in shooting up Native villages, destroying canoes, ruining fish weirs or places of cultivation, driving people from their homes or ruining their means of subsistence. Shows of naval force had been used at Cowichan, Kuper Island, the Queen Charlotte Islands, Hesquiat and many other places. Coercion often led to violence. Colonial secretaries and parliamentarians, missionaries and adherents to the Aborigines' Protection Society abhorred acts of vengeance on the frontiers of empire. Captains Prevost and Richards were but two of the high-minded officers who defended Indigenous interests but practised showing the flag. Prevost backed the Church Missionary Society and in doing so enabled William Duncan to establish his mission at Metlakatla. Richards knew the coast's First Nations from various close encounters in the surveying line during four years in these waters. He remarked:

> It appears to me that in the present relations existing between our people and the Indians, it cannot be a matter of surprise if many wrongs are committed on both sides, and my opinion is that the Natives in most instances are the oppressed and injured parties. The white man supplies him with intoxicating spirits under the influence of which most of these uncivilized acts are committed. The white man in too many instances considers himself entitled to demand their wives or their sisters, and if such demand is disputed, to proceed to acts of violence to gain their object.[10]

The service was not free from searing criticism. When bluejackets and marines clambered ashore in high spirits and with hopeful expectations after weeks and months at sea, they visited bars and brothels. They gambled and drank. They quarrelled and fought. Brawling sailors set no example for good conduct. Shore patrols did not always stop Jack Tar, when enflamed with spirits, from visiting Native villages, molesting women and creating a general nuisance. Local officers dealt with these matters using Admiralty regulations. In naval surgeons' records, reports of syphilis and other venereal diseases tell of cross-cultural interaction with lethal consequences.[11]

Battles with Demon Rum

On this frontier, as on others, a battle was joined between demon rum and Bibles, between traders and missionaries. Traders, like cannabis promoters nowadays, argued the benefits of free trade and keeping consumers happy. Missionaries reasoned that traders made a mockery of the concept of trusteeship (the protection of First Nations). "The white trader generally confirms by his practice all that the red man is warned against," wrote Richard Charles Mayne, RN in 1862.[12] Colonial governments of Vancouver Island and British Columbia invoked legislation to control the sale or gift of alcohol to the Natives. English law on the coast was seaborne, so the Navy was called upon to enforce liquor ordinances, but nefarious liquor peddlers were artful dodgers, the Native propensity to drink was no less determined than the peddlers' desire to sell their wares, and the number of warships was limited.

The gunboat *Forward* and the paddle-wheel sloop *Devastation* were used in many locations to police the liquor trade. One such was the Nass River, which flows to the Pacific at Portland Canal. The Reverend R.R.A. Doolan of Gonville and Caius, former teacher in the famous Sunday School of Jesus Lane, Cambridge, was sent to Metlakatla in 1864 by the London-based Church Missionary Society, and was then deployed by William Duncan to minister to the Nisga'a in the Nass River valley. Doolan never doubted that he was bound, in his own words, for "a centre of heathenism."[13] Optimistic, he was sure that the Nisga'a were desirous of having teachers. In his first season he experienced a degree of hardship that can only be described as a baptism of fire. The Nisga'a were always on the move, the language was difficult to learn, and preaching had to be done through a Tsimshian intermediary. What he saw as general social disorder, internecine violence, accidents, drinking bouts and related crimes were all devastating. Child mortality was high. The Nisga'a distrusted the ability of whites to check diseases. His letters home and his journal tell of how he found that pride and consciousness of status were disturbingly pervasive among the Nisga'a. Shamanism and ignorance stood in the way of healthy living conditions and enlightened minds. "The chiefs, as a body, keep aloof," he noted.

In December 1865, news swept through the Lower Nass villages: the steam-corvette *Clio*, Captain Turnour, patrolling the Skeena River, would come to their villages and take suspects and witnesses to internecine difficulties on the coast. The *Clio* impounded three whisky schooners in the vicinity. "Great excitement in the camp on account of the news about the man-of-war," wrote Doolan. However, liquor vendors continued to arrive in their schooners, and in April 1866, Doolan recorded sadly in his journal, "the camp is flooded with whisky." He feared that tensions between the Nisga'a and Tsimshian would be perpetuated and even increased, intertribal rivalries would grow into violence, and blood would flow. His appeal to Admiral Denman brought results, and in late September the *Forward*, Lieutenant D'Arcy Anthony Denny commanding, came to anchor in Nass Bay. News of this flashed upriver.

Denny went 14 miles upstream in the ship's gig to the Lower Nass villages and was greeted by Doolan. The priest told Denny of the Nisga'a's inclination to be insolent, adding that they were boastful, openly threatened the authority of Queen Victoria and defiantly indicated that they would traffic in whisky and get drunk whenever they pleased.

Denny wanted no trouble. He returned downstream in the gig, taking soundings as he went (for the river had not been surveyed), and after determining that there was a deep-enough channel, raised steam in the *Forward*, weighed anchor and inched upriver, anchoring in front of the villages. He trained his guns. He threatened the Natives with violence, firing four blank guns as warnings. He gathered the chief and other leaders together. He told them that the government had friendly intentions but would not shy away from the use of force if necessary. The Nisga'a, he proclaimed, must not traffic and consume whisky, for it was illegal and led to bloodshed and murder. In future, he said, such cases would be promptly punished. Some chiefs expressed pleasure at this; others were not so sure, though "the great bullies," as Denny said, had been dispersed. He ordered a 12-pounder rocket to be fired in celebration. The *Forward* weighed anchor and withdrew from the river.[14]

In later months the Reverend Doolan set out on rafts with 33 young Nisga'a from the Lower Nass villages, and after 18 hours, landing on the sandy flats of Kincolith ("the place of scalps"), they put up a new village. Thus was Kincolith founded by exodus—a parallel to Metlakatla. "The seed of the aboriginal race," Duncan told Doolan, had to be preserved, and the only way to conserve it was "within an ark." That ark was Kincolith. There was to be no liquor consumption there or trading, and no property distribution—potlatching—by the Natives.[15]

It was not easy to keep whisky out of the mission. The Navy, on periodic patrol, continued to seek out and seize trading schooners, but the region was so well travelled that Nisga'a near Kincolith could obtain booze easily. Kincolith remained "dry" and it remained besieged. The murder of three Nisga'a from Kincolith in 1868 threatened the existence of the mission. The gunvessel *Sparrowhawk* and Governor Frederick Seymour went there in 1869 to show the flag and prevent warring between parties of Tsimshian and Nisga'a.[16] The Nisga'a, having subsumed Anglicanism into their lives, claimed to have the best of both worlds. Passionately, they defended their aboriginal claims to land, and their own personal rights as proclaimed in the Nisga'a Declaration. Their struggle for compensation and fair treatment before the law continued and in due course resulted in independent municipal government and even the controversial right to sell their own lands.

Much missionary history, or the history of missions in coastal British Columbia, tells of missionaries and Natives, converts and opponents. Doolan stood for a classlessness alien to the Nisga'a; he was a social revolutionary. But he called in the floating authority to back his interests and his work. The story of the Nass involved the extension of British law and order, and the intervention by authorities in the form of British gunboats. Liquor trafficking was hard to control, but there are success stories. The paradox of progress in the Victorian age is here observed: liquor vendors subverted Indigenous lives, and missionaries seeking to get help to stop this called in the gunboats. In the specific case noted, Denny acted with discretion and only had to give a warning. In many other cases the official use of violence was the order of the day.

Mystery of the Missing Steamer and Her Crew

Among the last cases of the Navy's sanctioned use of violence against Northwest Coast peoples occurred at Kimsquit, north of Bella Coola, where the North West Company explorer-trader Alexander Mackenzie had reached Pacific tidewater in 1793. Once again authorities used force as a last resort, when the warship's commander thought it necessary to teach the Natives that crimes against white people and property could be repaid in kind by destruction of Native houses and other material possessions. The Kimsquit affair offers another example of "forest diplomacy," in which the Navy, at the government's request, employed forceful techniques of retribution that officials believed the Indigenes fully understood in advance of the use of force.

In early 1873 the *George S. Wright*, a steamer of American registry, carrying mail and cargo for the North Pacific Transportation Corporation, vanished without trace during her voyage from Kluvok, Alaska, to Nanaimo. Friends and family feared the fate of survivors. The US consul in Victoria requested that a gunboat be sent to investigate, and thus the sleek sloop-of-war *Peterel* steamed from Esquimalt to search the shoreline near Cape Caution, the mainland cape opposite the north tip of Vancouver Island. The ship examined the shoreline there, firing rockets and guns by day and night, hoping to attract the attention of survivors. The gunvessel *Rocket* joined in the search. Native informants could provide no information. The United States, at the request of President Grant, sent the *Lincoln* to join the quest. Bodies and property were discovered but the mystery remained unsolved. Not until 1877 did information come from a trading sloop, the *Ringleader*, that Billy Coma, a coal passer of the *George S. Wright*, was living in Nanaimo. Coma was part Owikeno and this had saved him, for 13 others from that steamer who had reached islands in Queen Charlotte Sound had been murdered. The Owikenos had released Coma, warning him that they would kill his father if authorities learned the fate of the others.[17]

On the strength of this news, Lieutenant Charles Reynold Harris, commanding the *Rocket*, received instructions to determine once and for all details of the disappearance of the *George S. Wright* and the fate of survivors. The *Rocket* steamed from Esquimalt carrying two members of the Victoria police, Dudower as interpreter and Bloomfield as representative of the civil power. It will be observed that the Navy was not acting on its own recognizance but as an aid to the civil power. The *Rocket's* voyage was difficult, with heavy fogs and high winds obliging her to seek shelter at various places, including Fort Rupert, where George Hunt came aboard as interpreter.[18] At various coves, intelligence was gathered and witnesses interrogated. Coma had now disappeared. All indications, and all information, led Harris to conclude that further inquiries at the village of Kimsquit, at the upper reaches of steep-faced Dean Channel, would bring results. It took the *Rocket* a full day to steam to a location off the village, which lay near the mouth of the Dean River.

Kimsquit, meaning "narrow" or "canyon," was one of some 35 villages of the Bella Coola. Well off the beaten track, the people of Kimsquit had had virtually no contact with the colonial world up to this time, except for their interactions with the Hudson's Bay Company. A tightly knit people whose interwoven ancestries were tied together by sentiment and pride of lineage, they sported an aggressive disdain for outsiders (they had harassed Mackenzie when he came through their territory) and bitterly resented their intrusion. This explains why they paid little attention to Harris and others on this mission of inquiry and examination. For their part, the authorities were not armed with anthropological studies and knew nothing of the subtle characteristics of Kimsquit chieftainship. To them a chief was simply a chief, irrespective of rank. They acted both as circumstances warranted and their own inclinations dictated.

The *Rocket* cast anchor off shore within view of the great houses that stood on pilings lining the river bank, their fronts adorned with huge red and black graphic designs of the raven as well as animals and fish. Harris sent Hunt to bring the Kimsquit chiefs aboard ship. He was told that very few of their people were in camp, and many of the principal chiefs were away at the neighbouring villages of Bella Coola and Kitlope. However, they expected the head chief to return that night and promised to come to the warship in the morning. Next day they failed to appear. Harris sent Bloomfield, Hunt and Dudower to the village to make inquiries. Their informants categorically denied that any chiefs were there, saying that the head chief had not returned. However, Bloomfield found four headmen, or chiefs, in camp and told them that they were to give up the Kimsquits who had been at the wreck of the *George S. Wright*.

Then came conflicting testimony. At first the Kimsquit denied any knowledge of the wreck. Then they admitted that two of the persons wanted were now dead and another was at Victoria. They eventually confessed that three men and one woman who had been at the wreck were indeed in the village. The police sprang into action and attempted to arrest all the suspects. They caught two who were trying to escape. An altercation followed, and when a call was made for the camp to resist by force, Harris warned the chiefs aboard the *Rocket* that unless the two suspects came on board the ship by nine o'clock the next morning, the village would be burned. The chiefs promised to cooperate, and Harris began his patient wait.

When no Natives appeared by the appointed hour, he weighed anchor and steamed to a position off the village. There he trained his guns on the houses. He sent an armed gig and also a galley ashore in a last attempt to secure the suspects. The landing party found the village almost deserted: only two chiefs and a few others remained. The suspects could not be found. The British gave those who stayed behind their characteristic imperial fiat— unless they surrendered the offenders, the village would be bombarded and burned to the ground. The gig and galley returned to the ship.

Harris ordered the firing of blank cartridges from the *Rocket*'s great guns, then fired two 20-pounder shells, one on either side of the village. He thought this would bring a response, and he was right. The chiefs immediately promised to deliver the guilty if the village was not burned. The hostages were rowed ashore in the gig and immediately fled to the bush with others who had been terrified by the ship's gunnery. A last-minute search of the village was made to see that no inhabitants remained. Then the warship's guns opened fire—blanks first, followed by shells around the village outskirts and finally shells into the village. A shore party completed the torching of the houses. The action complete, the *Rocket* steamed down Dean Channel, leaving Kimsquit in flames and smoke.

At the end of the day, Lieutenant Harris brought four persons to trial, two Owikenos and two Kimsquits. They knew about the wreck, and Harris believed their resistance to lawful authority indicated they knew more about the terrible scenario than they cared to let on. Perhaps he was mistaken. In any event, his efforts did not solve the mystery of the wrecked vessel and the murdered crew. "It is evident," he painfully admitted to his commander-in-chief, " that all the Indians from Alert Bay north were well aware of a great deal more in connection with this matter than they would reveal." And he complained, "There is the greatest difficulty in getting an Indian to tell the same story twice on this subject."[19] The Navy had carried out its retributive action, but without conclusive evidence, the Crown could not prove its case against the four brought to trial. As for the Kimsquit, they suffered terrible privations and over two harsh winters began to disperse to other settlements.

Here then was a coastal tragedy of strong naval action carried out in response to the best evidence, duly gathered, but which was inconclusive as far as the court was concerned. Such was the nature of frontier justice, and we are reminded of what Lord Glenelg said with wisdom when he was at the Colonial Office: the use of violence was uncalled for, but from the circumstances of the frontier derived the principles of war. These gratuitous

Officers, commissioned and non-commissioned, of the *Reindeer*, a 17-gun sloop launched in 1866, strike the imperial pose. They had added Caroline Island (now Kiribati) in the central Pacific to the imperial real estate in 1868. CFB ESQUIMALT NAVAL & MILITARY MUSEUM

aggravations were the byproduct of colonial expansion and commercial inroads into Native lands and seas. In some cases they induced distrust, even hatred, and they intensified Indigenous rivalries. Empires are based on force, and the guardians of empire made mistakes, many of which were unintended and were entirely in keeping with the precepts of their times, but which nowadays would fail to answer the requirements of justice and the limits of retribution. The process did not stop with the Kimsquit calamity: it was continued at Metlakatla in 1887 and in the Skeena "uprising" of 1888.[20]

Meanwhile, in England, Oscar Wilde was writing pensively:

> Set in this stormy Northern sea,
> Queen of these restless fields of tide
> England! what shall men say of thee.
> Before whose feet the worlds divide?

And England had reason to pause, for the Empire was an English product that changed England itself. These little wars of the frontier, these parades of power—countless in number, puzzlingly insignificant in their individual particularities of character, circumstance and place—were episodes of empire whose legacies of distrust and regret linger where the Northwest Coast peoples gather still.

The young naval commanders who did the bulk of this work were bona fide justices of the peace. These amphibious police, pursuing minimal intervention and acting as sailor-diplomats, answerable to civil authority, arrived on the scene in a show of force and exacted justice by peace if possible, by force if necessary. They attempted to check nefarious liquor traffic. They helped stamp out slavery by stopping intertribal marauding. They assisted missionaries, protected shipping, secured settlers and, in general, preserved law and order where and when they could. They were, in short, servants of an imperial cause, guardians of a Britannic peace and, in their own and reluctant way, pathfinders of empire. Paradoxically, their methods sometimes had to be warlike. They provided the technological advantage, the seaborne variant of Hilaire Belloc's:

> Whatever happens we have got,
> The Maxim gun, and they have not.

nine

Esquimalt,
ANCHOR OF EMPIRE

Ever since the Admiralty had deployed warships to the west coast of South America and the Pacific islands during the first decade of the nineteenth century, problems of provisioning and repairing vessels and providing hospital facilities had been manifest. Storeships—aging frigates—moored at Valparaiso after 1843 and at Callao after 1847 proved inadequate in terms of space. A good base of operations was sorely needed. Consequently, British warships investigated locations such as the Galapagos, Panama and islands off the coasts of Mexico and California as possible sites. As Admiralty interest in the Northwest Coast and its fine harbours grew after 1845, Esquimalt, near the southeastern tip of Vancouver Island, developed as a suitable place of refreshment and repair for ships and ships' companies of the Royal Navy. Some naval strategists argued that Esquimalt was disadvantaged by its nearness to the western United States, its undeniable attraction for seamen to desert and its apparent remoteness from those parts of the South Pacific where the Pacific squadron had heavy patrol duties. Still, with its delightfully sheltered harbour, healthy climate, timber and provisions, and proximity to ample supplies of coal, it afforded the best available situation in the eastern Pacific for a naval base.[1] And, not least, it was on British soil.

227

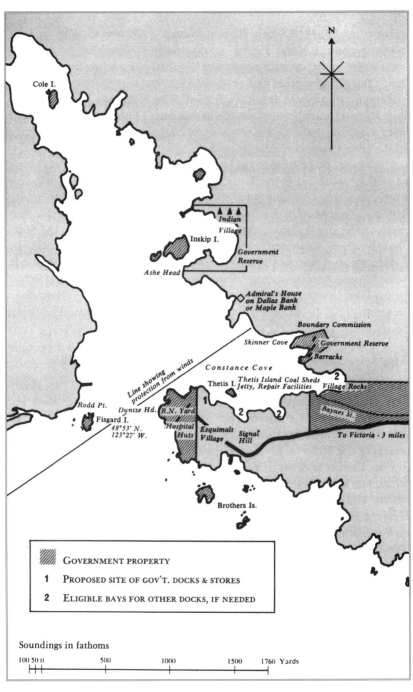

Soundings in fathoms

100 50 0   500   1000   1500   1760   Yards

Esquimalt Naval Base, Early 1860s

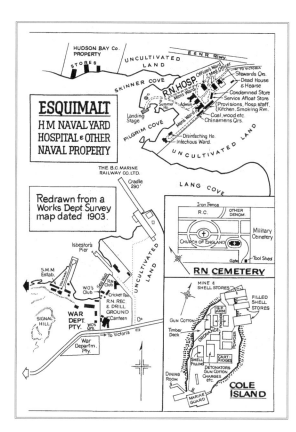

CFB ESQUIMALT NAVAL
& MILITARY MUSEUM

Heretofore, historians have contended that Esquimalt did not become a depot until 1865, when an official Order-in-Council authorized "a small establishment . . . for the custody, etc., of stores and provisions for Her Majesty's Ships in the North Pacific."[2] Actually, as will be shown, a more precise development occurred three years before, in 1862, when Esquimalt became the designated Pacific station headquarters. Even so, we know this port grew as a naval base much earlier—in the late 1840s and 1850s— although the exact date of the creation of an establishment remains elusive. The Admiralty merely was following the actual needs on these distant seas.

As early as the 1840s, the Navy began to search for a site for a base in the North Pacific during a period of international rivalry and naval operations in the Society Islands and along the north Pacific coast. The Earl of Ellenborough, the First Lord of the Admiralty, contended in 1846 that a base at Pago Pago, Samoa, would help check French expansion in the South Pacific, and that another on the north Pacific coast, preferably San Francisco

Bay, would control American aggrandizement in California and Oregon.[3] However, Lord Aberdeen at the Foreign Office would act on neither suggestion because to incorporate further territories within the Empire would involve "heavy direct and still heavier indirect expenditure, besides multiplying the liabilities of misunderstanding and collisions with Foreign Powers."[4]

Palmerston, who entered the Foreign Office as part of Lord John Russell's administration in July 1846, was more amenable to Ellenborough's suggestions; in 1847 and 1848 the Admiralty considered several locations, including the Galapagos, owned by Ecuador, and Panama, where the Navy had a coal depot. But both had unhealthy climates. Sites on the Mexican coast were similarly undesirable, though the islands of Cedros and Guadalupe near Baja California were classified as possibilities. In point of fact, however, neither Palmerston nor the Admiralty thought it expedient to acquire either of these, as such a move would appear to the United States to be a clandestine operation on the part of Britain.[5]

However, in 1846, when Britain gained uncontested title to lands bordering on the North Pacific, it was possible to establish a naval base somewhere on the British portion without fear of an international incident. The Oregon crisis had revealed that Vancouver Island could furnish many supplies to British warships. The Hudson's Bay Company's Fort Victoria usually could supply provisions. Timbers suitable for spars were available there, as was water. And coal deposits near the north end of the Island appeared promising.[6] Fear of war was good for trade.

Esquimalt, three miles to the west of Fort Victoria, provided easy access to sailing vessels, as it was large and virtually landlocked. Its upper or northern reaches entirely justified its Lekwungen name, *Iswhoymalth*, meaning "a place gradually shoaling." Along the harbour's southern and more rocky shores stood brooding hemlock and firs. By contrast to ports-of-call in the South Seas, however, Esquimalt was less than exotic. It lacked swaying palms, tropical sun and Polynesian hospitality. Even so, it was healthier, with a temperate climate. Sailors, after long sea passages, found some solace in the English society of nearby Victoria, in hunting and fishing in the area, in a welcome change of climate and, for a few, the chance to desert to nearby goldfields. There were brothels and public houses, and the first pub was opened at Parson's Bridge in 1855. Accordingly, Esquimalt was not entirely detested by seamen.

Growing Pains

An observer fortunate enough to be standing on Duntze Head on the east side of the entrance to Esquimalt Harbour on July 25, 1848, would have seen the approach of the first of Her Majesty's ships to anchor there: the fine frigate *Constance*, mounting 50 guns, and one of the many men-of-war built in Pembroke Yard, Wales. On that day, thousands of miles from Portsmouth, she quit the stormy waters of the Pacific by entering Juan de Fuca Strait at Cape Flattery and made her way, as winds, tides and currents would allow, up the 15-mile-wide strait until clear of treacherous Race Rocks islets. Then she came into full view, sails bright against the Olympic mountain ramparts on the far American shore. She then shaped a course so as to run directly into Esquimalt Harbour, taking Fisgard Island to port and Duntze Head to starboard. All the foretopmen were attentively in their place, ready to loosen sails on command as she swung around into the wind, and at the bosun's piercing call the canvas was furled, the hull gradually slowed as she came up into the prevailing wind. Almost as if by magic, the clanking of the anchor chain running out and finding its depth echoed round the harbour and through nearby forests, and she came safely to anchor, protected from the prevailing winds, in the snug cove in the southeast corner of Esquimalt Harbour that was to bear the ship's name. The *Constance* was later followed by over one hundred British warships that made Constance Cove their usual haven on the Northwest Coast. Britain had found its anchor of empire in the North Pacific, and from this Canada was to acquire the watchtower on its western shore, with tentacles to the high Arctic and potential influences reaching across the wide Pacific Ocean to Asian shores.

Little by little the Navy occupied lands to the east and south of Constance Cove. One prize possession was Thetis Island, first used as a refitting spot by the *Thetis* in 1852, on which crews of shore parties from various ships built primitive sawpits, coal sheds, and blacksmith and carpenter shops. In the course of the speculation in land that accompanied the Fraser River gold rush, James Douglas and John Work, as self-styled "Trustees for the Fur Trade," sold the island to one Jeremiah Nagle for £1. This transaction threatened to rob the Navy of the only land it used in the harbour, and the real-estate grab alarmed Rear-Admiral Bruce, Commander-in-Chief, Pacific. He pointed out that

231

possession was nine-tenths of the law and advised the secretary of the Admiralty that Thetis Island doubtless was naval property by virtue of its occupancy by the Navy for at least 15 years.[7] The struggle for Thetis Island had begun.

In subsequent discussions involving the Admiralty, the Colonial Office and the Hudson's Bay Company, which owned most of the land around the harbour, the Company acknowledged Admiralty title to Thetis Island.[8] This constituted a reservation of land for naval purposes, the first of its kind at Esquimalt, and it conformed to the provisions stipulated in the charter of grant of 1849 by which the Company obtained colonizing powers at Vancouver Island. The value of Thetis Island was enhanced in 1860 when the Admiralty approved construction of a depot there to hold 1,300 to 1,400 tons of coal. This project was designed to eliminate the necessity for all ships needing coal to go to the pit-heads at Nanaimo, some 80 miles by sea to the north.[9]

The grand occasion of the acceptance of the first vessel into the new graving dock at Esquimalt, 1887. The ship is the composite sloop *Cormorant*, the second of her name to visit this port. The dock, which revolutionized the geopolitics of the North Pacific and made Esquimalt into an imperial watchtower, was a triumph of Canadian politics, British Columbia's patience and imperial fixing. The powerful flagship *Triumph* can been seen in the distance. CFB ESQUIMALT NAVAL & MILITARY MUSEUM

As shipping in Juan de Fuca Strait increased with colonial development, particularly at the time of the Fraser gold rush, many marine tragedies occurred on the south end of Vancouver Island. Already in 1846, Captain Kellett, on survey in the *Herald*, warned about Race Rocks as "this dangerous group . . . for the tide makes a perfect race around it." Many merchant vessels came to grief nearby, with heavy loss of life. Colonial correspondence contains many accounts that make for melancholy reading. On the recommendation of that famed surveyor Captain George Henry Richards, who toiled in these seas in the late 1850s and early 1860s and directed what can be said to be one of the most magnificent surveys (conducted by various warships), the imperial government agreed that two lighthouses needed to be put up as aids to navigation for vessels in the waters of southernmost Vancouver Island and Juan de Fuca Strait. There was urgency to this work, as the toll of ships and lives mounted. At the narrowing entrance of Esquimalt, on a cluster of rocks called Fisgard Island, contractors and specialists put up a lighthouse in 1860. This lighthouse, visible to mariners for 10 miles in clear weather, was complemented by another built at hazardous Race Rocks Islets. The two lighthouses, which enabled ships to enter Esquimalt by day or night in good weather, are still in use, although nowadays navigating officers employ more sophisticated electronic devices for navigation. Fisgard Island was lit November 16, 1860; Race Rocks, December 26. Here was an imperishable British gift to British Columbia trade and navigation.

The Americans already had won the laurels, for they had lighthouses at high rocky Tatoosh Island (1857), Cape Flattery (1857), New Dungeness (1857) and Smith Island (1858). The US Coast Survey commenced in 1849 to find suitable places for lights and recommended 16 in all. Construction of Tatoosh proved difficult, for Haida and Nootkan peoples used it for summer whale hunts and for fishing. A smallpox epidemic broke out, killing at least five hundred in the local Makah village, and the Native Americans laid the blame for the plague on the newcomers. As a result, the Tatoosh Island light was built in an era of high tensions and fears, and the constructors put up a fortified blockhouse for defence. For years afterwards, Native tribes fought wars here, and many a lighthouse keeper quit early. The US Coast Guard made many more contributions to the safety of mariners in these seas, and when smuggling across the border into British territories led the federal government to establish the Puget Sound Collection District at Olympia, Washington Territory, in 1851—the first unit of the US Coast Guard stationed in the Washington and Oregon Territories—the cutter *Jefferson Davis* was soon ploughing the waters of Puget Sound and Juan de Fuca Strait.[10] Over time, Port Angeles, opposite Victoria, became operational base of the Coast Guard for the strait.

Across the strait on the British side, the marine infrastructure of naval supremacy continued to be enlarged. The southern shore of Esquimalt Harbour adjacent to Thetis Island provided several good bays, and auxiliary services were developed on these. This provided the foundation for a small dockyard complex that was constructed later. At the western extremity of this southern shore was Duntze Head, known locally as "Old Hospital Point," where hospital huts were erected in 1855 during the Crimean War.[11] These buildings were put in efficient condition in 1858, and their grounds generally were considered as government property. Nearby stood Esquimalt Village, a cluster of ship-chandleries, dwellings, public houses and brothels. To the east lay Signal Hill, its strategic position commanding

The admiral's residence, known as Maple Bank, on Admirals Road, was built by Rear-Admiral the Honourable Joseph Denman, the famous anti-slave trader and son of the Lord Chief Justice of England. The social nexus for invited officers and local worthies, it was the scene of many gatherings, as in this croquet party of the emblematic Victorian age when Britannia ruled the waves.
CFB ESQUIMALT NAVAL & MILITARY MUSEUM

the rocky peninsula that enclosed Esquimalt Harbour on the south, and along which rough roads led to Victoria on the east.

On the northeastern side of Constance Cove, barracks, which were constructed for the Royal Engineers engaged in the Boundary Commission survey of 1859–1862, were destined to become naval property—simply to keep them from falling into private hands. Farther north on this same shore stood "Dallas Bank," later known as "Maple Bank," where the commander-in-chief resided after 1864. In the upper reaches of Esquimalt Harbour lay Cole Island, chosen by naval and military officers as a site for a munitions depot in 1860, one year after the Admiralty decided to establish a powder magazine to supply Her Majesty's ships in the North Pacific.

Such a facility seemed especially necessary because the international tension between Britain and the United States appeared likely to develop into war. As Rear-Admiral Sir Thomas Maitland pointed out to the Admiralty, a powder magazine had to be built as soon as possible, for there was no secure place for ammunition. In case of war, months would pass before a supply could be sent out from England, and ammunition at

Royal Marine guard at Cole (Magazine) Island, the ammunition depot, upper Esquimalt Harbour. These soldiers of the Queen's Navy were essential for the security of the Service. It was vital that the ammunition and other stores of explosive materials be kept safe from theft and mischief.
IMAGE C-07551 COURTESY OF THE ROYAL BC MUSEUM AND ARCHIVES

Valparaiso was not only too far away but was also subject to the vagaries of politics in Chile.[12] By the end of 1862, the magazine had been constructed on Cole Island, and a marine guard posted day and night to prevent thefts. No longer were powder and shell sent to the storeships at Valparaiso and Callao. The Admiralty decision to erect a munitions depot at Esquimalt Harbour was consistent with its realization that the headquarters of the Pacific squadron would be transferred from Valparaiso to Esquimalt.[13]

Esquimalt Becomes Pacific Station Headquarters

The 1862 decision to transfer the station headquarters from Valparaiso was dictated mainly by political influences. Admittedly, the need for a depot to hold provisions and naval stores at Esquimalt had become evident as early as 1851, when Rear-Admiral Moresby, Commander-in-Chief, Pacific, recommended that the harbour be reserved for naval purposes.[14] A similar suggestion came four years later from Rear-Admiral Bruce.[15] But as we have seen, the Admiralty and Foreign Office neglected to give more than casual thought to the problem of a satisfactory base for the Pacific squadron until the Crimean War. At that time the rise of Russian naval power in the Pacific, and the suspected clandestine cooperation of the United States with Russia in 1856, alarmed Sir Charles Wood, the First Lord of the Admiralty. Wood knew that increasing the number of British warships in the Pacific would be expensive, though not difficult; but—as he advised the Earl of Clarendon, the foreign secretary—"the want of any good place for repairs and refitting is serious."[16] He hoped a remedy could be found; accordingly, instructions were sent to Bruce to report on the suitability of Esquimalt and other sites on Vancouver Island as a naval base.[17] No other locations were under consideration.

After his visit to Vancouver Island in the summer of 1856, Bruce advocated that a base be located at Esquimalt. In his opinion, this would strengthen the British Colony of Vancouver Island, "sandwiched" as it was between territories of two expanding powers, Russia and the United States.[18] But in the postwar period, in keeping with the ministry's concern for British interests in Central America that were threatened by American filibusters, the Admiralty considered Taboga Island off Panama as a possible base.[19] The Pacific Steam Navigation Company maintained a storehouse and hospital there, and the Navy, as already mentioned, possessed a coal depot. Esquimalt was momentarily forgotten.

However, the northward shift of the focus of station duties in 1858 and 1859 constituted one important reason for rejecting Taboga Island. The Northwest Coast was where most ships on station were needed, and to a degree that required more than the periodic attention of the commander-in-chief. Captain James Prevost, the senior naval officer at Vancouver Island, touched on this fact when he wrote to the secretary of the Admiralty in 1858 that the value of Vancouver Island to Britain increased with the rapid growth of American interests in the Oregon and Washington Territories. With more ships-of-war calling at Esquimalt, even a temporary establishment for coal and provisions would be useful.[20]

The lack of a base of operations in the North Pacific became even more noticeable during the Fraser River gold rush and the San Juan boundary dispute. The flagship *Ganges*, for example, was unable to proceed to the storeships at Callao and Valparaiso for nearly two years, and her return to England was delayed because she could not carry out a quick refit at Esquimalt.[21] It is not surprising that Rear-Admiral Baynes recommended establishing a supply depot at Esquimalt.[22]

The Admiralty wanted to find a solution and lost no time in reviewing the question of the best location for the Pacific station headquarters. The higher cost of sending supplies to Esquimalt compared to Panama caused some concern.[23] Nevertheless, by 1859 it had become apparent at the Admiralty that in Vancouver Island, Britain possessed a colony "offering all the advantages we can desire."[24] By frequenting this territory, the Navy would protect its trade, increase its commerce and develop its resources. Britain could expect freight rates to decline with the growth of trade. Above all, increased strategic advantages would arise from having a base in the North Pacific.[25] This convincing argument shifted Admiralty policy in favour of Esquimalt.

The supporting views of Vice-Admiral W.F. ("Fly") Martin, the Senior Naval Lord, were of powerful influence. Martin realized that the duties of the squadron were shifting gradually from southern to northern latitudes, and that the centre of British interests in the eastern Pacific was in actuality the British portion of the Northwest Coast of America. This judgement was accurate. Without reservation, he advocated that a harbour on

Vancouver Island should become the station headquarters—not necessarily Esquimalt, but certainly the best one available. And, with an eye to the future, he wrote:

> The sooner this is done, the sooner we shall be able to commence arrangements indispensable for operations in the Pacific in the event of a war with the United States or Russia. If these powers have dockyards & resources in the North Pacific and we have not, for every shilling spent by either of them, in that sea, in a war with us, we should spend a Guinea. Indeed, without some basis of operations in Vancouver island, we should have to abandon those seas in an American War. The duties of the station can be as well conducted from Vancouver's island as from Valparaiso or the Bay of Panama whilst the frequent visits of our ships will be of infinite importance to the colony.[26]

The Lords of the Admiralty were now in general agreement that a change from Valparaiso to Vancouver Island was desirable, but they deferred the decision until Rear-Admiral Baynes could report on matters of supply, depot ships, communications, sites for a naval yard and hospital, and, notably, the benefits that the presence of the Navy would confer on the colonies of Vancouver Island and British Columbia.[27] In connection with the last of these objectives, instructions subsequently sent to Baynes stated clearly that the proposed transfer to northern waters would not affect operations in the Pacific islands, and added: "While in a political point of view and in connection with Kamschatka [sic] and with China, the position of British Columbia may present important advantages which should be fully considered in your report."[28]

Baynes's reply testifies both to the shift of British interests to the North Pacific and to the superiority of Esquimalt over Panama as the Pacific naval station headquarters. Only on two counts did Baynes question the suitability of Esquimalt. He was concerned about the ease with which sailors could desert from there to the goldfields of Pacific America, and the ease with which enemy warships could shell the harbour.[29] In view of Esquimalt's military vulnerability, he was reluctant to recommend it as station headquarters until after Captain Richards of HMS *Plumper* completed surveys of the Island's harbours and an alternative site at Burrard Inlet, a commodious haven on the mainland shore near the mouth of the Fraser River.[30]

To Baynes, the obvious disadvantages of Esquimalt were of no consequence in comparison to its principal advantage: providing a base from which British warships could support the infant colony. Baynes firmly believed that the British possessions on the Northwest Coast promised to become "of immense importance," for their healthy climate and secure harbours would foster commercial development and population growth.[31] Their proximity to Russian America on the north and the United States on the south were proof to him that at all times they deserved as much care as the British government and the Commander-in-Chief, Pacific, could give them. This meant that a harbour on Vancouver Island should be designated as the Pacific station headquarters.

The surveys of Captain Richards showed not only that Esquimalt was unquestionably the most suitable harbour on the British portion of the Northwest Coast, but also that it could be properly defended.[32] This was all that Baynes required to press the Admiralty for the transfer of the headquarters.[33] Probably his recommendation would have been acted on at once if a change had not occurred in the Admiralty's membership when a new cabinet was formed in June 1859. Panic over the rapid construction of armoured ships by France, notably *La Gloire*, also caused the much less critical issue of the Pacific station headquarters to receive little if any attention until the following March. Even then, their Lordships seemed reluctant to follow the policy of their immediate predecessors. They instructed Rear-Admiral Sir Thomas Maitland, the incoming commander-in-chief, to report on the suitability of Esquimalt as station headquarters. This caused additional delay in resolving what the Comptroller of Victualling considered to be a most critical question.[34]

Maitland's recommendations were remarkably similar to those of Baynes and therefore need little comment here.[35] In the main, the Admiralty policy of 1862 on the change of station headquarters from Valparaiso to Esquimalt was based on these recommendations.[36] On only one matter was there a difference of opinion. Maitland recommended that an old frigate be used as a storeship at Esquimalt until storehouses were built. However, the Admiralty decided to construct storehouses immediately and allocated £1,000 for that purpose. This proved to be a hasty decision, for the Admiralty soon learned to its chagrin—as naval commanders had warned—that the Navy held no clear title to suitable land in Esquimalt Harbour other than Thetis Island, which by this time was almost entirely covered with coal sheds.[37] Consequently, the construction of the storehouses had to be deferred to a later date.[38]

The Admiralty's decision to transfer the station headquarters to Esquimalt represented a significant step in the growth of British commercial and political interests on the Northwest Coast.[39] This development, especially auspicious for the colonies of Vancouver Island and British Columbia, resulted in an expansion of naval base facilities in 1863 and 1864. A guardhouse was built on Duntze Head, and the hospital was removed to buildings vacated by the Royal Engineers on the northeastern side of Constance Cove.[40] The hospital now became a permanent facility, as opposed to a temporary one, in keeping with the importance Esquimalt had assumed as station headquarters.[41] In view of this expansion, the colonial administration at Vancouver Island refused permission to private individuals wishing to build wharves in Esquimalt Harbour until such time as the Admiralty formulated its plans for the naval establishment.[42] All this indicated a growing importance—albeit small in comparison to other parts of the world—of British interests in the Pacific.

A fur trader who later became a Collector of Customs summed up Esquimalt's importance to the British in 1863:

> Apart from its immense advantages of access for the larger class of vessels in a mercantile point of view, it [Esquimalt] has been selected as the rallying point for the squadrons commissioned to protect in the North Pacific the interests of Great Britain. Here in a landlocked harbour wherein large fleets may be safely moored with a thriving colony of British subjects around, and with a sister colony (that of British Columbia) teeming with mineral wealth, and within a few hours sail, commanding, too, as it does in the hands of Britain, should future difficulty arise, the whole commerce of the N. Pacific, from California to Siberia, from Siberia to Japan, Esquimalt it would seem, is destined to become a point of extreme importance on the Western Coast of America for the furtherance and protection of British interests and commerce.[43]

The Quickening Pace of Esquimalt after 1862

Although Esquimalt had become the chief haven of the Navy in the Pacific and the focal point of its operations in 1862, no proper depot for provisions, clothing or stores had been constructed. It was still necessary for ships to go to Valparaiso to replenish stores and for some refitting purposes. The limited facilities that Esquimalt did possess for storage—two small storehouses built on Duntze Head in 1862—were constructed of wood, which made them a fire hazard. What is more, they had been built unwisely in a position exposed to possible enemy bombardment. When Rear-Admiral John Kingcome reviewed the matter in 1863, he came to the conclusion that the storehouses should be moved to a more protected site within the harbour. In this he knew he had the support of the War Office, which had objected to buildings being constructed on Duntze Head, for this strategic position commanded the narrow harbour entrance and provided a likely site for future gun emplacements.[44] Henceforth, future structures were built of brick and in more secure positions.

By the close of 1863, Kingcome had realized some of his aims. A small staff consisting of an assistant paymaster, clerk, ship's steward, storeman and cooper had arrived from England to take charge of the storehouses.[45]

Pioneer Street in Esquimalt running down to a jetty, with various establishments for recreation, rest and repair. Then as now, the Navy was good for business and vice versa. CFB ESQUIMALT NAVAL & MILITARY MUSEUM

Ammunition was now stored on Cole Island and on Thetis Island, all "in sight of and under the immediate care of the Senior Officer at Esquimalt" and visited nightly by a guard boat.[46] Stores were transferred from Valparaiso to Esquimalt, and provisions were sent directly from England to Esquimalt along with machinery required for maintaining a navy then undergoing a technological transformation.[47] Valparaiso's role as a supply centre declined.

This formative period in Esquimalt's history, in the years between 1858 and 1864, occurred when Admiralty policy, reflecting British government attitudes, opposed spending large sums on shore establishments anywhere in the world. Accordingly, facilities at Esquimalt developed somewhat haphazardly and with great difficulty in view of the high costs of land brought about by the gold rush of 1858–1859 and the erection of mercantile establishments on the harbour shores. Even after plans for the naval and victualling stores depot were approved in 1865, the commander-in-chief considered stationing a storeship in Esquimalt Harbour as a cheaper measure than purchasing property ashore. When figures were cited to

Old Esquimalt Village, circa 1890s, with various British men-of-war at their moorings.
CFB ESQUIMALT NAVAL & MILITARY MUSEUM

show that the storeship *Naiad* at Callao cost over £6,000 yearly to operate and required the services of 35 men, the Admiralty dismissed the idea of stationing a storeship at Vancouver Island. The Board believed it better to spend money on shore establishments.[48]

What their Lordships had in mind in 1865, when they authorized a small "naval and victualling" depot at Esquimalt, was creating facilities to hold provisions and stores. Among other things, they felt that the increasing importance of the Colony of Vancouver Island made Esquimalt the best choice for such a depot for the Pacific squadron.[49] Actually, however, the Admiralty was merely authorizing the administration of an establishment that already existed.[50]

In 1866, more structures were erected to hold machinery for re-venting guns, to store spars and to house ordnance supplies. During the winter of 1866–1867, St. Paul's Anglican Church was built just south of Signal Hill.[51] A dry-dock was in the planning stage.

Commander Richard C. Mayne had deplored the fact that five British warships stationed at Vancouver Island were reliant on an American dry-dock at Mare Island in San Francisco Bay, the only facility of its kind in the North Pacific. In 1861 the surveying vessel *Hecate*, 6 guns, ran aground, and after provisional repairs were made at Esquimalt, she was convoyed by another British warship to Mare Island. Referring to the charged atmosphere in Anglo-American relations at the time of the *Trent* affair (see chapter 10), Mayne complained that this accident occurred when war with the Americans seemed imminent. "Had it broken out," he concluded, "the 'Hecate' must have been trapped, and the services of a powerful steamer would have been lost to the country."[52]

Retrenchment

With the planning of the much-needed dry-dock, it appeared that Esquimalt soon would be a naval establishment fully capable of serving a squadron of 12 to 15 ships, ranging in size from the ironclad *Zealous* to the gunboat *Forward*. However, the necessity for economy led the Admiralty to shelve all plans for expansion of the naval base in 1869.

This is not the place to examine fully the implications of drastic economy measures on the efficiency of the fleet. Suffice it to say that as early as the seventeenth century, men such as Samuel Pepys, that diligent historian of maritime affairs, realized that large economies could not be made without some decline in the condition of the naval service. Pepys wrote: "The ordinary way in all times in England, upon want of money and disquiets in government, [is] to find faults with the management of expensefulness of the Navy, determining generally in some insignificant retrenchments of charge for the better rectifying their complaints; but to the real disservice of the State, the retrenchments having [been] always such as have been afterwards found necessary to be revoked, with increase."[53]

Nonetheless, in Gladstone's first ministry, formed in 1868, H.G.C. Childers, the First Lord of the Admiralty, willingly supported his prime minister's ideas for retrenchment in armaments spending. Under Childers, the Admiralty opposed increasing the facilities at Esquimalt to meet all possible emergencies on the station and opposed keeping more than "ordinary stores."[54] The latter policy to limit naval stores was adopted against the advice of the Storekeeper General of the Admiralty, the Honourable Robert Dundas. He complained vehemently that as long as ships were on duty in the North Pacific, a port there for refit and replenishment was essential. He went even further, saying that any economy that might result from reverting to Valparaiso would reproduce the inconvenient system that the Order-in-Council of 1865 had tried to eliminate.[55] But his words went unheeded; in the interests of "economy," the station headquarters reverted to Valparaiso in 1869.[56] In addition, the naval force maintained in the Pacific was reduced to 10 ships (one ironclad as flagship, five corvettes or sloops, three smaller vessels and one stationary storeship) and about two thousand men.[57]

Esquimalt was not alone in suffering from government frugality in 1869. The China, East Indies, Cape, West Coast of Africa and South East Coast of South America stations were also reduced by a total of about 14 ships and 2,600 to 2,700 men.[58] To compensate for this reduction, as well as for other reasons, the Admiralty created a training or "Flying Squadron," as it became generally known, consisting of six screw-warships.[59] It made a round-the-world voyage in 1869–1870, calling briefly at various naval bases and coaling stations, including Esquimalt.[60] Rival powers may have been impressed by Britain's ability to spare so many ships for this purpose, but they must also have been aware of the decrease in naval strength abroad in subsequent years, as illustrated by the reduction of the Pacific station from 13 ships and 2,968 men in 1869 to 9 ships and 1,595 men by 1874.[61]

The development of Esquimalt as a naval base had been halted by 1869. However, the existing facilities continued to be useful to ships of the Pacific squadron, particularly those assigned to duties on the Northwest Coast. At that time there was always one frigate as "post ship" at Esquimalt, plus the gunvessel *Sparrowhawk* and the gunboat *Boxer* on permanent service for visiting coastal settlements, policing the Natives and checking illicit whisky traffic.[62]

Esquimalt's buildings still held half of all stores kept on the station. Its coal sheds, timber yards and hospital remained in operation. Its heavy machinery in the factory was still in use: a large screw-cutting lathe, a drilling machine, a forge and a furnace for casting metal were the only equipment of the kind available exclusively to ships of the Pacific squadron. In spite of demands for economy from inside or outside the cabinet, circumstances made Esquimalt, for strategic reasons, the naval base—although not the declared headquarters—of the Royal Navy's ships in the Pacific.[63]

ten

No NEED FOR GLORY:
ANGLO-AMERICAN TENSIONS

Of all the turbulent decades of British Columbia's history, arguably none matches the 1860s. Hard on the heels of the Fraser River gold-rush panic and the onset of the San Juan Island pig war came a new and urgent crisis—civil war in the United States, a war for the Union (of which more presently). Nagging defence needs of the Pacific colonies of Vancouver Island and British Columbia in the face of external threats, some real and others imagined or exaggerated, preoccupied the local press and the governors of that age, and spread to the thinking of strategists in London. The horrific and complicated Civil War in the United States brought unimagined problems to the British and the Empire, and so did the prospects of an invasion of British soil in North America by the feisty Fenian Brotherhood promoting Ireland's revolution. Added to this was the fact that Russia sold Alaska during this time, and suddenly British Columbia had a new, potentially aggressive, northern neighbour. In the circumstances, British investors were rightly alarmed by the perilous state of their capital as American expansionists looked eagerly for an opportunity to add to the real estate of the Republic. In the cozy corridors of power in Whitehall, the Colonial Office, driven by policies that made no sense out on the worried margins of empire, appeared reluctant to provide funds for local defence, though on request it did agree to ship rifles and ammunition for volunteer militia units. In New Westminster and Victoria, the press fumed at the neglect afforded patriotic colonists by an indifferent parent state. The Royal Navy, however, and the Admiralty never faded from view—and faithfully kept watch as they had done since the beginning of the Oregon crisis. Canada, the instant confederation of 1867, was anxious for an outlet on the Pacific Ocean, and the Colonial Office encouraged politicians in the two Pacific colonies to consider joining the new dominion. The union of the colonies of Vancouver Island and British Columbia in November 1868 was a preliminary to entry into the federation, even as it increased the rivalry between the two colonial capitals, Victoria and New Westminster. As the whirlwind decade closed, British Columbia stood at the crossroads. When annexation to the United States was rejected, union with Canada seemed the only way forward, but when it came on July 20, 1871, it offered a new but unpromising dawn.

These then are the complications of the 1860s, Canada's most critical decade—and its defining moment. Our long view taken on this era is that the greatest stimulus to development of British territories in North America during the nineteenth century was fear, whether real or imaginary, of American expansionist tendencies. This was a century of rivalry in continental aspirations and, increasingly, in maritime enterprise. Long-standing grievances were involved, some of which originated west of the Rocky Mountains. These differences remained unresolved through the War of 1812 and nearly resulted in hostilities during the Oregon crisis and the Crimean War. Now, in 1861, a new crisis loomed. In the course of the American Civil War, several incidents involving Britain endangered the peace. Once again the British exercised fleet and gunboat diplomacy on a large scale.

The policies of Britain and the activities of the Royal Navy in the decade of Anglo-American tensions extending from the beginning of the Civil War in 1861 to British Columbia's entry into the Canadian Confederation in 1871 were designed to safeguard British sovereignty on the Northwest Coast. In view of plans for a Canadian transcontinental railway, the headquarters of the Royal Navy's Pacific squadron at Esquimalt took on a new and bullish position in imperial defence. British strategists looked on Esquimalt as the eventual and natural terminus of a railway—the steel of empire—considered vital to the defence of the Empire. They saw it also (for profit was linked to power) as something much grander: a gateway to British possessions and trade in the Orient. All this lay in the future, for inasmuch as the Canadian Pacific Railway was not completed until 1885, British Columbia remained isolated from the rest of Canada, and because problems of military defence remained unresolved, the Royal Navy continued as the sure shield of British Columbia.

"Naval Security" during the American Civil War

Uncompromising differences between free and slave-holding states in the Union led to armed conflict between the mainly industrial North and the agrarian South, with war triggered at Charleston, South Carolina, April 12, 1861, when the Confederate Army opened fire on federally held Fort Sumter. The Confederate States of America alleged that Fort Sumter threatened their newly proclaimed sovereignty. These shots reverberated around the world. So began the most destructive conflict in the Western world since the end of the Napoleonic wars in 1815 and until the start of the First World War in 1914. The differences in question arose over the power of the national government to prohibit slavery in western territories not yet states. Then came the election of President Lincoln, and shortly thereafter seven states established the Confederate States of America. Others later joined. The war began in earnest in 1862, and it was not until the spring of 1865 that the principal Confederate armies laid down their arms. Union cavalry captured a fleeing President Jefferson Davis in Georgia in May 1865, Confederate resistance collapsed and the war ended. Then began the rebuilding of a united nation free of slavery.

The war between the Union and the Confederacy occurred pre-cisely at the time that the British Parliament was dominated by "little England" theories. Colonies were widely proclaimed to be a millstone round the neck of the mother country, and garrisons overseas were a drain on the Exchequer. The years between 1861 and 1871 found British politicians and public alike opposed to building costly fortifications abroad, manned by British troops, invariably at the expense of the taxpayer at home.[1] Self-government implied self-defence; or as the senior statesman W.E. Gladstone, a former colonial secretary, put it so aptly in 1864, it was "impossible to separate the blessings and benefits of freedom from its burdens."[2] Under successive secretaries of state for war and the colonies, the "burdens" were gradually shifted in the main to the self-governing parts of the Empire.[3] But in the case of Vancouver Island and British Columbia, the Select Committee of the House of Commons appointed in 1861 to consider the apportionment of colonial military expenditure reported quite correctly that considerable contributions could not be expected from these two colonies to defray costs for the Royal Engineers stationed there since 1859. The reason given was that these colonies had only just been settled.[4] Although they were not self-governing, as "Colonies Proper" they were classified, perhaps optimistically, as largely responsible for the costs of their own military defence. In March 1862, the Commons, on the basis of this report, adopted a resolution that self-governing colonies should be mainly responsible for their internal order and defence and ought to assist in their own "external defence."[5] Such were the government's intentions. In point of fact, the colonies of Vancouver Island and British Columbia were unable and unwilling to undertake their own defence. With a settler population of only about fourteen thousand in 1861, they could ill afford the detachment of Royal Engineers—which was disbanded subsequently in November 1863.

In these peculiar circumstances, defence of the Pacific colonies remained the responsibility of the Navy. As long as warships continued to visit settlements on Vancouver Island and British Columbia, a locally raised naval force—such as would eventually be permitted by the Colonial Naval Defence Act of 1865—was not required.[6] The colonists knew that the two gunboats *Forward* and *Grappler*, assigned permanently for coastal duties and assisted when necessary by steam frigates and corvettes that called at Esquimalt, would usually suffice. The use of these ships for the defence of these distant dependencies, however, did little to reduce burdens on the English taxpayer, as the government's reforms had intended. Instead of paying for garrisons they paid for gunboats.

From the outset of the American Civil War in April 1861, Britain occupied the position of observer of a conflict that would eventually cripple her trade with both the Union and the Confederacy. In order to avoid becoming involved in the struggle, she pursued a policy of neutrality. To this end, Governor James Douglas, previously censured by the secretary of state for the colonies for his belligerent plans in response to the American military occupation of San Juan Island in 1859, received carefully worded instructions, dated May 11, 1861, that in the event of an Anglo-American war, ships of the Royal Navy in the North Pacific were to show preference to neither Union nor Confederate forces.[7] Three months later, by August 7, the Commander-in-Chief, Pacific, possessed the Queen's Proclamation of May 15 ordering that neutrality was to be observed in all British dealings with the Union and Confederate governments.[8]

British warships, including the flagship and five of lesser force, gathered near the southern tip of Vancouver Island at the outbreak of the Civil War. Worry existed that the unresolved San Juan boundary dispute might lead to something more serious; a few American officials, spoiling for a fight, considered provoking quarrels with Britain, with the conquest of British North America in view.[9] Certainly, the colonies of Vancouver Island and British Columbia were likely targets. Realizing this, Lord Palmerston, the prime minister, suggested sending an infantry battalion from China to British Columbia and increasing the British squadrons in American waters.[10] The Colonial Office supported his view. But the First Lord of the Admiralty, the Duke of Somerset, who was shamefully ignorant of American naval strength in the Pacific, considered the British squadron of 12 ships adequate for the protection of the colonies on the Northwest Coast.[11] No troops were dispatched; the government recognized, in effect, that the security of these territories rested with "naval security."[12]

On November 8, 1861, an armed party from USS *San Jacinto* boarded the Southampton-bound British mail packet *Trent* in Bahama Channel. The *Trent* had sailed from Havana. Two envoys of the Confederate government, Mason and Slidell, who intended to visit London and Paris to petition for help in the Civil War, were taken forcibly from the British ship. British tempers flared. Feelings against the "Yankees" were potent in the north of England, where Lancashire was beginning its "cotton famine" and shutting down mills, a consequence of the Union blockade of Southern ports. Lord Palmerston fulminated, and Mason and Slidell were released, though they were not acclaimed when they arrived in England. To the British ministry, this incident constituted a flagrant violation of neutral rights at sea; from the British public it elicited some demands for war. The Foreign Office immediately sought redress from the United States government but, urging caution, made crystal clear to the Admiralty that all orders issued to admirals and officers commanding at sea should emphasize that they were to commence hostilities with United States forces only in self-defence.[13]

In these charged circumstances, the government took immediate steps to reinforce with men and munitions the British North American provinces that might be expected to bear the brunt in any Anglo-American war. All plans to withdraw regiments from British North America were cancelled, and between December 12, 1861, and January 4, 1862, the British government sent more than eleven thousand fully equipped troops to fortify the exposed Canadian frontier.[14] By the spring of 1862, some 18,000 regulars were stationed in British North America. While these figures seem impressive, it should not be overlooked that the British ministry recognized that superiority at sea—particularly on the Atlantic seaboard and the Great Lakes, the chief areas of contention and blockade—would be fundamental to British victory. In consequence, the North American and West Indies station was increased from 22 ships to about 30, the additions comprising mainly battleships and frigates; the Pacific squadron gained a corvette and sloop to bring the total to 14 vessels. The average number of warships on the Pacific station increased to its highest since the Oregon crisis—12 to 16 warships—during the years 1860 to 1867.[15]

Throughout the Civil War, the possibility existed that if Britain were to become involved, American shipping in the Pacific bearing letters-of-marque might prey on British interests scattered across the far reaches of that ocean. Rear-Admiral Sir Thomas Maitland, the Commander-in-Chief, Pacific, feared that 15 American clipper ships then at San Francisco might be converted into corvettes carrying 20 to 24 guns. He also feared that steamers plying the routes to Panama and Mexico could be similarly armed, not to mention numerous American ships in the guano trade and whaling industry.[16] To meet this contingency, he planned that in the event of war the British Pacific squadron would blockade San Francisco, thereby controlling the centre of American maritime activity on the Pacific coast. Further, at Panama, the flagship *Bacchante*, 51 guns, would watch all ship movements and protect British mail services and Pacific Steam Navigation Company establishments and vessels. But because the station headquarters at Esquimalt possessed no shore defences—it had neither a garrison nor a battery—Maitland had no plans to withdraw the four ships there—the steam frigate *Topaze*, the surveying paddle-sloop *Hecate* and the gunboats

Forward and *Grappler*—for service elsewhere on the north Pacific coast.[17] These vessels, the colonial guardians, remained at or near Esquimalt.

With full awareness of the critical state of affairs and the strength of the United States Navy in the Pacific, Maitland emphasized to the Admiralty the urgency of *"largely increasing without delay"* the Pacific squadron in order to protect British interests from Valparaiso to Vancouver Island.[18] By the time his urgent plea reached the Admiralty, the ministry, as noted above, had already strengthened the squadrons in American waters.

Ironically, American naval officers were similarly afraid of Britain's naval strength in the Pacific. Reports of "many" warships joining the British Pacific squadron from the China and East Indies station soon after the *Trent* affair duped the United States Commander-in-Chief, Pacific, into believing that the British were preparing for war with the United States.[19]

Actually, the British Pacific squadron was increased by only two ships, and one arrived from the Far East. But in another matter, the apprehensions of the American commander-in-chief were well founded. He feared that half the British squadron would suffice to "command" the city of San Francisco and take possession of the dockyard at nearby Mare Island owing to inadequate defences.[20] Certainly, he was right in concluding that these would be a British object of war. Because the British lacked docking facilities at Esquimalt and were dependent on the use of the Mare Island dock, British warships had no sure place to repair defects unless they seized and held San Francisco Bay and its environs.[21]

By contrast, neither the strange activities nor the numerical strength of the Russian imperial navy in the Pacific offered any serious threat to the British, although the more-than-friendly relations between Russia and the United States at this time must have concerned British naval commanders. Much has been written on the purpose of the visits in 1863 of six Russian corvettes to San Francisco Bay and a similar number to New York.[22] There can be little doubt, however, that this was a defensive measure on the part of the Russians. Probably they were in American ports seeking shelter from British and French forces, whose governments had opposed Russia's repression of the Poles in the preceding winter of 1862–1863. The inferiority of the Russian Navy in numbers and condition, as well as in supply and leadership, meant that rather than face the separate or combined British and French navies at sea, Russian warships preferred to seek refuge as they had during the Crimean War.[23] They represented a danger to the Royal Navy only in alliance with Lincoln's Union government.

Difficulties of Maintaining British Neutrality

From the outset of the Civil War, the Union Navy demonstrated its command of the seas by effectively blockading Confederate ports on the Atlantic coast and Gulf of Mexico. Because the blockade undermined the strength of the South, the secretary of the Confederate Navy believed that Confederate raiders preying on Northern commerce, which would compel the North to divert warships to protect her trade, could break it.[24] The South thus entered into contract with Liverpool shipbuilders for construction of the ironclad *Alabama* and others. These were designed with rams and the capacity to mount heavy guns. As a result, relations between Washington and London became severely strained, for the North thought that the supposedly neutral British were assisting the Confederacy. Their resentment was understandable. In July 1862 the *Alabama* sailed from Liverpool, under the watch of British officials, to prey on Union shipping.

New York merchants, bankers and shipping interests feared that English-built Confederate ships and other Confederate privateers would prey on Pacific Mail Steamship Company vessels that carried some $40 million annually from California to Panama for transshipment to New York.[25] The Union Navy, in consequence, was given orders to watch the Panama route.[26] The American consul at Panama knew that the task of the Union Navy would be easier if British warships on the Pacific station captured prizes taken by Confederate privateers. He endeavoured to solicit the support of his British counterpart at Panama by arguing that these prizes were a danger to British as well as to Union shipping, but without success.[27] British policy would not allow collaboration of this sort, and the Royal Navy adhered to strict neutrality.

On the question of the use of British ports, the Northern States realized that Victoria and Esquimalt were likely places for parties sympathetic to the Confederacy to equip privateers, because of the proximity of these harbours to the Pacific states. As a matter of fact, a large portion of the settler population of Vancouver Island favoured the Confederate cause, although the exact numbers cannot be known.[28] Consequently, the American consul at Victoria and captains of visiting Union warships watched for Confederate

activity, although early rumours that Confederates were outfitting privateers on the Pacific coast proved groundless.[29]

Simultaneously, United States government officials searched the Great
Lakes area for enemy vessels. Rumours in 1861 that the British ship *Peerless*,
at Toronto, was a Confederate privateer, aggravated the charged atmosphere
in Anglo-American relations.[30] At this time, British naval commanders were
under orders to prohibit the entry of belligerent warships and their prizes
into the neutral waters of the British colonies on the Northwest Coast.[31]
This measure was designed to prevent warships from converting prizes into
privateers in British ports. Moreover, the Foreign Office had instructed the
Admiralty to carry out the Queen's Proclamation of Strict Neutrality, dated
January 31, 1862, to prevent either side from using British territorial waters
and ports.[32] By these steps, the British government demonstrated a willingness to cooperate with the Union to ensure that Confederate privateers were
not outfitted in British ports. Failure to do this might have led to war, for the
United States was outraged that the Foreign Office did nothing to stop the
Confederate raider *Alabama* from sailing out of Liverpool in July 1862.

Early in 1863, when the American secretary of state William Seward
received information that a Confederate commodore was planning to purchase and man the British steamer *Thames* in Victoria, he asked Lord Lyons,
the British minister in Washington, to stop the project. Lyons was able to
pacify Seward with a promise that everything would be done by Governor
Douglas at Vancouver Island to halt such attempts.[33] But when Victor
Smith, the ill-informed Collector of Customs for Puget Sound, reported
that Confederate privateers were fitting out at Vancouver Island, that seces-
sionists were active there and that official authorities would not act to stop
them, Seward's fears were reinforced. The USS *Saginaw*, a side-wheel sloop
of war based on San Francisco, was sent to investigate.[34] She found that no
privateer had been fitted out at Victoria or elsewhere on the Pacific Coast.[35]

The Union undertook another search of Esquimalt and Victoria
in the following year, 1864. This occurred after the American consulate at Victoria had informed the Military Department of Oregon that a
Confederate privateer was preparing for sea with the purpose of capturing Union steamers carrying treasure on the Mexican Coast.[36] The USS
Narragansett, sent from San Francisco to reconnoitre, found no activity.
However, her use of Esquimalt Harbour for days at a time—ostensibly to

get in touch with a mail steamer from California and to coal, but actually to gain intelligence of Confederate activity—led the senior naval officer at Esquimalt, Captain Edward Hardinge, to complain to her commander that his action contravened the British policy of strict neutrality.[37] The Admiralty then forwarded instructions that the 48-hour limit for belligerent ships' visits was to be "strictly enforced at Vancouver Island."[38]

In the Pacific, the only real cause for alarm arose from the activities of the Confederate raider *Shenandoah*, commanded by the now-famous Raphael Semmes. After sailing from London in October 1864 and receiving armament and ammunition at Madeira, she set a course for Australia by way of the Cape of Good Hope. She made her way into the Pacific in early 1865. During June she destroyed the American whaling fleet in Bering Sea before turning south in search of American merchantmen bound for California from the Orient. When Semmes learned on August 2 that the Confederacy had capitulated, he decided to surrender his ship in England. After capturing 38 vessels in her brilliant career, the *Shenandoah*, in the guise of a merchantman, rounded Cape Horn and reached Liverpool on November 6.[39] So ended the career of the last of the famous Dixie raiders.

While this part of the drama was being played out, and until United States and British officials on the north Pacific coast learned of the surrender of the *Shenandoah*, they were forced to consider her still at large. Indeed, in July 1865 she was rumoured to be near Vancouver Island. American warships searched for her at the neutral port of Esquimalt, a likely place to dispose of her armament. The Royal Navy in the Pacific searched for her also, fearing that she would be a danger to neutral shipping should she decide not to surrender. The commander-in-chief, Rear-Admiral the Honourable Joseph Denman, wisely instructed his squadron that if the *Shenandoah* entered Esquimalt Harbour, she was not to leave without being disarmed.[40] In doing so, he anticipated the Foreign Office policy of detaining her by force in any British port she entered so that her case could be brought before courts of international law.[41]

Throughout the Civil War, British naval officers had followed instructions to the letter: they had maintained strict and impartial neutrality. With war swirling all around them, they had refused to be drawn into the quarrel of the North and the South. Tact and discretion ruled their actions. Admirals Kingcome and Denman steered the ship of state with cool heads

HMS *Grafton*, foreground, a protected cruiser first class, flagship on Pacific Station 1902–1904, recently arrived at Esquimalt. Beyond is HMS *Warspite*, an armoured cruiser, about to depart after her second tour of duty on this station. The naval yard can be seen in the left distance. Fisgard Light can be seen in the far distance. Note the steam launch.

and clever hands. Like their counterpart on the North American and West Indies Station, Vice Admiral Sir Alexander Milne, there was no need of naval glory. And when this dreadful war came to an end, their roles in keeping Britain out of the conflict won many awards and the highest praise.

Defence Measures at Esquimalt

The possibility that Britain would become embroiled in the Civil War resulted in the first meagre steps being taken to fortify Esquimalt. An opportunity to erect fortifications occurred in 1862 when 110-pounder Armstrong breech-loading guns were ordered for the *Bacchante* and *Topaze* and as replacements for the 68-pounders in the *Clio* and *Tartar*.[42] Rear-Admiral Sir Thomas Maitland decided to use the guns replaced from the *Clio* and the *Tartar*, plus some old 32-pounders, to fortify Esquimalt.[43] The Admiralty, supporting this initiative, sanctioned the building of a temporary powder magazine for the battery.[44] By September, work on emplacements for 16 guns—two 68- and fourteen 32-pounders—had begun on Duntze Head, the best position for commanding the narrow harbour entrance.[45]

These steps appeared to be timely. Within a few months of Maitland's proposal, reports reached him that three iron-plated ships of the Monitor class were being built for the use of the United States Navy, one each at San

Francisco, at the Columbia River mouth, and in Puget Sound. These vessels, with their revolving turrets and heavy armour, were useful in coastal and harbour operations during the Civil War.[46] Maitland thought that if one of them were actually stationed at Port Angeles, 15 miles distant from Esquimalt and Victoria, it would be proof that in the event of war it surely was intended "for no other purpose than to act against us."[47] He thus urged the Admiralty to send a vessel of the same type to defend the Colony of Vancouver Island. The Admiralty did not take up his suggestion.[48] In 1864 his successor, Rear-Admiral Denman, found Americans at San Francisco assembling an iron-cased turret vessel sent out in sections from the eastern United States. Like Maitland, he argued—again without success—that this necessitated a similar vessel to protect Vancouver Island, which was "defenceless except by the Squadron."[49]

If the Colony of Vancouver Island had been drawn into the Civil War, in all probability its defensive capabilities would have proved inadequate, particularly if the three British warships usually there (one corvette and two gunboats) had been overpowered. As already mentioned, the disbanding of the detachment of Royal Engineers in 1863, a critical moment, left the Island and mainland colonies "deprived of their Sole Military Force and altogether dependent for protection on the Naval Force stationed there," as Governor Douglas complained to Rear-Admiral John Kingcome.[50] Small militia units using arms sent from England were formed at Victoria in 1860, Nanaimo in 1861 and New Westminster in 1863, but apparently nothing was done to organize a volunteer force to man the fortifications on Duntze Head, Esquimalt. By 1865, all of the guns there had yet to be placed in position; the 32-pounders had carriages but the 68-pounders lacked the essential garrison slides.[51]

Rear-Admiral Denman, however, laboured to put the defences of the naval base on a more than temporary footing. He was at Valparaiso in early 1865 when he learned of the fall of the South's capital, Richmond, and, with it, the collapse of the Confederate cause. Well aware of the possibility that the Union, having defeated the Confederacy, would turn on the British territories in North America, he sailed for Vancouver Island in the *Sutlej*, 35 guns, to defend British interests from a possible American attack.[52] After he found that the Royal Navy was the sole defender of the remote British colonies, he recommended to the Admiralty that he be provided with forces adequate to combat those of the United States Navy in time of war. So urgent was the situation that he also recommended reinforcements should be sent from China or England "the first moment that hostilities appear probable."[53]

Frankness was Denman's characteristic quality. He was fully cognizant of anti-imperial views then prevailing—that is, that England would be better off without colonies, which were expensive to defend and difficult to govern—and he informed the Admiralty that it was not in Britain's interests "to maintain Colonies so remote," which could "only be secured to her by strong fortifications and a very considerable military force."[54] The British Pacific colonies, so sparsely populated, were not worth the costs of adequate defence, and "looking to the proximity of the American possessions on the Pacific Coast," he reasoned, "I do not consider that it would be possible at any expense, to preserve them to Great Britain for a prolonged period."[55] Either England should rid herself of these colonies or undertake to fortify them adequately.

In a second letter to the Admiralty, Denman re-emphasized his views on colonial defence. Foremost in his mind was the interdependence of the naval depot and the colonies of Vancouver Island and British Columbia. His cogent views on this matter deserve to be included here. In reference to the colonies he remarked:

> It appears to me that their value principally consists in the facility they might afford for maintaining our Naval forces in these Seas, and also for the means of repair and supply to the Squadrons on the North China Station and in Japan; but in every point of view it appears to me indispensable either to take immediate measures for securing the possession of them in case of hostilities for rendering them effective for these purposes; or on the other hand, to lose no time in relieving the Country of the responsibilities involved in continuing to hold them without making due provision for their defence.[56]

This frank statement gained the Admiralty's acceptance of a plan submitted by Denman for "a very formidable defence" of Esquimalt.[57] Its object was to release the Pacific squadron from merely guarding the naval base so that it could protect Victoria and the southern tip of Vancouver Island. Denman made several suggestions for local defence, including moving the shore establishments from Duntze Head to less exposed positions within Esquimalt Harbour and mounting guns in strategic places. He proposed mounting one 110-pounder Armstrong gun (pivot) at Signal Hill to bear on approaching vessels, one 40-pounder Armstrong gun (pivot) at Duntze Head to "command the approach to the harbour," two 68-pounder Armstrong guns (pivot) on Duntze Head to face the entrance and the harbour, three 32-pounder guns on Ashe Head, and one 40-pounder Armstrong gun on Inskip Island, within the harbour.[58] Captain G.H. Richards, at this time Hydrographer of the Admiralty and a frequent promoter of Esquimalt's development in London, supported Denman's plan. He raised the awkward question of who would man the guns and concluded that artillerymen would be required as it would be impossible for the naval force there to garrison the guns. The Admiralty adopted his proposal, and steps were taken for its implementation.[59]

For the commander-in-chief, the question of the security of the naval base became a matter of even greater importance when he learned that the United States Navy had decided to establish a depot at Port Angeles, across Juan de Fuca Strait from Esquimalt. As already mentioned, the possibility existed that a ship of the monitor type, similar to the *Monadnock*, which had called at San Francisco after the Civil War, would be stationed at Port Angeles. To defend Esquimalt against an attack by such a vessel, Denman believed mines would be best.[60] He asked the Admiralty to send him the necessary plans so that these new instruments of war could be built in the Esquimalt machine shop.[61] The request caught the Admiralty unprepared, for it had yet to reach a decision on the use of these underwater weapons.[62]

In 1866 the proposed union of the two colonies under the name "British Columbia" raised the important question of their protection in the event of war with the United States. American expansionists coveted Vancouver Island, with its magnificent harbours and rich coalfields, Denman told the Admiralty, and because it was the "key" to the defence of the united colony, it should have the aid of Britain both in colonization and defence.[63] He had come to realize that its importance in time of peace was "very small compared with what it would become in time of war."[64]

In order to strengthen British interests at Vancouver Island, he suggested various proposals of a maritime nature, including, first, making Esquimalt a port of call for trans-Pacific steamers plying the route between

Australia and Panama, thereby removing the mail service from American hands; second, building a dock; third, extending the depot; and fourth, defending the chief harbours of the Island.[65] Like commanders-in-chief before and after him, Denman had seen little if any value in these colonies initially. But he had been obliged to revise his thinking when he realized the growing importance of the Pacific and the value of the British possessions on the Northwest Coast.

The Fenian Problem

The danger of an American attack passed in 1866 with the restoration of sound Anglo-American relations, but it was replaced by a new fear that engaged the attention of the Royal Navy: possible invasions by the "Fenian Brotherhood," a militant society of Irish-Americans who believed that Irish independence could be won by involving Britain and the United States in war. Fear of the Fenians caused colonial legislatures from Nova Scotia to Vancouver Island to make hurried preparations.[66] In June 1866, some forty thousand Fenians were reported ready to sail from San Francisco for the Northwest Coast. Accordingly, at the request of the colonial governments of Vancouver Island and British Columbia, the Commander-in-Chief, Pacific, ordered the steam-sloop *Alert*, 17 guns, to the entrance of Victoria Harbour, the *Forward* to Cadboro Bay (facing San Juan Island, from where the Fenians might attack), and the gunvessel *Sparrowhawk* to New Westminster.[67] The *British Colonist* maintained that the residents of Vancouver Island should be prepared, Fenians or not, saying: "While the naval force stationed in our waters is always ready to maintain British supremacy on the seas, the inhabitants of Vancouver Island will be found equally willing to do their duty on the land."[68] This Victoria newspaper correctly interpreted the times, for during 1866 the ranks of the militia swelled to their greatest numbers for the colonial period, and an artillery company was formed at New Westminster.[69] An additional home guard was raised in the truly patriotic river city. The numbers were so few, however, that in an emergency, the chief means of defence doubtless would be the naval gunboats assisted by whatever warships were then present at Esquimalt. The New Westminster *British Columbian* of June 16, 1866, charged the imperial government with parental neglect, claiming the protection afforded was "utterly unworthy of a great and powerful nation, as it is wholly inconsistent with our idea of a liberal and paternal colonial policy."

The handy and well-gunned screw-sloop, or corvette, HMS *Alert*, launched 1856, was on Pacific Station 1858–1861 and 1865–1869. A guardian of colonial interests, she showed the flag during gold rush crises, the San Juan Island dispute and the Fenian raid scare. Alert Bay on Cormorant Island is named after her. CFB ESQUIMALT NAVAL & MILITARY MUSEUM

The Fenians, who were nothing more than a nuisance, kept the Royal Navy on the alert constantly. They were most effective in convincing British officials, more often on the local scene than in London, of their strength. A case in point is that of Rear-Admiral George F. Hastings, Commander-in-Chief, Pacific. En route to the Northwest Coast from England, his flagship, the *Zealous*, the first British ironclad in the Pacific, called at San Francisco on a goodwill mission.[70] It was July 4, 1867, and in recognition of American independence, as was the custom, the ship was dressed for the occasion and salutes were fired. Hastings received an invitation to take part in the official celebrations on shore, but when he learned that Fenians were to take prominent positions in the ceremonies, he concluded that no British officers should attend.[71] As will be seen, his knowledge of the numerical strength of Fenians at San Francisco came to dominate his attitudes about the use of the Royal Navy on the Northwest Coast.

At San Francisco, Hastings had also found a large number of American warships; his report, remarkable for its tone of alarm, convinced at least one lord of the Admiralty that the American Navy in the Pacific was "so superior to our small squadron that it would be overlooked" in a war with the United States, and thus the colony of British Columbia would be captured.[72] Although suggestions were made to strengthen the British squadron or fortify Esquimalt and Victoria, little was done to remedy the situation, partially because of an easing of Anglo-American tensions. The scarcity of ships at the commander-in-chief's disposal, however, forced him to keep the *Zealous* at Esquimalt for almost two years. When the Admiralty objected to this unusual and restrictive manner of using the powerful ironclad, Hastings countered, on April 16, 1869, that he was awaiting reinforcements and that the Fenian danger made the presence of the *Zealous* at Esquimalt "a matter of imperative necessity."[73]

An examination of the circumstances shows that Hastings had good reason for remaining on the Northwest Coast, because there were several alarms in 1868 and 1869. One incident occurred in March 1868, when an unknown number of Fenians were reported bound from San Francisco in a steamer. The *Forward* was sent to patrol the entrance to Victoria Harbour,

The ironclad *Zealous*, first of the sort sent to the Pacific to bolster British naval authority, had displacement tonnage of 6,096 tons. She could do 12.5 knots under steam power and a wonderful 10.5 knots under sail. She carried mighty muzzle-loading rifled Armstrong guns. She was the flagship of Rear-Admiral George F. Hastings and arrived Esquimalt in 1867 to give protection against imagined Fenian invasion from American territory. CFB ESQUIMALT NAVAL & MILITARY MUSEUM

and warships at Esquimalt, including the *Zealous*, made preparations to act on short notice.[74] Although St. Patrick's Day passed quietly, the fears of the British factions at Vancouver Island and British Columbia were increased when Colonel Walsh, fresh from disturbances in Ireland, arrived at San Francisco to a joyous reception from the Fenian Brotherhood.[75] In Victoria and New Westminster, police and militia were placed at the ready, warships were alerted and a marine guard patrolled the Esquimalt naval establishment day and night.[76]

Tensions continued throughout the summer of 1868. In late October, as the *Zealous* was preparing to leave Esquimalt for Honolulu, San Francisco and Mexico, Hastings received a copy of a telegram sent from the Colonial Office to the governor of British Columbia, warning that the Foreign Office had information on good authority that a Fenian attack might be made on Vancouver Island.[77] This disturbing information seemed to be substantiated by a report from the British consul in San Francisco that the Fenians had called for an attack on British Columbia, as well as on Nova Scotia and New Brunswick.[78]

The commander-in-chief's decisive steps during this "emergency" reveal his deep concern for British territory on the Northwest Coast. Militia and police units were readied, and all vessels arriving were examined for suspects. Again the Royal Navy was to act as the main deterrent. To aid the *Sparrowhawk* and *Forward* in defending the imperial establishments and stores in a colony that was "entirely defenceless and unprepared to meet any attack,"[79] Hastings again decided that the *Zealous* should remain at Esquimalt, this time until the arrival of the two steam-corvettes *Charybdis* and *Satellite*. Later he sent Captain R. Dawkins and Lieutenant L. Cling as private persons on a passenger steamer to make reconnaissance of various American harbours and settlements on Puget Sound, such as Townsend, Ludlow, Seattle and Olympia.[80] These officers found no cause for alarm, which served to reinforce the Admiralty's views that the Fenian danger was more imaginary than real and that Hastings was obsessed with keeping the *Zealous* on the Northwest Coast for the protection of British Columbia.[81]

The general preparations made during the scare of 1868–1869 were repeated on at least one other occasion. On December 29, 1871, the lieutenant-governor of British Columbia, Joseph Trutch, received a warning that Fenians were about to act against the colony. He asked the senior naval officer at Esquimalt, Captain R.P. Cator of the 17-gun corvette *Scout*, to station the gunboat *Boxer* inside Victoria Harbour.[82] This was done, and the *Sparrowhawk* took up a position outside the harbour, checking the movements of shipping while the *Scout* stood by in Esquimalt Harbour.

An ingenious signalling system was invented to warn of a Fenian attack from within or without. In the event of a raid, Victoria police would signal the *Sparrowhawk* by launching rockets from the government buildings. She then would fire three guns in rapid succession, thereby notifying the *Boxer*—with steam up and guns ready—to land a guard of 50 Royal Marines near Government House. After this, the *Boxer* would be employed in the harbour as required. This peculiar plan of defence, based on a communications system that now seems antiquated, would probably have been sufficient to face any challenge by armed but disorganized Irishmen. The British prepared for every contingency and overlooked nothing.

British Columbia had been a Canadian province since July 20, 1871, yet it still lacked an adequate militia and continued to rely almost solely on the Royal Navy for defence. Consequently, the executive council of the province appealed to the Dominion government, on whom the responsibility for the defence of this new part of Canada depended, to press the British government to restore the headquarters of the Pacific station to Esquimalt; it had been removed from there to Valparaiso in 1869. The British government also was asked to station at least one heavy frigate in addition to the gunboats already on the coast, to make proper arrangements for militia organization and to assign one hundred regular troops to British Columbia.[83]

To Captain Cator the whole Fenian "crisis" appeared to be without foundation. To his suggestion that the *Sparrowhawk* be withdrawn from the harbour entrance, however, the lieutenant-governor countered that this could not be done without risk to life and property in Victoria.[84] The threat was indeed exaggerated, and the crisis subsided, but all the same, for weeks the *Sparrowhawk* rode reassuringly at anchor at her appointed station in support of the civil power.

The duty undertaken by the *Sparrowhawk* was perhaps typical of the Royal Navy's vigilance over British territory on the Northwest Coast—particularly during the period after the establishment of the Colony of Vancouver Island in 1849 and of British Columbia in 1858, right down to the time of inclusion of these united colonies within the Dominion of Canada in 1871. This service continued at least until 1910, and without this presence of British warships on the Pacific coast, it is conceivable that the orderly development of the Province of British Columbia would not have taken place.

Changing Times in British Columbia

Several influences contributed to the growing importance of Esquimalt as a British naval base in the 1860s: the activities of Confederate and Union vessels along the Pacific seaboard, news of the intention of the United States to establish a naval station at Port Angeles, and fear of invasion by Fenians as the Civil War ended. Three additional influences deserve mention: the purchase of Alaska by the United States in 1867, proposals to construct a telegraph line and railroad across British North America to consolidate the Empire in matters of communication and defence, and, finally, the federation of British Columbia with the Dominion of Canada—consummated in 1871 after four years of negotiation.

In 1867, people in the new united Colony of British Columbia had good reason to be concerned about possible interference with their sovereignty. As previously mentioned, Rear-Admiral Hastings had found a large number of Fenians and a superior American naval force at San Francisco in July of that year. Three months later, the administration of Alaska was placed under the War Department of the United States government, which had purchased this Russian territory on March 30, 1867.

Negotiations for the acquisition of Alaska had been in progress since 1859, but the Civil War delayed their completion. These negotiations had prompted John A. Macdonald, later the prime minister of Canada, to declare that a railway to the Pacific would protect British Columbia from American designs. "I would be quite willing, personally," he wrote in 1865, "to leave that whole country a wilderness for the next half-century, but I fear if Englishmen do not go there, Yankees will."[85] An expansionist himself, Macdonald knew all too well the views of Americans such as William Seward, secretary of state and an adroit promoter of Manifest Destiny, who boasted that the purchase of Alaska made "the permanent political separation of British Columbia from Alaska and Washington territory impossible."[86]

The purchase of Alaska brought little reaction in British government circles. Lord Stanley at the Foreign Office believed that the United States had bought "a large amount of worthless territory" and, in any case, on no grounds could the Foreign Office object to the Americans establishing a military post across the inlet from Port Simpson.[87] Accordingly, the Royal Navy at Esquimalt remained an observer to the United States military occupation of Alaska, while at Victoria the British Colonist of May 16, 1867, warned that British Columbia, situated between Alaska and Washington territory, might now be "devoured at a single bite" by the Americans.[88]

The British position can be explained by the seeming uselessness of Alaska and also by the fact that limits existed as to how much Britain could now influence the course of events in North America. As one authority has explained: "The Northern victory in the Civil War destroyed any remaining possibility of a restoration of the balance of power in North America. Thereafter, Canadian-American relations and British policy with respect to the New World were posited upon the assumption that the United States had the preponderance of power on the continent. The provinces became a hostage to a subjective American judgement on the 'good behavior' of the British throughout the world."[89]

At the time of the Alaska purchase, American expansion into the British North American west and Far West could still be checked by the building of a Canadian railway; the transfer of Rupert's Land from Hudson's Bay Company to Canadian control, which was completed in 1869; and the confederation of British Columbia with Canada. Seward and his supporters for United States continental dominion were unaware of the speed with which certain Canadians and Britons were acting to thwart Manifest Destiny.

The tool of Canadian expansion was the railroad, with its twofold purpose of consolidating the British North American territories and facilitating the defence of the British Empire. Macdonald was not the first to imagine the day when British North America would serve as a vital part of an all-British route to link England with her possessions in the Far East.[90] As early as 1852, Captain M.F. Synge, RE, had been promoting the idea of a "great water route" to the Pacific.[91] His view was refuted by the British travellers Milton and Cheadle, who wrote in 1865 that "the North-West Passage by land" constituted "the real highway to the Pacific."[92] Referring to the fact that the Americans were spanning the continent with a railroad to San Francisco, they asked why the same could not be undertaken through British territory to British Columbia.[93] They held the belief—increasingly popular in the 1860s and afterward—that Vancouver Island, with its valuable coal mines, constituted an asset to the Royal Navy and, as such, should be the terminus of a Canadian transcontinental railway.[94]

In numerous contemporary writings on the subject, the related strategic matters of the projected railway and the presence of the Royal Navy in the Pacific overshadowed considerations of settlement and even commerce. For example, one strategist argued in 1861 that the existence of great gold and coal deposits on the Northwest Coast necessitated a strong British military and naval establishment at what he called "this half-way station between Halifax and India."[95] Such precautions would counteract Russian naval development and guard against American filibusters. A Pacific railway, he concluded, would be an economy measure because it "would dispense to a great extent with a standing army in time of peace on the Pacific coast, and facilitate its movements in time of war."[96]

Sir Edward Watkin, who proposed to the imperial government that the Grand Trunk Railway be extended to Pacific shores, voiced similar opinions.[97] He raised the question of whether the Admiralty intended to establish a naval station at Esquimalt.[98] And he was evidently satisfied with the Admiralty's answer that the small naval base there would gradually increase in importance.[99] With backing from the British ministry, London financial interests and the Canadian government, his "scheme for telegraphic, postal and passenger communications" from Lake Superior to British Columbia promised to end the isolation of the British colonies on the Northwest Coast and add to their security. It would, moreover, increase the importance of Esquimalt in an all-British route to the East.[100]

The entrance of the United Colony of British Columbia into the Canadian federation on July 20, 1871, affected the roles played by Esquimalt and the Royal Navy in the defence of Canada's west coast. The influences that led to this federation with other provinces of Canada resulted mainly from the exposed geographical location of British Columbia. Only five years earlier, in 1866, American expansionist tendencies along the exposed British frontier between Lake Superior and the Pacific had induced Governor Frederick Seymour to propose the union of the colonies of Vancouver Island and British Columbia in order to strengthen "British authority, British influence, and British power in the Pacific." From the point of view of the Royal Navy, union would eliminate difficulties faced by the Commander-in-Chief, Pacific, in dealing with two colonies instead of one.[101] Financial circumstances also compelled the greater association.

The choice of Victoria as the capital was based partially on its proximity to the naval base at Esquimalt and its communication links with San Francisco and Alaska.[102] In that era of optimism, it was easy to imagine that with imperial aid in defence, British Columbia could become the centre of a great maritime power in the North Pacific.[103] Esquimalt, watchtower of the North Pacific, assumed a new role as guardian of Canadian as well as imperial interests.

If the British Columbia government was motivated to seek a place in Confederation by a desire for protection from the United States, it was also lured by promises of prosperity and security. The final terms of entry—important here for their great attention to naval matters—called for the Dominion to assume the colonial debt, begin a public works program, guarantee a loan for a dry-dock at Esquimalt, exert influence on the imperial government to maintain Esquimalt as a British naval station and, above all, begin building a railway to the Pacific.[104] British Columbia joined Confederation in 1871, but because of political controversy, financial problems and geographic difficulties, 14 years were to elapse before the Canadian Pacific Railway reached Pacific tidewater at Port Moody on Burrard Inlet, to become an instrument of imperial defence. So for some considerable time after, the security of British Columbia depended on protection afforded by the Royal Navy.

As an aside, no account of the problems of British Columbia in the 1860s can skip over the rise of New Westminster, Queen Victoria's "Royal City," and the fight that Victoria waged to keep paramount position. The gold rushes continued to accentuate the importance of the Fraser River as conduit of transportation and trade, and New Westminster had been selected as the mainland capital for strategic reasons, situated as it was on the north side of the river, above where the north and south branches of the Fraser commence. Colonel Richard Clement Moody of the Royal Engineers, of wide vision, had laid out the townsite, while George Henry Richards of the Navy had completed, in 1858, the marine survey of the river. Richards tended to put the best face on navigating the Lower Fraser when, in fact, its shifting sands, to say nothing of tidal and seasonal variations and attendant challenges, were often treacherous. In any event, the Colony of British Columbia was a creation of the Crown, and it reflected the energy and professionalism of the Royal Engineers (sometimes aided by the Royal Marines). James Douglas himself had pointed out a route to the Interior via Lake Harrison, and other travellers, such as Richard Charles Mayne of the Royal Navy, had explored other possibilities. If the area beyond where Hope sits today, and Yale Bar, was little known before 1858, it became, with a rush, a matter for concern as to transportation possibilities. Thus began the romantic age of contending with the Fraser River beyond Hope, and the biggest construction project to date was begun by the colony, aided by the Royal Engineers. All river traffic, major and minor, needed to pass by New Westminster, and so its influence was increased. A powerful newspaper developed there, the *Royal Columbian*, under the strong-willed John Robson. Intensely monarchical and expressing robust civic pride on behalf of the colony, it fomented loyalty and went through none of the shifts of opinion (annexation or anti-annexation being the most significant) that wracked Victoria and the island colony.

New Westminster always rose to the occasion for a party on any significant day, especially May Day. The new governor, Frederick Seymour, loved such prospects and decided to give an entertainment on the eve of the birth of His Royal Highness the Prince of Wales (later Edward VII). The event was beyond all comparison, and the local paper proclaimed it as "the most brilliant affair of the kind which has taken place upon British soil to the westward of the Rocky Mountains," which goes without challenge. The band of the flagship *Sutlej* was invited for the occasion, carried from Esquimalt to the Queen City by the gunboat *Forward* (which, with its shallow draft, could navigate the river). Some band members must have brought their own refreshments, for as the *Victoria Daily Chronicle* noted (this detail not reported in the mainland paper), the band "was unfortunately incapacitated from furnishing music by the members becoming intoxicated in the early part of the day. Under the circumstances an orchestra was improvised consisting of professionals and amateurs." What punishments or demerits were meted out for the band of the *Sutlej* is not known.[105]

Meanwhile, even as the dreary, never-ending discussions about British Columbia's role in Confederation (and benefits accruing) went on, a quite different scenario was periodically enlivening the social scene in Victoria and Esquimalt. Every time a ship of the Royal Navy entered its west-coast base, the heartbeat of the city and surrounding community pounded a little stronger. In every port where Jack Tar, as the sailor was called, came ashore for recreation and repair, there was always a "fiddler's green"—a place of fun ashore, a netherland. In Victoria, of course, some sailors used the opportunity to desert to American territories or to British goldfields. Disreputable agents promoted such deserters, and in 1867 the Commander-in-Chief, Pacific, determined to put an end to this and began offering rewards of $100 for information that might lead to a conviction.[106] By and large, however, Jack Tar returned to his ship after a night on the town, and shore patrols along Old Esquimalt Road and elsewhere provided guidance and even safety for the men, to prevent mischief and misadventure ashore.

The more the ships, the more the men, and one pioneer remembered having five ships in Esquimalt "floating the white ensign at moorings." Much activity went on around the ships, and ship-to-ship "wig-wagging" using little flags from ship to shore was common. Speedy launches would be puffing from the ship to the canteen landing. Whalers manned by blue-jackets would be headed in the same direction. Sometime the admiral's barge would convey a gold-braided officer to the dockyard jetty. Whistle and bugle calls were the order of the day, denoting some of the oldest traditions in the Navy. At or near the canteen were the grounds on which were played cricket and "rugger"—"The Navy lads shone at both and it was on those grounds they acquired the skills which stood them in good stead when they engaged in their spirited clashes with local teams on Beacon Hill grounds to such established exhortations as 'Play up! Play up! The Navy.'" Over the rise and past the original grounds of St. Paul's Church (Church of England, naturally), also known as the garrison church, the road led to Esquimalt village. Of an excursion into Victoria, one citizen recalled, "It was quite a colourful experience to get down town of an evening when they were all ashore. The bulk of them came into Victoria, where the beer probably tasted different, if not better, than that procured at the Old Globe in the village or the several places of the Coach and Horses type along the Esquimalt Road." The local police left Jack Tar alone, by agreement with the shore patrols. And here's a final glimpse of a world lost:

What I could never understand, do not even now, why there was such hatred existing between the "jollies" and the "bluejackets" whenever it seemed to be promoted by a drink or three in a Victoria saloon. I can only attribute it to the fighting spirit seeking a temporary outlet. Always touched off in some beer resort, marines and sailors would barge through swinging doors of Johnson Street resorts. The marines swung their heavy-buckled belts and the sailors their lanyards weighted with heavy clasp knives, battling it out until the whistle of "Bobbie" brought the naval patrol to the scene and did what no civic custodian could do—put them where they could sober up.[107]

The writer surely must have known there was a difference between a sailor and a soldier that made for natural rivalry.

On Christmas Day 1862, the ship's company of the *Topaze* gave a party, and Esquimalt shore resident Robert Preston wrote about it under the heading "peep through the lower deck." When he went on board he found several citizens of Victoria and Esquimalt, and the ship's band playing "The Roast Beef of Old England." A seaman arrived with a large pudding, indicating more to come. The captain led the visitors to the lower deck, where on the tables, groaning under the weight of food, a great feast was on offer. The ship was bedecked in flags and evergreen arches. There was much ale and porter, even Imperial Champagne. As Lancashire was then in a state of vast unemployment due to the Union naval blockade of Southern cotton shipments, a fund was established to send aid "to their starving brethren in the Old Land," as Preston put it. A theatrical presentation followed, then a concert with a full-throated soprano with the unlikely name of Mlle. A. Lacharme (not a cross-dresser) holding everyone in rapture. A shower of bouquets arrived at her feet.[108] On another occasion, in February 1863, the *Devastation* gave a party: awnings were spread, guns decorated, flags arranged, booms squared and a grand amateur performance and ball occurred on board that evening. At dusk, horse-drawn conveyances arrived, "filled with the fair sex from Victoria, with smiling faces and fancy dresses, who seemed to enliven the wharf as they eagerly awaited for a boat to take them off to the good old 'Devy.'" "Dancing commenced as soon as the performance terminated, and, as Byron says:

'No sleep till morn, when youth and pleasure meet,' and so the drowsy Morpheus was discarded, the company kept the spirits up till about 4 a.m., and thus came to an end one of the best entertainments that has ever been given on the waters of Esquimalt harbour."[109]

A few years later, when the first and only Flying Squadron cast anchor in Esquimalt in 1870, early historian Edgar Fawcett estimated that officers and men of the Navy in port as of that date probably numbered 3,500. The whole population of the area turned out in welcome, and it was a beautiful sight as the six warships came into view under full sail from Race Rocks, through the entrance and past Fisgard Light and Duntze Head. Then they came to anchor and swung round into the wind. Admiral Farquhar welcomed Admiral Sir Geoffrey Phipps Hornby of the *Liverpool*, flagship of the Squadron.[110]

The commander-in-chief could order up a naval ball whenever he wished, and so it was when the *Repulse*, flagship of Vice Admiral Hillyar, was about to leave for the last time. The Repulse Ball, as remembered, was in every respect the best and most brilliant on the station. The hosts were ever so kind and attended to the guests. The ladies were "tastefully dressed in full 'ball' costume." The decorations were superb, with shining cutlasses and ramrods arranged so as to form immense chandeliers for a thousand lights. On the quarterdeck was a giant H, for the admiral, and jets of flames like so many stars surrounded it. The big ship was thrown open to persons of all classes, and in the gunroom the tables were spread with food and drink. Dancing continued till dawn. Carriages and boats took the guests back to Victoria, and in the cool of the morning, "with the sun gilding the eastern horizon," another pleasure of a wonderful day was experienced.[111]

There were other occasions for the Navy to strut its stuff, as in 1882 when the Governor General of Canada, the Marquis of Lorne, and his wife, the Princess Louise, daughter of Queen Victoria, arrived in HMS *Comus*, fresh from San Francisco. They arrived safe from train bumps on the Central and Union Pacific and from torpedo threats. The locals looked forward to a time when viceregal parties could come by Canadian trains across the Dominion.[112] So it was when Lord Stanley, a later Governor General, and Lady Stanley visited in 1889. The City of Victoria put on its best attire. Every flagstaff floated the Union Jack. At the corner of Government and Douglas streets, an arch had been erected; over it were more Union Jacks, and three mottos adorned the pine-clad arch: God Bless our Wide Dominion, 138 Degrees West and Still in Britain, and In the Name of our Sovereign, Greetings. The viceregal party arrived off Ogden Point in HMS *Champion* and was taken into the Inner Harbour by the Dominion government steamer *Sir James Douglas*. Once again Esquimalt was bedecked in bunting and flags. A parade and civic reception followed, and a ball was given by the Navy aboard the flagship, the fine string band of the *Swiftsure* providing music. In downtown Victoria another party was in progress, with a civic ball at the Assembly Hall, Fort and Vancouver Streets. The string band of C Battery provided the music here. "As you can see," James K. Nesbitt, local writer and history enthusiast, wrote decades later, "Victoria always went all-out when it came to entertaining the representative of Queen Victoria. Nowhere in all this wide Dominion, it was said, were people so loyal as in Victoria."[113]

Years of Transition

In summary, the decade beginning in 1861 constituted a most difficult period in the history of Anglo-American relations. Residents of the colonies of Vancouver Island and British Columbia, before and after their union in 1866, feared invasion and suffered anxiety for their personal security, a state of mind only partially eased on joining Confederation in 1871.[114] The danger of becoming involved in the American Civil War, threats of Fenian raids, and the purchase of Alaska by the United States contributed to the difficulties of this decade. Annexation to the United States was discussed, even voted on, and was thrown out as a possibility. Local patriotism had been steeled by the events and the fears felt so near at hand. British Columbians became vocal, for the first time, in matters of their future, and the colonial press was influential.

The imperial government was not apathetic to the precarious position of British Columbians, as demonstrated by the actions of successive commanders-in-chief to fortify Esquimalt Harbour. In spite of demands for economy after 1868—and not a few statements in public and parliamentary circles that Britain should rid herself of her burdensome colonies in North America—no change occurred in the policy pursued after 1846: ships of the Royal Navy remained on the coast for the preservation of British interests.

273

And so closed the miserable decade of the 1860s, one of crises for Britain, Canada and the Empire, and yet, strange to tell, the greatest gift had been given to the Empire—the Dominion of Canada. The imperial consolidation that followed led to the end of Anglo-American antagonism by the late 1890s and to a phase of solidarity essential to imperial interests when the guns of August exploded in anger in 1914.

By 1871, Esquimalt had assumed greater prominence in imperial defence. Strategists began to view the base as the eventual terminus of the projected transcontinental Canadian railroad—a Northwest Passage by rail, so to speak—as well as a link in a telegraphic system to stretch eventually across British North America and the Pacific Ocean, thus reducing the remoteness of the Northwest Coast and enhancing the value of Esquimalt.

The last comments belong to the *Daily British Colonist* of Victoria, reluctant on the matter of Confederation but now celebratory of the achievement. British Columbia and Canada had joined hands and hearts, and now "John Bull the younger stands with one foot on the Atlantic and the other on the Pacific." At midnight, just as July 20, 1871, began, there was much celebration in the streets. "They were celebrating the Birth of Liberty." From Esquimalt could be heard the 21-gun salute from the great guns of the flagship *Zealous*. It was a day to put out more flags, to celebrate a new triumph in brinkmanship. Almost five years to the day earlier, Martha Douglas, daughter of ex-governor James Douglas, had written in her diary: "Alternate rain and sunshine . . . the Union of Vancouver Island with British Columbia was proclaimed today. The Ships of War fired a salute on the occasion." And to this Sir James Douglas, founder of the city of Victoria and on-the-spot architect of colonial development, added, in his handwriting, "A funeral procession, with minute guns, would have been more appropriate to the sad melancholy event."[115] The career of this remarkable figure also closed in those frenetic 1860s. His firm and wise rule as governor of Vancouver Island, 1851–1864, and of British Columbia, 1858–1864, had laid the foundations of the Province of British Columbia. No person had passed through a greater transition, from days in the North West Company through those of the Hudson's Bay Company and into the age of turbulent frontiers that commanded the greatest of skills. But time and tide had swept away the old order, and with it came a new and uncertain dawn.

eleven

$\mathcal{T}$HE LENGTHENING SHADOWS:
ARMAGEDDON APPROACHES

After British Columbia joined the Canadian federation in 1871, the Navy continued to use Esquimalt as a base in the Pacific for almost 40 years. This was the long watch of British sea power on all oceans and annexes, and the mother country cried out for military support. Not until May 4, 1910, when the Parliament at Ottawa passed the Canadian Naval Service Act, did the British government relinquish the operation and maintenance of Esquimalt to Canadian authorities. During the intervening years, Canadian statesmen were satisfied with arrangements made at the time of Confederation for Britain to look after the sea defences and Canada gradually to assume those of the land. In defence matters, Canadian politicians generally left matters to Mother England, for this was always the simplest political solution. It bred dependency. In Britain, knowing politicians cried out to cut Canada adrift on the world stage—"cut the painter" was the phrase. In Ottawa, the government played a different game. It constantly refused to provide monetary contributions toward the costs of imperial defence as advocated, for example, by the Imperial Federation League at the first colonial conference in London in 1887. It did assist with manning garrisons.

By 1910, however, a necessary policy of imperial-Dominion naval defence had been established, under which a small Canadian navy and a reluctant Canadian government began to assume the duties formerly

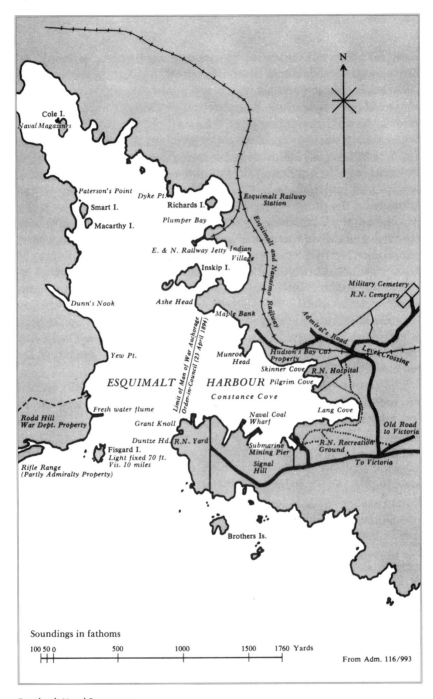

Cole I.
Naval Magazine

Paterson's Point
Smart I.
Macarthy I.

Dyke Pt.
Richards I.
Plumper Bay

Esquimalt Railway
Station

E. & N. Railway Jetty
Inskip I.

Indian
Village

Dunn's Nook

Ashe Head

Maple Bank

Esquimalt and Nanaimo Railway

Military Cemetery
R.N. Cemetery

Admiral's Road

Yew Pt.

Munroe
Head

Hudson's Bay Co.
Property

Level Crossing

Skinner Cove

R.N. Hospital

ESQUIMALT   HARBOUR Pilgrim Cove

Constance Cove

Lang Cove

Rodd Hill
War Dept. Property

Fresh water flume

Grant Knoll

Limit of Man of War Anchorage
Order-in-Council (23 April 1894)

Naval Coal
Wharf

Old Road
to Victoria

Duntze Hd. R.N. Yard

Fisgard I.
Light fixed 70 ft.
Vis. 10 miles

Submarine
Mining Pier

R.N. Recreation
Ground

To Victoria

Rifle Range
(Partly Admiralty Property)

Signal
Hill

Brothers Is.

276

Soundings in fathoms

100 50 0   500   1000   1500   1760 Yards

From Adm. 116/993

Esquimalt Naval Base, 1910

The ship's company of the protected cruiser second class, HMS *Leander*, shown here after having arrived safely into the dock at Esquimalt. These men, and their ship, had sailed the seven seas. Note the barbettes, or casements, housing the machine-moveable guns. On station 1897–1900.

carried out by the Royal Navy. These were very feeble first steps in self-defence, reflecting the astounding complexity of the confederation. The first prime minister, Sir John A. Macdonald, thought it was best to leave things very much as they were as the government built up the communications and transportation networks of the new dominion.

As will be seen in this chapter, imperial authorities were by no means certain that Esquimalt ought to continue as station headquarters, and there was much muddled thinking on whether it was the base that supported the Navy or the other way round. Throughout all this time, Esquimalt's value as an anchor of empire increased, and it was the awakening power of Imperial Russia and two related crises—the first in 1877—that exposed the difficulties of Britain retaining a powerful naval force in the North Pacific in support of seaborne trade and imperial communications. If, from our perspective, the British authorities seem confused in the face of the unravelling scenarios, it is worth remembering that they lived in a world going through its own communications revolution.

Railways, Submarine Cables and Sea Power

At the colonial conference of 1887, Canadian spokesmen declared that the Canadian Pacific Railway, completed in 1885, constituted a valuable contribution to the Empire's security. Although it was built primarily to consolidate the new nation and open new lands to colonization, it enabled Britain to assist in the defence of her base at Esquimalt. It allowed her to supply the Pacific squadron with munitions, provisions and men, and to transport troops and stores through the Queen's North American territories to Pacific shores and beyond.[1] Indeed, certain urgent and perishable stores could be sent from Halifax to Esquimalt in seven days, in contrast to the previous three months or more via Cape Horn. Moreover, mail and telegrams could be dispatched across Canada to colonial authorities and to naval and military officers in British Columbia, rather than over the American-dominated Panama route or through the United States, thus eliminating a situation that was potentially dangerous in the event of war. Further—and of vital importance to Britain—the new railway reduced her dependence on two traditional water routes for conveying troops to the East and importing foodstuffs—one by the Cape of Good Hope and the other through the Mediterranean, particularly after the opening of the Suez Canal in 1869. By the 1880s, strategists in Cabinet offices in Whitehall had come to realize that the Suez route could be blocked in wartime by a European belligerent, regardless of international law that provided for its being open in war as in peace.[2]

The naval base at Esquimalt had been named the terminus of the railroad by an Order-in-Council dated June 7, 1873. This was promising, but because of the cost and because of difficulties in crossing the Strait of Georgia, that decision proved to be a hasty one, which led to dispute between the governments of Canada and British Columbia. Burrard Inlet, Howe Sound and Bute Inlet were considered less expensive alternatives. Finally, Burrard Inlet was chosen as the end of the rail line, against the formidable opposition of the Commander-in-Chief, Pacific, Rear-Admiral Algernon de Horsey.[3] He favoured Esquimalt because he believed that Burrard Inlet occupied a location with questionable security from an attack, especially overland from the United States.[4]

Ultimately, however, the naval base was also served by a railroad—the Esquimalt and Nanaimo Railway, or E&N. In 1874, Prime Minister Mackenzie sent J.D. Edgar to pacify British Columbia, with instructions that the railway to Esquimalt was to be "wholly and purely a concession" to the province. Mackenzie, who was never able to see railway politics as a national and imperial benefit, and who said that Canadian commerce across the continent could easily travel on American rails, with spur lines running north and south into the Dominion as required, was lukewarm, even indifferent. Edgar, to his credit, viewed the east coast of Vancouver Island from HMS *Myrmidon* and concluded that an Island railway would link the Nanaimo coal mines with Esquimalt, "said to be the finest harbour upon the shores of the North Pacific."[5] Upon its completion in 1886, the E&N constituted an extension of the Canadian Pacific Railway when steamer service began from Burrard Inlet to Nanaimo.[6] Together, the railroad and steamer service answered the needs for an ocean terminus at Esquimalt, for a railroad on Burrard Inlet and for a transportation link to the settlements of the Fraser River Valley. Although slight navigational hazards on the inland waters between the open Pacific and the then infant town of Vancouver on Burrard Inlet were not yet overcome, this network of railways and steamers allowed Vancouver Island and the so-called Lower Mainland of British Columbia to develop apace. These improved transportation facilities greatly increased the strategic value of the Esquimalt naval base, which the Governor General of Canada, the Marquis of Lansdowne, and others considered to be the foundation of an imperial "stronghold" on the shores of the North Pacific. On October 10, 1885, Lord Lansdowne addressed a civic banquet in Victoria, saying:

> You have here a naval station likely, I think, in time to become one of the greatest and most important strongholds of the empire. You have a coal supply sufficient for all the navies of the world. You have a line of railway . . . which is ready to bring that coal up to the harbor of Esquimalt. You will shortly have a graving dock, capable of accommodating all but one or two of Her Majesty's ships. You have, in short, all the conditions requisite for the creation of what I believe is spoken of as a *place d'armes*.[7]

Canada had acquired a gateway to the Far East. Here was a triumph of capital, technology, engineering and corporate development that had eradicated unbelievable difficulties of geography. Once on Pacific shores and waters, subsequent extensions of the Canadian Pacific Railway by steamers and telegraph systems, by means of trans-Pacific steamers and a submarine cable, achieved in effect the objective British mariners had long sought: a Northwest Passage from England to the East. In 1887 the Canadian Pacific Railway Company initiated a regular steamer service between Vancouver and Hong Kong via Yokohama. The three vessels in service—which eventually became five—were steamers with a maximum speed of 15 knots, faster than any others in those seas. They could be converted rapidly into armed merchant cruisers to strengthen the British Pacific squadron and give it a still wider grasp in the Pacific, if required. This service, as the chairman of the Colonial Defence Committee predicted in 1886, linked the Empire together in a "chain of communications between British stations" which did "literally girdle the globe."[8]

The world seemed to be shrinking; space was being compressed. In addition to steamships and railways, telegraph and submarine cable installations promised to reduce the time required to communicate between London and distant colonial possessions from months to minutes. Already the Atlantic and Australian cables, completed in 1858 and 1872 respectively, were serving British strategic and commercial interests. In any discussion on a proposed trans-Pacific cable, consideration had to be given the Royal Navy, on whose force the defence of the cable stations depended. The positions of these cable terminals determined, in large measure, the centre or centres of operations of the squadron. In other words, the Navy would defend and act from these points. Thus, Esquimalt, Hong Kong and Melbourne, functioning as communications "nerve centres," would enable the Admiralty to better control ship movements and at the same time greatly reduce the decision-making powers required of the commanders-in-chief on the various foreign stations.

The Canadian engineer Sir Sandford Fleming possessed vision and imagination on the grandest of scales, and he championed the strategic value of a communications link from Britain to Australia via Canada and the Pacific. He thought in terms of continents and oceans. Even before the

Canadian Pacific Railway reached tidewater, he was expounding the opinion that a Pacific cable would play a vital part in the defence of the Empire. The cable would facilitate naval operations, he contended, and that could make sea power more effective. He was breathing the spirit of the age. In terms of economy, he estimated that total cost of the cable would actually be less than that of a single ironclad. Optimistically, Fleming envisaged that a private company, with a small amount of imperial financial assistance, could establish "a work which would add incalculable strength to Great Britain as a great naval power."[9]

Laying a trans-Pacific submarine cable was easier said than done. Implementing the project proved to be an expensive and difficult matter. The cable from Bamfield on Vancouver Island to Auckland, Brisbane and, ultimately, Hong Kong by way of Fanning Island, Suva and Norfolk Island was not laid until 1902. Henceforth, imperial power was strengthened by almost instant contact between Britain and her colonies within the Pacific Rim. These advances in communications technology did not reduce the importance of admirals and their fleets as instruments of diplomacy and force; in fact, they made more effective the deployment of British warships. (Incidentally, we note that Fleming gave birth to the idea of 24 time zones, with the new International Date Line jogging westwards so as to leave the Aleutian Islands in a North American zone.)

Esquimalt Naval Base in the Ascendant

During the last phase of British naval operations in the North Pacific, the sinews of power resided as much in the naval base at Esquimalt as in the ships operating from there. "Sea-power does not consist entirely of men-of-war," Admiral Sir Cyprian Bridge wrote in 1907. He added that, among other things, "There must be docks, refitting establishments, magazines, and depots of stores."[10] Esquimalt was essentially the supply and repair depot for the Pacific station, yet, because supplies such as Welsh coal came from overseas, control of the sea in wartime was vital: "Thus the primary defence of the out-lying base is the active, sea-going fleet," Bridge explained. "Moderate local defence, chiefly of the human kind in the shape of a garrison, will certainly be needed."[11] In the case of Esquimalt, then, strategists were concerned with the interrelated questions of the necessity of a dry-dock and the defence of the shore establishment.

The need for a dry-dock at Vancouver Island was long apparent both to naval commanders in the Pacific and to the Admiralty. The only dock in the North Pacific to which the Royal Navy had access was the floating dock at Mare Island, near San Francisco, opened in 1854.[12] But this was in American—and therefore potentially enemy—territory. Moreover, it was inadequate for vessels larger than two thousand tons burthen, such as the flagship *Sutlej*. In any event, it had not always proved safe for Her Majesty's ships, such as the *Termagant*, 1,547 tons burthen, which nearly met with disaster in 1861 when she fell from the blocks within the Mare Island dock.[13] Although a larger dock was opened there in 1868, it could not hold the British flagship *Zealous*.[14] Other docks existed at Callao, Valparaiso, Hong Kong and Singapore, but the only facility in the Pacific capable of receiving the *Zealous* was at Melbourne, far across the ocean from her place of employment. As the commander-in-chief correctly understood this situation in 1868, if a ship her size were to be kept on the Pacific station, a dock at Vancouver Island was a necessity.[15]

Projects to overcome this deficiency date from 1864, but early ones proved abortive because of prohibitive costs. The danger of a war between Britain and Russia in 1877–1878—over Russia's designs in the Balkans—made British strategists more aware of the unprotected state of British Columbia. Because that province was dependent on the Royal Navy for protection, it was of "paramount importance," a provincial Executive Council committee reported in 1877, that facilities such as a dock should exist to maintain its very means of defence.[16] From the point of view of naval operations, Rear-Admiral de Horsey considered a dockyard to be an imperial need and, further, a "mercantile necessity," because Esquimalt would become the terminus of the railroad to the Pacific, and steamers would soon be plying the ocean between British Columbia and the Far East. As he saw it, the real question was not one of funds but of imperial needs—"first for the necessities of the Navy—and secondly for the prosperity of this portion of the Empire."[17]

Although the commander-in-chief and the Executive Council committee shared the view that building a dock and defending the base were imperial rather than colonial responsibilities, the task of building the dock fell to British Columbia, which lacked the necessary financial resources, even when promises of Admiralty support under the terms of the Colonial

Docks Loan Act (1865) were taken into consideration.[18] Construction began in 1880 but was soon suspended for lack of funds. Then in 1883, to pacify British Columbians who claimed that the federal authority had not fulfilled the terms of union, the Canadian government undertook the responsibility. Thereafter, development went ahead steadily.

March 21, 1876, was a superb day for Esquimalt's citizens, a day in which, a reporter noted, "the sun shone approvingly on the scene." This was the day the contractor was placed in possession of the locale on which the new dock was to be constructed. One citizen remarked that he had waited 18 years for the commencement of the project, and as a sign of faith in the public utility of the project, he took axe in hand and proceeded to level the fence, one hundred feet in length, that marked one side of his property. The fence had run along the easterly shore of Thetis Cove, a natural basin, enclosed on two sides with rock walls, between which the tide ebbed and flowed, allowing a mean depth of 19 feet at high water. The eastern wall of the basin was Thetis Island, a huge rock topped by three warehouses; the western wall was a rocky promontory forming a breakwater of sorts. To the south lay a beach backed by land easily excavated, and to the north was the great basin, the finest harbour from Cape Horn to the North Pole on the Pacific side of the continent, save for San Francisco Bay. It was in this natural location that the dock was to be built, a cofferdam to be placed at the entrance of the cove—that is, from Thetis Island to the rocky promontory opposite. It had taken 18 years, and government after government, before a contract could be made, but it was anticipated that Esquimalt would soon have a graving dock of sufficient capacity to accommodate the largest ironclad of the British fleet.[19]

The long-overdue, long-promised Esquimalt graving or dry-dock was officially opened and used for the first time on July 20, 1887.[20] It measured 400 feet long and 90 feet wide at the coping on top, and it could hold ships of 7,322 tons burthen. It was later lengthened.[21] The economies and advantages it made possible were soon apparent. By November the *Cormorant* and *Caroline* had been repaired for about half what would have been charged at San Francisco.[22] As further proof of its value, 24 merchant ships and 70 British warships used the facility during the first seven years.[23] In 1891, HMS *Warspite*, a first-class armoured cruiser of 8,400 tons

HMS *Cormorant*, the second vessel bearing this name, this one a composite sloop of the Wild Swan class, is seen here in the dock at Esquimalt undergoing repair and inspection of the hull. She could do equally well under sail or steam. CITY OF VANCOUVER ARCHIVES, BO P490, VIA WIKIMEDIA COMMONS

displacement, was in the dry-dock for three months. She was probably the largest British warship to enter it. The dockyard greatly increased the importance of the naval base at Esquimalt. Not only did it furnish a vital service for the Royal Navy, but also it led to the rapid expansion of mercantile shipping in the Pacific and to maritime development on the Northwest Coast.

At the time of the war scare of 1877–1878 over differences with Russia, Esquimalt was listed with 11 other imperial coaling stations and naval establishments as virtually unprotected.[24] In an era when it was argued that Britain's strength depended on her world trade, secure bases from which the Royal Navy could operate to guard this commerce were prime requisites; thus it was contended that these "outposts of the United Kingdom" should be fortified and defended.[25] Although Esquimalt ranked eighth in importance among 12 such establishments, its value to the Royal Navy remained high: "The necessity of a Naval Station in the Pacific is obvious, and Esquimalt is the only British place at present available."[26] But in fact no further precautions had been taken at Esquimalt to keep pace with the great advances in armaments after Rear-Admiral Denman made improvements to its defences in 1866.

The Russian "Bombardment Bogies"

The inadequate state of these defences was evident to Rear-Admiral de Horsey. He knew that the declaration of war between Russia and Turkey in April 1877 would force Britain to take strong measures to strengthen Turkey, her ally in the Middle East, in order to check Russia's drive to the Mediterranean, where British strategic and other interests were considerable.[27] Although Britain considered her Mediterranean interests paramount and thus tended to concentrate her forces there, Russia's reply could be to attack elsewhere, such as at British Columbia and the naval base at Esquimalt.[28] Safeguarding these places was given high priority by the Pacific squadron; Admiral de Horsey's flagship, the iron-hulled *Shah*, steamed from South American waters to Esquimalt where, on August 4, she joined four other ships of the squadron, the *Opal*, *Fantome*, *Darling* and *Rocket*.

By this time the torpedo had become a determinant in naval warfare but had never been used by the Royal Navy in combat. However, on May 29, 1877, the *Shah* and the corvette *Amethyst* fought an inconclusive action

With naval ratings manning the yards in preparation, the white-hulled battleship *Triumph*, 6,640 tons and 280 feet length (draft 26 feet), is about to sail. She had a formidable armament of ten 9-inch muzzle-loading rifled guns, plus secondary weapons, and was belt-armoured. Fast under sail or steam, she was one of two units designed specifically as a flagship for distant stations, the other being the *Swiftsure*. The *Triumph* was present at the official opening of the Canadian Pacific in Vancouver harbour 1887. She was built by Palmers of Jarrow 1870. CFB ESQUIMALT NAVAL & MILITARY MUSEUM

with a very small but actual ironclad, the turret ship *Huascar*, which had broken away from the Peruvian fleet to turn pirate. The British ships opened their guns on the *Huascar* and scored hits but to no immediate purpose. Then the *Shah* fired a Whitehead torpedo against the fast-fleeing pirate vessel and missed. The poor results brought the Admiralty's displeasure, and de Horsey became a political sacrifice. Moreover, the *Shah* was relieved by the battleship *Triumph*, and thereafter the vessel deployed by the Admiralty flagship was a battleship until cruisers were greatly improved in their speed.[29]

Russian warships were rumoured to be at San Francisco, and the *Opal* and *Darling* were sent to report. The *Opal* found the Russian vessels *Ernack*, *Tonngouss*, *Vostock* and *Japonetz* of the Siberian detachment, and the *Bayan*, *Vasdnick*, *Abrek* and *Gornoski* on commission in the Pacific. Some of these ships had "fish" torpedoes, which were fired through bow tubes under water. When these vessels sailed from San Francisco under sealed orders on May 17, the *Opal* steamed immediately for Esquimalt.[30] In reality, the nine Russian ships reported at San Francisco represented no great threat: the largest was a corvette of two thousand ton's displacement, while the rest were sloops and gun-vessels. Yet, by their number, they could provide considerable nuisance value by seizing shipping and threatening the British Columbia coast. In London the crisis prompted a discussion at the Royal United Service Institution in which most participants made a strong case for Britain to greatly strengthen Esquimalt's defences, increase its fortifications and guns, and maintain a strong squadron.[31] The British world was becoming one in imperial thinking and imperial defence, and the growing worry was Russia at sea.

On February 18, 1878—nine days after Victoria newspapers reported a second visit by a Russian squadron to San Francisco[32]—an excited lookout on Race Rocks flashed a telegraphic message to Esquimalt warning that a Russian warship was bearing down on Victoria. The corvette *Kreyzer*, 11 guns, steamed right into Esquimalt Harbour and, as might be imagined, caused considerable concern on shore.[33] Her commander, amazingly ignorant of the dispute between his government and that of Britain, had entered Esquimalt—or so he said—because of bad weather and the need for repairs. But in the opinion of the senior naval officer at Esquimalt, these were merely pretexts. He believed that the object of the visit, clearly, was to determine the defences of the British naval base.[34]

In the crisis, the Canadian government and local militia units were understandably anxious to assist the Royal Navy in protecting British Columbia against an expected cruiser raid. Some steps had been taken to improve the defences at the southern tip of Vancouver Island after the 1877 alarm. In 1878 a volunteer artillery corps was raised to man obsolete navy guns placed to guard the entrances to Victoria and Esquimalt harbours.[35]

But these meagre preparations were insufficient according to both the Commander-in-Chief, Pacific, and the Admiralty. On June 28, de Horsey sent the following confidential report to the Admiralty, revealing his concern:

> The Dockyard [at Esquimalt] is Imperial property, and bears the same relative position to our Squadron in the Pacific as Halifax does to the Squadron in the North Atlantic, but with three fold force, as there is no Bermuda or Jamaica in these waters—no British possession within possible reach for supplies and repairs. It is lamentable to think that in the present defenceless condition of this harbour, and viewing the trifling number of Volunteer Militia, any fairly organized enemy's expedition should suffice to destroy the Dockyard and be masters of the position, until again ejected by hard fighting. This is assuming the absence of Her Majesty's Ships, which, in case of War, must be counted upon. They could not remain here as mere floating batteries, and even if used for that purpose, it is easy to conceive their being enticed away by a feint, or even by false information.[36]

The commander-in-chief thus had raised the awkward issue of the extent to which the Navy should be held responsible for securing the naval base. He believed that Esquimalt ought to be defended by "Imperial resources" under "Naval Control."[37] In this the Lords Commissioners of the Admiralty agreed. But in their opinion, the responsibility for shore defence rested with the War Office, to which they recommended strongly that Esquimalt should be made secure from attack "as it is probably the only harbour to which Her Majesty's Ships would have access in time of War on the entire Pacific Coast of America."[38]

The crisis, ended by the Congress of Berlin, did bring some results in that reports were made by military officers on the defences of British

Columbia.[39] Generally speaking, however, confusing divisions of authority existed between the imperial and Dominion governments. Canada was not much interested in contributing funds for permanent works at Victoria and Esquimalt, and the number of men available for militia was insufficient for local defence. Therefore, it was not surprising that when a similar although less serious crisis occurred in 1885, this time over Afghanistan, the meagre precautions taken at Esquimalt after 1878 against a potential hit-and-run attack by Russian cruisers were considered inadequate. To increase the deterrent against such a raid, the Admiralty bought two Yarrow first-class torpedo boats from Chile—Torpedo Boats No. 39, the *Swift*, and No. 40, the *Sure*. They were sailed 6,000 miles to Esquimalt, where they remained until early in the twentieth century.[40] They were 100 feet long and 40 tons displacement. Originally, they seem to have had spar torpedoes only, but later were fitted with dropping gear. They were escorted on their coasting hop by the *Pelican* as far as Acapulco, then by the *Satellite* to Esquimalt, where they were overhauled, commissioned from time to time, taken on cruises and exercised. Finally placed in reserve at the end of 1903, they were sold, probably in 1905.

As a further precaution, especially for the protection of trade in the Pacific, the Admiralty commissioned the *Britannia* and *Coptic* as mercantile

Torpedo boats 39 (*Swift*) and 40 (*Sure*) arrived on station to provide coastal and harbour defence from any intended "fitful" raid by an enemy cruising formation. Carrying torpedoes as well as deck guns, these fast craft were designed to carry the war to the enemy. They are a form of early destroyer.
CFB ESQUIMALT NAVAL & MILITARY MUSEUM

cruisers. The Admiralty also decided on two armed mercantile cruisers for the Australian station (*Lusitania* and *Massilia*), and one for the China station (*Pembroke Castle*). The *Britannia* was armed at Coquimbo, but the success of peace negotiations with Russia meant that none of these ships had to be deployed.[41]

The Russian war scares led to several effects that were auspicious for the development of Esquimalt. Among these were detailed examinations of naval defence protection and, in the case of Esquimalt, eventual cooperation between the British and Canadian governments. On the recommendation of the Colonial Defence Committee (CDC), some emergency measures were taken to fortify Esquimalt in the summer of 1878.[42] This included the construction of four earth batteries. At about the same time a Royal Commission was appointed "to enquire into the Defence of British Possessions and Commerce Abroad." The Carnarvon Commission, as it was generally called, stated in its Third Report (1882) that Esquimalt must be fortified if the British squadron were kept on the west coast of North America. At the same time, the commission questioned the importance of Esquimalt as a naval base because of the insignificance of British trade on the north Pacific coast in comparison to other areas. Moreover, the report stated, the Navy would be better able to protect British interests in China and could deal with Russian warships in the northwestern Pacific more effectively if the Pacific station headquarters were at Hong Kong rather than Esquimalt.[43]

The war scare of 1885 forced a reappraisal of the Carnarvon Commission's arguments, and both the CDC and the Committee on Colonial Garrisons pressed for cooperation between the imperial and Dominion governments on the defence of Esquimalt. The CDC contended that the Canadian government should participate in harbour security, for if Esquimalt and Victoria possessed adequate shore defences, this would aid the Royal Navy in guarding "the whole seaboard of British Columbia," including the coal port of Nanaimo and the railway terminus at Burrard Inlet.[44] The Committee on Colonial Garrisons recommended that the British supply the armament and an officer-in-charge, and that the Dominion government construct the works and man the garrison.[45] In other words, the major result of the war-scare period was the reawakening of imperial and Dominion interest in the necessity of defending the naval base.[46] From this arrangement came "C" Battery, Royal Canadian Artillery, which was raised in 1887 and made its headquarters at Work Point Barracks, lying between Victoria and Esquimalt harbours. "C" Battery served a total of 10 guns, with arcs of fire so arranged as to guard the sea approaches to these ports—and deal with any hostile intruder. The gunners' work can only be regarded as prosaic but, even so, 85 members of this unit, along with special constables, found themselves employed in "showing the flag" in response to the Skeena "uprising" of 1888, and took to the sea in this unusual amphibious operation for a northern cruise in HMS *Caroline*. In 1893 the Royal Marine Artillery took over the manning of the guns. Royal Engineers later established an extensive underwater mines network designed to be exploded so as to hinder the passage of a hostile torpedo boat destroyer or other enemy vessel. These measures, as well as the great articulated guns at Fort Rodd Hill, are examples of how shore installations were designed to protect the base and the warships that depended on just such a fleet headquarters.

Shifting Strategy for the Pacific

In addition to its naval base and dockyard at Esquimalt, the Navy required coaling stations at places throughout the Pacific islands and along Pacific shores. However, between Esquimalt and the Falkland Islands, no coaling stations existed on British soil. The "Foreign Coaling Stations" used by the Pacific squadron were, from north to south, San Francisco, San Diego, Mazatlan, Acapulco, Panama, Guayaquil, Payta, Callao, Coptapo, Coquimbo, Valparaiso and Ancud.

The Hawaiian Islands lay at the crossroads of the Pacific—on the direct routes between Panama and Japan, Vancouver and Australia. Thus the possible establishment of a coal depot on this mid-Pacific position was important to British maritime interests.[47] The advantage that would accrue to Britain in having a coaling depot there was evident in 1886 when Rear-Admiral Sir Michael Culme-Seymour informed the Hawaiian king that, unofficially, Britain "could not approve of any other nation having a coaling station or other establishment in the Sandwich Islands."[48]

Having at last awakened to the strategic value of the Hawaiian Islands, the British ministry favoured establishing a depot somewhere in the

290

Rear-Admiral Sir Michael Culme-Seymour, Bart, perhaps the greatest fleet handler of his day, was a firm and forceful personification of Rule Britannia. Commander-in-Chief, Pacific, 1885–87. He flew, or wore, his flag in the third-class battleship *Triumph*, the hull painted a conspicuous white.

CFB ESQUIMALT NAVAL & MILITARY MUSEUM

Islands, but it was too late. When news reached London in November 1887 of the cession of Pearl Harbor to the United States as a coaling and repairing station, all the Foreign Office could do was remind the Hawaiians and the United States that British warships were free by treaty to "enter into all harbours, rivers, and places within those Islands to which the Ships of War of other nations are or may be permitted to come to anchor there and to remain and refit."[49] In effect, however, Britain was excluded from the Islands. Admiral Alfred Thayer Mahan, USN, strongly promoted the acquisition of the Islands as beneficial to American security and power projection in the face of rising naval powers in the western Pacific. The cession of Pearl Harbor gave the United States a foothold that led finally to the annexation of the Hawaiian Islands in 1898. By that time, in the new period of Anglo-American *rapprochement*, capped by the Hay–Pauncefote Treaty of 1901, British protests had all but died away.[50]

As a result of exclusion from Hawaii, the Admiralty immediately considered other positions in the eastern Pacific for a coaling station. In 1881 and 1883, surveys had been made of the Galapagos Islands off Ecuador; although Tagus Cove was found to be the best site there, it did not meet with Admiralty approval.[51] The Admiralty realized in 1893 that, although a depot midway between Esquimalt and the Falklands was required, the growth of American interests in Hawaii and naval power in the Pacific, coupled with the likelihood that Panama would cede a canal zone to the United States, made the Galapagos a questionable location for a British depot. The Admiralty reasoned soundly that in an Anglo-American war, a coaling station there would have to be defended by the squadron, while in a war with any other power its necessity would diminish.[52]

As late as 1897–1898, the British government was still considering the Galapagos, and it had once more added the Revillagigedo group off Mexico to the list of possibilities.[53] But again the Admiralty and Foreign Office took no action. Aware that the United States government would complain vehemently if the Galapagos became a British coaling station, the senior Naval Lord bemoaned, "A naval base at the Galapagos is what we have long wanted and might have had without difficulty thirty years ago, but times have changed."[54] In brief, the proximity of American interests in Panama coupled with the necessity of defending the position determined the decision to do without a coaling station in these latitudes. The implication seems clear. In order to uphold her interests in the Pacific, Britain was becoming more and more dependent on good relations with the United States.

While American influence in the Pacific increased, the centre of gravity of British activity continued to shift from the Pacific shores of Latin America to British Columbia, even though the station headquarters had reverted, for reasons of alleged economy, from Esquimalt to Valparaiso in 1869. The relocation of the headquarters to Valparaiso prompted the Canadian government, on behalf of British Columbia, to urge Britain to maintain a naval base at Esquimalt as part of the terms under which the Pacific province entered Confederation in 1871. Accordingly, Esquimalt was not closed.

By 1882, an anomalous situation had developed at Valparaiso. It was almost deserted by Royal Navy ships and was visited only on annual cruises by the squadron, whose main duties lay in the North Pacific.[55]

Consequently, in 1883, Coquimbo and Esquimalt became headquarters of the Southern and Northern Divisions respectively.[56] But by 1900 the Northern Division, for all intents and purposes, was the sole operational region of the Pacific squadron, except for the annual patrol of the Pacific islands.[57]

All this while, the size of British warships, and warships in general around the world, increased in tonnage, propulsion, armour and armament. On the Pacific station, the number of ships may have been fewer as the 1880s flowed into the 1890s, but they packed more punch, so to speak, and were powerful instruments of naval war. W.E. Gladstone, the British prime minister, seeing such formidable vessels, expressed alarm at their destructive potential in an age of progress, and at one time he resigned in protest of the bloated naval estimates to be voted by Parliament. The Navy was moving toward the crisis of 1892, when the French appeared to be outbuilding the British fleet, and the Admiralty, under Sir Frederick Richards, brought through a plan, duly effected, to maintain Britannia's pre-eminence.

The flagship *Warspite* arrived at Esquimalt in July 1890. She was an armoured cruiser of the first class, mounting 14 big guns. She had the appearance of a British bulldog, a local said, adding: "Viewed from a distance, she is seen to sit sullenly down in the water, black and forbidding." Aboard, the bright work gleamed, and briskness and business were the human order of the day. "*Warspite* is a little world of its own, and its customs, laws and manners are as clearly (possibly more clearly) defined than the great world outside. It has its departments, which are as sacred to each other as the prescribed realms of [the] autocratic world." No one would overstep the boundaries, but those in command had access to the whole ship. Each member of the lower deck knew his station, had entered the service on this understanding and abided by his decision. The officers' quarters were best, but the rank and file were also comfortably housed, well fed and clothed both comfortably and cleanly. The officer commanding was Captain the Honourable Hedworth Lambton. The commander-in-chief was Admiral Charles F. Hotham. Among the officers were scions of a number of British families. One of them, the Honourable Henry Stanhope, the Earl of Chesterfield's heir, asked the hand in marriage of Miss Kathleen O'Reilly of Point Ellice House. She had her eye on Robert

A powerful instrument of naval authority at the time, the first class armoured cruiser *Warspite* was twice the flagship on Pacific Station, 1890–93, 1899–1902. Some observers thought she had the appearance of a bulldog, and among her officers and men were many who fought at the Battle of Jutland. Here she is dressed in royal celebration. CFB ESQUIMALT NAVAL & MILITARY MUSEUM

Falcon Scott, destined for the Antarctic, so turned Stanhope down. One of the ship's surgeons, Oswald Meredith Jones, came ashore, fell in love with Kathleen Brady and became one of Victoria's best-loved medicos.[58]

The charming, vivacious and fun-loving females of Esquimalt and Victoria attracted much interest from the Navy. Rear-Admiral Algernon Charles Fieschi Heneage, or "Pompo" Heneage, as he was lovingly called, for he liked pomp and circumstance and was well known for his effervescent humour, is reported to have told the admiral about to relieve him in the command, "You will like the gals, m'boy, but the men are just damn Yankees."[59] The *Warspite* had two peaceful commissions on the Pacific station, and the only incident of professional note was that in 1892, on a circumnavigation of Vancouver Island, she struck a rock, hitherto unknown, in Discovery Passage.

During the 1890s, some doubt existed as to whether or not Esquimalt was the best site in British Columbia for the northern headquarters of the squadron. The major objection was that it faced Port Angeles across Juan de Fuca Strait, a common resort of American warships. It was also within easy steaming of the new (1891) United States naval base at Bremerton. For a time, the big battleship *Oregon* was based at Bremerton.[60] American naval files show fears that an attack by torpedo boats based on Esquimalt might materialize. Shore batteries were erected at critical choke points on Puget Sound so as to guard the narrow approaches to the cities and railheads of Seattle and Tacoma. Whidbey Island's Camp Casey is an example of these. The growth of American naval forces in the Pacific forced the Admiralty to be as hesitant about maintaining and expanding Esquimalt as it had been in discussions on the suitability of the Galapagos for a coaling station. Not surprisingly, and for some time, Their Lordships contemplated removing the dockyard and naval establishments from Esquimalt to a position farther from the border of the United States, where they could be better defended against attack.[61] Alternatives considered in 1891 were Burrard Inlet, Toquart in Barkley Sound, Port Simpson (also proposed as a continental railway terminal) and even Naden in Haida Gwaii, which could be used to shelter armed cruisers protecting British shipping on the Great Circle route between British Columbia and Asia.

In 1892 the Admiralty reviewed several burning questions relating to retention of Esquimalt as a naval base and its proper defence against a raid by American cruisers. All things considered, Esquimalt provided the best site available and thus would have to be protected. But to what degree and in what fashion? The defence of Esquimalt lay not so much in shore fortifications as in naval power. According to one Lord of the Admiralty, so long as the Royal Navy had command of the sea and patrolled Juan de Fuca Strait, Esquimalt would be "practically secure."[62] Here was a reassertion of the "blue water" doctrine that the security of the Empire depended on sea power. After the Crimean War, British naval thinking had assumed a questionable defensive attitude, relying largely on fortifications and coastal craft for naval defence throughout the Empire. The American Civil War had emphasized riverine or "brown water" warfare, and mines, spar torpedoes and even the submarine had come into prominence. So had commerce raiding, and protection against the same by arming merchant cruisers. "Ships versus forts" became a British strategic conundrum, with a good deal of support being given by Royal Engineers and Royal Marine Artillery to the benefits of shore-based defence. The Admiralty fought hard, and the cobwebs were swept away with the so-called Blue Water School, which by the 1890s claimed that the strength of the nation at sea would best secure

Britain against invasion and at the same time protect the communications and trade of a widely extended empire.

But such thinking did not eliminate the necessity of shore defences, either at home or abroad. Once the Admiralty knew with certainty that Esquimalt was to be maintained, it became the responsibility of the British and Canadian governments to reach a decision on how the base could be made secure. This was resolved in April 1893.[63] The two governments reached agreement whereby the War Office would defray half the cost of extensive new works and the whole of the cost of armaments, while Canada would contribute the other half of the cost of the new works, supply the sites for batteries and provide £10,000 toward the cost of the barracks for the Canadian troops and Royal Marines who were to garrison the fortress. Parks Canada, now the custodian of these battery sites, gives a summary of the powerful deterrents against a cruiser attack by an imagined enemy:

> The most powerful battery was to be that of Signal Hill, whose two 9.2-inch B[reech] L[oading] guns would reach some 10 miles to counter-bombard any ships attempting to shell the harbour installations from long range. The Fort Rodd Hill and Macaulay Point 6-inch BL gun batteries were for medium-range work of up to 10,000 yards and the three other batteries—Belmont, Duntze Head and Black Rock—were each equipped with two 12-pounder Q[uick] F[iring] guns with fighting ranges of 400 yards and maximum ranges of 8000 yards. Search-lights also were mounted at the quick-firing batteries so covering fire could be brought to bear, by night as well as by day, over the shore-controlled submarine minefield that would be laid to protect the approaches to Esquimalt Harbour in time of war.[64]

When completed in 1895, these preparations were deemed adequate to defend Esquimalt and Victoria against a raid by one or two enemy cruisers. At last one of the most difficult problems in imperial defence cooperation had been solved.[65]

Throughout all these later decades of the nineteenth century, and throughout all the vicissitudes described here, the Navy served not only as the security of empire, but also as a celebrant of empire—a visual force to promote the institutional strength of the Crown and of British dominions, colonies and dependencies that girdled the globe. As such, the Navy was a begetter of the spectacle of the British Empire. On every birthday of the Queen-Empress, the ships lying at Esquimalt would be dressed splendidly in honour, and to this day May 24 is the local day of celebration. So it was similarly on the celebration of her golden jubilee in 1887 and diamond jubilee in 1897. When the venerated monarch died in January 1901, ships' yards were dressed in black, and at the appointed hour the sound of the 21 muffled guns fired in solemn salute at three-minute intervals began to thunder across the water and reverberate to the near and distant hills. Soon thereafter, with Edward VII's coronation, the men-of-war were brilliantly dressed once more and a new salute fired. The Empire never lost its sense of élan, its sense of occasion, and what occurred in Esquimalt occurred elsewhere wherever the White Ensign flew or the Union Jack blew in some distant outpost far away in the frontiers of India, Natal or Burma. As has been said, around the world the sun never set on the British Empire, and British Columbia was the gift of Empire.

Britain at a Disadvantage

British naval policy underwent a revolution between 1896 and 1905 to deal with the rising strength of foreign naval powers. The United States Navy, for example, made the eight ships of the Royal Navy in the Pacific appear small by contrast. When the Commander-in-Chief, Pacific, Rear-Admiral A.K. Bickford, complained bitterly to the Admiralty in 1901 of the disparity between British and American naval forces in the Pacific and of the "dangerously weak state" of the squadron under his command, the Admiralty could do nothing; the necessity of maintaining large forces in European and Chinese waters prohibited an increase in the Pacific squadron.[66] As the First Naval Lord concluded in a noteworthy document, "The very fact of the great superiority of the U.S. Squadron in the Pacific should shew us how impossible it is for us in view of the requirements elsewhere to maintain a Squadron in the Pacific capable of coping with it. It is impossible for this country in view of the greater development of foreign navies to be a superior force everywhere."[67] As Rear-Admiral Bickford knew, in the event of a diplomatic crisis over the Alaska boundary or the inter-ocean canal across Panama, the Pacific squadron would be unable to support British interests and would have to acquiesce to American demands.[68] The

Admiralty refused to increase the British squadron and chastised Bickford for his impertinence.

As early as 1897, the simultaneous rise of American naval power and hemispheric interests, particularly in the Pacific, had made the question of the defence of Esquimalt purely academic, for in that year the Committee on Colonial Defence reported that the cost of defending the base against a full-scale attack by United States cruisers would be out of all proportion to Canada's resources.[69] The Board of Admiralty, however, was not in agreement.

The northern course of empire had been drawing British warships into more northern waters in protection of imperial interests for more than 50 years. In 1886, for example, Victoria-based sealing schooners were seized by an American revenue cutter in the Bering Sea, which the United States claimed was *mare clausum*. Britain protested that the Bering Sea was open and the captures flagrant violations of international law. The ensuing dispute nearly led to war in 1888 when Rear-Admiral Heneage planned to halt these "unjustifiable acts" by ordering the retaking of some Canadian schooners that American vessels were convoying through British waters from Sitka to Port Townsend on Puget Sound. The Foreign Office intervened and Heneage's orders were cancelled. This was but one incident that endangered the peace. During 1891–1893 British and American warships patrolled the sea, from which sealers had been excluded by a *modus vivendi*. In 1903 a Paris tribunal upheld the case of Britain, and Canadian sealing interests received compensation for damages. The duties of the Royal Navy in these northern waters constituted their principal operations during 1890–1903, involving two or three vessels for the patrol and the concentration of the remainder of the Pacific squadron (usually six or seven) at Esquimalt during the critical periods of Anglo-American disagreement.[70]

New wasps' nests ensued. In 1896 the Klondike gold rush started. The prospectors' route lay across the Alaska Panhandle to the White and Chilkoot Passes and to the Canadian interior. In 1898, precipitated by the Klondike, HM steam screw-sloop *Egeria*, 940 tons, arrived at Esquimalt to take up surveying duties after a considerable gap in such activities. The task was to resurvey and continue the work of Richards and of Pender, more particularly in northern waters of British Columbia and in southern Alaska. Noteworthy as a commander was Commander John F. Parry, later

Hydrographer to the Navy, who took a strong interest in the history of the coastal surveys dating from the time of Wood and Kellett. The demands multiplied: the Pacific cable on the west coast of Vancouver Island, the First Narrows of Vancouver Harbour, Nanaimo, Seymour Narrows, Johnstone Strait and Queen Charlotte Sound. The prospect of a railway coming to Port Simpson or Prince Rupert necessitated these extensive and demanding surveys, and even at that late time, and perhaps afterward, soundings were taken by crews in open boats. Extra rum rations were issued as compensation for their hard work at the oars in wet, exposed and dreary conditions.[71]

Considering the gold discoveries in the Yukon, the long-standing quarrel over the Panhandle and the contentious matter of sealing in the Bering Sea, the Admiralty wisely refused to discount the possibility of an American attack on British Columbia.[72] In a fiery dispatch to the Colonial Office dated March 8, 1898, the Admiralty Board strongly advocated that Esquimalt be provided with defences beyond the 1893 standard so that it could contribute more adequately to the protection of Canada and the Empire, and serve as a base of operations for the Royal Navy in wartime.[73] As their Lordships explained, "Deprived of their base and coaling station, Her Majesty's ships could not be maintained in those waters, and without naval defence, the trade and ports of British Columbia would become prey to every enemy, and the province be at [the] mercy of the United States."[74] At all costs British Columbia must be saved from Manifest Destiny.

The plea of the Admiralty Board for "adequate" defences elicited only a partial response. Together, the Admiralty, Colonial Office, War Office and Treasury reached a decision for what now can be considered the final step toward imperial protection of Esquimalt. This decision acknowledged that although Esquimalt's defence was primarily a Canadian obligation, the responsibility for maintenance of the garrison of some 323 troops at the base should be assumed jointly by the War Office and Canada because of the inadequate strength and organization of the Dominion's permanent forces.[75]

The United States Navy's Pacific fleet grew in strength, particularly after the Spanish–American War of 1898. One of the prominent Lords of the Admiralty, Admiral Walter Kerr, complained of the limits of Britain's role as sovereign of the sea and self-appointed world policeman. "The very fact of the great naval superiority of the U.S. Squadron in the Pacific," he said, "should show us how impossible it is for us in view of the requirements elsewhere to maintain a Squadron in the Pacific capable of coping with it. It is impossible for this country, in view of the greater developments of foreign navies to be a superior force everywhere."[76] The growth of American military and sea power caused British policy increasingly to centre on avoiding war with the United States, so that by 1905 it was fully recognized in Whitehall that the best defence of Canada, and thus of Halifax and Esquimalt, rested in a cordial Anglo-American understanding.[77] One of the chief architects of the Anglo-American naval rapprochement was Admiral Sir John Fisher, who had been Commander-in-Chief, North America and West Indies. He was a strong critic of Canada's dependency status and stance, and he thought the withdrawal of the squadrons from Halifax and Esquimalt would encourage Canadians to get on better with their American neighbours.

All the same, the ever-so-welcome Anglo-American *rapprochement* did not eliminate the necessity of providing protection from other powers—notably Germany, France, Russia and Japan—all of which, at the turn of the century, were making remarkable increases in their naval forces in the Pacific as well as advances in matériel.[78] China lay in chaos, while Germany, Russia, France, Britain and Japan wrested concessions from the old empire and seized territories of economic and strategic value. Under the influence of these circumstances, the British ministry sought and gained an ally that strengthened her sagging naval power in the Pacific. The Anglo-Japanese Alliance of 1902 brought together two powerful "island empires" with overwhelming naval superiority in the Atlantic and Pacific Oceans respectively.[79] The agreement was really an insurance policy, effective only if the other partner was attacked by, or at war with, two or more powers. For Britain, the alliance had implications of economy for it meant that more warships could be withdrawn from the Pacific and China stations and stationed in or near the North Sea to guard against the growing German menace. As counterfactual history can be the greatest fun to the student of history, the following may be considered. Had the German East Asiatic squadron under Admiral Graf von Spee steamed north from the Chilean coast after defeating the outmatched British squadron at Coronel in November 1914, Japanese, rather than British or Canadian, warships would have protected British Columbia, a fact that alarmed many British

Columbians at a time when Asian immigration was a hotly debated issue. From the commencement of hostilities until the United States entered the conflict in 1917, Japan supplied the main naval protection for British Columbia.[80]

The Anglo-Japanese Alliance, and the signing of the *Entente* with France in 1904, marked the end of Britain's "splendid isolation." The system of distributing warships among nine foreign stations had been rendered obsolete by changes in strategy and in instruments of war. Technological advances in wireless telegraphy, torpedoes, torpedo boat destroyers, mines, submarines, guns, armour, steel hulls and steam propulsion—in short, a great advance over the naval equipment of 1856—made sea power potentially more effective provided that ships, and especially bases, were available. Because her strength at sea remained as essential to Britain's survival as ever—and could serve as a restraining influence on her probable enemies—the "new conditions" that Admiral Sir John Fisher, now First Sea Lord, mentioned in his famous recommendation to the British cabinet of October 1904 necessitated a concentration of naval strength in home waters and a reorganization of the squadrons overseas.[81] The alliance with Japan was renewed twice, but was abrogated in 1921 under pressure from Canada and the United States, though resisted by New Zealand and Australia. The Pacific world was being rapidly reordered while Britain concentrated naval forces in home waters in the face of rivalry from the German imperial navy, led by Admiral Tirpitz and backed strongly by Kaiser Wilhelm II.

Step by step, Fisher, Selborne, Kerr and other naval lords worked to counter the German challenge. In the sweeping fleet reorganizations of 1905, the Pacific, southeast coast of America and North American stations were abolished.[82] Only the Channel, Atlantic, Mediterranean and Eastern commands remained, the last of these comprising the old China, East Indies, Australian and Pacific squadrons. Naval establishments such as Bermuda, Halifax and Trincomalee, which had served the needs of the Navy handsomely under the former distribution system, were drastically reduced. This permitted savings of £192,000 from an annual total of £1,292,000—funds vital to the building of new capital ships such as the revolutionary *Dreadnought*.

The Pacific station was closed at sunset on March 1, 1905, when

Commodore J.E.C. Goodrich lowered his broad pendant on the *Bonaventure* at Esquimalt, terminating a command dating from 1837.[84] He then sailed for distant Hong Kong, leaving Commander A.T. Hunt of HMS *Shearwater* as commander-in-charge for station duties on the west coast of America. The victualling depot and hospital at Esquimalt were closed, and the munitions and stores transferred to Hong Kong. Only the dockyard and certain bunkering facilities remained in operation at Esquimalt. The grand old naval base, Britain's anchor of empire in the eastern Pacific, and Canada's western guardian, was now a shadow of its former self.

The closure of the station did not mean that the Pacific, in particular British Columbia, was ignored by the Royal Navy and the imperial government. Instead of one unarmoured cruiser, first-class, and two unarmoured cruisers, second-class, the Pacific Ocean was allotted four unarmoured cruisers, second-class. These were all placed under the charge of the commander-in-chief of the Eastern Fleet based in Hong Kong and other Chinese ports.[85] However, in 1908, the only ships of the Royal Navy actually on the Northwest Coast—the sloops *Algerine* and *Shearwater* and the survey ship *Egeria*—were scarcely sufficient for coastal defence. London

Here we see the steel sloop HMS *Shearwater* serving as tender to the new submarines *CC1* and *CC2*, purchased by the British Columbia government of Sir Richard McBride, 1914, to give much-needed protection against a possible German cruiser attack. Here was the origin of the RCN's submarine service. CFB ESQUIMALT NAVAL & MILITARY MUSEUM

gave reassurances, of course, even when the material assets of power were recalled or reassigned. The advantages of the telegraph, wireless telegraphy, crack cruisers, trans-Pacific cable and Canadian Pacific Railway now were such that even if assistance were not available immediately at Esquimalt or Vancouver, troops could be sent from eastern Canada in six days or from England in 26 days (including seven for preparation), while warships could be sent from Hong Kong in 20 days. These technological advances actually made British Columbia less remote and probably provided her with more potential military defence than ever before. All the same, it did not assuage British Columbians' opinion that their interests had been sold out.

Canada's Reluctance to Assume Defence

The successor to the Royal Navy on the Northwest Coast was, symbolically, the Royal Canadian Navy.[86] Initially, in 1907, a scheme inviting Canada and the other self-governing Dominions to contribute financially to imperial defence had received strong opposition from Canadian delegates to the imperial conference in London. They maintained that Canada was already doing her share by protecting the Great Lakes, policing her fishing grounds, providing transcontinental railways and assuming the upkeep of Esquimalt and Halifax. It was a fine presentation, but it lacked substance and conviction. Self-satisfaction had been expressed, a common Canadian narrative in such matters.

Canada could have had a powerful position in an imperial navy. But it was all a matter of control, of what had been proclaimed righteously as Dominion autonomy. Under the leadership of the Liberal prime minister, Sir Wilfrid Laurier, the Canadian government determined to create a separate Canadian navy; in 1910 it passed the Canadian Naval Service Act that established the organizational structure of the force under a department of marine and fisheries. At the same time, pre-war cooperation with Britain and Australia in the naval defence of the Empire was reaching its zenith.[87] The Canadians took no lead and shied away from responsibilities as well as benefits. They would not play. And so it was that all the Royal Canadian Navy could boast in terms of units were two obsolete cruisers bought from the Admiralty as training ships—the *Niobe* in the Atlantic and the *Rainbow* in the Pacific.[88] On account of British naval withdrawals, politicians in Victoria were horrified by lack of seaborne protection from fitful enemy cruisers or of the commerce flowing in and out of British Columbia's burgeoning ports. Not until Britain and Germany declared war in 1914 was the Canadian force in the Pacific augmented by the hurried purchase of two submarines (built in Seattle) to protect British Columbia from a seemingly imminent attack by the German light cruiser *Leipzig*. Even then, this was not Ottawa's doing but Victoria's. As the submarines—*CC1* and *CC2* (known affectionately to university students of Canadian naval annals as Canadian Club 1 and Canadian Club 2)—were purchased by the patriotic premier of the province, Sir Richard McBride, British Columbia can be said to have been the only province with its own navy, if only for a short time. Eventually they sailed for Halifax by way of the Panama Canal and were based there for the duration of the war.[89]

Nonetheless, Canada did acquire, somewhat reluctantly, the foundations of two great shore establishments. Arrangements for the transfer of garrisons at Halifax and Esquimalt from imperial to Dominion control were completed in 1906.[90] When British troops left Esquimalt on May 22, a milestone in Canadian self-defence had been reached. It now remained to transfer the two dockyards; this was done at Halifax in 1906 and at Esquimalt on November 9, 1910. It was only a matter of necessary paperwork before the Admiralty formally relinquished these bases, and this was done at Halifax on October 13, 1910, and at Esquimalt on May 4, 1911. The terms of transfer, briefly stated, stipulated that Canada would maintain the existing facilities of supply and repair, and they would be available to the Royal Navy should they be needed at any time.[91]

A secret Admiralty memorandum of 1912 commented on the costs of the Royal Navy's naval defence of Canada in the previous hundred years. It reads:

> Mere statements of the cost of keeping certain ships near Canada, or of the expense of particular naval establishments in Canada are no measure of the value of the naval defence by which her territory and interests have been protected. The British Navy as a whole and the sea power which its supremacy ensures, and not the squadrons on the North American or Pacific Stations have given Canada the security she has enjoyed. The truth should never be darkened with detail.

HMCS *Rainbow*, a light cruiser acquired from the Royal Navy in 1910 and one of the two original vessels of the Royal Canadian Navy, is welcomed in Esquimalt Harbour by the lovely sloop *Algerine*, fully dressed for the occasion. CFB ESQUIMALT NAVAL & MILITARY MUSEUM

No more cogent statement representing the principles of British strategy in relationship to Canadian development can be found. Ships might provide local service, but the overall power of the Royal Navy was the key to the security of British possessions overseas and of British trade. The Admiralty, nonetheless, took pains to detail the costs of maintenance, personnel and property directly accruing to Canada in the 50-year period after 1851 and estimated that a staggering £25 million to £30 million had been spent on keeping ships in Canadian waters. "Apart from what is referred to in the foregoing obligations," the memorandum concluded, "there is no record available of any naval expenditure properly attributed to the relations of the Mother country to the Dominion of Canada."[92] In other words, naval protection had cost Canada, whether as colonial territories or as a self-governing federation or nation, not one penny in the nineteenth century.

When the Admiralty formally closed the Pacific station at Esquimalt, and the naval base and dockyard were transferred to the Canadian government, the responsibility the Royal Navy had fulfilled for nearly a century in patrolling and protecting British territory on the Northwest Coast of North

America virtually terminated. But the benefits of the long service rendered by successive commanders-in-chief and ships under their command since early in the nineteenth century endured. Under the protection of the Royal Navy, the infant Pacific colonies had grown into a province comprising a part of a dominion. It is no less significant that the Royal Navy contributed to the permanent establishment of British traditions in British Columbia.

All the same, and with much regret to all connected to the old Navy at Esquimalt, an unwelcome end had come to an era, which had been marked by great change, changes hard to imagine now from our distant times. Naval officers such as Mayne, Moresby or Bridge, committing to writing their memories of change, often commented on how they hardly recognized Victoria and Esquimalt when they returned to the area even 10 or 15 years after they first sailed to Vancouver Island in the 1840s. They had seen the landscape transformed from wilderness.

The old Vancouver Island had passed away. Here is Admiral Moresby reflecting years later on events at Newcastle Island, 1853, when Native men found guilty of murder had been hanged, and the mother of one of the dead had implored authorities that the fatal rope might be given to her, which it was. "Then all moved towards the woods and vanished slowly into the gathering gloom, bearing their dead. Such was the old Vancouver." He concludes:

> As I lean backward the vision of the forest primeval and its children fades, and there arises in its place the roar of civilization, the teeming life of the cities that are and will be throned on the North Pacific. So the world changes, so our feverish activities fill the space between the two silences; but to an old sailor, who recalls many men and things in the peace of his last days, it is difficult sometimes to distinguish phantom and reality, and easier to believe that the pines are still waving in their solitude, and the rivers running undisturbed to the great ocean.[93]

Another admiral, Sir Cyprian Bridge, born in Newfoundland and one of the great officers of the Navy during *Pax Britannica*, rising to commander-in-chief of the Australian Station and then the China Station, was wined and dined in Esquimalt in 1901 when en route to become Commander-in-Chief, China, the most exciting sea appointment. He had recently been director of naval intelligence, and he knew as well as anyone of Britannia's worldwide obligations and challenges. But he had a soft spot for Esquimalt and for Victoria. He had sailed into Juan de Fuca Strait from Sitka and, before that, Petropavlovsk in the *Brisk*. His description is a reminder of how quickly the world had changed to that point in time.

When we reached the entrance to the Straits of Juan de Fuca, a couple of canoes came off from the southern shore. In each canoe there were several Indians, all stark naked, except where mud was caked on their skins. They brought off fish to barter for tobacco. We anchored for a day and night at [Port] San Juan, where two or three Englishmen had established a sawmill. There were trees of great size in the neighborhood; some lying on the beach had trunks of vast diameter. There was a curious Indian cemetery here. The remains of the dead were put into rough wooden boxes and fixed rather high up the trees.

On entering the snug harbour of Esquimalt we could see only one house, the residence of the magistrate or judge, on our port hand as we came in, and three neatly-built wooden huts on the opposite shore. These had just been put up to serve as hospitals for casualties occurring at Vladivostok.

Vancouver's Island was then under the Hudson Bay Company, whose governor lived near Fort Victoria, the site of what is now the capital. Esquimalt as a settlement did not exist. What afterwards became the dockyard was an island which at low water one could reach by wading. There were three or four farms but not one of these was visible from the anchorage.

There was a road from the harbour to Fort Victoria, on nearing which a river had to be crossed by a substantial wooden bridge. Close to the bridge, on the side farthest from the fort, was an Indian town, known as King Freezy's town, which consisted of several long wooden sheds or lodges. Near the other end of the bridge there were four or five pleasant-looking cottages. These, the governor's house some distance off, and the fort were the only buildings of any kind in the place. The people who lived in them, probably less than fifty, formed the whole population. One or two of us went to the fort. It was a strong and rather extensive stockade of logs. Within it two or three Hudson Bay Company's officers lived; and there were also the Company's storehouses, containing the goods to be bartered with the Indians for furs and the furs themselves.

The fort stood on ground rather like an English common, a nearly level area studded with bushes. As we walked toward it we were joined by a troop of young Indians, all of whose faces were daubed with bright red paint. They each had on a striped cotton shirt but no other clothes. They were made to stop at a respectful distance from the gateway of the fort, as no Indian was allowed inside except under strict precautions. The officers in the fort were very hospitable, and showed us much civility.

That was the old Victoria, and the old Esquimalt, just on the eve of the Fraser River gold fever. Admiral Bridge takes up his tale of what he saw half a century later:

I visited Vancouver's Island again in 1901. The change in the place was very great. At the time of my first visit in 1855, British Columbia, as a province, did not exist even in name. Esquimalt and Victoria were still unfounded. We could, and usually did, cut down trees for ship's spars within a few yards of the spot at which we landed from our boats.

When I visited the island in 1901, Esquimalt had become a town, connected by electric tramway with the capital. There was now a dockyard with a considerable dry dock, and workshops of respectable size. Fort Victoria had grown into Victoria, a beautiful capital city, with its park, great public buildings, library, museum, hospital, banks, and hotels. The memory of the fort was preserved only by the name of Fort Street, which ran near its site. Close to the spot on which the fort had stood there was now a cathedral, in which I attended divine service.

Outside the city, near where King Freezy's town had been, there were handsome private houses. Victoria harbour was provided with great wharves, and the place was full of shipping. At my first visit, two steamers only entered it, the *Otter* and the *Beaver*, both belonging to the Hudson Bay Company, and both carrying guns. They took stores for barter and supplies to the Company's posts near the coast, picked up the furs brought from the Indians, and took them to San Francisco.

We were all sorry to leave Esquimalt, where the few settlers' families, well-bred and pleasant people, had been most kind and hospitable.[94]

In review, ships of the Royal Navy were not the first belonging to any European nation to penetrate the vast waters of the Pacific, for the Portuguese, Spanish, French and Dutch had all claimed pre-eminence in that line. But it was the British, fresh from the success of their great explorations under James Cook and George Vancouver, who had acquired the ascendancy there, and when the search for new trading partners and the quest for markets had been joined with the nagging business of keeping a narrow eye on rivals who sought to take up imperial gains in islands and coastal zones, the future of the Pacific had entered the files of the Foreign Office and become a matter of concern for the Colonial Office. British imperial expansion in the Pacific occurred in irregular patterns and was reactive in nature—usually to pre-empt a rival. All the same, the pursuit of profit and power led to entanglements ashore. Through the activities of these vessels between 1810 and 1914, Britain could expand her overseas trade and, when necessary, acquire numerous territories within the Pacific Rim. That Britain was able to extend her frontiers beyond her own immediate shores to include a section of the Pacific Northwest can be attributed, at least partially, to her strength at sea.

It may safely be said that the British acquired Vancouver Island and the mainland cordillera area (later British Columbia) not because it wanted to but because it had to. It was American ambitions that forced the British hand. Vancouver Island was defensive empire, to stay the tide of American settlement. British Columbia was defensive empire, too, to prevent lawlessness in the new jurisdiction, and thus Crown Colony government was founded there—a direct act of state. Vancouver Island was corporate empire, a creature of the Hudson's Bay Company. The long arm of British sea power never failed British aspirations, no matter how uncertain, and it is equally important to note that in London, and especially in the offices of government in Whitehall, the official mind of British imperialism never failed to make sure that the trading area became in time the colonial real estate, and that it, too, in turn, became part of Canada. At no time were Vancouver Islanders or mainland British Columbians able or willing to shoulder the burdens of their own defence. They rode the waves of international politics and were carried along by British and Canadian statesmen. They weathered many a storm in the process.

British warships constituted a shield behind which the fur-trading posts of the North West Company and the Hudson's Bay Company and the colonial settlements of Vancouver Island and British Columbia could prosper and mature. These vessels provided protection from attacks by First Nations. They stopped lawless gold miners and foreign encroachments. When assaults by Russians in the North Pacific seemed imminent during the Crimean War, and then again during the war scares of 1877–1878 and 1885, the Royal Navy's presence served to allay the fears of British settlers on the Northwest Coast. When difficulties with the United States erupted over the Oregon boundary and the ownership of the San Juan Islands, again the Navy stood by and helped to resolve the disputes. When American Manifest Destiny threatened to absorb the greater part of British North America into the United States, the Royal Navy supplied the deterrent. Officers acting on strict instructions, duly followed, adhered to a policy of neutrality during the Civil War. And when the new Dominion of Canada showed economic inability, and even a strong disinclination, to undertake the defence of her own coasts, the Royal Navy provided the principal means of protection for 40 years after British Columbia entered Confederation.

The influence of the Royal Navy in the history of British Columbia was therefore decisive. Ships of war, as instruments of British policy, played a role that still has not yet been sufficiently appreciated. In histories of British Columbia and the Pacific Northwest, attention is frequently given to the impact of explorers, fur traders, settlers and railway builders, with little reference to the importance of British ships and seamen. Canadians have a great seafaring history, but their historians and their history teachers far prefer giving attention to other matters. A pity—not because other themes are not important, for they are, but because an incomplete story is being told. National boundaries speak to sea power's influence.

Yet the division of the greater part of the North American continent between the United States on the one hand and Britain and Canada on the other is due in part to British naval supremacy. Britain's national strategy was based on primacy at sea. Her rivals in the nineteenth century, including Russia and the United States, could never afford to ignore this. Both in the Atlantic and Pacific Oceans, maritime factors decided the course of empires, and the exercise of sea power by the Royal Navy constituted a determining influence in Canada's possession of a Pacific shore: a fact of certain significance to Canada, to North America and, ultimately, to the Commonwealth and the Pacific rim. "Rule, Britannia" proclaims Britain's greatness at sea over the years, and even now echoes can be heard on distant margins—in anti-piracy and anti-slavery actions, showing the flag, protecting the commerce of all nations and guarding old islets of empire that cannot be left unguarded, "the limpet colonies," the hangers-on, including Pitcairn Island, the Falklands and South Georgia.

In Canadian waters, the traditions of the old British Navy are not totally forgotten, even as time passes and those vibrant years of the nineteenth century, the chrysalis years of Canada's formation, seem ever so remote. The pride, prestige and traditions of the Royal Navy were inherited by the Royal Canadian Navy, but the new service had to face diplomatic requirements far different from Britain's splendid isolation during the *Pax Britannica*, an isolation that painfully came to an end in the period 1880–1910 and foreshadowed the great world crisis of 1914. The Canadian naval traditions, based on their British legacies, were to find full glory in the next war, in the Battle of the Atlantic, the Royal Canadian Navy's finest hour.

The era of oak, canvas and cordage has gone the way of all flesh. From our distant time, only romance can call up the vision of one of the great "wooden walls" of Old England sailing into Esquimalt, or Halifax, providing reassurance in perilous days. Only romance can conjure up the image of a landing party from one of Her Majesty's warships recently arrived in Constance Cove, Esquimalt, out stretching their legs on a bright summer's morning on Old Esquimalt Road. There they are now, six abreast and thirty or more deep, flanked by young midshipmen and grizzled old warrant officers, summer hats of sennet providing shade, webbing and puttees indicating a possibility of some imaginable shore action.

The Navy had swank, and the officers and men of all distinctions shared in the majesty and the privilege of being in the great sea service of Nelson and his Band of Brothers. "England Expects that Every Man will Do His Duty" was the mantra of them all, from the highest, most exalted admiral to the lowest cadet and recent volunteer. They sailed the seven seas, regarding them cheekily as their own. They did so with justifiable élan and abundant style. Admiral Sir John Fisher used to say that "the Navy travels First Class"—an exaggeration, but the fact was that the Navy was the guardian of empire and of seaborne commerce on a global scale. Profit and power were jointly to be considered in all things.

Lord Palmerston, arguably the greatest architect of the Britannic imperial project, liked to proclaim Britain's eternal interests, and having a strong navy was the best insurance for Britain's future. This could not stop Imperial Germany from trying to build, under the Kaiser's enthusiasms and Tirpitz's bold shipbuilding plans, from rising to test Britain's authority on and over the seas. But once the Germans made this challenge, this extraordinarily foolish plot to seize the Trident of Neptune, they brought about the beginnings of the grand maritime alliance that finally, by blockade and war at sea, brought Imperial Germany to its knees in 1918. Canada formed part of that grand maritime alliance, as did many British dominions and colonies. Imperial Japan, France, Russia, Italy and the United States joined in common cause with the Royal Navy. Out on the coasts of British Columbia, war was hardly ever thought about. Canada's Pacific interests had lain so long under the watchful British presence, and now that, too, was gone in 1914 when the catastrophe swept down on Europe and embroiled the world in Armageddon. By that war's end, a new revolution had occurred in naval affairs and international politics: the United States Navy, under President Woodrow Wilson's scheme, began a construction project to make it "second to none." That meant parity with the Royal Navy. In the aftermath of the First World War, the British primacy sagged, and a new order began in the Pacific Ocean. Through a reversal of fortune, the US Navy became the Canadian ally and Imperial Japan the new enemy.

For a brief period of time, only a century really, between the War of 1812 and the First World War, British supremacy at sea yielded many benefits—and among the greatest of these is British Columbia, a child of the sea and of sea power, and acquired without a shot being fired. The naval traditions and the naval influences continue even from those distant days. The enduring principles of sea power remain much the same, though the weapons of war continue to evolve. All the same, morale and training are essentials, and in this final anecdote may be perceived a telling lesson about fighting spirit. In August 1914, when HMCS *Rainbow* was sent to protect trade off the coast southward toward Mexico, she was as well prepared for war as could be expected—well provisioned and well fuelled. Her ship's company, raised as trainees and well led and managed by the warrant officers and petty officers who really ran the ship, or any other ship for that matter, had brought her to fighting trim. She went out in search of the German light cruiser, the *Leipzig*, known to be ranging off San Francisco. The *Rainbow* never encountered the *Leipzig*—probably a good thing—but the spirit of Nelson was on board this Canadian warship. When about to depart Esquimalt, this message had been sent to her: "Remember the Spirit of Nelson. All Canada is Watching."

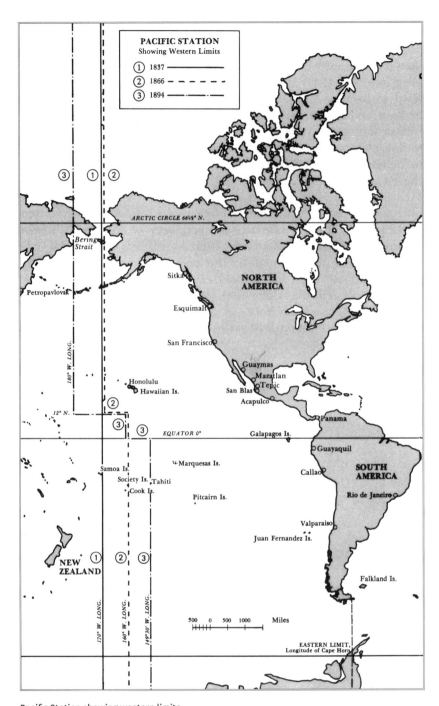

Pacific Station showing western limits

This map is reprinted with permission of the original publisher from *The Royal Navy on the Northwest Coast of North America, 1810–1914* by Barry Gough © University of British Columbia Press 1971. All rights reserved by the publisher.

APPENDIX A

Changing Boundaries of the Pacific Station

In 1808, the Royal Navy's South American station (or Brazil's station) was created. It included within its limits the entire eastern Pacific.[1] From this command evolved the Pacific station, created in 1837, which assumed the duties of the old South America station west of Cape Horn. This development represented a further recognition of British political influence and maritime activity in the Pacific. Rear-Admiral C.B.H. Ross was appointed to the command on September 4, 1837, but did not assume "command of Her Majesty's ships and vessels employed on the Western Coast of America, and in the Pacific" until he entered the station limits in early March 1838.[2]

The extension of the Navy's influence beyond the Horn paralleled that in the seas east of the Cape of Good Hope. After the Napoleonic Wars, the Indian Ocean, the China Seas and the waters of the Antipodes were visited more frequently by British men-of-war. The task of ensuring that British traders, missionaries and consular agents would be free from attack or interference in these vast tracts of water rested initially with the East Indies and China station.[3] After 1820, that command extended to 170° west longitude, where it met the western extremity of the South American station. Several subdivisions of the East Indies and China station followed, but by 1859 the increasing importance of Australia, New Zealand and the islands of the western Pacific led to the creation of an independent command: the Australian station.[4] Five years later, the China station became a separate entity charged with halting piracy and protecting British trade and colonial dependencies in those seas.[5] Thus, by 1864 the waters of the Pacific rim had been divided into three naval districts: the Pacific, Australian and China stations.

Britain's largest naval station was the Pacific, bounded on the north by Bering Strait; on the south by the Antarctic Circle; on the east by the longitude of Cape Horn; and on the west by 170° west longitude.[6] As such, this command encompassed

---

1. The South American station's limits, as defined in 1816, were "to the southward of the line and to the westward of the 30th meridian of west longitude." Admiralty Minute, December 18, 1816, Adm. 3/88; Gerald S. Graham and R.A. Humphreys, eds., *The Navy and South America, 1807–1823: Correspondence of the Commanders-in-Chief on the South American Station*, vol. 104 (London: Navy Records Society, 1962), xii.

2. Ross to Wood, March 19, 1838, Adm. 1/51; see John Bach, "The Royal Navy in the South Pacific, 1826–1876" (Ph.D. thesis, University of New South Wales, 1964), chapter 2.

3. For the boundaries of this and the Cape of Good Hope command, see Gerald S. Graham, *Great Britain in the Indian Ocean: A Study of Maritime Enterprise, 1810–1850* (Oxford: Clarendon Press, 1967), Appendix, 455–59.

4. Admiralty Minute of March 25, 1859, Adm. 1/5716.

5. Grace Fox, *British Admirals and Chinese Pirates, 1832–1869* (London: Regan Paul, Trench, Trubner and Co., 1940), 51.

6. S. Herbert (Adm.) to Rear-Admiral Sir George Seymour, July 25, 1844, Adm. 172/4.

all the American shores west of the Horn and all the islands westward to Samoa. The Navy gave special attention to Pacific South America and to the Galapagos, Hawaiian, Marquesas, Society and Cook Islands. Pitcairn Island, the landing place of the *Bounty* mutineers in 1790, was also closely watched. So, too, were the guano-clad Chincha Islands off the Peruvian coast, where the horrors of coolie labour never ceased to shock naval commanders who called to guard British ships engaged in transporting this fertilizer to Europe and elsewhere.

At other places along the coasts of the Americas, as developments warranted, the Pacific command undertook various tasks: encouraging Spanish colonies to win their independence; freighting silver and gold; watching British spheres of influence and communications in Central America; guarding British fur traders on the Northwest Coast; securing the British colonies there from Indians, American gold seekers, Fenians and Britain's two North Pacific rivals, Russia and the United States; and protecting Canadian sealing schooners out of Victoria from American interference.

As for the Pacific islands, the western limit of the station receded with the expanding influence in Pacific affairs of the Antipodes and, after 1878, the Western Pacific High Commission. From 1837 to 1866, the meridian of 170° west longitude constituted the western boundary; then the Admiralty redefined it as "on the west by the Meridian of 160° West longitude to 12° North latitude thence along the Meridian Northward to Behring Strait."[7] This change established that the Phoenix, Samoan and Friendly Islands were clearly under the control of the Australian station. In 1894 there was a further limitation of the Pacific station, along with a subsequent expansion of its Australian counterpart to include the Cook Islands and others brought under the jurisdiction of the Pacific Order-in-Council of 1893. At that time all major groups, exclusive of the Hawaiian, Tuamotu and Marquesas Islands, and Fanning and Christmas Island, were to be served by the Australian station. Consequently, the intricate western periphery of the Pacific station became "the meridian of 149°30' West longitude [Tahiti], from the Antarctic circle to the equator; thence along that line west to the meridian of 160° West longitude; thence on that meridian northward to 12° North latitude, along that parallel to the meridian of 180°; thence on that meridian north to the shores of Asia."[8] Such was the complex western limit until closure of this station in 1905.

7. Revised Standing Orders to Rear-Admiral C.F. Hillyar, September 13, 1872, Adm. 1/6236, pt. 2.
8. Evan MacGregor to Rear-Admiral H.F. Stephenson, January 1, 1894, RG 8, IIIB, Vol. 3, fol. 2, LAC.

$\mathcal{A}$PPENDIX B

Pacific Station: Ships and Complements, 1847–1867

YEAR	SHIPS	COMPLEMENTS	YEAR	SHIPS	COMPLE-MENTS
1847	16	3,864	1858	11	2,764
1848	12	3,495	1859	12	2,845
1849	12	2,709	1860	15	3,625
1850	13	2,558	1861	15	3,805
1851	13	2,767	1862	12	2,760
1852	12	2,058	1863	15	3,615
1853	10	1,893	1864	14	3,178
1854	9	1,764	1865	14	2,928
1855	10	2,602	1866	16	3,861
1856	11	2,562	1867	14	3,321
1857	12	2,794			

Source: "Return showing the number of Her Majesty's ships and vessels on the different stations on the 1st day of March of each year from 1847–1867 . . . ," *Parliamentary Papers*, 1867–1868, 45 (H. of C. 167), pp. 2–3.

PPENDIX C

Distribution of the Royal Navy, 1861–1874

Showing Naval Estimates, Number of Ships and Men by Area and Date

AREA	1861* SHIPS	1861* MEN	1865* SHIPS	1865* MEN	1869* SHIPS	1869* MEN	1874* SHIPS	1874* MEN
CHINA	66	7,970	39	5,153	35	4,118	20	2,428
EAST INDIES			8	1,590	9	2,063	9	1,499
AUSTRALIA	7	1,325	8	1,566	4	775	9	924
PACIFIC	15	3,805	14	2,928	13	2,968	9	1,595
SOUTH EAST COAST OF AMERICA	9	1,772	9	930	11	1,727	5	542
CAPE OF GOOD HOPE	11	1,775	3	456	16	1,769	11	1,656
WEST COAST OF AFRICA	15	1,868	22	1,901				
NORTH AMERICA & WEST INDIES	23	3,616	29	6,522	21	3,724	16	2,313
MEDITERRANEAN	40	17,474	25	7,642	18	3,901	16	2,733
SQUADRON OF EVOLUTION (HOME WATERS)	14	9,485	8	4,381	10	4,504	7	3,654
TOTAL SEAMEN, BOYS, AND MARINES VOTED		77,000		69,000		63,000		60,000
TOTAL NAVAL ESTIMATES		£12,640,588		£10,392,224		£9,996,641		£10,440,105

*As of April 1 each year.

Source: *Parliamentary Papers*, 1867–1868, 45 (167), 638–39; 1868–1869, 38 (422), 480; and 1876, 45 (225), 522–23; in C.J. Bartlett, "The Mid-Victorian Reappraisal of Naval Policy," in K. Bourne and D.C. Watt, eds., *Studies in International History: Essays Presented to W. Norton Medlicott* (London: Longmans, Green and Co., 1967), p. 208.

$\mathcal{A}$PPENDIX D

Commanders-in-Chief and Senior Naval Officers: Pacific Station, 1837–1914[1]

1. Rear-Admiral of the White Charles Bayne Hodgson Ross, CB, appointed Commander-in-Chief, Her Majesty's ships and vessels employed and to be employed on the Pacific Station, September 4, 1837; flag in HMS *President*, 50 guns, sail.

2. Rear-Admiral of the White Richard Thomas, appointed May 5, 1841; flag in HMS *Dublin*, 50 guns, sail.

3. Rear-Admiral of the White Sir George Francis Seymour, Kt., CB, appointed May 14, 1844; flag in HMS *Collingwood*, 80 guns, sail.

4. Rear-Admiral of the White Phipps Hornby, CB, appointed August 25, 1847; flag in HMS *Asia*, 84 guns, sail.

5. Rear-Admiral of the Blue Fairfax Moresby, CB, appointed August 21, 1850; flag in HMS *Portland*, 50 guns, sail.

6. Rear-Admiral of the White David Price, appointed August 17, 1853; flag in HMS *President*, 50 guns, sail.

7. Rear-Admiral of the White Henry William Bruce, appointed November 25, 1854; flag in HMS *Monarch*, 84 guns, sail.

8. Rear-Admiral of the Red Robert Lambert Baynes, CB, appointed July 8, 1857; flag in HMS *Ganges*, 84 guns, sail. Note: Each flagship after HMS *Ganges* was steam-screw powered.

9. Rear-Admiral of the White Sir Thomas Maitland, Kt., CB, appointed May 5, 1860; flag in HMS *Bacchante*, 51 guns, screw.

10. Rear-Admiral of the White John Kingcome, appointed October 31, 1862, promoted Vice-Admiral of the Blue whilst holding appointment, March 5, 1864; flag in HMS *Sutlej*, 35 guns, screw.

1. From NS 1440-102/2, Canadian Forces Headquarters, Department of National Defence, Ottawa, and published through the courtesy of S.F. Wise of the Directorate of History. This list was compiled by E.C. Russell, to whom credit is given; it corrects a number of errors in J.F. Parry, "Sketch of the History of the Naval Establishments at Esquimalt from Their Commencement until the Abolition of the Pacific Squadron in 1905 and Miscellaneous Matters Connecting British Columbia with His Majesty's Navy" (typescript of a paper read before the Natural History Society of BC, February 19, 1906; from *Victoria Daily Times*, February 20 and 21, 1906), 34–35.

11. Rear-Admiral of the White the Honourable Joseph Denman, appointed May 10, 1864; flag in HMS *Sutlej*, 35 guns, screw. Note: Ranks such as "Admiral of the Red" were abolished by Order-in-Council dated July 9, 1864.[2]

12. Rear-Admiral the Honourable George Fowler Hastings, CB, appointed November 21, 1866; promoted Vice-Admiral whilst holding appointment September 10, 1869; flag in HMS *Zealous*, 20-gun armoured frigate.

13. Rear-Admiral Arthur Farquhar, appointed November 1, 1869; flag in HMS *Zealous*, 20-gun armoured frigate.

14. Rear-Admiral Charles Farrel Hillyar, CB, appointed July 9, 1872; promoted Vice-Admiral whilst holding appointment, May 29, 1873; flag in HMS *Repulse*, 12-gun armoured frigate.

15. Rear-Admiral the Honourable Arthur Auckland Leopold Pedro Cochrane, CB, appointed June 6, 1873; flag in HMS *Repulse*, 12-gun armoured frigate.

16. Rear-Admiral George Hancock, appointed April 15, 1876; flag in HMS *Repulse*, 12-gun armoured frigate.

17. Rear-Admiral Algernon Frederick Rous de Horsey, appointed August 6, 1876; flag in HMS *Shah*, 26-gun iron screw/sailing ship.

18. Rear-Admiral Frederick Henry Stirling, appointed July 21, 1879; flag in HMS *Triumph*, iron screw/sailing ship.

19. Rear-Admiral Algernon McLennan Lyons, appointed December 10, 1881; flag in HMS *Triumph*, iron screw/sailing ship.

20. Rear-Admiral John Kennedy Erskine Baird, appointed September 13, 1884; flag in HMS *Swiftsure*, iron screw/sailing ship.

21. Rear-Admiral Sir Michael Culme-Seymour, Bart., appointed July 4, 1885; flag in HMS *Triumph*, iron screw/sailing ship.

22. Rear-Admiral Algernon Charles Fieschi Heneage, appointed September 20, 1887; promoted Vice-Admiral whilst holding appointment, November 29, 1889; flag in HM Ships *Triumph* and *Swiftsure*.

23. Rear-Admiral Charles Frederick Hotham, CB, appointed February 4, 1890; flag in HMS *Warspite*, armoured cruiser.

24. Rear-Admiral Henry Frederick Stephenson, CB, appointed March 2, 1893; flag in HMS *Royal Arthur*, armoured cruiser.

2. Before 1864, flag-officers were appointed to fleets that had their own "squadron colours"—"the Red," "the White," or "the Blue." After this date they were called Admiral, Vice-Admiral or Rear-Admiral without the colour designation, although Admiral of the Fleet was retained. In fact, after the Napoleonic Wars, only the White squadron's colours were flown, and the White Ensign became the symbol of the Royal Navy, the Red Ensign that of the Merchant Navy, and the Blue Ensign that of the Reserve. Michael Lewis, *The Navy in Transition, 1814–1864: A Social History* (London: Hodder and Stoughton, 1965), 126–27.

25. Rear-Admiral Henry St. Leger Bury Palliser, appointed March 5, 1896; flag in HMS *Imperieuse*, armoured cruiser.

26. Rear-Admiral Lewis Anthony Beaumont, appointed March 20, 1899; flag in HMS *Warspite*, armoured cruiser.

27. Rear-Admiral Andrew Kennedy Bickford, CMG, appointed October 15, 1900; flag in HM Ships *Warspite*, armoured cruiser, and *Grafton*, protected cruiser.

28. Commodore James Edward Clifford Goodrich, MVO, RN, appointed October 15, 1903; broad pendant in HM Ships *Grafton*, protected cruiser, and *Bonaventure*, cruiser second-class (until February 28, 1905).

29. Commander Allen Thomas Hunt, RN, appointed Commander-in-Charge for Station Duties on the West Coast of America, succeeding Commodore Goodrich, March 1, 1905; pendant in HMS *Shearwater*, screw-powered sailing sloop.

30. Commander Adrian George Allgood, RN, appointed August 1, 1906; pendant in HMS *Shearwater*.

31. Commander Charles Wispington Glover Crawford, RN, appointed December 31, 1907; pendant in HMS *Shearwater*.

32. Commander Gerald William Vivian, RN, appointed April 1, 1910; pendant in HMS *Shearwater*.

33. Commander Frederic Henry Walter, RN, appointed April 24, 1912; pendant in HMS *Shearwater*.

34. Captain Robert Gwynne Corbett, RN, appointed Senior Naval Officer West Coast of America, December 10, 1913; pendant in HMS *Algerine*, screw-powered sailing sloop.

34. (a) Captain Frederick A. Powlett, RN, Senior Naval Officer West Coast of America, August 30, 1914, HMS *Newcastle*.[3]

35. Commander Walter Hose, RCN, succeeded Captain Corbett, August 15, 1914; pendant in HMCS *Rainbow*, cruiser.

36. Rear-Admiral William Oswald Story, RN (Retired), appointed October 12, 1914, Admiral Superintendent Esquimalt Dockyard.

---

3. If there appears to be confusion with respect to the identities of Senior Naval Officers at Esquimalt in 1914, such represents quite accurately the confused state of affairs at Esquimalt at the outbreak of war. Even after the transfer of the dockyard to the Canadian Government, there was still a Royal Navy officer responsible to the Admiralty for the West Coast of America. At the same time, the infant Royal Canadian Navy had Commander Hose as the Senior Canadian Naval Officer on the coast. With the outbreak of war, Captain Powlett of HMS *Newcastle* arrived from the Far East and was by seniority the Senior Naval Officer. Meanwhile Commander Hose in the *Rainbow* was trying to cope with his sea responsibilities as well as the dockyard. Mostly owing to intransigence on the part of Captain Powlett, there were frictions with the Canadian Government. The problem was resolved by the Canadian Government sending Rear-Admiral Story, a retired RN officer resident in Canada, to take over the dockyard but not the operational control of ships.

$\mathcal{A}$PPENDIX E

Changing Technology in British Warships, 1810–1914

The British warship *Racoon*, a sloop-of-war on the Northwest Coast of America, Columbia River, in 1813, had little in common with HMS *Algerine*, stationed at Esquimalt from 1908 to 1919. Both were "sloops," it is true, but they were markedly dissimilar in a number of respects. The following note is an attempt, in limited space, to explain some of the fascinating technological changes that occurred in the British fleet in the nineteenth and early twentieth centuries. For this purpose, a few vessels that served in the Pacific or called at Esquimalt have been chosen to illustrate the various innovations in propulsion, basic material, armament and hull design.

Naval architects of the eighteenth century continued to perfect the wooden fighting ship, and by the end of the Napoleonic Wars had probably reached the limits of improvement, except for the internal iron cross-reinforcing of hulls. Issues of the *Navy List* show that in 1813 there were about 900 ships in the fleet available for service; of these, some 650 were in commission at sea. It is not surprising, therefore, that with British naval supremacy solidly established and with great reductions in the naval estimates occurring over approximately the next 20 years, little was done to modify ship design. (However, even in times of retrenchment, warship building continued as a national and imperial necessity, and some improvements were undertaken on the basis of admirable French and American hull designs.) Britain's strength at sea was based on the wooden fighting ship, it was argued, and any deviation from this would undermine the *Pax Britannica*, which was in any case more illusory than real. Hence Viscount Melville, the First Lord of the Admiralty, could write in 1828, in words that have been much quoted, "Their Lordships feel it their bounden duty to discourage to the utmost of their ability the employment of steam vessels, as they consider that the introduction of steam is calculated to strike a fatal blow at the naval supremacy of the empire." This observation is not as ridiculous as it appears at first glance.

A warship is essentially a weapons-carrying platform. British warships of this time were classified into six "rates" according to the number and weight of guns mounted, which of course also indicated the number of seamen necessary to man them and service the other onboard requirements. The rates were approximately as follows:

Ships-of-the-Line (that is, fit to stand in line of battle):

1ST RATES	3-deckers, usually 90 guns or more
2ND RATES	3-deckers and later 2-deckers large enough to carry up to 90 guns
3RD RATES	2-deckers, usually mounting 74 guns

Ships below the Line (or not fit to be in the line of battle):

4TH RATES	Single-deckers (frigates) with 50 to 56 guns on one complete gun deck and some guns on the forecastle and quarterdeck
5TH RATES	Frigates of 32 to 44 guns
6TH RATES	Small frigates (and later large sloops)

Ships below the Rates:

Sloops, bomb vessels, gun brigs, cutters and others

The larger the ship the higher the command. Flagships were invariably ships of the line, that is 1st, 2nd and 3rd rates, and had captains. But all of the six rates were "post ships" in the early nineteenth century. A post ship was a ship sufficiently large, or important, to justify the appointment of a "post captain"—a captain of the Royal Navy who had his name "posted" on a list compiled by the Admiralty, and who was so called to distinguish him from a commander (originally master and commander). Aboard ship, the latter had the courtesy title of "Captain," a practice that survived so-cially until after the First World War. Sloops were commanders' commands. In this context, "sloop" had nothing to do with the rig: the larger sloops were generally ship-rigged; the smaller ones were brig sloops. Bomb vessels, gun brigs, gunvessels, gun-boats, fireships and others were lieutenant's commands. Strictly speaking, a "ship" is a three-masted vessel, but sloppy and ill usage of the term means it has come to be applied to any vessel that floats on water. Please note: boats are not ships; they are water craft attendant to a warship. Launches, gigs, pinnaces and whalers are boats.

Shortly after 1815 the French term "corvette" began to be used in the Royal Navy to indicate a new class of post ship below the 6th rates but above the sloops. They were of two varieties. The first were old 5th rates cut down to one deck. (The French used the term *razeed*, or cut down.) The *Trincomalee* and *Amphitrite* on the Pacific station at the time of the Crimean War were of this type—38 to 44-gun frigates reduced to 24-gun corvettes. (This practice was also followed with line-of-battleships, such as the *America*, 74 guns, which was cut down to a frigate of 50 guns in 1835.) The second variety of corvette was the new large sloop designed by Sir William Symonds, surveyor of the Navy and an opponent of steam. The *Dido* and *Daphne* of 18 guns and the *Calypso* (originally 20 and later 18 guns) are some in this category. Sometimes they were referred to as sloops, but they were usually commanded by a post captain.

In terms of aesthetics, brigs appeared squat and thick, sloops more racy, corvettes more muscular. Larger or heavier frigates bristled menacingly with guns on a powerful frame; they were prominent on all foreign stations during *Pax Britannica*. Ships of the line carried an inherent majesty as the capital ships of the era. Such was the old sailing navy. When steam came, mast positions needed adjusting to accommodate funnels. Gunboats were sleek and close to the waterline, with raked masts. Gunvessels bespoke elegance, power and speed. Early cruisers and battleships, armoured and heavily gunned, combined function with firepower but looked awkward and unsettled when compared with later designs. When at last the Queen Elizabeth, or super-dreadnought class, came into commission, the great majesty of fine warship design had arguably reached its pinnacle.

Beginning in the 1840s, the introduction of steam—first paddle-wheel, then screw—new and heavier guns, which accordingly meant fewer of them, and armour made any classification based simply on number of guns meaningless. In this transitional period, chaos reigned in describing ships. The frigate *Sutlej*, flagship in 1863–1867, was classified as 35 guns. She was launched in 1855 as a wooden sailing ship of the 4th rate, was converted to steam with screw propulsion in 1859–1860, and carried Armstrong breech-loading guns of varying sizes, her armament making her far superior in this category to a 36- or 42-gun frigate of a decade earlier mounting the standard 32-pound guns and carronades.

Gradually, the old terminology, in use since the reign of Charles I, gave way to a new nomenclature. For instance, the *Zealous*, on the Pacific station 1867–1872, was a battleship but not of the first order. She was an ironclad classified as a "screw-ship, armour plated." Her displacement tonnage was 6,096, indicating that she was a large ship for her day, on a "foreign station" at least. HMS *Triumph*, flagship for 1878–1882 and 1885–1888, was a "third-class battleship" of 6,650 tons displacement. Another flagship, the *Grafton*, on station 1902–1904, was a "first-class cruiser." By that time, the classification of the ship itself as a "first-class cruiser" would provide a good indication of its tonnage, armament, range and speed. These ships were made obsolete by the building of the *Dreadnought*, the first all-big-gun turbine battleship, in 1905–1906.

The mine, spar torpedo and self-propelled torpedo all came into existence during this era, the mine being the first. Torpedo boats were designed and constructed, and torpedo boat destroyers developed as countermeasures. Hull armour needed to be developed below the water line to defend against mines and torpedoes, and anti-torpedo nets that could be lowered or retracted as required were fitted to warships.

The pace of innovation in terms of mechanical production accelerated after the 1830s, as low-pressure steam engines gave way to higher-pressure engines (with the availability of better materials and engineering, better lubricants and maintenance). Developments in boilers sped the process. The turbine marks the greatest propulsion advance, used first in commercial and then in naval vessels. Coal remained the fuel of battleship design as late as 1912 (Jellicoe's *Iron Duke*), but thereafter oil supplanted coal, another revolution changing the nature of war at sea.

By 1914 the fleet had witnessed great changes in matériel—in propulsion (from sail to steam), in basic materials (from wood to iron and steel), in offence (armament changes, particularly the revolution in the gun, with the smoothbore replaced by the rifled gun, giving greater range and accuracy; the introduction of shell; and cordite replacing black power) and in defence (the addition of armour). These technological changes reflected the changing industrialism and gradual mechanization of the age, and they coincided with advances in communications (railways, telegraphs, submarine cables and wireless telegraphy), reforms in naval administration, modifications in tactics and improvements in the methods of officer selection and recruitment of seamen. Britain was a leader in the professionalization of naval architecture, ship design and armaments manufacturing, partly driven by American patents and design innovation and by German chemical industries and steel production. All in all, the old navy had disappeared; industry had transformed sea power. The natural world of wood, hemp, oakum, tar and canvas had given way to iron and steel, steam propulsion and electrical devices. The submarine and naval aviation revolutionized sea power, spelling the ultimate end of the battleship. By 1914, the machine age had triumphed. Britain's security now rested on something quite different from the venerable wooden fighting ship of Nelson's day, but the objectives and discipline of the Royal Navy remained the same. To the end of this age, there were many admirals ("the fossils," Admiral Sir John Fisher, the reformer, dubbed them) who insisted that Britain's naval primacy rested on seamanship learned at sea under canvas, "learning the ropes" (and much else). Some navies of the world still have sailing ships as training vessels, but the ironical point is that Britain's naval primacy began to slip, though not completely, with the passing of the age of sail. Before long, the Dreadnought race had begun. It continues to this day.

$\mathscr{A}$PPENDIX F

British Warships on the Northwest Coast of North America or in British Columbia Waters, 1778–1908

The list of ships and date of visit that follows originated in the work of Captain (later Rear-Admiral Sir) John Parry, KCB, Hydrographer of the Navy, 1914–1919, as given in his "Sketch of the History of the Naval Establishments at Esquimalt from Their Commencement until the Abolition of the Pacific Squadron in 1905 and Miscellaneous Matters Connecting British Columbia with His Majesty's Navy" (typescript, 1906). A number of errors have been corrected here, and several additions and deletions made. The list is essentially confined to British warships that visited Esquimalt; it also includes ships more generally on the Northwest Coast, 1778–1845, but omits ships that completed full commissions in the Pacific without calling at Esquimalt. It excludes ships of the Flying Squadron (*Liverpool*, *Liffey*, *Endymion*, *Phoebe*, *Scylla* and *Peart*) that visited Esquimalt in 1870, except the *Scylla*, which remained on station. Not included are HMCS *Rainbow* and the submarines *CC1* and *CC2*, acquired by the Province of British Columbia in 1914.

Further information on a particular ship's movements can be found in the ship's log, kept in the National Archives (TNA), Kew, Surrey. Beginning in 1837 with the establishment of the Pacific station, and ending in 1854, there are also manuscript volumes in the Adm. 8 series (in TNA) that give the list of ships on station for each month. From 1855, these monthly lists are printed, and a set is available in the Naval Library, Ministry of Defence, London. There is an index of ships' names at the end of each annual volume. The *Navy List*, a periodic publication, gives some information on the ship in question, its officers, size of complement and place of service. Further information on various ships that were in the Pacific and are related to the history of British Columbia will be found in the excellent dossiers compiled by Rear-Admiral P.W. Brock, CB, DSO. Digitalized copies of these are in the Maritime Museum of British Columbia, Victoria, while resumés of the design and history of a number of these ships are to be found in past editions of *The Bulletin* of this same institution.

Date of launch or purchase is given in parentheses.

Acorn (1884) 1889

Alert (1856) 1860, 1861, 1867

Algerine (1895) 1908—to Royal Canadian Navy

America (1810) 1845

Amethyst I (1844) 1858

Amethyst II (1873) 1875, 1877, 1878

Amphion (1883) 1879–1880, 1889–1890, 1901–1904

Arethusa (1882) 1900

Bacchante (1859) 1861–1863

Blossom (1806) 1818

Bonaventure (1892) 1904–1905

Boxer (1868) 1869–1874

Brisk (1851) 1855

Calypso (1845) 1858–1859

Cameleon (1860) 1868, 1870–1873

Caroline (1882) 1886–1889

Champion I (1824) 1849

Champion II (1878) 1881–1882, 1889–1895

Chanticleer (1861) 1868–1871

Charybdis (1859) 1862–1865, 1869–1871

Chatham (1788) 1791–1794

Clio (1858) 1864–1868

Cockatrice (1832) 1854

Colombine (1862) 1864–1866

Comus (1878) 1882–1883, 1896–1897

Condor (1898) 1900–1901

Conquest (1878) 1886–1889

Constance I (1846) 1848

Constance II (1880) 1883–1885

Cormorant I (1842) 1846

Cormorant II (1877) 1886–1889

Daedalus I (1790) 1791–1794

Daedalus II (1826) 1850–1853

Daphne I (1838) 1851

Daphne II (1888) 1889–1892

Daring (1874) 1875–1878

Devastation (1841) 1861–1864

Dido (1836) 1855

Discovery I (1776) 1778–1779

Discovery II (1789) 1791–1794

Driver (1840) 1850

Egeria (1873) 1898–1905

Espiègle (1880) 1888–1891

Fantome (1873) 1875–1878

Fawn (1856) 1871–1874

Fisgard (1819) 1871–1874

Flora (1893) 1903–1905

Forward (1855) 1860–1869

Ganges (1821) 1858–1860

Gannet (1878) 1879–1883

Garnet (1877) 1891–1894

Grafton (1892) 1902–1904

Grappler (1856) 1860–1868

Havannah (1811) 1858

Hecate (1839) 1861–1863

Herald (1823) 1846, 1847

Heroine (1881) 1883–1886

Hyacinth (1881) 1886–1888, 1893–1895

Icarus (1885) 1889, 1896–1902

Imperieuse (1883) 1896–1899

Inconstant (1836) 1849

Kingfisher (1879) 1881–1884

Leander (1882) 1897–1900

Magicienne (1849) 1857

Malacca (1853) 1866–1867

Melpomene (1888) 1890–1893

Modeste (1837) 1844–1847

Monarch (1832) 1855–1856

Mutine I (1859) 1861–1862

Mutine II (1880) 1882–1885

Myrmidon (1867) 1873–1876

Nymphe (1888) 1890–1895

Opal (1875) 1876–1878

Osprey (1876) 1877–1880

Pandora (1833) 1846, 1848

Pelican (1877) 1879–1881, 1884–1887

Penguin (1876) 1877–1880

Peterel (1860) 1872–1876

Phaeton (1883) 1897–1903

Pheasant (1888) 1890–1901

Pique (1834) 1854

Plumper (1848) 1857–1861

Portland (1822) 1851–1853

President (1829) 1854–1855

Providence (1791) 1796–1797

Pylades (1854) 1859–1861, 1869–1871

Racoon (1808) 1813

Reindeer (1866) 1868–1875

Repulse (1868) 1873–1876

Resolution (1771) 1778–1779

Ringdove (1867) 1870

Rocket (1868) 1875–1882

Royal Arthur (1891) 1893–1896

Sappho (1873) 1882–1886

Satellite I (1855) 1856–1860, 1869

Satellite II (1881) 1884–1885, 1894–1897

Scylla (1856) 1866–1867, 1871–1873

Shah (1873) 1876–1879

Shannon (1875) 1870–1880

Shearwater I (1861) 1867

Shearwater II (1901) 1902—to Royal Canadian Navy

Sparrowhawk I (1856) 1866–1872

Sparrowhawk II (1897) 1898–190

Starling (1829) 1837, 1839

Sulphur (1826) 1837, 1839

Sutlej (1855) 1863–1867

Swift (1835) 1852

Swiftsure (1870) 1882–1885, 1888–1889

Tartar (1854) 1861–1862

T[orpedo]. B[oat]. 39 (1885) 1885–1904

T.B. 40 (1885) 1885–1904

Tenedos (1870) 1872–1876

Termagant (1847) 1860

Thetis I (1846) 1852–1857

Thetis II (1871) 1870–1882

Topaze (1858) 1860–1863, 1867–1869

Tribune (1853) 1859–1860, 1864–1865

Trincomalee (1817) 1853, 1885–1888

Triumph (1870) 1879–1882, 1885–1888

Turquoise (1876) 1878–1880

Virago I (1842) 1854

Virago II (1896) 1897–1903

Warspite (1884) 1890–1893, 1899–1902

Wild Swan (1876) 1885–1888, 1895–1897

Zealous (1866) 1867–1872

*A*PPENDIX G

Types and Classes of British Warships on the Northwest Coast of North America or in British Columbia Waters, 1778–1914

1. SAILING SHIPS

SHIPS-OF-THE-LINE—*2ND RATE*

Canopus Class
- *Asia*, 84 guns, 1824
- *Ganges*, 84 guns, 1821
- *Monarch*, 84 guns, 1832

Superb Class
- *Collingwood*, 80 guns, 1841

FRIGATES—*4TH RATE*

Razée (cut down) 3rd Rate
- *America*, 50 guns, 1810
- *Portland*, 52 guns, 1822
- *President*, 50 guns, 1829

FRIGATES—*5TH RATE*
- *Fisgard*, 46 guns, 1819
- *Inconstant*, 36 guns, 1836
- *Pique*, 36 guns, 1834
- *Thetis*, 36 guns, 1846

FRIGATES—*6TH RATE*
- *Amethyst*, 26 guns, 1844
- *Imogene*, 28 guns, 1831
- *Samarang*, 28 guns, 1822

OTHERS—*DISCOVERY SHIPS*
- *Blossom*, 26 guns, 1806 (6th rate)
- *Chatham*, 1788 (armed tender, brig)
- *Daedalus I*, 1790 (hired store ship)
- *Discovery I*, 1776 (Cook's ship)
- *Discovery II*, 1789 (Vancouver's ship)
- *Resolution*, 1771
- *Providence*, 1796

OTHERS—*SURVEYING SHIPS*
- *Herald*, 1823 (ex-*Termagant*, ex-5th rate)
- *Pandora*, 10 guns, 1833
- *Starling*, 4 guns, 1829
- *Sulphur*, 8 guns, 1826 (ex-bomb vessel)

OTHERS—*CORVETTES*

Designed as Corvettes
- *Calypso*, 18 guns, 1845
- *Dido*, 18 guns, 1836
- *Daphne*, 18 guns, 1838

Razée (cut down) Frigates
- *Havannah*, 19 guns (launched 1811 and cut down 1844)
- *Daedalus*, 20 guns (launched 1826 and cut down 1844)
- *Amphritite*, 24 guns (launched 1816 and cut down 1846)
- *Trincomalee*, 26 guns (launched 1817 and cut down 1847)

OTHERS—*SLOOPS*
- *Champion*, 18 guns, 1824
- *Modeste*, 18 guns, 1837
- *Racoon*, 24 guns, 1808

OTHERS—*BRIG*
- *Swift*, 8 guns, 1835

OTHERS—*SCHOONER*
- *Cockatrice*, 6 guns, 1832

Adapted from a list compiled by Rear-Admiral P.W. Brock, CB, DSO, and published by courtesy of the Maritime Museum of British Columbia. With date of launch or purchase.

2. STEAM ASSISTED

PADDLE-WHEEL VESSELS—*SLOOPS*

Driver Class
- *Cormorant*, 6 guns, 1842
- *Devastation*, 6 guns, 1841
- *Driver*, 6 guns, 1840
- *Virago*, 6 guns, 1842
- *Vixen*, 6 guns, 1841

PADDLE-WHEEL VESSELS
—*SURVEYING SHIPS (EX-SLOOP)*

Hydra Class
- *Hecate*, 1839

PADDLE-WHEEL VESSELS—*FRIGATE*

- *Magicienne*, 16 guns, 1849

SCREW FRIGATES

Shannon Class
- *Bacchante*, 51 guns, 1859
- *Liffey*, 51 guns, 1856
- *Topaze*, 51 guns, 1858
- *Liverpool*, 51 guns, 1860
- *Phoebe*, 51 guns, 1854 (converted to screw 1860)
- *Constance*, 50 guns, 1846
- *Sutlej*, 1855

Large Iron Teak-Sheathed Frigate
- *Shah*, 1873

Last Wooden Frigate
- *Endymion*, 51 guns, 1865

Other Classes
- *Termagant*, 31 guns, 1847
- *Tribune*, 31 guns, 1853

SCREW-CORVETTES, SLOOPS,
GUNVESSELS AND GUNBOATS

—*CORVETTES*

Pearl Class
- *Pearl*, 21 guns, 1855
- *Satellite*, 21 guns, 1855
- *Scout*, 21 guns, 1856
- *Scylla*, 21 guns, 1856
- *Charybdis*, 21 guns, 1859

Covered Deck
- *Clio*, 22 guns, 1858

Wooden Ram-bowed Class
- *Tenedos*, 1870, smaller type
- *Thetis*, 1871, larger type

Last Wooden Class
- *Amethyst*, 1873

"Gem" Class, Composite
- *Opal*, 1875
- *Turquoise*, 1876
- *Garnet*, 1877

Other Classes
- *Brisk*, 16 guns, 1851
- *Pylades*, 21 guns, 1854
- *Malacca*, 13 guns, 1853
- *Tartar*, 20 guns, 1854

—*SLOOPS*

3rd Class (later Surveying Vessel)
- *Plumper*, 1848

Cruiser Class
- *Alert*, 17 guns, 1856
- *Fawn*, 17 guns, 1856

Greyhound Class
- *Mutine*, 17 guns, 1859

Cameleon Class
- *Cameleon*, 17 guns, 1860
- *Chanticleer*, 17 guns, 1861
- *Reindeer*, 17 guns, 1866

Rosario Class
- *Peterel*, 11 guns, 1860
- *Shearwater*, 11 guns, 1861
- *Columbine*, 1862

—*SLOOPS COMPOSITE*

Daring Class
- *Daring*, 1874
- *Albatross*, 1873
- *Egeria*, 1873
- *Fantome*, 1873
- *Sappho*, 1873

Wild Swan Class
- *Wild Swan*, 1876
- *Osprey*, 1876
- *Penguin*, 1876
- *Cormorant*, 1877
- *Pelican*, 1877
- *Gannet*, 1878
- *Kingfisher*, 1879

- *Mutine*, 1880
- *Espiègle*, 1880
Reindeer Class
- *Acorn*, 1884
- *Icarus*, 1885
Buzzard Class
- *Nymphe*, 1888
- *Daphne*, 1888

— GUN VESSELS

Wanderer Class
- *Sparrowhawk*, 4 guns, 1856
Cormorant Class
- *Myrmidon*, 4 guns, 1867
Plover Class
- *Ringdove*, 6 guns, 1867
Beacon Class
- *Boxer*, 4 guns, 1868
- *Rocket*, 4 guns, 1868

— GUNBOATS

Forward Class
- *Forward*, 2 guns, 1855
- *Grappler*, 2 guns, 1856
Pheasant Class
- *Pheasant*, 1888

3. ADVANCED STEAM
ASSISTED/POWERED

— IRONCLADS

- *Zealous*, 1866
- *Repulse*, 1868
- *Swiftsure*, 1870
- *Triumph*, 1870

— ARMOURED CRUISERS

- *Shannon*, 1875
- *Imperieuse*, 1883
- *Warspite*, 1884

— PROTECTED CRUISERS

1st Class
- *Royal Arthur*, 1891
- *Grafton*, 1892
2nd Class
- *Arethusa*, 1882
- *Leander*, 1882
- *Amphion*, 1883

- *Phaeton*, 1883
- *Melpomene*, 1888 (later 3rd Class)
- *Rainbow*, 1891
- *Bonaventure*, 1892
- *Flora*, 1893
3rd Class (ex-Corvettes)
- *Champion*, 1878
- *Comus*, 1878
- *Conquest*, 1878
- *Constance*, 1880
Satellite Class
- *Satellite*, 1881
- *Heroine*, 1881
- *Hyacinth*, 1881
- *Caroline*, 1882

— SLOOPS, STEEL

- *Algerine*, 1895
- *Condor*, 1898
- *Shearwater*, 1901

— TORPEDO CRAFT

Torpedo Boats
- *T.B. 39*, 1885
- *T.B. 40*, 1885
Torpedo Boat Destroyers
- *Virago*, 1896
- *Sparrowhawk*, 1897

$\mathcal{A}$CKNOWLEDGEMENTS

I cannot begin to pay tribute to all persons who have guided my studies or answered my questions over the course of the half century that I have been researching the subject of this book. Here's a feeble attempt. For academic advice about theme and touch: G.S. Graham, Willard Ireland, Glyn Williams, John Semple Galbraith, Margaret A. Ormsby, John Bach, Douglas Cole, Raymond Dumett, Eugene Rasor. For naval advice: Vice-Admiral Sir James Watt, Rear-Admiral P.W. Brock, Commodore Jan Drent, John Hattendorf, Michael Whitby, Michael Hadley, James Boutilier, Lt. Cdr. L. Phillips. For additional naval advice, particularly on hydrography: Rear-Admiral George S. Ritchie, Captain Michael Barritt, Lt. Cdr. Andrew David, R.W. Sandilands, Andrew Cook. For expertise on the nineteenth century and various navies: Roger Sarty, Andrew Lambert, Robert Erwin Johnston, C.I. Hamilton, Malcolm Murfett, Kenneth Hagan, Ian Nish. For knowledge of local history: Jack Bates, Sherri Robinson, Rick James, Ken Gibson, Lorraine McConkey, Mike Vouri. For the company and encouragement of other working historians: C.R. Boxer, John Grenville, A.G. Hopkins, Peter Cain, Antony Low, Derek Fieldhouse, R.E. Robinson, John Darwin, Peter Clarke, Abraham Nasatir, Doyce Nunis, Vernon F. Snow. For technical knowledge and friendship: Norman Collingwood, Len McCann, Steve Mayo, Bill Wolferstan. For editorial advice: John Gough, Tony Blicq, Jane Fredeman, Kenneth Pearson, Audrey McClellan. To archivists and librarians of the following collections: Hudson's Bay Company Archives, Manitoba Archives, British Columbia Maritime Museum, Library and Archives Canada, Archives of British Columbia, Esquimalt Archives, National Maritime Museum, British Library, Institute of Historical Research University of London, Warwickshire Record Office, Oregon Historical Society, British Library, Bodleian Library, the Athenaeum, the London Library, the Royal Commonwealth Society, University of Cambridge Library. For grants: Canada Council, British Council, Koerner Foundation, Western Washington University, Wilfrid Laurier University and University of London. The basis for every map was drawn by my late father, John Gough. Thank you to him, for this and many more contributions over the years. To those who have provided photographs, secured permissions, proofread copy, compiled indexes and turned, as a form of alchemy, a typescript into a printed book, abundant thanks. I alone am responsible for errors and omissions.

✏️OTES

INTRODUCTION

1. Admiral John Moresby, *Two Admirals* (London: John Murray, 1909; rev. ed., London: Methuen and Co., 1913), 52–53.

2. Ibid., 55–59.

3. Admiral Sir Cyprian Bridge, *Some Recollections, 2nd ed.* (London: John Murray, 1919), 118–19.

4. See Barry M. Gough, "Sea Power and South America: The 'Brasils' or South Station of the Royal Navy 1808–1837," *The American Neptune*, 50, no. 1 (1990): 26–34.

5. See Barry M. Gough, *Pax Britannica: Ruling the Waves and Keeping the Peace before Armageddon* (Basingstoke, UK: Palgrave Macmillan, 2014), 185–86, and sources used.

6. Journal of the *Grampus*, July 28, 1846, Byam Martin Papers, Add. MSS. 41, 472, BL.

7. Leonard B. Irwin, *Pacific Railways and Nationalism in the Canadian-American Northwest, 1845–73* (New York: Greenwood Press, 1968), 222.

PROLOGUE

1. Harold A. Innis, *The Fur Trade in Canada*, rev. ed. (New Haven, CT: Yale University Press, 1962), 205.

2. Waging wars with France and the United States was a factor that brought a rapid decline of British vessels in the maritime fur trade (primarily that for sea otter). See F.W. Howay, "An Outline Sketch of the Maritime Fur Trade," in *Canadian Historical Association Annual Report, 1932* (Ottawa: CHA, 1932), 7. Also James R. Gibson, *Sea Otter Skins, Boston Ships, and China Goods: The Maritime Fur Trade of the Northwest Coast, 1785–1941* (Montreal and Kingston: McGill-Queen's University Press, 1992).

3. William McGillivray [?], "Some Account of the Trade Carried on by the North-West Company," fol. 20, Royal Commonwealth Society Collections, University of Cambridge Library.

4. McTavish, McGillivrays and Company to McTavish, Fraser and Company, January 23, 1810, Q/113, pp. 228–30, LAC; published as "Appeal of the North West Company to the British Government to Forestall John Jacob Astor's Columbia Enterprise," *Canadian Historical Review*, 17 (September 1936): 306.

5. G.C. Davidson, *The North West Company* (Berkeley: University of California Press, 1918), 134.

6. For details, see James P. Ronda, *Astoria and Empire* (Lincoln: University of Nebraska Press, 1990). On the loss of the Tonquin, see the brief account, written the year after the event, in Robert F. Jones, *Astorian Adventure: The Journal of Alfred Seton, 1811–1815* (New York: Fordham University Press, 1993), 91–94.

7. S. McGillivray to Lord Liverpool, November 10, 1810, Q/113, pp. 221–23, LAC.

8. See Richard Glover, ed., *David Thompson's Narrative, 1784–1812*, vol. 40 (Toronto: Champlain Society, 1962), 358–59; and see also A.S. Morton, "The North

West Company's Columbian Venture and David Thompson," *Canadian Historical Review*, 17 (1936): 284–88. For various historians' interpretations of Thompson's apparently faltering progress, see Barbara Belyea, "The 'Columbian Enterprise' and A.S. Morton: A Historical Exemplum," *BC Studies*, 86 (Summer 1990): 3–27.

CHAPTER ONE

1.   For sources and further discussion, see Barry M. Gough, *Pax Britannica: Ruling the Waves and Keeping the Peace before Armageddon* (Basingstoke, UK: Palgrave Macmillan, 2014), p. xxx.

2.   Instructions, J.W. Croker (secretary of the Admiralty) to Captain J. Hillyar, March 13, 1813, Adm. 2/1380, pp. 367–79.

3.   Quoted in F.W Howay, W.N. Sage and H.F. Angus, *British Columbia and the United States* (New Haven, CT: Yale University Press, 1942), 34.

4.   John Macdonald of Garth, "Journal from England to the Columbia River, North West Coast of America," MG 19, A 17, LAC; printed in B.C. Payette, ed., *The Oregon Country under the Union Jack* (Montreal: privately printed, 1961), v–x. Hereinafter cited as *Macdonald Journal*, with date.

5.   Rear-Admiral Sir Manley Dixon to Croker, June 21, 1813. Adm. 1/21; also Gerald S. Graham and R.A. Humphreys, eds., *The Navy and South America, 1807–1823: Correspondence of the Commanders-in-Chief on the South American Station*, vol. 104 (London: Navy Records Society, 1962), 93–95. Hereinafter cited as *Navy and South America*.

6.   Ibid.

7.   Ibid.

8.   A.T. Mahan, *Sea Power in Its Relations to the War of 1812* (Boston: Little, Brown and Co., 1905), 2:248.

9.   On the early activities of the *Racoon*, see the indispensable John A. Hussey, ed., *The Voyage of the "Racoon": A "Secret" Journal of a Visit to Oregon, California and Hawaii, 1813–1814* [by Francis Phillips] (San Francisco: Book Club of California, 1958), ix–xi.

10.   Dixon to Croker, June 9, 1813, Adm. 1/21.

11.   Reasons are given in Dixon's secret instructions to Hillyar of July 1, 1813, ibid.

12.   *Macdonald Journal*, July 9, 1813.

13.   Dixon to Croker, March 12, 1813, Adm. 1/21; *Navy and South America*, 98.

14.   Admiralty Instructions to Hillyar, March 12, 1813, most secret, Adm. 2/1380, pp. 370–75. The instructions were to be opened 30 leagues south of Rio.

15.   Ibid.

16.   Ibid.

17.   Dixon to Croker, June 21, 1813, Adm. 1/21.

18.   Macdonald Journal, July 10 and 12, 1813.

19.   Dixon to Hillyar, July 1, 1813, secret, encl. in Dixon to Croker, July 12, 1813, Adm. 1/21.

20.   Ibid. See also Bowes to Dixon, September 14, 1813, encl. in Dixon to Croker, October 20, 1813, Adm. 1/22; *Navy and South America*, 110; and Kenneth W. Porter, *John Jacob Astor, Business Man* (Cambridge, MA: Harvard University Press, 1931), 1:218–19. On the leak of information, see W. Kaye Lamb, ed., *Journal of a Voyage to the North West Coast of North America during the Years 1811, 1812, 1813 and 1814*, by Gabriel Franchère, vol. 45 (Toronto: Champlain Society, 1969), 20–21.

21.   Mahan, *War of 1812*, 2:245. Principal documents concerning naval activities

of both US and British naval forces in the Pacific are printed in William Dudley and Michael Crawford, eds., *Naval War of 1812: A Documentary History* (Washington, DC: Naval Historical Center, 1992, 2002), 2:683–714, for 1813, and 3:707–87, for 1814–1818.

22. See Mahan, *War of 1812*, 2:246.

23. *Macdonald Journal*, July 22, 1813.

24. Ibid., September 18, 1813.

25. Ibid., October 2, 1813.

26. Mahan, *War of 1812*, 2:248.

27. Ibid., 2:247; Dudley and Crawford, *Naval War of 1812*, 3:707.

28. Mahan, *War of 1812*, 2:248–49. See also Hillyar to Croker, February 28, 1814, copy, encl. with Dixon to Croker, May 13, 1814, Adm. 1/22; *Navy and South America*, 132–33.

29. For action accounts see Andrew Lambert, *The Challenge: Britain against America in the Naval War of 1812* (London: Faber and Faber, 2012), 285–98. For deep-seated, contested history, compare Theodore Roosevelt, *The Naval War of 1812*, new ed. (Annapolis, MD: Naval Institute Press, 1987); and William James, *Naval Occurrences of the War of 1812* (London: Conway Maritime, 2004), with a convincing introduction by A. Lambert.

30. Hillyar's description of the engagement is in his letter to Croker of March 30, 1814, copy, encl. in Dixon to Croker, June 10, 1814, Adm. 1/22; *Navy and South America*, 141–42.

31. Log of the *Essex*, March 28, 1814, in Payette, *Oregon Country*, 197.

32. See Harold and Margaret Sprout, *The Rise of American Naval Power, 1776–1918* (Princeton, NJ: Princeton University Press, 1939), 73–85.

33. Kenneth W. Porter, "The Cruise of the *Forester*," *Washington Historical Quarterly*, 23 (1932): 262–69.

34. Hillyar to Captain Thomas T. Tucker, April 14, 1814, encl. in Dixon to Croker, September 8, 1814, Adm. 1/22; *Navy and South America*, 147–48; Tucker to Dixon, June 20, 1814, Adm. 1/22.

35. Howay, Sage and Angus, *British Columbia and the United States*, 33.

36. Earl S. Pomeroy, *The Pacific Slope* (New York: Knopf, 1966), 17.

37. Robert Greenhow, *Memoir, Historical and Political, on the North West Coast of North America* (Washington, DC: Blair and Rives, 1840), 159.

38. Washington Irving, *Astoria* (London: R. Bentley, 1836), 3:214. Also, Alexander Henry the Younger, "Journal Across the Rocky Mountains to the Pacific," March 2, 1814, Coventry Transcript, MG 19, A13, LAC. Published in Barry M. Gough, ed. *The Journal of Alexander Henry the Younger, 1799–1814*, 2 vols. (Toronto: Champlain Society, 1988, 1992); also printed in Payette, Oregon Country. Hereinafter cited as Henry Journal, with date.

39. Sale documents are in *Oregon Historical Quarterly*, 33 (1932): 43–50.

40. Captain William Black to Dixon, April 10, 1814, from San Francisco, Adm. 1/22.

41. This is based on the narrative in Hussey, *Voyage of the "Racoon,"* 4.

42. *Henry Journal*, November 30, 1813, and April 4 and 10, 1814.

43. Ross Cox, *Adventures on the Columbia River, including the Narrative of a Residence of Six Years on the Western Side of the Rocky Mountains* (London: H. Colburn and R. Bentley, 1831), 1:266. For other versions of what Black said, see Elliot Coues, ed., *New Light on the Early History of the Greater Northwest: The Manuscript Journals of Alexander*

Henry . . . and of David Thompson (London: Suckling and Co., 1897), 2:770–71, note 36.

44. *Henry Journal*, December 13, 1813.

45. Black's report, December 15, 1813, deciphered, Adm. 1/22. A copy in cipher reached the Admiralty October 14, 1814.

46. Hussey, ed., *Voyage of the "Racoon,"* 5.

47. See, for example, Hubert H. Bancroft, *The Northwest Coast* (San Francisco: A.L. Bancroft and Co., 1884), 1:233; and see also Robert Greenhow, *The History of Oregon and California* (London: John Murray, 1844), 304.

48. Payette, *Oregon Country*, xii–xiii.

49. Dixon to Croker, December 24, 1814, Adm. 1/22.

50. *Henry Journal*, April 24, 1814.

51. Hussey, ed., *Voyage of the "Racoon,"* 15ff.

52. Ibid., 20. Vernon D. Tate, ed., "Spanish Documents Relating to the Voyage of the *Racoon* to Astoria and San Francisco," *Hispanic American Historical Review*, 18 (May 1938): 190–91.

53. Captain Peter Corney of the *Columbia* described Fort George's substantial defences in his *Voyages in the North Pacific* (Honolulu: Thorn. G. Thrum, 1896), 79a and 80a.

54. "Statement relative to the Columbia River [1815]," encl. in McGillivray to Sir C. Bagot, November 15, 1817, and fur traders' demands, May 7, 1814, FO 5/1230. This subject is examined more fully in Barry M. Gough, *Fortune's a River: The Collision of Empires in Northwest America* (Madeira Park, BC: Harbour Publishing, 2007), 319–41.

55. J. Monroe to Plenipotentiaries, March 22, 1814, in United States, *American State Papers, Foreign Relations* (Washington, DC: Gales and Seaton, 1832–59), 3:731.

56. See Katherine B. Judson, "The British Side of the Restoration of Fort Astoria," *Oregon Historical Quarterly*, 20 (1919): 243–60 and 305–6.

57. A.L. Burt, *The United States, Great Britain and British North America, from the Revolution to the Establishment of Peace after the War of 1812* (New Haven, CT: Yale University Press, 1940), 371.

58. Monroe to A. Baker, July 18, 1815, encl. in Baker to Lord Castlereagh, July 19, 1815, FO 5/107.

59. Baker to Monroe, July 23, 1815, encl. in Baker to Castlereagh, August 13, 1815, ibid.

60. Baker to Dixon, July 24, 1815, encl. in ibid. For the full diplomatic interplay, see Burt, *United States, Great Britain and British North America*, 411–22.

61. See Frederick Merk, "The Genesis of the Oregon Question," *Mississippi Valley Historical Review*, 36 (March 1950): 593–94.

62. S. McGillivray to Sir C. Bagot, November 15, 1817, encl. in Bagot to Castlereagh, December 2, 1817, FO 5/123.

63. Bagot to Castlereagh, November 24, 1817, cypher, ibid.

64. Ibid.

65. Bagot to Sir John Sherbrooke (Governor General of Canada), December 1, 1817, ibid.

66. Bagot to Castlereagh, December 2, 1817, ibid.

67. Commodore J. Yeo to Croker, August 30, 1817, encl. in J. Barrow to Hamilton (FO), September 3, 1817, FO 5/128.

68. Ibid.

69. Sir Charles K. Webster, *The Foreign Policy of Castlereagh, 1812–1815* (London: G. Bell and Sons, 1931), 196. See also Gerald S. Graham, *Empire of the North Atlantic:*

the Maritime Struggle for North America, 2nd ed. (Toronto: University of Toronto Press, 1958), 262–64.

70. Merk, "Genesis of the Oregon Question," 603–4.

71. F.V. Longstaff and W. Kaye Lamb, "The Royal Navy on the Northwest Coast, 1813–1850, Part I," *British Columbia Historical Quarterly*, 9 (January 1945): 6; Bowles to Croker, April 29, 1818, Adm. 1/23.

72. J. Keith to Captain F. Hickey, October 7, 1818, encl. in Barrow to Hamilton, August 10, 1819, FO 5/147.

73. Hickey to Keith, October 4, 1818, encl. in Barrow to Hamilton, August 10, 1819, FO 5/147.

74. Burt, *United States, Great Britain and British North America*, 422.

CHAPTER TWO

1. Admiral Sir Cyprian Bridge, *Sea-Power and Other Studies* (London: Smith, Elder and Co., 1910), 63–64.

2. See Albert H. Imlah, *Economic Elements in the "Pax Britannica"* (Cambridge, MA: Harvard University Press, 1958), 186.

3. Sir Halford J. Mackinder, *Democratic Ideas and Reality* (London: Constable and Co., 1919), 73.

4. See Gerald S. Graham, *The Politics of Naval Supremacy: Studies in British Maritime Ascendancy* (Cambridge: Cambridge University Press, 1965), chapter 4.

5. William Laird Clowes, *The Royal Navy: A History from the Earliest Times to the Present* (London: Sampson Low, Marston and Co., 1901), 6:vii.

6. See Barry M. Gough, *Pax Britannica: Ruling the Waves and Keeping the Peace before Armageddon* (Basingstoke, UK: Palgrave Macmillan, 2014).

7. For the boundaries of this station, see Appendix A.

8. *Navy and South America*, xi–xii and xxiii–xxxiv. The genesis of the Pacific station is explained in John Bach, "The Royal Navy in the South Pacific, 1826–1876" (Ph.D. thesis, University of New South Wales, 1964), chapter 2. See also Appendix A.

9. During the California gold rush, British men-of-war called at San Francisco to receive merchants' treasure for shipment to England.

10. On this rivalry, see Frederick Merk, *The Oregon Question: Essays in Anglo-American Diplomacy and Politics* (Cambridge, MA: Belknap Press, 1967).

11. See John S. Galbraith, *The Hudson's Bay Company as an Imperial Factor, 1821–1869* (Berkeley and Los Angeles: University of California Press, 1957), 133 and note 62.

12. John Franklin to John Barrow (Adm.), November 26, 1823, copy, A. 8/1, fols. 224–29, HBCA.

13. John H. Pelly (HBC governor) to Barrow, November 29, 1823, ibid., fol. 220. Further details on British plans and strategy at this time are given in John E. Caswell, "The Sponsors of Canadian Arctic Exploration, Part III—1800 to 1839," *The Beaver*, Outfit 300 (Autumn 1969): 29–30.

14. Governor and Committee to George Simpson, February 27, 1822, A. 6/20, HBCA; printed in R. Harvey Fleming, ed., *Minutes of Council of the Northern Department of Rupert Land 1821–31*, vol. 3 (London: Hudson's Bay Record Society, 1940), 303.

15. Galbraith, *Hudson's Bay Company*, 134.

16. For an attack on the thesis of H.W.V. Temperley that Russia "was extending a long arm over the Pacific," see Irby C. Nichols Jr., "The Russian Ukase and the

Monroe Doctrine: A Re-evaluation," *Pacific Historical Review*, 36 (February 1967): 16ff.

17. G. Canning (FO) to R. Rush (American minister in London), January 1824, draft, FO 5/194; and Dexter Perkins, *The Monroe Doctrine, 1823–1826* (Cambridge, MA: Harvard University Press, 1932), 33. Russia had, in fact, sent three frigates to the Northwest Coast in 1822 to exclude foreigners; Nichols, "Russian Ukase and the Monroe Doctrine," 21, 24. See also Kenneth Bourne, *Britain and the Balance of Power in North America, 1815–1908* (London: Longmans, Green and Co., 1967), 64–71.

18. Merk, *Oregon Question*, 137.

19. For general accounts of American and French interest, see Harold W. Bradley, "Hawaii and the American Penetration of the Northeastern Pacific, 1800–1845," *Pacific Historical Review*, 12 (September 1943): 277–86; George Vern Blue, "The Policy of France toward the Hawaiian Islands from the Earliest Times to the Treaty of 1846," in *The Hawaiian Islands*, Publication of the Archives of Hawaii No. 5 (Honolulu: Archives of Hawaii, 1930), 51–93; and Christian Schefer, "La monarchie de Juilliet et l'expansion coloniale," *Revue des Deux Mondes*, 6e série, 11 (1912): 152–84.

20. Canning to Lord Liverpool, July 7, 1826; in Edward J. Stapleton, ed., *Some Official Correspondence of George Canning* (London: Longmans, Green and Co., 1887), 2:74.

21. Ibid.

22. Admiral Sir Cyprian Bridge, *Some Recollections*, 2nd ed. (London: John Murray, 1919), 127–31. The statute is 59 Geo. 3 (1819), c. 25.

23. For the increase of British naval strength in the Pacific at this time, including sending a ship-of-the-line to the west coast of South America, see Liverpool to Earl Bathurst, October 16, 1823, in Historical Manuscripts Commission, *Report on the Manuscripts of Earl Bathurst, at Cirencester Park* (London: HMSO, 1923), 548–49; and C.J. Bartlett, *Great Britain and Sea Power, 1815–1853* (Oxford: Clarendon Press, 1963), 67–69.

24. Canning to George IV, July 14, 1824, FO 83/3; Jean I. Brookes, *International Rivalry in the Pacific Islands, 1800–1875* (Berkeley and Los Angeles: University of California Press, 1941), 50. Details of the mission are in Lord G.A. Byron, *Voyage of the "Blonde" to the Sandwich Islands, 1824–25* (London: John Murray, 1826).

25. Board of Trade to Planta, June 30, 1825, FO 58/3; quoted in W.P. Morrell, *Britain in the Pacific Islands* (Oxford: Clarendon Press, 1960), 64.

26. Morrell, *Britain in the Pacific Islands*, 66.

27. M. Seymour, "Remarks on the Capabilities, etc. of the Sandwich Islands [1834]," Adm. 1/43.

28. See Morrell, *Britain in the Pacific Islands*, 70–71.

29. Captain E. Russell to Commodore Mason, February 3, 1837, Adm. 1/48.

30. Rear-Admiral Sir Graham Eden Hamond, Hamond Journal, III (HAM/127), p. 31, NMM. His fears that the Americans were about to seize the whaling centre of the Pacific were conveyed in letters to the Admiralty, December 10, 1836 (Adm. 1/47), and August 28, 1837 (Adm. 1/48). The *North Carolina*, however, spent all her time in South American waters; see Robert E. Johnson, *Thence Round Cape Horn: The Story of United States Naval Forces on Pacific Station, 1818–1923* (Annapolis, MD: United States Naval Institute, 1963), 46–53.

31. Russell to Mason, February 3, 1837, Adm. 1/48.

32. Views of Lord Stanley (CO) quoted by Lord Aberdeen (FO) to Richard Pakenham (British minister, Mexico), December 15, 1841, FO 50/143; see also Sister Magdalen Coughlin, "California Ports: A Key to Diplomacy for the West Coast, 1820–1845," *Journal of the West*, 5 (April 1966): 162.

33. Sir John Pelly to Russell, February 6, 1841, CO 42/485. An earlier plea that American expansion in the northeastern Pacific would deprive Britain of commercial and colonizing advantages had no influence on the ministry: Pelly to Lord Palmerston, February 26, 1840, CO 6/14.

34. Russell to James Stephen, Minute, February 9, 1841, CO 42/485.

35. Sir John Barrow to Stephen, February 11, 1841, CO 42/482.

36. Ibid.

37. Barrow was not without his critics, one of whom was Sir Thomas Byam Martin: "Mr. Barrow has, in his time, greatly and mischievously misled the First Lords of the Admiralty; no public servant has done more harm for so little good." Admiral Sir R. Vesey Hamilton, ed., *Journals and Letters of Admiral of the Fleet Sir Thom. Byam Martin*, vol. 1 (London: Navy Records Society, 1903), 115. For a different view, see Sir John Henry Briggs, *Naval Administrations, 1827 to 1892* (London: Sampson Low and Co., 1897), 72.

38. Stephen to Pelly, draft, February 16, 1841, CO 42/485.

39. G. Simpson to Pelly, March 10, 1842, FO 5/388; in Joseph Schafer, ed., "Letters of Sir George Simpson, 1841–1843," *American Historical Review*, 14 (October 1908): 86–93.

40. Ibid.

41. Ibid.

42. Rear-Admiral R. Thomas to S. Herbert (Adm.), April 15, 1842, Adm. 1/5512.

43. Ibid.

44. Thomas to Herbert, August 16, 1842, ibid.; see also Morrell, *Britain in the Pacific Islands*, chapter 4.

45. Captain J. Jones to Rear-Admiral Ross, November 6, 1841, encl. in Thomas to Herbert, April 15, 1842, Adm. 1/5512.

46. H.U. Addington (FO) to Herbert, October 4, 1842, and Admiralty Minute, October 8, 1842, Adm. 1/5525.

47. Lord Paulet to W.A.B. Hamilton, March 11, 1843, Adm. 1/5562. Paulet's instructions from Rear-Admiral Thomas, January 17 and 18, 1842, are in Adm. 1/5531. A good account of the Paulet episode is in Ralph S. Kuykendall, *The Hawaiian Kingdom, 1778–1854* (Honolulu: University of Hawaii Press, 1938), 206–26.

48. Foreign Office Memorandum, July 1843, FO 58/19; Brookes, *International Rivalry*, 135. On American influence, see Morrell, *British in the Pacific Islands*, 83.

49. Quoted in Morrell, *British in the Pacific Islands*, 85.

50. As early as 1846, the disadvantageous British position was recognized by Captain Henry Byam Martin of HMS *Grampus*. He regretted that Paulet's treaty had been cancelled because Britain would have derived great advantage from possessing these islands that lay on the high road of trans-Pacific trade and were the rendezvous of whalers. He claimed that France would not have objected. *Grampus* Journal, August 15 and 24, 1846, Byam Martin Papers, Add. MSS. 41, 472, BL.

51. Sir John Barrow, *Autobiographical Memoir* (London: John Murray, 1847), 333 and 470.

52. Sir John Barrow, *Voyages of Discovery and Research within the Arctic Regions, from the Year 1818 to the Present Time* (London: John Murray, 1846), 16–17.

53. Ibid., 12.

54. Admiralty instructions, May 11, 1825; in Frederick W. Beechey, *Narrative of a Voyage to the Pacific and Beering's Strait to Co-operate with the Polar Expeditions, 1825–28* (London: Colburn and Bentley, 1831), 1:ix–xiii. Commander L.S. Dawson, comp., *Memoirs of Hydrography . . . 1750–1885* (Eastbourne, UK: Henry W. Keay, 1885), 1:112.

55. Beechey to J.W. Croker (Adm.), November 18, 1826, Adm. 1/1574.

56. Beechey, *Narrative of a Voyage*, 2:63–64.

57. Beechey to Captain F. Beaufort (Hydrographer), August 15, 1831, File No. Misc. 15, Folder 1, item 3, HO.

58. Beechey to Beaufort, June 17, 1835, ibid., item 4; Beechey to Beaufort, November 1, 1836, S.L. 21, item 4, HO.

59. F.V. Longstaff and W. Kaye Lamb, "The Royal Navy on the Northwest Coast, 1813–1850, Part 1," *British Columbia Historical Quarterly*, 9 (January 1945): 10n18.

60. Beechey to Beaufort, November 1, 1836, S.L. 21, item 4, HO. The reference is to Samuel Purchas, who published Michael Lok's interview with Juan de Fuca—and other discovery narratives.

61. A.S. Hamond to Mason, June 17, 1837, encl. in Rear-Admiral G.E. Hamond to G. Wood (Adm.), August 25, 1837, Adm. 1/48.

62. G.E. Hamond to Wood, August 25, 1837, ibid.

63. Captain Sir Edward Belcher, *Narrative of a Voyage round the World, Performed in Her Majesty's Ship "Sulphur," during the Years 1836–1842* (London: Henry Colburn, 1843), 1:313–17. No special report by Belcher on Bodega Bay and Ross Colony is to be found among the Admiralty papers in the PRO.

64. See duplicate of Admiralty Board Instructions to Rear-Admiral Richard Thomas, Commander-in-Chief, Pacific, August 21, 1841, Admiral Thomas Papers, G. 4, article 6, HSL.

65. A.P. Nasatir, "International Rivalry for California and the Establishment of the British Consulate," *California Historical Society Quarterly*, 46 (March 1967): 61–63; Johnson, *Thence Round Cape Horn*, 57 and note 4.

66. Ephraim D. Adams, "English Interest in the Annexation of California," *American Historical Review*, 14 (July 1909): 745. Professor Adams mistakenly concluded that no British naval activity followed.

67. Thomas to secretary of the Admiralty, December 28, 1841, Adm. 1/5512; and Jenkin Jones to Ross, December 27, 1841, No. 38, copy, JON/5, NMM.

68. Belcher to Wood, December 28, 1837, Cap B 101, Adm. 1/1586; and Belcher to Wood, June 10, 1839, Cap B 223, Adm. 1/1587. See also Richard E. Pierce and John H. Winslow, eds., *H.M.S. Sulphur on the Northwest and California Coasts, 1837 and 1839* (Kingston, ON: Limehouse Press, 1979).

69. Hydrographic guidance to Captain Beechey, n.d., S.L. 21, item 6, HO.

70. Belcher, *Narrative of a Voyage*, 1:xx.

71. *Proceedings of the Royal Geographical Society*, 4 (1859–60), 35.

72. B.223/b/10, fol. 76d. HBCA; quoted in E.E. Rich, *The Fur Trade and the Northwest to 1857* (Toronto: McClelland and Stewart, 1967), 278. Hamond to Wood, August 28, 1837, Adm. 1/48. Slacum's memorial to Congress is printed in *Oregon Historical Quarterly*, 13 (1902): 175–224.

73. With Palmerston at the Foreign Office, the Hudson's Bay Company could be assured that such views were unacceptable. See Rich, *Fur Trade and the Northwest*, 279.

74. George M. Douglas, ed., "Royal Navy Ships on the Columbia River in 1839," *The Beaver*, Outfit 285 (Autumn 1954): 39–41, based on Belcher's *Narrative of a Voyage*.

75. Belcher to Ross, extract, December 17, 1839, CO 6/14.

76. The Company was then busy meeting the demands for provisions of the Russian American Company, according to a contract of 1839; Longstaff and Lamb, "Royal Navy on the Northwest Coast," 14–15.

77. Pelly to Russell, May 18, 1840, CO 6/14. For the Company's position, see Galbraith, *Hudson's Bay Company*, 220–21.

78. Ellenborough to Lord Aberdeen (FO), May 16, 1846, private, Aberdeen Papers, Add. MSS. 43,198, BL.

79. *Proceedings of the Royal Geographical Society*, 4 (1859–1860): 35.

80. In 1823, HMS *Cambridge*, 80 guns, sailed from England to convey British consuls to the east and west coasts of South America. She was probably the first British ship-of-the-line to enter the Pacific since Anson's *Centurion*, 60 guns, to be followed in 1844 by the *Collingwood*, 80 guns, flagship of Rear-Admiral Sir George Seymour, Commander-in-Chief, Pacific. For the voyage of the *Cambridge*, see John Cunningham, Surgeon, "Voyage to the Pacific, 1823–5," JOD 21, NMM.

81. The eight that called on the north Pacific coast were HMS *Blossom*, 1818; *Blossom* 1826–1827; *North Star*, 1836; *Imogene*, 1837; *Sulphur* and *Starling*, 1837, 1839; *Curaçoa*, 1841; *Carysfort*, 1843.

82. William Stanton, *The United States Great Exploring Expedition of 1838–1942* (Berkeley and Los Angeles: University of California Press, 1975). On the growing value of Puget Sound ports, see Norman A. Graebner, *Empire on the Pacific, a Study in American Continental Expansion* (New York: Ronald, 1955).

CHAPTER THREE

1. The full claims are given in "Correspondence Relative to the Negotiation of the Question of the Disputed Right to the Oregon Territory," *Parliamentary Papers*, 1846, 52 (Cmd. 695). On the British case, see Travers Twiss, *The Oregon Question Examined in Respect to Facts and the Law of Nations* (London: Longman, Brown, Green and Longmans, 1846); and Adam Thom, *The Claims to the Oregon Territory Considered* (London: Smith, Elder and Co., 1844).

2. W. Kaye Lamb, "The Founding of Fort Victoria," *British Columbia Historical Quarterly*, 7 (April 1943): 71ff.

3. John H. Pelly (HBC governor) to Lord Palmerston (FO), February 26, 1840, copy, CO 6/14.

4. See Norman Graebner, "Maritime Factors in the Oregon Compromise," *Pacific Historical Review*, 20 (November 1951): 331–46.

5. J. McLoughlin to Governor, March 28, 1845, B.223/b/33, fols. 170–72, HBCA.

6. These instructions, noted in IND. 4761, PRO, were received by Rear-Admiral Richard Thomas on February 11, 1843.

7. Lord Aberdeen's instructions to the Admiralty, October 23, 1843, are in R.C. Clark, *History of the Willamette Valley, Oregon* (Chicago: S.J. Clarke, 1927), 1:327–28.

8. See "HMS *Modeste* on the Pacific Coast 1843–47: Log and Letters," *Oregon Historical Quarterly*, 61 (December 1960): 408–36; and T. Baillie to Thomas, August 4, 1844, Adm. 1/5550.

9. F.V. Longstaff and W. Kaye Lamb, "The Royal Navy on the Northwest Coast, 1813–1850, Part I," *British Columbia Historical Quarterly*, 9 (January 1945): 19.

10. This report and those of other officers, naval and military, relating to the defences of British North America at this time are in Adm. 7/626.

11. Baron Metcalfe to Lord Stanley, July 4, 1846, confidential, WO 1/552.

12. Sir Robert Peel to Aberdeen, February 23, 1845, Aberdeen Papers, Add. MSS. 43,064, fols. 178–81, BL.

13. G. Simpson to Pelly, March 29, 1845, copy, FO 5/440; on this proposal see E.E. Rich, *The History of the Hudson's Bay Company, 1670–1870* (London: Hudson's Bay Record Society, 1958–1959), 2:724; and C.P. Stacey, "The Hudson's Bay Company and Anglo-American Military Rivalries during the Oregon Dispute," *Canadian Historical Review*, 18 (September 1937): 285–301.

14. See Simpson to Lts. Warre and Vavasour, May 30, 1846, confidential, WO 1/552; and Alvin C. Gluek, Jr., *Minnesota and the Manifest Destiny of the Canadian Northwest: A Study in Canadian-American Relations* (Toronto: University of Toronto Press, 1965), 60–71.

15. CO Memorandum on HBC Defence, November 27, 1845, CO 537/96.

16. H.U. Addington (FO) to J. Stephen (CO), April 3, 1845, confidential, WO 1/553. The planned meeting with officers of the Royal Navy is mentioned in Henry J. Warre, "Travel and Sport in North America, 1839–1847," typescript, RG 24, F71, p. 52, LAC. Also Simpson to Pelly, May 4, 1845, D. 4/67, fols. 13–15, HBCA.

17. Warre and Vavasour to secretary of state for the colonies, No. 1, June 10, 1845, WO 1/552.

18. Simpson to P.S. Ogden, SO, May 1845, confidential, copy, ibid.

19. Warre and Vavasour to secretary of state for the colonies, No. 2, October 26, 1845, ibid. (received July 7, 1846).

20. Vavasour to Colonel N.W. Holloway, RE (Officer Commanding, Canada), March 1, 1846, copy, FO 5/457.

21. Simpson to Pelly, March 29, 1845, copy, FO 5/440. See the sketch of the river entrance in Warre Notebook, RG 24, F71, LAC.

22. Vavasour to Holloway, March 1, 1846, copy, FO 5/457.

23. Warre, "Travel and Sport," p. 143, LAC.

24. Peel to Aberdeen, September 28, 1844, no. 270, Add. MSS. 44,454, BL. He suggested that the flagship *Collingwood*, "when she has leisure," might visit the mouth of the Columbia.

25. Addington to Corry, March 5, 1845, secret, encl. in W.A.B. Hamilton (Adm.) to Seymour, March 10, 1845, confidential, Adm. 172/4.

26. The hardening of policy was announced in the Commons. Great Britain, *Hansard's Parliamentary Debates*, 3rd series, 79, 199 (4 April 1845).

27. Aberdeen to Pakenham, April 2, 1845, private, Aberdeen Papers, Add. MSS. 43,123, fol. 2476, BL.

28. Rear-Admiral Sir George Seymour, Private Diary, CR 114A/376/21, *passim*, WRO. On Seymour's career and the Pritchard Affair at Tahiti, see *Dictionary of National Biography* (London, 1897), 51:321

29. Seymour, Private Diary, CR 114A/374/22, July 14, 1845, WRO.

30. For more on this mission, see Barry M. Gough, "H.M.S. *America* on the North Pacific Coast," *Oregon Historical Quarterly*, 70 (December 1969): 292–311.

31. Seymour to Corry, July 14, 1845, Seymour Order Book I, CR 114A/414/1, WRO. A copy of Seymour's instructions to Gordon, February 13, 1845, are in ibid.

32. McLoughlin to Governor, March 28, 1845, B. 223/b/33, fols. 170–72, HBCA.

33. On Lieutenant Peel, see Captain J. Gordon to Seymour, October 22, 1845, Adm. 1/5564; Admiral Sir Albert H. Markham, *The Life of Sir Clements R. Markham* (London: John Murray, 1917), 39–41. Markham thought Peel "the perfect model of what a British naval officer ought to be."

34. T. Larkin to Dr. John Marsh, August 19, 1845, Marsh Collection, California State Library, Sacramento; in John A. Hawgood, ed., *First and Last Consul: Thomas Oliver Larkin and the Americanization of California—a Selection of Letters* (San Marino, CA: Huntington Library, 1962), 33.

35. Gordon to Officer-in-Charge, Fort Victoria, August 31, 1845, Port Discovery, B. 226/b/1, fols. 35–36d, HBCA.

36. Lt. Thomas Dawes, "Journal of HMS 'America,'" JOD/42, MS 57/055, p. 85, NMM.

37. Gordon to Lt. Wm. Peel, September 2, 1845, encl. in Corry to Addington, February 13, 1846, FO 5/459.

38. Wm. Peel to Gordon, September 27, 1845, encl. in Hamilton to Addington, February 10, 1846, FO 5/459. Inscribed on the back, probably in Aberdeen's hand, is "a very good report."

39. Gordon to Admiralty, October 19, 1845, Adm. 1/5564.

40. Peel to R. Pakenham, January 2, 1846, FO 5/459.

41. R. Finlayson to McLoughlin, September 24, 1845, Fort Victoria, B. 226/b/1, fol. 37d, HBCA.

42. [Roderick Finlayson], *Biography* [of Roderick Finlayson] (Victoria, BC: [1891]), 15; see also his "History of Vancouver Island and the Northwest Coast," typescript, 34, BCA.

43. From Finlayson's Journal, BCA, quoted in Captain John T. Walbran, *British Columbia Coast Names, 1592–1906* (Ottawa: Government Printing Bureau, 1909), 210. See also Leigh Burpee Robinson, *Esquimalt: "Place of Shoaling Waters"* (Victoria, BC: Quality Press, 1947), 29–30.

44. Finlayson, "History of Vancouver Island," 35. On R. Haig-Brown, see Reginald Eyre Watters, ed., *British Columbia: A Centennial Anthology* (Toronto: McClelland and Stewart, 1958), 198–204.

45. James Douglas to Simpson, March 20, 1846, private, D. 5/16, HBCA. Douglas was indeed correct in his views on Gordon, for the latter thought Oregon of little importance, especially in comparison to California. See Gordon to secretary of the Admiralty, October 19, 1845, Adm. 1/5564.

46. Baillie's instructions from Seymour, August 12, 1845, are in Adm. 1/5561.

47. Seymour to Corry, July 14, 1845, Y158, Adm. 1/5550.

48. Douglas to Baillie, October 8, 1845, copy, B. 223/b/33, fols. 107–107d, HBCA.

49. Report of Lts. Warre and Vavasour to secretary of state for the colonies, December 8, 1845; in Joseph Schafer, ed., "Documents Relative to Warre and Vavasour's Military Reconnoissance [*sic*] in Oregon, 1845–6," *Quarterly of the Oregon Historical Society*, 10 (March 1909): 64.

50. McLoughlin to Governor, November 20, 1845; in E.E. Rich, ed., *The Letters of John McLoughlin from Fort Vancouver to the Governor and Committee, Third Series, 1844–46* (London: Hudson's Bay Record Society, 1944), 48.

51. Seymour to Gordon, August 12, 1845, private, Tahiti, CR 114A/418/1, WRO.

52. Seymour to Corry, October 3, 1845, Honolulu, Y7, Adm. 1/5561.

53. Ibid.

54. Seymour, Private Diary, CR 114A/374/22, Appendix, WRO.

55. Seymour, Private Diary, CR 114A/374/23, February 26, 1846, WRO.

56. Ibid.

57. Ibid., March 7, 1846.

58. Seymour to secretary of the Admiralty, March 6, 1846, Adm. 1/5568.

59. Ibid.

60. See, for example, Report of William Wilkins (secretary of war), November 30, 1844, *Senate Documents*, 28th Cong., 2nd Sess., vol. 1, pp. 113ff.

61. Seymour to Lord Ellenborough, March 7, 1846, Ellenborough Papers, PRO 30/12/4/20, TNA.

62. Corry to Smythe (under-secretary of state for foreign affairs), June 6, 1846, FO 5/461.

63. Ibid.

64. See C.J. Bartlett, *Great Britain and Sea Power, 1815–1853* (Oxford: Clarendon Press, 1963), 148–74.

65. Corry to Smythe, June 6, 1846, FO 5/461.

66. Ibid.

67. Addington to Corry, June 19, 1846, confidential, Adm. 1/5568.

68. Ibid.

69. Peel to Lord Egerton, January 6, 1846, Peel Papers, BL.

70. Ellenborough to Peel, March 5, 1846, Peel Papers, Add. MSS. 40,473, fols. 78–78b, BL.

71. Peel to Ellenborough, March 17, 1846, secret, Peel Papers, ADD. MSS. 40,473, fols. 120–23, BL. The naval estimates of 1846 were 12 percent higher than those of the previous year because of developments in steam engineering, fear of war with France and, according to Peel, "relations with the United States." Julius W. Pratt, "James K. Polk and John Bull," *Canadian Historical Review*, 24 (1943): 346.

72. Ellenborough to Seymour, June 28, 1846, Ellenborough Papers, PRO 30/12/4/20, PRO. On Ellenborough at the Admiralty, see Albert H. Imlah, *Lord Ellenborough: A Biography*, Harvard Historical Studies, vol. 43 (Cambridge, MA: Harvard University Press, 1939), 236–38; and Bartlett, *Great Britain and Sea Power*, 182.

73. See Hunter Miller, ed., *Treaties and Other International Acts of America* (Washington, DC: US Government Printing Office, 1936), 5:58; and Frederick Merk, *The Oregon Question: Essays in Anglo-American Diplomacy and Politics* (Cambridge, MA: Belknap Press, 1967), 341–42.

74. On this point, see the convincing article by Wilbur D. Jones and J. Chal Vinson, "British Preparedness and the Oregon Settlement," *Pacific Historical Review*, 22 (November 1953): 361–64. Merk, *Oregon Question*, 362–63, in discounting the importance of sea power in this crisis, makes no reference to the above-mentioned work.

75. Seymour to Corry, April 7, 1846, San Blas, Y63, Adm. 1/5561.

76. Ibid.

77. Seymour to Captain J. Duntze, January 14, 1846, copy, Adm. 1/5561.

78. Seymour, Private Diary, July 19, 1846, CR 114A/374/22, WRO.

79. On Seymour's policy for California, see Ephraim D. Adams, "English Interest in the Annexation of California," *American Historical Review*, 14 (July 1909): 756–61. Seymour to Corry, April 7, 1846, San Blas, Adm. 1/5561.

80. Seymour, Private Diary, August 14, 1846, CR 114A/S74/23, WRO.

81. Ibid., Appendix, 129. Seymour expressed his displeasure on this subject to Captain H. Byam Martin, CB, of the *Grampus*, and the latter knew that "with so great a probability of an American war," Gordon would be "called to account." *Grampus* Journal, Byam Martin Papers, Add. MSS. 41, 472, BL.

82. Dawes, "Journal of HMS 'America' . . . ," p. 107, NMM.

83. Courts Martial Books, Adm. 13/103 and 104 for August 26, 1846.

84. Seymour to Senior Naval Officer of HM Ships in Oregon, October 3, 1846, Honolulu, CR 114A/481/2, WRO.

85. These became points of dispute later. John S. Galbraith, *The Hudson's Bay Company as an Imperial Factor, 1821–1869* (Berkeley and Los Angeles: University of California Press, 1957), 253–55, 260–61 and 271.

86. Frank E. Ross, "The Retreat of the Hudson's Bay Company in the Pacific Northwest," *Canadian Historical Review*, 18 (September 1937): 262–80.

87. Company agents at Honolulu had advised Seymour of the great necessity "to leave one of HM Ships at the River until everything was finally settled." Reported in Pelly and Allan to HBC governor, October 1, 1846, A, 11/62, fols. 139–139d, HBCA.

88. Seymour to Ward, September 27, 1847, Y174, Adm. 1/5578.

89. This advice was forwarded to the next Commander-in-Chief, Pacific. W.A.B. Hamilton to Rear-Admiral T. Phipps Hornby, December 10, 1847, instructions, PHI/3/5, NMM.

90. Directors of HBC at Fort Vancouver to Captain T. Baillie, May 1, 1847, extract, in Seymour to Ward, September 27, 1847, Y174, Adm. 1/5578.

91. Douglas to Governor and Committee, Hudson's Bay Company, July 28, 1846, extract, encl. in Pelly to Earl Grey, December 11, 1846, CO 305/1.

92. Statistics on the relative strength of British, American and French warships, both sail and steam, are in Merk, *Oregon Question*, 348.

93. Harold and Margaret Sprout, *The Rise of American Naval Power, 1776–1918* (Princeton, NJ: Princeton University Press, 1939), 132.

94. Quoted in Robert E. Johnson, *Thence Round Cape Horn: The Story of United States Naval Forces on Pacific Station, 1818–1923* (Annapolis, MD: United States Naval Institute, 1963), 75.

CHAPTER FOUR

1. Among studies of HBC and imperial policies, see Hartwell Bowsfield, ed., *Fort Victoria Letters, 1846–1851* (Winnipeg: Hudson's Bay Record Society, 1979), with introduction by Margaret A. Ormsby; Richard Mackie, *Trade Beyond the Mountains: the British Fur Trade on the Pacific, 1793–1843* (Vancouver: UBC Press, 1997); Daniel W. Clayton, *Islands of Truth: the Imperial Fashioning of Vancouver Island* (Vancouver: UBC Press, 2000); and Stephen Royle, *Company, Crown and Colony: the Hudson's Bay Company and Territorial Endeavour in Western Canada* (London: I.B. Tauris, 2011). Quotes from W. Kaye Lamb, "The Founding of Fort Victoria," *British Columbia Historical Quarterly*, 7 (April 1943): 71–92.

2. Lamb, "The Founding of Fort Victoria," 87.

3. Richard C. Mayne, *Four Years in British Columbia and Vancouver Island: An Account of Their Forests, Rivers, Coasts, Gold Fields, and Resources for Colonization* (London: John Murray, 1862), 26–28.

4. B.A. McKelvie, "Sir James Douglas: a New Portrait," *British Columbia Historical Quarterly*, 7 (April 1943): 97.

5. Paul Knaplund, "James Stephen on Granting Vancouver Island to the Hudson's Bay Company, 1846–1848," *British Columbia Historical Quarterly*, 9 (October 1945): 264.

6. One estimate of the capital needed for the enterprise was £50,000. A.S. Morton, *A History of the Canadian West to 1870–71*, 2nd ed. (Toronto: University of Toronto Press, 1973), 751.

7. For an account of Hudson's Bay Company motives, see John S. Galbraith, *The Hudson's Bay Company as an Imperial Factor, 1821–1869* (Berkeley and Los Angeles: University of California Press, 1957), 284–92, esp. 287, and 307.

8. Earl Grey, *The Colonial Policy of Lord John Russell's Administration* (London: R. Bentley, 1853), 1:1–49; W.P. Morrell, *British Colonial Policy in the Age of Peel and Russell* (Oxford: Clarendon Press, 1930), 444–46.

9. E.E. Rich, *The History of the Hudson's Bay Company, 1670–1870* (London: Hudson's Bay Record Society, 1959), 2:750.

10. Minute of Earl Grey, September 16, 1846, on J. Pelly to Grey, September 7, 1846, CO 305/1. The "politics" of how the Hudson's Bay Company eventually received the charter of grant to Vancouver Island are examined more completely in Barry M. Gough, "Crown, Company, and Charter: Founding Vancouver Island Colony—A Chapter in Victorian Empire Making," *BC Studies*, 176 (Winter 2012/13): 9–54.

11. Paul Knaplund, "Letters from James Edward Fitzgerald to W.E. Gladstone Concerning Vancouver Island and the Hudson's Bay Company, 1848–1850," *British Columbia Historical Quarterly*, 13 (January 1949): 12n26; Minutes of B. Hawes and Grey, June 7, 1848, CO 305/1.

12. Adam Dundas to Grey, May 30, 1848, CO 305/1; printed in BCA, *Report of the Provincial Archives Department of the Province of British Columbia for the Year ended December 31st, 1913* (Victoria, BC, 1914), V49.

13. Ibid.

14. See Great Britain, *Hansard's Parliamentary Debates*, 3rd Series, vol. 101, 263ff.; Knaplund, "Letters from James Edward Fitzgerald," 1–21; and John S. Galbraith, "Fitzgerald versus the Hudson's Bay Company: The Founding of Vancouver Island," *British Columbia Historical Quarterly*, 16 (1952): 191–207.

15. Draft of grant, encl. in Order-in-Council, September 4, 1848, BT 1/470/2506.

16. H. Merivale (CO) to Pelly, March 13, 1848, encl. in Merivale to Le Marchant, September 8, 1848, ibid.

17. Ibid.

18. Draft of grant, encl. in Order-in-Council, September 4, 1848, ibid.

19. Ibid.

20. Rich, *Hudson's Bay Company*, 2:755–56.

21. Willard E. Ireland, "The Appointment of Governor Blanshard," *British Columbia Historical Quarterly*, 8 (July 1944): 213–26; and W. Kaye Lamb, "The Governorship of Richard Blanshard," *British Columbia Historical Quarterly*, 14 (April 1950): 1–40.

22. Knaplund, "James Stephen," 268.

23. This argument was made as late as October 1848; J. Douglas to Captain G.W.C. Courtenay, October 10, 1848, copy B. 223/b/37, fols. 39–41, HBCA.

24. Rear-Admiral Phipps Hornby to H.G. Ward (Adm.), August 23, 1848, Adm. 1/5589.

25. Ibid.

26. Courtenay to William Miller (British consul, Honolulu), September 12, 1848, extract, in Miller to Addington (FO), October 23, 1848; in BCA, *Report of the Provincial Archives . . . 1913*, V77.

27. Ibid.

28. Allan Pritchard, "What's in a Name? Captain Courtenay and Vancouver Island Exploration," *British Columbia Historical News*, 37, 4 (Winter 2004): 3–4.

29. Ogden and Douglas to Simpson, March 16, 1848, B.223/b/37, fol. 6d, HBCA; Ogden and Douglas to Simpson, February 23, 1849, B.223/b/38, fol. 72, HBCA.

30. Captain J. Shepherd to officer-in-charge, Fort Victoria, May 12, 1849, B. 226/b/2, fols. 18d-19, HBCA.

31. R. Finlayson to Shepherd, May 13, 1849, ibid., fols. 19d-20. Finlayson to Douglas, May 23, 1849, ibid., fols. 21d-22.

32. F.V. Longstaff and W. Kaye Lamb, "The Royal Navy on the Northwest Coast, 1813–1850, Part II," *British Columbia Historical Quarterly*, 9 (April 1945): 123–24.

33. Finlayson to Douglas, May 23, 1849, B. 226/b/2, fol. 21d, HBCA.

34. Hornby to J. Parker (Adm.), August 29, 1849, PHI/2/1, NMM; in BCA, *Report of the Provincial Archives . . . 1913*, V74.

35. Pelly to B. Hawes (CO), November 22, 1849, A.8/6, fols. 14–15, HBCA.

36. Ibid.

37. A. Barclay to secretary of the Admiralty, November 22, 1849, A.8/17, fol. 46, HBCA.

38. Driver's log, Adm. 53/3837; Rear-Admiral P.W. Brock, "H.M.S. Driver, 1840–1861," undated memo prepared for author.

39. Letter to George Simpson, in Robin Percival Smith, *Captain McNeill and His Wife the Nishga Chief* (Surrey, BC: Hancock House, 2001), 219.

40. Commander Johnson to Hornby, June 21, 1850, Valparaiso, PHI/3/5, NMM.

41. Blanshard to Grey, September 18, 1850, encl. in Grey to Pelly, February 25, 1851, ibid., fols. 149–51.

42. R. Blanshard to Grey, September 18, 1850, CO 305/2. See also Willard E. Ireland, "Pre-Confederation Defence Problems of the Pacific Colonies," in *Canadian Historical Association Annual Report*, 1941 (Toronto: CHA, 1941), 44.

43. Ibid., 44n13.

44. See Barry M. Gough, *Gunboat Frontier: British Maritime Authority and Northwest Coast Indians, 1846-1890* (Vancouver: UBC Press, 1984), 32–49.

45. Blanshard to Grey, September 18, 1850, encl. in Grey to Pelly, February 25, 1851, ibid., fols. 149–51.

46. Pelly to Grey, December 2, 1850, ibid., fol. 143.

47. A. Colvile (HBC governor) to Grey, December 18, 1850, ibid., fols. 146–47; Pelly to Grey, February 28, 1851, ibid., fols. 152–53.

48. Douglas to J. Blenkinsop, October 27, 1850, B.226/b/3, fol. 14d, HBCA.

49. Rear-Admiral Moresby to Blanshard, August 27, 1851, F. 1217, BCA.

50. Barry M. Gough, *Pax Britannica: Ruling the Waves and Keeping the Peace before Armageddon* (Basingstoke, UK: Palgrave Macmillan, 2014), 192–97.

51. Douglas to P.S. Ogden, August 6, 1851, B. 226/b/3, fols. 116–17; and Douglas to Grey, October 31, 1851, A.8/6, fol. 244, HBCA

52. Law Officers of the Crown to Lord Clarendon (FO), July 28, 1853, encl. in Osborne to Rear-Admiral Price, August 9, 1853, Adm. 172/3, No. 6.

53. Galbraith, *Hudson's Bay Company*, 294.

54. Douglas to Governor and Committee, November 15, 1853, B.226/b/14, fol. 11, HBCA.

55. Rich, *Hudson's Bay Company*, 2:762.

56. Douglas enjoyed the prestige of double office. "It is to the credit of the man that he was, on the whole, true to both offices and betrayed neither trust." Morton, *History of the Canadian West*, 762.

57. Moresby to secretary of the Admiralty, July 7, 1851, encl. in Peel to Pelly, December 20, 1851, A.8/6, fols. 203–211, HBCA.

58. Ibid.

59. Ibid. Moresby had complained about the price of provisions; Galbraith, *Hudson's Bay Company*, 294–96.

60. Pelly to Grey, January 14, 1852, A.8/6, fol. 219, HBCA.

61. Douglas to Simpson, March 20, 1854, B. 226/b/11, fols. 38–38d, HBCA. The Company agent at Fort Vancouver believed that the Colony of Vancouver Island, as conceived, was "injurious to the concern and ruinous to the Colonists." John Ballenden to Douglas and Work, November 2, 1852, B. 223/b/40, fol. 38, HBCA.

62. Several projects and plans were put forward during this period to extend American communications, trade and empire to the Pacific, and even to Asia. See Charles Vevier, "American Continentalism: An Idea of Expansionism, 1845–1910," *American Historical Review*, 65 (January 1960): 326–30. One British writer, probably Lt. Adam Dundas, RN, had warned against such American continental growth and expansion into the Pacific Northwest in 1848; "Oregon and Vancouver Island," *Nautical Magazine*, 17 (October 1848): 517–23.

63. Douglas to Pelly, April 13, 1852, B.226/b/6, fols. 60–61, HBCA.

64. Ibid.

65. Sir J. Crampton to Clarendon, February 7, 1853, in Richard W. Van Alstyne, ed., "Anglo-American Relations, 1853–57," *American Historical Review*, 42 (April 1937): 494–95.

66. See Kenneth Bourne, *Britain and the Balance of Power in North America, 1815–1908* (London: Longmans, Green and Co., 1967), 170–85.

67. Ibid., 184–205.

68. John Meares, *Voyages Made in the Years 1788 and 1789, from China to the North West Coast of America* (London, 1790), 224; quoted in W. Kaye Lamb, "Early Lumbering on Vancouver Island," *British Columbia Historical Quarterly*, 2 (January 1938): 32.

69. Frederick Merk, ed., *Fur Trade and Empire: George Simpson's Journal*, rev. ed. (Cambridge, MA: Belknap Press, 1968), 122 and 298. Simpson's 1829 Report, D.4/93, fol. 57d, HBCA, quoted by W. Kaye Lamb, "Introduction," in E.E. Rich, ed., *The Letters of John McLoughlin from Fort Vancouver to the Governor and Committee, First Series, 1825–38* (London: Hudson's Bay Record Society, 1941), xcii. See also John A. Hussey, *The History of Fort Vancouver* (Tacoma: Washington State Historical Society, 1957), 64.

70. Rear-Admiral Seymour to J. Gordon, February 13, 1845, Seymour Order Book I, CR 114A/414/1, WRO.

71. As Third Lord of the Admiralty, 1841–1844, his knowledge of these matters grew. See his Adm. Notebook, CR 114A/409, pp. 1–89, WRO.

72. Seymour, Private Diary, CR 114A/373/23, p. 138, WRO. HMS *Blossom's* crew had cut Monterey pines (*Pinus radiata*) near the San Rafael mission in 1826; Lt. Geo. Peard, Journal of HMS *Blossom*, 1825–1828, Add. MSS. 35, 141, fols. 99, BL. The firs from the Pacific Northwest, which Seymour preferred, were probably Douglas fir (*Pseudotsuga menziesii*), a wood valued for construction but which is not a true fir.

73. Lamb, "Early Lumbering," 32–33.

74. Report of December 27, 1847, encl. in J. Meek to Seymour, January 10, 1848, Adm. Corr. I, BCA. Robert G. Albion, *Forests and Sea Power: The Timber Problem of the Royal Navy, 1852–1862* (Cambridge, MA: Harvard University Press, 1926), 141.

75. Lamb, "Early Lumbering," 33. R. Dundas (Storekeeper General, Admiralty) to Barclay, July 7, 1847, A.8/14, fol. 234, HBCA.

76. Lamb, "Early Lumbering," 33–34; F.W. Howay, W.N. Sage and H.F. Angus, *British Columbia and the United States* (New Haven, CT: Yale University Press, 1942), 134; and Ogden to Sir G. Simpson, June 14, 1850, private, B.223/b/39, fol. 42, HBCA.

77. Douglas to Blenkinsop, September 30, 1850, B.226/b/3, fols. 15–15d, HBCA.

78. Brotchie to Governor and Committee, March 21, 1851, B.226/b 5b, fols. 1–1d and enclosures; Douglas to Brotchie, February 16, 1852, B.226/b/4, fols. 46–46d; Douglas to Barclay, December 7, 1852, B.226/b/6, fol. 151; Douglas to Simpson, March 17, 1853, ibid., fols. 195–96, HBCA. Prevost to Moresby, June 7 and July 23, 1853, Adm. 1/5630; Lamb, "Early Lumbering," 34–38.

79. Bruce Journal, June 14, July 14, September 14, 1855, Adm. 50/308; Bruce to Osborne, September 11, 1855, Adm. 1/5656.

80. Technological advances during the mid-nineteenth century are considered in Appendix E. See also Gerald S. Graham, "The Transition from Paddle-Wheel to Screw Propeller," *Mariner's Mirror*, 44 (1958): 35–48; and Geoffrey Penn, *"Up Funnel, Down Screw!" The Story of the Naval Engineer* (London: Hollis and Carter, 1955).

81. Commodore Mason to Rear-Admiral Hamond, November 29, 1836, Callao, Adm. 1/48.

82. Alexander Forbes, *California: A History of Upper and Lower California* (London: Smith, Elder and Co., 1839), 332–42.

83. Gordon's *"Cormorant* Remark Book from 1 January to 31 December 1846" was kept by the Hydrographer's Office for reference purposes. File No. Misc. 16, Folder 1, item 3, HO. In this document, Gordon referred to Esquimalt harbour as "Fisgard Harbour."

84. W.S. Jevons, *The Coal Question*, 3rd ed., rev. (London: Macmillan and Co., 1906), 133.

85. Rear-Admiral Thomas to Commander A.S. Hamond, May 23, 1843, extract, encl. in Thomas to S. Herbert (Adm.), October 26, 1843, Adm. 1/5538. See also John Bach, "The Royal Navy in the South Pacific, 1826–1876" (Ph.D. thesis, University of New South Wales, 1964), 53–54.

86. John H. Kemble, "Coal from the Northwest Coast, 1848–1850," *British Columbia Historical Quarterly*, 2 (April 1938): 123–30.

87. Douglas to Captain J. Duntze, September 7, 1846, CO 305/1.

88. In 1845 and 1846, Rear-Admiral Seymour sent instructions to captains to report on coals fit for the Navy. Seymour to J. Gordon, February 13, 1845, Seymour Order Book I, CR 114A/414/1, WRO, and Seymour to Duntze, January 14, 1846, Adm. 1/5561.

89. Reported in G. Gordon to Duntze, October 7, 1846, copy, CO 305/1.

90. Seymour to Ward, February 8, 1847, Official Letter Book II, CR 114A/416/2, WRO.

91. Sir Henry De la Beche to Hamilton, January 30, 1848, A.8/17, fols. 28, 30, HBCA.

92. Hamilton (Adm.) to Hawes, October 19, 1848, and Merivale to Hamilton, November 2, 1848, "Papers re: Vancouver's Island," Great Britain, *Parliamentary Papers*, 1849, 35 (103), p. 12.

93. Minute to Earl Grey, February 9, 1848, CO 305/1.

94. S. Cunard to Ward, January 3, 1848, encl. in Ward to Seymour, February 5, 1848, Parliamentary Papers, 1849, 35 (103), p. 11.

95. Acknowledged in Merivale to Adm., February 18, 1848, ibid., p. 12.

96. "Memorandum of an Agreement for 30 years' Lease . . . ," in "Labuan Papers," Parliamentary Papers, 1847–1848, 62, (460), p. 8. On Wise and Labuan, see Gerald S. Graham, *Great Britain in the Indian Ocean: A Study of Maritime Enterprise, 1810–1850* (Oxford: Clarendon Press, 1967), 395–98.

97. Pelly to Grey, March 4, 1848, CO 305/1.

98. See "Principal Services required from the Squadron in 1848," by Rear-Admiral Seymour, PHI, 3/16, NMM. Courtenay sent letters to the officer-in-charge of Fort Victoria and to Chief Factor Douglas at Fort Vancouver. Both, dated July 25, 1848, from Esquimalt, are in B.223/b/37, fols. 31–33, HBCA.

99. Courtenay to Douglas, July 29, 1848, ibid., fol. 33d.

100. Courtenay to Douglas, August 17, 1848, copy, ibid., fols. 37–38.

101. Douglas and J. Work to Governor and Committee, December 5, 1848, B. 223/b/38, fol. 63d, HBCA; and Hornby to Ward, November 28, 1848, Adm. 1/5589.

102. Men were brought from the Stikine and Columbia basins for this task.

103. Johnson to Hornby, June 21, 1850, Valparaiso, PHI/3/5, NMM.

104. On the growth of Company interest in coal, see Walter N. Sage, *Sir James Douglas and British Columbia* (Toronto: University of Toronto Press, 1930), 172–76; and James Audain, *From Coalmine to Castle: The Story of the Dunsmuirs of Vancouver Island* (New York: Pageant Press, 1955), 8–23. On Nanaimo specifically, see B.A. McKelvie, "The Founding of Nanaimo," *British Columbia Historical Quarterly*, 8 (July 1944): 169–88.

105. Gerald S. Graham, *The Politics of Naval Supremacy: Studies in British Maritime Ascendancy* (Cambridge: Cambridge University Press, 1965), 102–3.

106. Hornby to Moresby, February 12, 1851, PHI/2/2, NMM.

107. Price and not quality of Vancouver Island coal determined its use by the Royal Navy at this time. Rear-Admiral Fairfax Moresby to secretary of the Admiralty, October 13, 1853, Adm. 1/5630.

108. See note in *Nautical Magazine*, 20 (January 1851): 56.

109. Ibid. Native people of the area made rope from shredded cedar.

110. See chapter 3.

111. Blanshard to Grey, June 15, 1850, encl. in Hawes to Pelly, September 21, 1850, A. 8/6, fol. 110, HBCA.

112. See Leigh Burpee Robinson, *Esquimalt: "Place of Shoaling Waters"* (Victoria, BC: Quality Press, 1947), 39–42.

113. Commander Wood to secretary of the Admiralty, September 19, 1848, Adm. 1/5596. PHI/1, November 15, 1848, and February 25, 1849, NMM. Reports on the First Nations of Juan de Fuca Strait are in Wood to secretary of the Admiralty, November 11, 1848, Adm. 1/5596. The *Herald*, meanwhile, was bound with HM Discovery Ship *Plover* for the western Arctic in search of the Arctic expedition of Sir John Franklin. See Flora Hamilton Burns, "H.M.S. *Herald* in Search of Franklin," *The Beaver*, Outfit 294 (Autumn 1963): 3–13.

114. Seymour to Ward, February 26, 1847, Adm. 1/5577; printed in Robert M. Martin, *The Hudson's Bay Territories and Vancouver's Island with an Exposition of the Chartered Rights, Conduct, and Policy of the Honourable Hudson's Bay Corporation* (London: T. Brettell, 1849), 44.

115. Commander James Wood, "Vancouver Island, British Columbia," *Nautical Magazine*, 27 (December 1858): 664.

116. Moresby to secretary of the Admiralty, July 3, 1851; in W. Kaye Lamb, ed., "Correspondence Relating to the Establishment of a Naval Base at Esquimalt, 1851–57," *British Columbia Historical Quarterly*, 6 (October 1942): 280.

117. Geo. Allan to Barclay, April 7, 1849, A.11/64, fol. 27d, HBCA.

118. Ibid.

119. Douglas to Barclay, November 23, 1848, Ft. Victoria, B.223/b/38, fol. 69, HBCA.

120. Ibid.

121. Ibid.

122. See chapters 5 and 8.

123. A. Colville to Pakington, November 24, 1852, A.8/7, HBCA.

124. Andrew Lambert, *Trincomalee: The Last of Nelson's Frigates* (London: Chatham, 2002), 8, ch. 5.

CHAPTER FIVE

1. This was an imperial war on a grand scale, involving many states. See Andrew C. Rath, *The Crimean War in Imperial Context, 1854–1856* (New York: Palgrave Macmillan, 2015).

2. Navy Records Society volumes deal with aspects of the war other than the Pacific: D. Bonner-Smith and Captain A.C. Dewar, eds., *Russian War, 1854, Baltic and Black Sea: Official Correspondence*, vol. 83 (London: Navy Records Society, 1943); D. Bonner-Smith, ed., *Russian War, 1855, Baltic: Official Correspondence*, vol. 84 (London: Navy Records Society, 1944); and Captain A.C. Dewar, ed., *Russian War, 1855, Black Sea: Official Correspondence*, vol. 85 (London: Navy Records Society, 1945).

3. Previous accounts include C.D. Yonge, *The History of the British Navy* (London: R. Bentley, 1866), 3:323–25; William Laird Clowes, *The Royal Navy: A History from the Earliest Times to the Present* (London: Sampson Low, Marston and Co., 1901), 6:429–32; Captain John Franklin Parry, "Sketch of the History of the Naval Establishments at Esquimalt from their Commencement until the Abolition of the Pacific Squadron in 1905 and Miscellaneous Matters Connecting British Columbia with His Majesty's Navy" (typescript of a paper read before the Natural History Society of British Columbia, February 19, 1906; reprinted from *Victoria Daily Times*, February 20 and 21, 1906); and Michael Lewis, "An Eye-Witness at Petropaulovski, 1854," *Mariner's Mirror*, 49 (November 1963): 265–72.

4. Hector Chevigny, *Russian America: The Great Alaskan Venture, 1741–1867* (New York: Viking Press, 1965), 214. See also Commodore C. Elliot to Rear-Admiral Sir James Stirling (commander-in-chief, China), November 25, 1855, S22, Adm. 1/5672.

5. The best compendium used by mariners at this time was A.G. Findlay, *Directory for Navigation of the Pacific*, 2 pts. (London: R.H. Laurie, 1851). For Petropavlovsk, see pt. 2, pp. 594–604.

6. See, for instance, Stirling to secretary of the Admiralty, February 13, 1856, S64, Adm. 1/5672.

7. Frank A. Golder, *Russian Expansion in the Pacific, 1641–1850* (Cleveland: Arthur H. Clark Co., 1914), 263–64.

8. Ibid.

9. Ernest G. Ravenstein, *The Russians on the Amur: Its Discovery, Conquest and Colonization* (London: Trubner and Co., 1861), 116–25.

10. The text of the agreement is printed in E.H. Oliver, ed., *The Canadian North-West: Early Development and Legislative Records*, Publication No. 9 of the Public Archives of Canada (Ottawa: Government Printing Bureau, 1915), 2: 791–97. See also Donald C. Davidson, "Relations of the Hudson's Bay Company with the Russian American Company on the Northwest Coast, 1829–1867," *British Columbia Historical Quarterly*, 5 (January 1941): 33–51.

11. John S. Galbraith, *The Hudson's Bay Company as an Imperial Factor, 1821–1869* (Berkeley and Los Angeles: University of California Press, 1957), 154, 163.

12. W. Politkowiski and others to HBC, February 2/4, 1854, encl. in A. Colvile (HBC governor) to Clarendon (FO), February 28, 1854, A. 8/19, fols. 23–24, HBCA; Galbraith, *Hudson's Bay Company*, 165–69; and S.B. Okun, *The Russian-American Company*, trans. C. Ginsburg (Cambridge, MA: Harvard University Press, 1951), 235–43.

13. H.U. Addington (FO) to Colvile, March 22, 1854, A. 8/19, fols. 24–25, HBCA.

14. Ibid.

15. Lord Palmerston (Home Office) to Lord Clarendon, (FO), August 29, 1854, Clarendon dep., c. 15, fol. 172, Bod. L.

16. A.R. Roche, *A View of Russian America in Connection with the Present War* (Montreal, 1885); see also W.L. Morton, *The Critical Years: The Union of British North America, 1857–1873* (Toronto: McClelland and Stewart, 1964), 26.

17. Galbraith, *Hudson's Bay Company*, 165–66.

18. Admiralty Circular, February 24, 1854, Adm. 116/857.

19. Stirling to secretary of the Admiralty, March 6, 1854, S64, Adm. 1/5629, acknowledging receipt of these instructions.

20. Initially, Sir James Graham, the First Lord of the Admiralty, was cognizant of the need to give the Commander-in-Chief, Pacific, some warning of the critical state of European affairs, especially as it was intended to send a frigate for the protection of Vancouver Island. J. Graham to Clarendon, January 25, 1854, private, Clarendon dep., c. 14, fol. 150, Bod. L. The signing of the Anglo-Russian neutrality agreement for the Northwest Coast removed the need for sending this ship.

21. General Memo No. 11, May 9, 1854; in "Journal kept by Alexander V. Maccall, Clerk's Assistant, 1854–1856, in H.M.S. *Victory, Pique and Amphitrite*," LOG/N/P/1, MS 9397, NMM. Hereafter cited as *Maccall Journal* (unpaginated).

22. W.P. Morrell, *Britain in the Pacific Islands* (Oxford: Clarendon Press, 1960), 194.

23. Rear-Admiral Price to R. Osborne (secretary of the Admiralty), July 25, 1854, Y136, Adm. 1/5630. On British and French consular pressure, see Merze Tate, "Hawaii: A Symbol of Anglo-American Rapprochement," *Political Science Quarterly*, 79 (December 1964): 555–56. See also Richard W. Van Alstyne, "Great Britain, the United States, and Hawaiian Independence, 1850–1855," *Pacific Historical Review*, 4 (1935): 15–24.

24. Jean I. Brookes, *International Rivalry in the Pacific Islands, 1800–1875* (Berkeley and Los Angeles: University of California Press, 1941), 208.

25. The *Pique*, 40 guns, joined the others at Honolulu, July 22, 1854.

26. Price to Osborne, July 25, 1854, Y136, Adm. 1/5630.

27. The Hudson's Bay Company agent at Honolulu reported that the *Aurora* left there May 28, 1854, for Kamchatka and the Northwest Coast on a surveying expedition. R. Clouston to A. Barclay (secretary, HBC), June 3, 1854, A. 11/63, fol. 64, HBCA. HMS *Trincomalee*, with supplies for British Arctic expeditions, left the following day. She did not pursue the Russian warship because news of war had not yet reached the islands.

28. Ravenstein, *Russians on the Amur*, 120–21.

29. De Castries Bay, south of the Amur's mouth, is on the mainland facing across to Sakhalin. There the Russians planned to establish "a Naval Station of some magnitude"; Lieutenant Dent (HMS *Sybille*) to Commander Forsythe, May 29, 1855, S109, Adm. 1/5657.

30. On this point generally, see A.T. Mahan, *The Influence of Sea Power upon History, 1660–1783* (London: Sampson Low and Co., 1890), 14.

31. "Avatska" and "Awatska" are common spellings, but "Avatcha" is used in Admiralty charts and Pilot.

32. Captain Fenton Aylmer, ed., *A Cruise in the Pacific: From the Log of a Naval Officer* (London: Hurst and Blackett, 1860), 2:59.

33. Rear-Admiral P.W. Brock, "H.M.S. *President*," typescript, n.d., p. 9, MMBC.

34. Captain Nicolson to Commodore Frederick, September 19, 1854, Cap N52 Adm. 1/5631.

35. Ravenstein, *Russians on the Amur*, 124. There were four Paixhans guns. The rest were mainly 36- and 24-pounders. See the plan of Petropavlovsk in *Illustrated London News*, December 16, 1854, 622.

36. Quoted by Captain J.C.R. Colomb, "Russian Development and Our Naval and Military Position in the North Pacific," *Journal of the Royal United Service Institution*, 21 (1877): 665. Throughout the late nineteenth century, the importance of Petropavlovsk to Russia increased, which led to much debate among strategists in London. The expert Ravenstein, whose work is frequently referred to here, was often in attendance at meetings at the Royal United Service Institution.

37. See Bernard Brodie, *Sea Power in the Machine Age* (Princeton, NJ: Princeton University Press, 1941), chapter 5.

38. *Maccall Journal.*

39. Captain R. Burridge to Nicolson, August 30, 1854, Cap N52, Adm. 1/5631.

40. Lewis, "Eye-Witness at Petropaulovski," 267, 269–70. Also Michael Lewis, *The Navy in Transition, 1814–1864: A Social History* (London: Hodder and Stoughton, 1965), 79, 81, 124.

41. *Maccall Journal.*

42. Hubert H. Bancroft, *History of Alaska, 1730–1885* (San Francisco: A.L. Bancroft and Co., 1886), 571.

43. Nicolson to Frederick, September 19, 1854, Cap N52, Adm. 1/5631. This official report, written sometime after the action, was carefully worded to protect all concerned. Despite this, it is the best extant account of those strange, confusing events.

44. Clowes, *Royal Navy*, 6:430.

45. Nicolson to Frederick, September 19, 1854, Cap N52, Adm. 1/5631.

46. Fevrier-Despointes to Nicolson, September 2, 1854, ibid.

47. See *Maccall Journal.*

48. Nicolson to Fevrier-Despointes, September 2, 1854, Cap N52, Adm. 1/5631.

49. Nicolson to Fevrier-Despointes, September 3, 1854, ibid. The Americans, deserters from a whaler, proposed that they were prepared to guide a landing party in the attack in return for a passage to Hawaii; Brock, "H.M.S. *President*," p. 12, MMBC. An agreement was made and adhered to: 11 Americans were taken to Honolulu.

50. Nicolson to Fevrier-Despointes, September 3, 1854, Cap N52, Adm. 1/5631.

51. Nicolson to Frederick, September 19, 1854, ibid.

52. Burridge to Nicolson, September 5, 1854, encl. in Nicolson to Frederick, September 19, 1854, ibid.

53. Ibid.

54. Brock, "H.M.S. *President*," p. 13, MMBC.

55. Rear-Admiral H.W. Bruce to Sir Charles Wood (First Lord of the Admiralty), February 24, 1856, confidential, Halifax Papers, Add. MSS. 49, 549, BL. In a second letter on this subject, dated April 1, 1856, ibid.

56. According to the final tally, the *Virago* lost 5 men; the *Pique*, 17; and the President, 11. Frederick to Osborne, November 15, 1854, Y1, Adm. 1/5656.

57. Quoted in Lewis, "Eye-Witness," 268.

58. See, for example, ibid., 271.

59. Admiralty Minute, December 6, 1854, Cap N52, Adm. 1/5631.

60. Brodie, *Sea Power*, 71.

61. Nicolson to Frederick, September 19, 1854, Cap N52, Adm. 1/5631.

62. The *Anadis*, given over to the French, was evidently destroyed. The new *Sitka*, 800 tons, was a valuable prize. See below, note 69.

63. J. Douglas to Duke of Newcastle (secretary of state for war and the colonies), May 16, 1854, WO 1/551, fols. 143–47. See also Donald C. Davidson, "The War Scare of 1854: The Pacific Coast and the Crimean War," *British Columbia Historical Quarterly*, 5 (October 1941): 243–54; Walter N. Sage, *Sir James Douglas and British Columbia* (Toronto: University of Toronto Press, 1930), 180–82. On the defence of the colony, see Willard E. Ireland, "Pre-Confederation Defence Problems of the Pacific Colonies," in *Canadian Historical Association Annual Report, 1941* (Toronto: CHA, 1941), 45–46.

64. G.C. Manby (War Department) to J. Sheperd (HBC deputy governor), August 31, 1854, A. 8/7, fol. 139, HBCA.

65. Douglas planned to conscript men of the colony, including Natives, but the Legislative Council felt that there were too few whites to be of any use, and that armed Natives might turn on the colonists. *Minutes of the Council of Vancouver Island, 1851–1861*, British Columbia Archives Memoir No. 2 (Victoria, BC: BC Archives, 1918), 24–25.

66. Ibid. According to the charter of grant for Vancouver Island (1849), the Hudson's Bay Company was to defray costs of defence "except nevertheless during time of Hostilities between Great Britain and any Foreign European or American Power"; Draft of Grant, encl. in Order-in-Council, September 4, 1848, BT 1/470/2506.

67. Frederick to Osborne, November 13, 1854, Y15, Adm. 1/5656.

68. Rumours of these vessels caused great excitement; see J. Parker (Adm.) to Clarendon (FO), September 28, 1855, Adm. 116/857; and Bruce to Osborne, July 11, 1856, Y106, Adm. 1/5672.

69. The *Plover* had been with the *Herald* in the Arctic, 1849–1850. She was sold in San Francisco, and her officers and men sailed the prize *Sitka* to England. See Rochfort Maguire, "Journal kept on bd. H.M.S. Plover" (Dublin: National Library), vol. 2, entries for October and November 1854. See also Maguire to secretary of the Admiralty, April 8, 1855, Cap M 103, Adm. 1/5658.

70. The *Amphitrite*, Captain Matthew Connolly now in command, returned to Honolulu Roads to find the *Trincomalee, Pique, Alceste, Eurydice* and *Artemise*. *Amphitrite's* log, Adm. 53/5018, December 11, 1854. These ships were there to prevent an American seizure of the Hawaiian Islands; Graham to Clarendon, December 7, 1854, Clarendon dep., c. 14, fols. 535–36, Bod. L.

71. See Barry M. Gough, *Pax Britannica: Ruling the Waves and Keeping the Peace before Armageddon* (Basingstoke, UK: Palgrave Macmillan, 2014), 179–81.

72. Bruce Journal, Adm. 50/308, February 13, 14 and 25, 1855.

73. Bruce to Douglas, February 14, 1855, extract in Bruce to Osborne, September 14, 1855, Y116, Adm. 1/5656. Original in BCA; published in W. Kaye Lamb, ed. "Correspondence Relating to the Establishment of a Naval Base at Esquimalt, 1851–57," *British Columbia Historical Quarterly*, 6 (October 1942): 281–82.

74. Douglas to Bruce, May 8, 1855, Adm. Corr. I, BCA.

75. Parry, "Sketch of the History of the Naval Establishments at Esquimalt," 2. The four ships were the *Dido, Amphitrite, Trincomalee* and *Cockatrice*.

76. Graham to Clarendon, September 25, 1854, Clarendon dep., c. 14, fol. 443, Bod. L. The *Monarch* did not reach Petropavlovsk until June 23, 1855.

77. The position was 50°N, 160°E. J.M. Tronson, *Personal Narrative of a Voyage . . . in H.M.S. Barracouta* (London: Smith, Elder and Co., 1859), 85–90.

78. Rear-Admiral Sir James Stirling to secretary of the Admiralty, April 15 and October 1, 1855, S76, Adm. 1/5657.

79. At a second rendezvous, 20 miles southeast of Avatcha Bay, the following assembled: the *President*, 50 guns, *Pique*, 40 guns, *Trincomalee*, 24 guns, *Amphitrite*, 24 guns, *Dido*, 18 guns, and *Brisk*, 14 guns, from the Pacific squadron; the *Encounter*, 14 guns, and *Barracouta*, 6 guns, from the China squadron; and the *Forte*, 60 guns, *Alceste*, 54 guns, *Eurydice*, 32 guns, and *Obligado*, 8 guns, from the French Navy. Clowes, *Royal Navy*, 6:475n. For the *Brisk's* voyage, see Admiral Sir Cyprian Bridge, *Some Recollections*, 2nd cd. (London: John Murray, 1919), 117–19.

80. Reported in Stirling to secretary of the Admiralty, October 1, 1855, S141, Adm. 1/5657.

81. Tronson, *Personal Narrative*, 94.

82. Bruce to Osborne, July 17, 1855, Sitka, Y83, Adm. 1/5656. See also Major F.V. Longstaff, *Esquimalt Naval Base: A History of Its Work and Its Defences* (Victoria, BC: Victoria Book and Stationery Co., 1941), 16.

83. Commodore C. Elliot to Stirling, June 7, 1855, S109, Adm. 1/5657.

84. Bruce found emplacements for 72 guns. See his report to Osborne, June 15, 1855, enclosing map of defences, Y95, Adm. 1/5656.

85. Remark Book of Captain C. Frederick, No. 7, Adm. 172/2.

86. Golder, *Russian Expansion*, 265–66; and Paul Bernard Whittingham, *Notes on the Late Expedition against the Russian Settlements in Eastern Siberia* (London: Longman, Brown, Green and Longmans, 1856), 94–99.

87. See Admiralty Minutes of October 9, 1855 (S109), and December 8, 1855 (S141), Adm. 1/5657.

88. Fevrier-Despointes, like his unfortunate counterpart Price, died in the Pacific, but of natural causes. His successor, Fourichon, reached Petropavlovsk in the *Forte*. Bruce Journal, Adm. 50/308, June 8, 1855.

89. Ibid., July 13, 1855. See also Captain Voevodsky to Tsar, August 18, 1855 (OS); extract in Report of Russian American Company, November 16, 1855; *Alaska Boundary Tribunal, Counter Case of the United States. Appendix II* (Washington, 1903), 20; and Longstaff, Esquimalt Naval Base, 17. No British account of the meeting with Russian officials exists.

90. The *Brisk* to Vancouver Island, San Francisco, Mexico; the *Trincomalee*, expected from Petropavlovsk, to await the *Amphitrite* at Sitka until August 20 before sailing to Esquimalt, San Francisco, Honolulu; the *Dido* to watch the coast of Russian

America and await the *Trincomalee* near Sitka, then proceed to San Francisco. Bruce Journal, Adm. 50/308, July 13, 1855.

91. See Sir James Graham to Clarendon, October 25, 1854, in Richard W. Van Alstyne, ed., "Anglo-American Relations, 1853–1857," *American Historical Review*, 42 (April 1937): 498. Also Kenneth Bourne, *Britain and the Balance of Power in North America, 1815–1908* (London: Longmans, Green and Co., 1967), 179–83.

92. Bruce Journal, Adm. 50/308, particularly September 18, 1855. This information came from Captain Frederick of the *Amphitrite*, off Cape Edgecumbe, August 8. The British minister in Washington had reason to believe that American privateers might be operating out of Sitka. See Sir John Crampton to Clarendon, March 12, 1855, Clarendon dep., c. 43, fols. 121–22, Bod. L.

93. See Agatha Ramm, "The Crimean War," in J.P.T. Bury, ed., *The Zenith of European Power, 1830–1870*, vol. 10 of *The New Cambridge Modern History* (Cambridge: Cambridge University Press, 1967), 468–92.

94. Reports by commanders of HMS *Calypso* and *Havannah* are in Adm. Pac. St. Rec., RG 8, IIIB, vol. 34, LAC. See also *Nautical Magazine*, 26 (February 1858): 96–98.

95. The introduction of shell spelled the end of wooden warships; see James P. Baxter, *The Introduction of the Ironclad Warship* (Cambridge, MA: Harvard University Press, 1933), passim, esp. 17 and 69.

96. Great Britain, *Hansard's Parliamentary Debates*, 3rd. Series, 145, col. 426; Brodie, *Sea Power*, 73.

97. Great Britain, *Hansard's Parliamentary Debates*, 3rd. Series, 149, col. 915; Brodie, *Sea Power*, 73.

98. *Transactions of the Institution of Naval Architects*, Vol. 34, 33; see also Brodie, Sea Power, 76.

99. Quoted in Captain S.W. Roskill, *The Strategy of Sea Power: Its Development and Application* (London: Collins, 1962), 91.

100. Ibid.

101. Madge Wolfenden, "Esquimalt Dockyard's First Buildings," *British Columbia Historical Quarterly*, 10 (July 1946): 235–40.

102. Bruce to Osborne, September 14, 1855, Y116, Adm. 1/5656.

103. Ibid.

104. Douglas to Smith (CO), October 10, 1855, encl. in Smith to secretary of the Admiralty, December 22, 1855, ibid.

105. Rath, *The Crimean War*, 122–29.

CHAPTER SIX

1. This gold rush and subsequent naval exploration revealed the existence of more than one island.

2. General considerations relative to the rush are given in F.W. Howay and E.O.S. Scholefield, *British Columbia, from the Earliest Times to the Present* (Vancouver: S.J. Clarke, 1914), 2:1–9; and Corday McKay, *Queen Charlotte Islands* (Victoria, BC: Province of British Columbia, Department of Education, 1953), 39 and 45.

3. W.P. Morrell, *British Colonial Policy in the Age of Peel and Russell* (Oxford: Clarendon Press, 1930), 445.

4. J. Douglas to Rear-Admiral Moresby, January 29, 1852, Adm. Corr. I, BCA; Douglas to Earl Grey, secretary of state for the colonies, January 29, 1852, CO 305/3.

5. Douglas to Earl Grey, ibid.

6. Lord Malmesbury (FO) to secretary of the Admiralty, May 13, 1852, copy, Adm. Corr. I, BCA.

7. Rear-Admiral Moresby to secretary of the Admiralty, August 30, 1852, encl. in Stafford to Merivale, October 22, 1852, A. 8/7, fol. 22, HBCA.

8. Ibid.

9. Ibid.

10. Admiral John Moresby, *Two Admirals* (1st ed. London: John Murray, 1909; revised ed. London: Methuen and Co., 1913), 205–7.

11. Moresby place names and naval connections are enumerated in Captain John T. Walbran, *British Columbia Coast Names, 1592-1906* (Ottawa: Government Printing Bureau, 1909), 342–43.

12. Douglas to A. Barclay (secretary, HBC), July 12, 1852, B.226/b/6, fol. 97, HBCA.

13. In the main, reports of the quantity of gold found were highly exaggerated. Nonetheless, there were some large findings. See A. Kuper to Moresby, July 20, 1852, San Francisco; in W. Kaye Lamb, ed., "Four Letters Relating to the Cruise of the 'Thetis,' 1852–53," *British Columbia Historical Quarterly*, 6 (July 1942): 192–99.

14. Commander J.C. Prevost to Moresby, June 7, 1853, Y73, Adm. 1/5630.

15. At this time there was no warship permanently stationed on the Northwest Coast. But the Admiralty advised that it was "highly desirable" that a warship "frequently" visit Vancouver Island. R. Osborne (Adm.) to Moresby, March 2, 1852, Adm. Corr. I, BCA.

16. Prevost to Rear-Admiral Baynes, May 7, 1858, encl. in Prevost to secretary of the Admiralty, May 7, 1858, Y108, Adm. 1/5694.

17. Ibid.

18. Ibid.

19. As communications between Whitehall and many colonial governors were so slow before the advent of the telegraph, governors were often required to assume authority in direct violation of their instructions. The Provisional Regulations of Governor Douglas, December 29, 1857, are printed in BCA, *Report of the Provincial Archives Department of the Province of British Columbia for the Year ended December 31st, 1913* (Victoria, BC, 1914), v112.

20. Douglas to H. Labouchère (CO), May 8, 1858, CO60/1.

21. Douglas to Baynes, May 12, 1858, encl. in Baynes to secretary of the Admiralty, June 25, 1858, Y132, Adm. 1/5694.

22. Douglas to Lord Stanley (secretary of state for the colonies), May 19, 1858, "Papers Relative to the Affairs of British Columbia, I," *Parliamentary Papers*, 1859, 17 (Cmd. 2476), p. 11.

23. Douglas to Prevost, May 21, 1858, Cap P 102, Adm. 1/5696.

24. Lt. T.S. Gooch, RM, and five marines. A Native man was hired as pilot.

25. Prevost to Baynes, June 7, 1858, Cap P 102, Adm. 1/5696.

26. Ibid.

27. F.W. Howay, W.N. Sage and H.F. Angus, *British Columbia and the United States* (New Haven, CT: Yale University Press, 1942), 147.

28. Richard C. Mayne, *Four Years in British Columbia and Vancouver Island: An Account of Their Forests, Rivers, Coasts, Gold Fields, and Resources for Colonization* (London: John Murray, 1862), 53; and Margaret A. Ormsby, *British Columbia: A History* (Toronto: Macmillan, 1958), 159.

29. Prevost to Baynes, June 7, 1858, Cap P 102, Adm. 1/5696.

30. Prevost to Douglas, June 28, 1858, Adm. 1/5713.

31. Ibid.

32. Ibid.

33. Admiralty instructions to Baynes, June 28, 1857, Adm. Corr. II, BCA.

34. On this matter, see Baynes to secretary of the Admiralty, June 25, 1858, Y132, Adm. 1/5694. See also W.G. Romaine (Adm.) to Baynes, August 16, 1858, "Papers relative to the Affairs of British Columbia, I," p. 52, and related correspondence.

35. By the time Douglas's alarm of July 1, 1858 (CO 60/1), reached London, the Admiralty had already informed the Colonial Office of the intended visit of Baynes to Vancouver Island. Minute of N. Irving, October 10, 1858, ibid.

36. The fact that the *Calypso* lacked auxiliary power could have had two effects: (1) she might be compelled to lie farther out from the river entrance than a steam ship, and (2) the size of landing parties might be small because of the need to retain sufficient hands to man the sails in an emergency. Some of the difficulties of entering the river at this time were described by Captain George Henry Richards in *Vancouver Island Pilot: Sailing Directions for the Coasts of Vancouver Island and British Columbia*, Part 1 (London: Hydrographic Office, Admiralty, 1861), 97–101.

37. Baynes to secretary of the Admiralty, June 26, 1858, Y135, and July 22, 1858, Y156; both in Adm. 1/5694.

38. Douglas to Stanley, July 1, 1858, CO 60/1. According to the report in the *Nautical Magazine*, 37 (December 1858): 687, "Some idea of the extent of the trade and travel created by the Fraser River mania, may be gathered from the fact that in the 'Alta California' of July 14th, besides the six large steamships running into Puget Sound, there were advertised, six clipper ships, (including one of 2,200 tons), three barques, five brigs, and seven schooners—in all twenty-seven vessels on the berth." See also E.W. Wright, ed., *Lewis and Dryden's Marine History of the Pacific North-West* (Portland, OR: Lewis and Dryden Printing Co., 1895), 69.

39. Douglas to Stanley, July 1, 1858, CO 60/1.

40. Ibid.

41. Alfred Waddington, *The Fraser Mines Vindicated* (Victoria, VI: Printed by P. de Garro, 1858), 16–17; quoted in Walter N. Sage, *Sir James Douglas and British Columbia* (Toronto: University of Toronto Press, 1930), 204.

42. Prevost to Douglas, August 26, 1858, Cap P 141, Adm., 1/5696.

43. The 65-man detachment of Royal Engineers had arrived in HMS *Havannah*, 18 guns, Captain Thomas Harvey, on July 12, 1858. They were originally sent from England via Panama for Boundary Commission duty. The *Plumper* carried them to the Fraser.

44. Douglas to Sir E. Bulwer Lytton, secretary of state for the colonies, September 29, 1858, CO 60/1; Douglas to Lytton, October 12, 1858, encl. in H. Merivale to secretary of the Admiralty, January 26, 1859, Adm. 1/5621; Sage, *Sir James Douglas*, 227.

45. Prevost to Baynes, August 31, 1858, Cap P 141, Adm. 1/5696.

46. Douglas to Lytton, September 29, 1858, CO 60/1. Douglas noted that he was obliged to Prevost and Richards for their "cordial and unflinching support in every emergency."

47. Ibid. Lytton shared these views. See his Minute No. 2 to Douglas, n.d., and the resulting Lytton to Douglas, October 16, 1858, ibid.

48. Sir J. Pakington to Vice-Admiral Martin, August 24, 1858, Martin Papers, Add. MSS. 41,409, fols. 45–48, BL.

49. Ibid. See Francis Martin Norman, *"Martello Tower"* in *China and the Pacific in H.M.S. "Tribune,"* 1856–60 (London: George Allen, 1902); also F.V. Longstaff,

Esquimalt Naval Base: A History of Its Work and Its Defences (Victoria, BC: Victoria Book and Stationery Co., 1941), 173–74.

50. This was the opinion of Sir John Pakington, First Lord of the Admiralty, as reported in Lytton to Douglas, October 16, 1858, draft, CO 60/1.

51. These gunboats were ordered by the Admiralty on February 13, 1859. Minute of A. Blackwood (Adm.), June 17, 1859, CO 60/6.

52. Douglas to Stanley, August 27, 1858; and Lytton (who had replaced Stanley in May 1858) to Douglas, October 16, 1858, draft, CO 60/1.

53. Baynes to secretary of the Admiralty, October 20, 1858, Adm. 1/5713.

54. Quoted in Minute No. 1, Lytton to Douglas, n.d. (early October 1858), and Minute No. 2, Lytton to Douglas, n.d. (probably October 14, 1858), CO 60/1.

55. Prevost to Baynes, October 11, 1858, Cap P 163, Adm. 1/5696.

56. Baynes to secretary of the Admiralty, November 16, 1858, copy, CO 60/5.

57. An Act to Provide for the Government of British Columbia, 21 and 22 Vic., c. 99.

58. Quoted in A.S. Morton, *A History of the Canadian West to 1870–71*, 2nd ed. (Toronto: University of Toronto Press, 1973), 772.

59. Ibid., 773.

60. Ibid.

61. Baynes to secretary of the Admiralty, November 16, 1858, copy, CO 60/5.

62. See Ormsby, *British Columbia*, 162; and Sage, *Sir James Douglas*, 232–34.

63. Baynes to Douglas, December 7, 1858, "Papers relative to the Affairs of British Columbia, II," *Parliamentary Papers*, 1859 (Session 2), 22 (Cmd. 2578), p. 49.

64. Baynes to Douglas, December 14, 1858, Ships' letters, F 1212a, BCA.

65. Douglas to Lytton, December 27, 1858, "Papers relative to the Affairs of British Columbia, II," p. 47.

66. Prevost to Baynes, January 10, 1859, copy, CO 60/5; H. Corry to Merivale, March 21, 1859, ibid.

67. C. Brew (Inspector of Police) to Douglas, January 12, 1859, in F.W. Howay, ed., *The Early History of the Fraser River Mines*, British Columbia Archives Memoir, No. 3 (Victoria, BC: BC Archives, 1926), 68 and notes.

68. G.H. Richards to Prevost, January 12, 1859, copy, CO 60/5.

69. Dorothy Blakey Smith, ed., "The Journal of Arthur Thomas Bushby, 1858–1859," *British Columbia Historical Quarterly*, 21 (January–October, 1957–1958): 126–27.

70. Merivale to secretary of the Admiralty, April 11, 1859, Adm. 1/5721; Prevost to Baynes, January 29, 1859, CO 60/5; Mayne, *Four Years in British Columbia*, 66–73.

71. Log of HMS *Plumper*, January 17, 1859, Adm. 53/6854.

72. Prevost to Baynes, January 10, 1859, copy, CO 60/5.

73. The *Tribune* arrived from Hong Kong on February 13, 1858; the *Pylades* from Singapore three days later. Baynes to secretary of the Admiralty, April 30, 1859, Y84, Adm. 1/5713. See Mrs. Fred (Mary Augusta) Egerton, *Admiral of the Fleet Sir Geoffrey Phipps Hornby, G.C.B., A Biography* (Edinburgh: Wm. Blackwood and Sons, 1896), 55–61; and Norman, "Martello Tower," 229, 246.

74. Baynes to secretary of the Admiralty, April 30, 1859, Y84, Adm. 1/5713, and September 9, 1860, Y169, Adm. 1/5736; Vice-Admiral Seymour to secretary of the Admiralty, November 27, 1858, extract, CO 60/5; and Willard E. Ireland, "Pre-Confederation Defence Problems of the Pacific Colonies," in *Canadian Historical Association Annual Report*, 1941 (Toronto: CHA, 1941), 48.

75. Baynes to secretary of the Admiralty, October 20 and November 9, 1858, and Admiralty Minutes thereon, Adm. 1/5713.

76. Irving to under-secretary of state, War Office, October 3, 1859, CO 60/5; Lugard (WO) to Merivale, June 16, 1859; Minute of Blackwood, June 17, 1859; and H. Corry to under-secretary, War Office, June 9, 1859, CO 60/6.

77. Charles W. Wilson, in Reginald Eyre Watters, ed., *British Columbia: A Centennial Anthology* (Toronto: McClelland and Stewart, 1958), 18–19.

78. M. de Courcy to Baynes, February 24, 1859, copy, CO 60/5.

79. R. Quine to his brother and sister, April 22, 1861, Manx Museum, Isle of Man; transcripts in London School of Economics Library.

80. Morton, *History of the Canadian West*, 774.

81. Report of Douglas on the State of the Colony, August 23, 1859, CO 60/5.

82. Baynes to secretary of the Admiralty, September 13, 1859, Adm. 1/5713.

83. Rear-Admiral Sir T. Maitland to secretary of the Admiralty, May 24, 1861, Y164, and September 30, 1861, Y292, Adm. 1/5761; Rear-Admiral P.W. Brock, "H.M.S. *President*" typescript, n.d., p. 19, MMBC.

84. Mayne, *Four Years in British Columbia and Vancouver Island*, 206–7.

85. Commander L.S. Dawson, comp., *Memoirs of Hydrography . . . 1750-1885* (Eastbourne, UK: Henry W. Keay, 1885), 134–55. For his time as Hydrographer, see George S. Ritchie, *The Admiralty Chart: British Naval Hydrography in the Nineteenth Century*, new ed. (Edinburgh: Pentland Press, 1995), 342–57.

86. Mayne, *Four Years in British Columbia and Vancouver Island*, 214.

87. Ibid., 215–16.

88. Address from New Westminster, November 1862, printed in Linda Dorricott and Deidre Cullon, eds. *The Private Journal of Captain G.H. Richards: The Vancouver Island Survey (1860–1862)* (Vancouver: Ronsdale Press, 2012), 228–29.

89. Dorricott and Cullon, *Private Journal of Captain G.H. Richards*, 226.

90. The *Beaver* closed her surveying assignments in November 1870 and ended her career at Prospect Point, entrance of Vancouver harbour, in 1888.

91. Territorial and trading matters are considered in John S. Galbraith, *The Hudson's Bay Company as an Imperial Factor, 1821–1869* (Berkeley and Los Angeles: University of California Press, 1957), 169–74; and in C. Ian Jackson, "The Stikine Territory Lease and Its Relevance to the Alaska Purchase," *Pacific Historical Review*, 36 (August 1967): 289–306, and "A Territory of Little Value: The Wind of Change on the Northwest Coast, 1861–67," *The Beaver*, Outfit 298 (Summer 1967): 40–45.

92. See Maitland to secretary of the Admiralty, July 12, 1862, Y124, Adm. 1/5790. Copies of this and other reports relative to the Stikine Rush are in RG 8, IIIB, Vol. 34, LAC.

93. Maitland to secretary of the Admiralty, July 12, 1862, Y214, Adm. 1/5790.

94. J. Pike to Maitland, October 6, 1862, encl. in Maitland to secretary of the Admiralty, December 2, 1862, Y306, ibid.

95. J. Furuhjelm (Governor of Russian Colonies in America) to Maitland, September 25/6, 1862, RG 8, IIIB, Vol. 34, LAC.

96. James Cooper (Harbour Master, BC) to colonial secretary, October 17, 1862, in Ships' letters, F 1210, 3, BCA.

97. Order-in-Council, July 19, 1862; Howay and Scholefield, *British Columbia from the Earliest Times*, 2:84.

98. Maitland to secretary of the Admiralty, September 3, 1862, Y246, Adm. 1/5790.

99. Maitland to secretary of the Admiralty, February 7, 1863, Y30, Adm. 1/5826.

100. Governor Seymour to Rear-Admiral Honourable G.F. Hastings, August 29, 1867, encl. in F. Rogers (CO) to secretary of the Admiralty, November 11, 1867, Adm. 1/6026.

101. These were defined in Admiralty instructions to Rear-Admiral J. Denman, July 16, 1864, copy, CO 60/30.

102. Rogers to secretary of the Admiralty, December 19, 1867, Adm. 1/6026.

103. Minute of Blackwood, December 31, 1867, ibid. The Admiralty informed the Colonial Office that the Commander-in-Chief, Pacific, was correct. See Lennox to Elliot, October 28, 1867, Y12, Adm. 1/6056.

104. *General Orders for Her Majesty's Squadron on the Pacific Station, 1865* (printed Valparaiso 1865), 13; copy in Adm. 13/184/13.

105. See, for example, Morton, *History of the Canadian West*, 787.

106. The development of colonial jurisdiction on the Northwest Coast has been elucidated by Willard E. Ireland in "The Evolution of the Boundaries of British Columbia," *British Columbia Historical Quarterly*, 3 (October 1939): 263–82.

CHAPTER SEVEN

1. Charles Wood to Alfred Martin, October 31, 1859, EB W851, BCA.

2. Another British naval officer thought the island only important for its strategic value: Richard C. Mayne, *Four Years in British Columbia and Vancouver Island: An Account of Their Forests, Rivers, Coasts, Gold Fields, and Resources for Colonization* (London: John Murray, 1862), 42. Some even have referred to it as the "Cronstadt of the Pacific," as in note 3 of this chapter.

3. Best accounts of the dispute are Mike Vouri, *The Pig War: Standoff at Griffin Bay* (Friday Harbor, WA: Griffin Bay Bookstore, 1999), and *Outpost of Empire: The Royal Marines and the Joint Occupation of San Juan Island* (Seattle: Northwest Interpretive Association, 2004); James O. McCabe, *The San Juan Water Boundary Question* (Toronto: University of Toronto Press, 1964); Keith A. Murray, *The Pig War* (Tacoma: Washington State Historical Society, 1968); and Hunter Miller, *San Juan Archipelago: Study of the Joint Occupation of San Juan Island* (Bellows Falls, VT: printed at the Wyndham Press, 1943). See also Vol. 8 of Hunter Miller's *Treaties and Other International Acts of the United States of America* (Washington, DC: US Government Printing Office, 1948). Of lesser value are Viscount Milton, *History of the San Juan Boundary Question* (London: Cassell, Petter and Galpin, 1869); Scott Kaufman, *The Pig War: The United States, Britain, and the Balance of Power in the Pacific Northwest, 1846–72* (Lanham, MD: Lexington Books, 2003); Archie W. Shiels, *San Juan Islands: The Cronstadt of the Pacific* (Juneau, AK: Empire Printing Co., 1938).

4. J. Neilson Barry, ed., "Broughton's Log of a Reconnaissance of the San Juan Islands in 1792," *Washington Historical Quarterly*, 21 (1930): 55–60; Edmond S. Meany, ed., *Vancouver's Discovery of Puget Sound* (Portland, OR: Binfords-Mort, 1942), chapters 8 and 9.

5. Captain Prevost to Rear-Admiral Fairfax Moresby, June 7, 1853, Y73, Adm. 1/5630.

6. Miller, *Treaties*, 8:307–9.

7. Reported in J. Douglas to A. Barclay (secretary, HBC), December 19, 1854, B 226/b/11, fol. 92, HBCA.

8. Rear-Admiral H.W. Bruce to Sir Charles Wood (First Lord of the Admiralty), September 18, 1855, Halifax Papers, Add. MSS. 49,549, BL.

9. Ibid.

10. Wood to Bruce, November 16, 1855, Halifax Papers, Add. MSS 49, 565, fol. 33, BL.

11. Wood to Bruce, February 16, 1856, ibid.

12. E. Hammond (permanent under-secretary, FO), to secretary of the Admiralty, September 16, 1856, Adm. 1/5678.

13. Prevost to Lord Clarendon (FO), August 12, 1857, Cap P, 60, Adm. 1/5684.

14. The Royal Engineers were transported from Panama to Vancouver Island in HMS *Havannah*. Admiralty Minute of October 30, 1857; Prevost to secretary of the Admiralty, August 14, 1857, ibid.; Admiralty Minute of November 11, 1857, Adm. 1/5687.

15. F. Napier (British minister, Washington) to Clarendon, January 9, 1858, encl. in FO to Adm., February 4, 1858, Adm. 1/5699. Prevost had instructions from the Foreign Office stipulating that Rosario Strait fitted the description given in the Oregon Treaty. See McCabe, *San Juan*, 20–21.

16. Prevost to secretary of the Admiralty, December 17, 1857, Adm. 1/5699.

17. See Prevost to secretary of the Admiralty, December 7, 1847, ibid. The Foreign Office was satisfied with the position taken by Prevost; Malmesbury (FO) to Prevost, May 14, 1858, ibid.

18. Prevost to Hammond, April 13, 1858, FO 5/810; quoted in McCabe, *San Juan*, 26.

19. Series 1393, U.S. Senate Ex. Doc. 8, 41st Cong., 1869, I, Engineer's Report, 2; quoted in McCabe, *San Juan*, 32.

20. Sir John Pakington, the First Lord of the Admiralty, thought the advantages of possessing the island questionable. See Minute of Sir J. Pakington, March 11, 1858, Adm. 1/5699. His views were the opposite of his predecessor. See Sir C. Wood to Clarendon, February 17, 1858, Clar. dep., c. 82, fols. 150–151, Bod. L.

21. Adm. to FO, April 6, 1858, draft, ibid. (sent April 8, 1858).

22. Admiralty Board Minute, March 2, 1859, on Hammond to secretary of the Admiralty, February 5, 1859, Adm. 1/5719.

23. Encl. in Prevost to Malmesbury, November 30, 1858; copy sent in Hammond to secretary of the Admiralty, February 5, 1859, ibid. Richards noted that charts by Vancouver (1792) and Kellett (1847) were still valuable.

24. Memorandum of Hammond, April 20, 1858, FO 5/813; in McCabe, *San Juan*, 30.

25. An indication of the interest in this subject is registered in the mass of writing on it. See note 3 of this chapter for the principal works.

26. Hubert H. Bancroft, *British Columbia, 1792–1887*, vol. 27 *in History of the Pacific States of North America* (San Francisco: History Company, 1887), 607–8.

27. See McCabe, San Juan, 37–39.

28. Walter N. Sage, *Sir James Douglas and British Columbia* (Toronto: University of Toronto Press, 1930), 266.

29. General W.S. Harney to Douglas, August 6, 1859, CO 305/12.

30. Rear Admiral R.L. Baynes to secretary of the Admiralty, August 12, 1859, Adm. 1/5713.

31. Dallas to Harney, May 10, 1860, B.226/b/19, fol. 127, HBCA.

32. Quoted in Richard W. Van Alstyne, *The Rising American Empire* (Oxford: Basil Blackwell, 1960), 118.

33. McCabe, San Juan, 39.

34. For a close examination of Harney, see Murray, Pig War, 15–22.

35. See his biography in *The Dictionary of American Biography* (New York: Scribner, 1932), 8:280–81.

36. Lord Lyons to General Lewis Cass (US secretary of state), May 12, 1859, copy, CO 305/30.

37. Hammond to H. Merivale (CO), April 27, 1859, CO 305/12.

38. Sage, *Sir James Douglas*, 39.

39. M. de Courcy to Baynes, August 5, 1859; and A.G. Young (colonial secretary, Vancouver Island) to J. de Courcy, July 23, 1859, encl. in Baynes to secretary of the Admiralty, August 8, 1859, Y146, Adm. 1/5713.

40. Douglas to M. de Courcy, July 29, 1859, encl. in Baynes to secretary of the Admiralty, August 8, 1859, ibid.

41. Douglas to Prevost, July 29, 1859, encl. in Baynes to secretary of the Admiralty, August 8, 1859, ibid.

42. Ibid.

43. M. de Courcy to Prevost, August 1, 1859, ibid.

44. Douglas to M. de Courcy, July 30, 1859, ibid.

45. M. de Courcy to Baynes, August 5, 1859, encl. in Baynes to secretary of the Admiralty, August 8, 1859, ibid.

46. Reported in ibid.

47. Douglas to Captain G. Phipps Hornby, August 2, 1859; in Sage, *Sir James Douglas*, 270.

48. See, for example, Douglas to M. de Courcy, two letters of July 29, 1859, and Douglas to Baynes, August 17, 1859, in ibid., 266, 267, 272–73.

49. Hornby to Baynes, August 5, 1859, Adm. 1/5713.

50. Ibid.

51. G. Pickett to Harney, August 3, 1859; Miller, *Treaties*, 8:358.

52. In the *Tribune* were 69 Royal Marines and 15 Royal Engineers. Hornby to Baynes, August 5, 1859, Y146, Adm. 1/5713. Mrs. Fred (Mary Augusta) Egerton, *Admiral of the Fleet Sir Geoffrey Phipps Hornby, G.C.B., A Biography* (Edinburgh: Wm. Blackwood and Sons, 1896), 66.

53. The disembarkation of 120 Americans constituted "a most unprecedented and unjustifiable act of aggression." Prevost to Malmesbury, August 3, 1859, CO 305/12.

54. Commander Norman claimed that Pickett tricked the naval officers by inviting them to a picnic, a "preconcerted device for denuding the British frigate of most of her officers in anticipation of what had been planned to come off." Francis Martin Norman, "Martello Tower," in *China and the Pacific in H.M.S. Tribune, 1850–60* (London: George Allen, 1902), 269.

55. Ibid, 271. The earlier orders were "to prevent the landing of United States Troops and the erection of military works by the detachment occupying San Juan." Douglas to Hornby, August 2, 1859; in Sage, *Sir James Douglas*, 270.

56. F.W. Howay and others, eds., "Angus McDonald: A Few Items of the West," *Washington Historical Quarterly*, 8 (July 1917): 196. According to McDonald, chief factor at Fort Colville, Baynes told Douglas he would refuse an order from the governor to attack the American camp on San Juan; ibid., 195.

57. Baynes to Admiralty, August 12, 1859, Adm. 1/5713; Egerton, *Admiral of the Fleet*, 68.

58. Baynes to Douglas, August 13, 1859, confidential, Ships' letters, F 1213, BCA.

59. Ibid.

60. Douglas to Baynes, August 17, 1859, Vancouver Island Misc. Letter-Book, No. 2, 216–20, BCA; in Sage, *Sir James Douglas*, 272–73.

61. Colonel R.C. Moody, RE, to Sir John T. Burgoyne (Inspector-General of Fortifications), August 8, 1859; Egerton, *Admiral of the Fleet*, 66–67. Moody's plans for the defence of British Columbia, mainly by the Royal Navy, are given in this letter.

62. Baynes to secretary of the Admiralty, August 12, 1859, Adm. 1/5713.

63. Baynes to secretary of the Admiralty, August 19, 1859, ibid.

64. Duke of Newcastle to Douglas, October 21, 1859, G/336, pp. 114–16, LAC; in Sage, *Sir James Douglas*, 277.

65. Hammond to secretary of the Admiralty, October 2, 1859, and W.G. Romaine to Hammond, October 11, 1859, CO 305/12.

66. Admiralty to Baynes, October 3, 1859, encl. in FO papers, Adm. 1/5720 (received December 2, 1859). Baynes did not leave Vancouver Island for England until September 10, 1860, leaving Captain J.W.S. Spencer of HMS *Topaze* as Senior Officer, Vancouver Island.

67. Duke of Somerset to W.E. Gladstone, October 12, 1859, Gladstone Papers, Add. MS. 44, 304, fols. 13–14, BL.

68. Somerset to Gladstone, October 15, 1859, ibid., fols. 17–18.

69. Ibid.

70. *Navy Estimates, Ships and Men, 1860–1*, printed for the Cabinet, confid., ibid., fol. 52.

71. See C.J. Bartlett, "The Mid-Victorian Reappraisal of Naval Policy," in K. Bourne and D.C. Watt, eds., *Studies in International History: Essays Presented to W. Norton Medlicott* (London: Longmans Green and Co., 1967), 189–208.

72. Baynes to secretary of the Admiralty, October 26, 1859, Adm. 1/5713; and Baynes to secretary of the Admiralty, November 9, 1859, Y1, Adm. 1/5736.

73. Hammond to secretary of the Admiralty, October 21, 1859, encl. in FO papers, Adm. 1/5720.

74. Baynes to secretary of the Admiralty, January 25, 1860, Y30, ibid.

75. Admiralty Minute, March 19, 1860, on Baynes to secretary of the Admiralty, January 25, 1860, Y30, ibid.

76. Hammond to secretary of the Admiralty, December 22, 1859, in FO Papers, Adm. 1/5720.

77. Baynes to Captain G. Bazalgette, RMLI, Memo of March 20, 1860, encl. in Baynes to secretary of the Admiralty, March 28, 1860, Y71, Adm. 1/5736.

78. *British Colonist* (Victoria, BC), August 17, 1859.

79. Baynes to secretary of the Admiralty, November 9, 1859, Y1, Adm. 1/5736.

80. Somerset to Baynes, March 31, 1860, BAY/2, NMM.

81. Somerset to Baynes, May 17, 1860, 36 MS 1061, NMM. Baynes received a KCB the following day.

82. See H.C. Allen, *Great Britain and the United States: A History of Anglo-American Relations (1783–1952)* (New York: St. Martin's Press, 1955), 511–17.

83. Prevost prepared the British case with the aid of F.S. Reilly of the Foreign Office and, before him, Sir Travers Twiss, famed international jurist, professor of law in King's College, London, and author of *The Oregon Question Examined in Respect to Facts and the Law of Nations* (London: Longman, Brown, Green and Longmans, 1846).

84. McCabe, San Juan, 114–17.

85. *Supplement to the London Gazette*, October 30, 1872.

86. The theme was repeated in the Alaska Boundary Tribunal Award (1903), with more repercussions in Canada.

87. The *Times*, October 30, 1872; Milton to Clarendon, December 22, 1869, Clar. dep., c. 510 (fol. 1), Bod. L.

88. Sir John A. Macdonald to Charles Tupper, n.d. [1871?], Macdonald Papers, Macdonald-Tupper Correspondence, II, 165ff., LAC; in Goldwin Smith, "Notes on the Problems of San Juan," *Pacific Northwest Quarterly*, 31 (1940): 185.

89. See Appendices B and C for the number of ships on the station.

CHAPTER EIGHT

1. As mentioned in Chapter 7, his son took an active part in the San Juan crisis and, like his father, became a prominent Lord of the Admiralty in later years.

2. Mrs. Fred (Mary Augusta) Egerton, *Admiral of the Fleet Sir Geoffrey Phipps Hornby, G.C.B., A Biography* (Edinburgh: Wm. Blackwood and Sons, 1896), 25–37.

3. T. Phipps Hornby to J. Parker, August 29, 1849, in BCA, *Report of the Provincial Archives Department of the Province of British Columbia for the year ended December 31st 1913* (Victoria, BC, 1914), V74.

4. A more complete analysis of these is given in my book *Gunboat Frontier: British Maritime Authority and Northwest Coast Indians, 1846–1890* (Vancouver: UBC Press, 1984).

5. Quoted in James Morris, *Heaven's Command, An Imperial Progress* (New York: Harcourt Brace Jovanovich, 1971), 86. Also, for discussion of Glenelg, G.R. Mellor, *British Imperial Trusteeship 1783–1850* (London: Faber and Faber,1951), 250.

6. The Select Committee was appointed in May 1835 under these general terms. See Mellor, *British Imperial Trusteeship*, 249.

7. Quoted in W. Ross Johnston, *Sovereignty and Protection: A Study of British Jurisdictionalism in the Late Nineteenth Century* (Durham, NC: Duke University Press, 1973), 15.

8. For more extensive treatment of the theories and application of "Native policy" in Vancouver Island and British Columbia, see Gough, *Gunboat Frontier*. The current discussion draws heavily on Barry M. Gough, *Pax Britannica: Ruling the Waves and Keeping the Peace before Armageddon* (Basingstoke, UK: Palgrave Macmillan, 2014), ch. 9.

9. See Appendixes E, F and G for information on the changing technology in British warships and lists of the warships on the Northwest Coast during this period.

10. G.H. Richards to R.L. Baynes, August 21, 1859, encl. in Baynes to J. Douglas, August 26, 1859, F1212a 24, BCA; quoted in Gough, *Gunboat Frontier*, 80.

11. Gough, *Pax Britannica*, 155–57.

12. Richard C. Mayne, *Four Years in British Columbia and Vancouver Island: An Account of Their Forests, Rivers, Coasts, Gold Fields, and Resources for Colonization* (London: John Murray, 1862), 210.

13. Doolan's correspondence with the CMS, as well as his journal, is distilled in Barry M. Gough, "Pioneer Missionaries to the Nishga: The Crosscurrents of Demon Rum and British Gunboats, 1860–1871," *Journal of the Canadian Church Historical Society*, 26, 2 (October 1984): 81–95. See also E. Palmer Patterson II, *Mission on the Nass: The Evangelization of the Nishga, 1860–1890* (Waterloo, ON: Eulachon Press, 1982).

14. Denny's report of proceedings, October 24, 1866, Adm. 1/5969.

15. Doolan, Journal, December 9, 1865, January 8 and 29, April 18, May 15, 1866, and other entries for that year, CMS Archives, C C2/0, 7/14.

16. Commander-in-Chief to Admiralty, June 16, 1868, Adm. 1/6056, Y76; Gough, *Gunboat Frontier*, 195–98.

17. This account is drawn from Gough, *Gunboat Frontier*, 198–204, where full references are to be found. Other episodes of similar type are recounted in that work.

18. Hunt was later an assistant to the esteemed anthropologist Franz Boas of Columbia University.

19. Lieutenant Charles Reynold Harris to Rear-Admiral de Horsey, April 10, 1877, Y84, Adm. 1/6414.

20. See Gough, *Gunboat Frontier*, chs. 12 and 13 respectively.

CHAPTER NINE

1. Alexander Rattray, MD, an assistant surgeon in HMS *Topaze*, showed statistically that Esquimalt had a more healthy climate than England. Alex Rattray, *Vancouver Island and British Columbia: Where They Are, What They Are, and What They May Become* (London: Smith, Elder and Co., 1862), 54, 148.

2. Order-in-Council, June 29, 1865, copy, Adm. 1/5961; printed in Admiralty, Orders-in-Council, Vol. 3 (London, 1873), 79–80. See also F.V. Longstaff, *Esquimalt Naval Base: A History of Its Work and Its Defences* (Victoria, BC: Victoria Book and Stationery Co., 1941), 21.

3. Lord Ellenborough to Lord Aberdeen, May 16, 1846, private, Aberdeen Papers, Add. MSS 43, 198, BM. The Revillagigedo Islands off the west coast of Mexico were an alternative of lesser promise.

4. Aberdeen to R. Pakenham (British minister, Mexico), December 15, 1841, FO 50/143. See also Ephraim D. Adams, "English Interest in the Annexation of California," *American Historical Review*, 14 (July 1909): 747.

5. H.G. Ward (Adm.) to Rear-Admiral Phipps Hornby, March 17, 1848, PHI/3/15, NMM. See also Kenneth Bourne, *Britain and the Balance of Power in North America, 1815–1908* (London: Longmans, Green and Co., 1967), 176–77 and notes. For a good description of what a naval base should afford, see Gilbert N. Tucker, *The Naval Service of Canada: Its Official History* (Ottawa: King's Printer, 1952), 1:45–46.

6. See chapter 4.

7. Rear-Admiral H.W. Bruce to R.B. Osborne (secretary, Adm.), January 21, 1858, and enclosures, Adm. 1/5694. Bruce was incorrect: the earliest claim of the Navy to Esquimalt was the visit of the *Constance* in 1848, and the *Thetis*, after which the island was named, was there in 1852–1853. The first survey of the harbour was in 1846.

8. Rear-Admiral R.L. Baynes to Governor J. Douglas, October 26, 1858, Adm. 1/5713.

9. Baynes to secretary of the Admiralty, January 10, 1860, Adm. 1/5969.

10. Dennis Noble, *The Coast Guard in the Pacific Northwest* (Washington, DC: US Coast Guard, 1988), 1–8.

11. See chapter 5.

12. Rear-Admiral Sir T. Maitland to secretary of the Admiralty, February 1, 1862, Adm. 1/5790. The problems of keeping stores at Valparaiso are considered in John Bach, "The Maintenance of Royal Navy Vessels in the Pacific Ocean, 1825–1875," *Mariner's Mirror*, 56 (August 1970): 262–64.

13. Minute of Admiral Milne, June 6, 1859, on Baynes to secretary of the Admiralty, March 28, 1859, Adm. 1/5713.

14. Rear-Admiral F. Moresby to secretary of the Admiralty, July 3, 1851; in W. Kaye Lamb, ed., "Correspondence Relating to the Establishment of a Naval Base at Esquimalt, 1851–57," *British Columbia Historical Quarterly*, 6 (October 1942): 280.

15. Bruce Journal, September 11, 1855, Adm. 50/308. He thought the storeship *Naiad* should be moved from Callao to Esquimalt.

16. Sir Charles Wood to Lord Clarendon, January 2, 1856, Halifax Papers, Add. MSS. 49, 565, BL.

17. Wood to Bruce, February 16, 1856, ibid. In these instructions, the First Lord noted of Esquimalt: "It is so far from us, and the access to it overland is so difficult that it would be impossible to succour it in time to preserve it from an unforeseen assault. On the other hand, there is coal, wood and supplies of various kinds of which it might be well to avail ourselves in a good climate."

18. Bruce to Wood, September 22, 1856, ibid.

19. Minutes of A. Blackwood (Adm.), February 20, 1858, on H. Vansittart (FO) to secretary of the Admiralty, November 17, 1857, Adm. 1/5696. Neither Baynes nor Maitland favoured a permanent naval depot at Panama, but merely sought the use of the Pacific Steam Navigation Company's facilities. Maitland to secretary of the Admiralty, February 22, 1861, Adm. 1/5761.

20. Prevost to secretary of the Admiralty, June 7, 1858, Adm. 1/5696.

21. Baynes to secretary of the Admiralty, December 18, 1860, Adm. 1/5761.

22. Baynes to secretary of the Admiralty, December 1, 1859, Adm. 1/5969.

23. Minute of Rear-Admiral Sir Richard Milne, February 10, 1859, ibid. According to Milne, Panama would be the main depot with a subsidiary storeship kept at Esquimalt.

24. Minute of Vice-Admiral Sir Richard Dundas, February 11, 1859, ibid.

25. Ibid.

26. Minute of Vice-Admiral W.F. Martin, February 17, 1859, ibid.

27. Minute of Sir John Pakington (First Lord of the Admiralty), February 19, 1859, ibid.

28. Admiralty instructions to Baynes, March 10, 1859, draft, ibid.

29. Baynes to secretary of the Admiralty, May 12, 1859, ibid.

30. In 1859 a public debate began as to whether Esquimalt or Burrard Inlet should become the headquarters. See *The Times* (London), March 15 and June 22, 1860; Matthew Macfie, *Vancouver Island and British Columbia: Their History, Resources, and Prospects* (London: Longman, Green, Longman, Roberts and Green, 1865), 127; and J.D. Pemberton, *Facts and Figures Relating to Vancouver Island and British Columbia* (London: Longman, Green, Longman and Roberts, 1860), 12. Actually, lands on Burrard Inlet did not go unnoticed, for in 1860 some were reserved "for naval purposes." See Douglas to the Duke of Newcastle (CO), December 23, 1859, and enclosures, CO 60/5; Plan of Sections reserved for Naval Department, item 16, Adm. Corr. II, BCA; File Misc. 4 (Parry Papers I), Item 8, HO. For sailing ships, access to Burrard Inlet was "entirely unsuitable"; Rear-Admiral the Honourable George Hastings to secretary of the Admiralty, October 18, 1867, Adm. 1/6008.

31. Baynes to secretary of the Admiralty, May 12, 1859, Adm. 1/5969.

32. Report of Captain George H. Richards on the Harbours of Vancouver's Island and British Columbia, encl. in Richards to Douglas, October 23, 1859; "Papers re: British Columbia, Pt. II," *Parliamentary Papers*, 1859 (Session 2), 22 (2578), with charts and maps. See also Admiral J. Washington, hydrographer, Memorandum of May 5, 1859, encl. in H. Merivale (CO) to secretary of the Admiralty, June 26, 1859, Adm. 1/5721.

33. Baynes to secretary of the Admiralty, November 14, 1859, Adm. 1/5969. He also thought that the War Office should consider the matter of shore batteries.

34. Victualling Department to secretary of the Admiralty, March 13, 1860, and Minute of Eden, March 19, 1860, Adm. 1/5761.

35. See his three reports to the secretary of the Admiralty for January 25, 1861 (Adm. 1/5761), August 27, 1861 (Adm. 1/5969), and January 10, 1862 (Adm. 1/5790).

36. Instructions to Rear-Admiral Kingcome, December 2, 1862, Adm. 13/5. See also John Bach, "The Royal Navy in the South Pacific, 1826–1876" (Ph.D. thesis, University of New South Wales, 1964). A commodore at Valparaiso was in charge of the Southern Division (south of the equator).

37. Maitland to secretary of the Admiralty, August 8, 1861, Adm. 1/5761.

38. Maitland, Colonel R.C. Moody, RE, and Captain Richards recommended that two sites would be suitable for a naval establishment of docks and storehouses. One, adjacent to Thetis Island (finally selected), was most convenient for ships, yet would be exposed to enemy bombardment. The second was at the head of Constance Cove. Maitland to secretary of the Admiralty, April 24, 1861, Adm. 1/5969.

39. Instructions to Kingcome, December 2, 1862, Adm. 13/5.

40. Elevations and plans of these buildings are in File No. Misc. 18, Item 2, HO.

41. See Kingcome to secretary of the Admiralty, November 23, 1863, and Minute of Richards (now Hydrographer of the Admiralty), January 14, 1864, ibid.

42. Maitland to Douglas, June 26 and September 2, 1862, F 1206, 28 and 34, Ships' letters, BCA.

43. Alexander Caulfield Anderson, "History of the Northwest Coast" (typescript in BCA from the original in the Academy of Pacific Coast History, University of California at Berkeley, 1878), 106–7. Anderson was not alone in his enthusiasm, as the works of Mayne, Pemberton, Macfie and Rattray cited in this chapter will attest.

44. Kingcome to secretary of the Admiralty, July 14, 1863, Esq. Nav. Estab. Rec, I, MMBC.

45. Admiralty to Kingcome, December 18, 1863, ibid.

46. Kingcome to secretary of the Admiralty, December 5, 1863, ibid.

47. Rear-Admiral the Honourable J. Denman to secretary of the Admiralty, November 21, 1864, ibid.

48. Denman to secretary of the Admiralty, August 17, 1865, Adm. 1/5969.

49. Order-in-Council, June 29, 1865. See note 2 of this chapter.

50. Ibid.

51. That position proved too exposed, for in 1875 a severe storm nearly blew the wooden structure down, and the vibrations of gunfire broke numerous windows. In 1904 the church was moved to its present position at the corner of Esquimalt Road and Grafton Street.

52. Richard C. Mayne, *Four Years in British Columbia and Vancouver Island: An Account of Their Forests, Rivers, Coasts, Gold Fields, and Resources for Colonization* (London: John Murray, 1862), 24–25.

53. J.R. Tanner, ed., *Samuel Pepys's Naval Minutes* (London: Navy Records Society, 1926), 39–40.

54. Admiralty Minute, March 18, 1869, Adm. 1/6137.

55. R. Dundas to secretary of the Admiralty, March 9, 1869, ibid.

56. Admiralty instructions to Rear-Admiral Hastings, January 26, 1869, Adm. 13/40.

57. Admiralty Minute, January 25, 1869, Adm. 1/6127.

58. Admiralty Minute, January 23, 1869, ibid. There was no reduction on the Australian station at this time.

59. According to Admiralty draft instructions to Rear-Admiral G. Phipps Hornby, dated June 10, 1869 (Adm. 1/6108), the cruiser squadron was being sent "with the

two-fold purpose of effecting reliefs to Ships and Crews on distant Foreign Stations, the force on which has been somewhat reduced—and also of improving the efficiency of officers and men, especially in handling Ships in Squadrons, upon which so much depends." Final instructions to this effect were sent to Hornby on November 25, 1869 (Adm. 1/6113).

60. For this cruise and the visit to Esquimalt (May 15–27, 1870), see J.B., *The Cruise Round the World of the Flying Squadron, 1869–1870, under the Command of Rear-Admiral G.T. Phipps Hornby* (London: J.D. Potter, 1871); and William Haynes, *My Log: A Journal of the Proceedings of the Flying Squadron* (Devonport, UK: Clarke and Son, 1871).

61. See Appendix C for sources and further details on the distribution of the Royal Navy, 1861–1874.

62. Hastings to Rear-Admiral A. Farquhar, January 18, 1870, Y28, Adm. 1/6151.

63. See, for example, Hastings to secretary of the Admiralty, February 22, 1870, ibid., and Longstaff, *Esquimalt Naval Base*, 27–28.

CHAPTER TEN

1. See C.P. Stacey, *Canada and the British Army, 1846–1871*, rev. ed. (Toronto: University of Toronto Press, 1963), 43ff.; and Robert L. Schuyler, "The Recall of the Legions: A Phase in the Decentralization of the British Empire," *American Historical Review*, 26 (October 1920): 18–36.

2. Lord John Morley, *The Life of William Ewart Gladstone* (London: Macmillan, 1903), 1:573.

3. A separate War Office was established in 1854.

4. Resolution of Lord Stanley, June 21, 1861, "Report . . . Colonial Military Expenditure," *Parliamentary Papers*, 1861, 21 (423), p. xiv. At that time, British Columbia's contribution (£11,000) to support 138 Royal Engineers (165 were originally sent) engaged on "colonial" not "imperial duties" remained unpaid. Actually, the engineers had been sent at the time of the gold rush, in keeping with the policy that "wherever England extended the sway of her sceptre, there she pledged the defence of her sword." Minutes of Evidence, April 18, 1861, ibid., p. 4.

5. Great Britain, *Hansard's Parliamentary Debates*, 3rd Series, 165, col. 1060. On the labours of the committee, see Donald C. Gordon. *The Dominion Partnership in Imperial Defense, 1870–1914* (Baltimore: Johns Hopkins University Press, 1965), 12–23.

6. 28 Vic., c. 14; under this statute, self-governing colonies could commission their own naval forces. See B.A. Knox, "Colonial Influence on Imperial Policy, 1858–1866: Victoria and the Colonial Defence Act, 1865," *Historical Studies: Australia and New Zealand*, 11 (November 1963): 66–67.

7. Duke of Newcastle to Governor James Douglas, May 11, 1861, confid., encl. in A.G. Young to Ozzard, September 23, 1861, RG 8, IIIB, Vol. 35, LAC.

8. Queen's Proclamation, May 15, 1861, encl. in C. Paget (Adm.) to Rear-Admiral Sir T. Maitland, May 16, 1861, ibid.

9. Robin W. Winks, *Canada and the United States: The Civil War Years* (Baltimore: Johns Hopkins University Press, 1960), 35–36; and Kenneth Bourne, *Britain and the Balance of Power in North America, 1815–1908* (London: Longmans, Green and Co., 1967), 210–11.

10. Lord Palmerston (prime minister) to the Duke of Somerset (Adm.), May 26, 1861, Palmerston Papers, Add. MSS. 48, 582, BL.

11. Ibid. Somerset mistakenly thought the US Navy had only one small vessel in the Pacific (see Bourne, *Britain and the Balance of Power*, 215). He evidently failed to check the quarterly returns of commanders-in-chief on foreign stations that gave the strengths of foreign navies. For the period under review, the annual composition of United States naval forces in the Pacific, as given in Robert E. Johnson, *Thence Round Cape Horn: The Story of United States Naval Forces on Pacific Station, 1818–1923* (Annapolis, MD: United States Naval Institute, 1963), App. 3, was:

YEAR	SHIPS	YEAR	SHIPS
1861	9	1867	16
1862	7	1868	15
1863	5	1869	11
1864	8	1870	12
1865	8	1871	12
1866	11		

Statistics on the British naval strength for the Pacific during this period are given in Appendix B of this book.

12. This strange phrase was used often in the 1860s. See W.C.B. Tunstall, "Imperial Defence, 1815–1870," in *Cambridge History of the British Empire* (Cambridge: Cambridge University Press, 1961), 2:831.

13. Lord John Russell (FO) to Lord Lyons (British minister, Washington), and Russell to Adm., November 30, 1861, in United States, *Official Records of the Union and Confederate Navies in the War of the Rebellion* (Washington, DC: Government Printing Office, 1894–1922), ser. 1, 1:158ff.

14. Bourne, *Britain and the Balance of Power*, 229; Stacey, *Canada and the British Army*, 118.

15. See Appendix B.

16. Rear-Admiral Maitland to secretary of the Admiralty, January 13, 1862, Adm. 1/5790.

17. Ibid.

18. Ibid.

19. Report of Flag Officer Charles H. Bell to Gideon Welles (secretary of the Navy), May 29, 1862; United States, *Official Records of the Union and Confederate Navies*, ser. 1, 1:391.

20. Ibid. The British consul at San Francisco urged Rear-Admiral Maitland to station a British warship there for the protection of British interests; C. Brooker to Maitland, September 28, 1861, Adm. 1/5761.

21. Incidentally, about this time Lieutenant Edmund Verney, commanding the gunboat *Grappler*, wrote privately to Arthur Mills, MP, influential in discussions on colonial defence in London, to ask the secretary of the Admiralty "what dock accommodation would be available for H.M. fleet in the Pacific, in the event of war with America, and whether H.M. Government contemplates the establishment of a dockyard in Vancouver Island." He added, "Everybody knows that Nature intended there should be a dockyard at Esquimalt." Verney to Mills, August 30, 1862, BF1214, BCA. See also the views of R.C. Mayne, given in the previous chapter, on the necessity of a dockyard at this time.

22. The Russians were willing to aid in the defence of San Francisco against Confederate ships rumoured to be found there. Frank A. Golder, "The Russian Fleet and the Civil War," *American Historical Review*, 20 (July 1915): 801–14.

23. Rear-Admiral A.A. Popov instructed the Pacific squadron "to make the acquaintance of the colonies of the European sea powers, to seek out their valuable points, and constantly to be on guard." A. Belomer, "The Second Pacific Squadron," *Morskoy Sbornik*, 283 (1914): 54–55; in E.A. Adamov, "Russia and the United States at the Time of the Civil War," *Journal of Modern History*, 2 (1930): 598. These do not necessarily imply aggressive tactics on the part of Russia, however.

24. On the naval objectives of the South, see James D. Bulloch, *The Secret Service of the Confederate States in Europe or How the Confederate Cruisers Were Equipped* (London: R. Bentley and Son, 1883; reprint, New York and London: T. Yoseloff, 1959), 1:46.

25. Brainerd Dyer, "Confederate Naval and Privateering Activities in the Pacific," *Pacific Historical Review*, 3 (1934): 433.

26. Secretary of Navy to Flag Officer J.B. Montgomery, commanding United States Pacific squadron, April 27, 1861; United States, *Official Records of the Union and Confederate Navies*, ser. 1, 1:15.

27. Amos Corwine to Charles Henderson, May 29, 1861, encl. in Henderson to Captain Wm. Graham, Senior Officer at Panama, May 31, 1861, RG 8, IIIB, Vol. 35, LAC.

28. Estimating the amount of sympathy for the Confederacy is a difficult matter. However, support for both sides existed in Britain and the Pacific colonies. See the views of Lord Lyons, expressed in his letter to Lord John Russell, May 6, 1861, Russell Papers, TNA.; in Ephraim D. Adams, *Great Britain and the American Civil War* (London: Longmans, Green, and Co., 1925; reprint, London: Peter Smith, 1957), 1:88n2.

29. Maitland to secretary of the Admiralty, July 14, 1861, Adm. 1/5761.

30. Copies of correspondence between the two governments were sent to the Commander-in-Chief, Pacific. See RG 8, IIIB, Vol. 35, LAC

31. Maitland to Douglas, August 2, 1861, ibid.

32. Russell to Adm., January 31, 1862, ibid.

33. Copies of this correspondence were sent to the Commander-in-Chief, Pacific, encl. in Paget to Kingcome, May 11, 1863, ibid. Governor Douglas, incidentally, had his own plan for conquering American territory as far south as the Columbia River by means of the Royal Navy. See Benjamin F. Gilbert, "Rumours of Confederate Privateers Operating in Victoria, Vancouver Island," *British Columbia Historical Quarterly*, 18 (1954): 240–41.

34. Wm. Seward to Lyons, April 15, 1863, enclosing telegram from Collector of Customs, San Francisco, April 14, 1863, RG 8, IIIB, Vol. 35, LAC. Instructions to Lt.-Cdr. W.D. Hopkins of the *Saginaw*, April 23, 1863, United States, *Official Records of the Union and Confederate Navies*, ser. 1, 2:165–66.

35. Selfridge (Commandant, Mare Island) to Welles, June 3, 1863, ibid., 259–60.

36. Bell to Welles, January 9, 1864. ibid., 583.

37. In Rear-Admiral Kingcome to secretary of the Admiralty, March 5, 1864, copy, RG 8, IIIB, Vol. 35, LAC.

38. W.G. Romaine (Adm.) to Kingcome, April 27, 1864, ibid.

39. Documents relating to her cruise are in United States, *Official Records of the Union and Confederate Navies*, ser. 1, 3:749–838.

40. Rear-Admiral Denman to Governor A.G. Kennedy, August 9, 1865, F 1223, BCA, and Denman to secretary of the Admiralty, September 7, 1865, Adm. 1/5924.

41. Circular of secretary of state for the colonies, September 7, 1865, encl. in Kennedy to Denman, November 15, 1865, RG 8, IIIB, Vol. 35, LAC.

42. The Armstrong gun, which made its appearance in the 1850s, incorporated striking advances. It was a built-up, wrought iron, rifled, breech-loading gun, but had an unhappy history because its breech was by no means foolproof, and the Admiralty reverted in the 1860s and 1870s to muzzle-loading rifled guns until technological problems were overcome.

43. Maitland to secretary of the Admiralty, February 1, 1862, Adm. 1/5790.

44. Admiralty Minute, March 11, 1862, ibid.

45. Maitland to Douglas, September 8, 1862, F. 1206, 36, BCA. Two days earlier, the *British Colonist* misreported the number of guns to be mounted as 50.

46. Their fighting value on the high seas was doubtful. See Harold and Margaret Sprout, *The Rise of American Naval Power, 1776–1918* (Princeton, NJ: Princeton University Press, 1939), 171–72.

47. Maitland to secretary of the Admiralty, August 9, 1862, Adm. 1/5790.

48. Ibid.

49. Rear-Admiral Denman to secretary of the Admiralty, August 22, 1864, Adm. 1/5878.

50. Douglas to Kingcome, September 15, 1863, Adm. Corr. III, BCA.

51. Denman to secretary of the Admiralty, January 24, 1865, Adm. 1/5924.

52. Denman to secretary of the Admiralty, June 3, 1865, ibid.

53. Ibid.

54. Ibid.

55. Ibid.

56. Denman to secretary of the Admiralty, September 5, 1865, Adm. 1/5924.

57. Denman to secretary of the Admiralty, June 15, 1865, ibid.

58. Ibid.

59. Memo by Richards, August 24, 1865, appended to ibid. The secretary of state for the colonies, Edward Cardwell, concurred with Denman on the need for defence. F. Rogers (CO) to secretary of the Admiralty, September 19, 1865, Adm. 1/5951.

60. He actually used the term "torpedo," which was the original name for a mine. In this same year (1866), British engineer Robert Whitehead was perfecting his "locomotive" or "fish" torpedo with its secret deep-keeping mechanism. See note 62 of this chapter.

61. Denman to secretary of the Admiralty, July 14, 1866, Adm. 1/5969.

62. Admiralty Minute, August 29, 1866, ibid. Probably no actual torpedoes reached the Pacific until 1876, when HMS *Shah* brought her Whitehead outfit. This was used without success against the Peruvian ironclad *Huascar.* See Admiral G.A. Ballard, "British Frigates of 1875; The 'Shah,'" Mariner's Mirror, 20 (July 1936): 305–15; and F.G.H. Bedford, *The Life and Letters of Admiral Sir Frederick George Denham Bedford, G.C.B., G.C.M.G.* (Newcastle-Upon-Tyne: printed for private circulation, [1960]), 52–59.

63. Denman to secretary of the Admiralty, August 26, 1866, Adm. 1/5969.

64. Ibid.

65. Ibid.

66. W.L. Morton, T*he Critical Years: The Union of British North America, 1857–1873* (Toronto: McClelland and Stewart, 1964), 169.

67. Denman to secretary of the Admiralty, June 25, and July 14, 1866, Adm. 1/5969.

68. *British Colonist*, June 13, 1866, in Willard E. Ireland, "Pre-Confederation Defence Problems of the Pacific Colonies," in *Canadian Historical Association Annual Report, 1941* (Toronto: CHA, 1941), 52–53.

69. Reginald H. Roy, "The Early Militia and Defence of British Columbia, 1871–1885," *British Columbia Historical Quarterly*, 18 (1954): 1.

70. Britain's first iron-hulled battleship, the *Warrior*, was laid down in 1860, but during the Civil War several wooden ships under construction, such as the *Zealous*, were modified to carry armour. The displacement tonnage of the *Zealous* was 6,096. She was 252 feet long and carried 3 to 4½ inches of armour amidships, tapering to 2½ inches forward and aft. Her 800 nominal horsepower engine with boiler pressure of 22 pounds per square inch gave her a speed of 12.5 knots on trial. She was capable of 10.5 knots under sail. Her armament consisted of twenty 7-inch, 6½-ton muzzle-loading rifled Armstrong guns in the battery, plus two bow and two stern chasers.

71. The US commandant supported Hastings in this decision. Rear-Admiral Hastings to secretary of the Admiralty, July 5, 1867, Adm. 1/6008.

72. Rear-Admiral Sir Alexander Milne to Henry Corry (Adm.), August 17, 1867, appended to "Return of Foreign Ships of War to 30th June 1867," encl. in Hastings to secretary of the Admiralty, July 5, 1867, ibid.

73. Hastings to secretary of the Admiralty, April 16, 1869, Adm. 1/6092.

74. Hastings to secretary of the Admiralty, March 12, 1868, Adm. 1/6056.

75. Hastings to secretary of the Admiralty, May 7, 1868, ibid.

76. Hastings to secretary of the Admiralty, July 7, and November 9, 1868, ibid.

77. Hastings to secretary of the Admiralty, October 30, 1868, ibid.

78. The consul's ability to gather information in San Francisco about Fenian movements was hampered by lack of funds. Such intelligence might have been vital for protecting the colony.

79. Hastings to secretary of the Admiralty, October 30, 1868, ibid.

80. Hastings to secretary of the Admiralty, December 26, 1868, ibid.

81. Noted in Hastings to secretary of the Admiralty, April 16, 1869, Adm. 1/6092.

82. The account here is based heavily on Roy, "Early Militia," 2–6.

83. Ibid., 5.

84. J. Trutch to Captain Cator, January 31, 1872, Papers of the Deputy Minister of Militia and Defence, Canada, No. 6322, LAC; in ibid., p. 6.

85. John A. Macdonald to Edward Watkin, March 27, 1865, private, Macdonald Papers, LAC; in P.B. Waite, *The Life and Times of Confederation, 1864–1867* (Toronto: University of Toronto Press, 1962), 307.

86. Quoted in Charles Vevier, "American Continentalism: An Idea of Expansion, 1845–1910," *American Historical Review*, 65 (January 1960): 332. Similar views are given in Alvin C. Gluek Jr., *Minnesota and the Manifest Destiny of the Canadian Northwest: A Study in Canadian-American Relations* (Toronto: University of Toronto Press, 1965), 215.

87. Quoted in Bourne, *Britain and the Balance of Power*, 302. E.H. Hammond (FO) to under-secretary of state, Colonial Office, December 9, 1867, CO 60/30.

88. Quoted in Winks, *Canada and the United States*, 165.

89. Ibid., 375.

90. See, for example, Sandford Fleming's *Observations and Practical Suggestions on the Subject of a Railway through British North America, submitted to the Province of Canada, 1863*, in CO 807/7, No. 74, p. 39; and his first publication on the matter, *A Railway to the Pacific through British Territory* (Port Hope, ON: 1858).

91. Captain M.F. Synge, "Proposal for a Rapid Communication with the Pacific and the East, via British North America," *Journal of the Royal Geographical Society*, 22 (1852): 174–200.

92. Viscount Milton and W.B. Cheadle, *The North-west Passage by Land . . . An Expedition from the Atlantic to the Pacific, Undertaken with the View of Exploring a Route across the Continent through British Territory, by One of the Northern Passes in the Rocky Mountains* (London: Cassell, Petter, and Galpin, 1865), 395–96.

93. The first transcontinental railroad was completed to San Francisco in 1868.

94. See R.I. Murchison's presidential address to the Royal Geographical Society, 1861, in the Society's *Proceedings*, 5 (1860–61): 203.

95. T.T. Vernon Smith, "Pacific Railway," *Nautical Magazine*, 31 (1861): 251.

96. Ibid.

97. For Watkin's activities, see E.E. Rich, *The History of the Hudson's Bay Company, 1670–1870* (London: Hudson's Bay Record Society, 1959), 2:822, 825–33, 843–44.

98. Watkin to Newcastle, December 29, 1862, encl. in CO to Adm., January 22, 1863, Adm. 1/5948.

99. Minute of C. P[aget], January 23, 1863, ibid.

100. Similarly, the Duke of Newcastle, the secretary of state for the colonies, favoured Esquimalt as the terminus of the cable, for obvious strategic reasons. CO to Adm., January 22, 1863, ibid. Later that year he supported Collins's proposed America–Asia–Europe telegraph on the same grounds. See John S. Galbraith, "Perry McDonough Collins at the Colonial Office," *British Columbia Historical Quarterly*, 17 (1953): 212.

101. Seymour to E. Cardwell (CO), February 17, 1866, CO 880/5, Confidential Print, No. 37, p. 38.

102. Seymour to the Duke of Buckingham and Chandos (CO), December 10, 1867, "Correspondence . . . Capital of British Columbia," *Parliamentary Papers*, 1867–1868, 48 (H. of C. 483), p. 8.

103. J.L. Sinclair to Buckingham and Chandos, September 2, 1867, CO 60/31.

104. Margaret A. Ormsby, *British Columbia: A History* (Toronto: Macmillan, 1958), 245–57.

105. Details from Reginald Eyre Watters, ed., *British Columbia: A Centennial Anthology* (Toronto: McClelland and Stewart, 1958), 77.

106. *Daily British Colonist*, November 18, 1867.

107. Frank Kelley, "When British Ships Rode at Anchor," *Daily Colonist*, Victoria, October 26, 1952.

108. "James K. Nesbitt Discovers a Witness [Robert J. Preston, writer and poet]," *Daily Colonist*, April 18, 1965, 16.

109. Ibid.

110. *Daily Colonist*, May 17, 1870. In Edgar Fawcett, *Some Reminiscences of Old Victoria* (Toronto: William Briggs, 1912), 127–28.

111. James K. Nesbitt, "By B.C. Attempts to Woo Settlers . . . ," *Daily Colonist*, July 22, 1873, 2 and 15.

112. James K. Nesbitt, "Victoria Was at Fever Pitch for Marquis of Lorne Visit," *Daily Colonist*, November 4, 1979, 14–15.

113. James K. Nesbitt, " In 1889 Victoria Put on a Show . . . ," *Daily Colonist*, October 20, 1974, 6–7.

114. The need for common defence by the British North American colonies had led to the union of four of these colonies in 1867, and the British North America Act allowed for the organizing of military security and a standardized militia scheme. Richard A. Preston, *Canada and "Imperial Defense"* (Durham, NC: Duke University Press, 1967), 56–57.

115. Watters, ed., *British Columbia*, 24–25 and 79 respectively.

CHAPTER ELEVEN

1. "Proceedings of the Colonial Conference," *Parliamentary Papers*, 1887, 56 (Cmd. 5091), 275–76.

2. Gerald S. Graham, *Empire of the North Atlantic: The Maritime Struggle for North America*, 2nd ed. (Toronto: University of Toronto Press, 1958), 282.

3. See Rear-Admiral A. de Horsey to secretary of the Admiralty, October 26, 1877, Adm. 1/6414.

4. D.M. Schurman, "Esquimalt: Defence Problem, 1865–1887," *British Columbia Historical Quarterly*, 19 (1955): 57nl. Compare the views of General R.C. Moody in L.J. Burpee, *Sandford Fleming, Empire Builder* (London: H. Milford, 1915), 155.

5. Mackenzie to Edgar, February 19, 1874, CO 807/7, no. 74, p. 4; Edgar to secretary of state for Canada, June 17, 1874, ibid., p. 109.

6. Margaret A. Ormsby, *British Columbia: A History* (Toronto:: Macmillan, 1958), 265–69, 304; J. Michael Jones, "The Railroad Healed the Breach," Canadian *Geographical Journal*, 73 (September 1966): 98–101.

7. Marquis of Lansdowne, *Canadian North-west and British Columbia: Two Speeches by His Excellency the Marquis of Lansdowne* (Ottawa: Department of Agriculture, 1886), 13.

8. Memo. by Major-General Andrew Clarke, April 16, 1886, in "Report of the Committee on the Proposals of the C.P.R. for the Establishment of a Line of Steamers in the Pacific," June 1886, CO 880/9, Vol. 116, p. 21.

9. Sandford Fleming, *Memorandum in Reference to a Scheme for Completing a Great Inter-Colonial and Inter-Continental Telegraph System by Establishing an Electric Cable Across the Pacific Ocean, 20 November 1882* (London, 1882), 9.

10. Admiral Sir Cyprian Bridge, *Sea-Power and Other Studies* (London: Smith, Elder and Co., 1910), 253. Sea power is also based on a strong national economy and on manpower.

11. Ibid., 251.

12. With a floating dock, the dock floods its tanks, and sinks, allowing the ship to steam or be warped into the dock. It then pumps out and rises, bringing the ship up.

13. Richard C. Mayne, *Four Years in British Columbia and Vancouver Island: An Account of Their Forests, Rivers, Coasts, Gold Fields, and Resources for Colonization* (London: John Murray, 1862), 159–60; also *British Colonist*, December 7, 1861, in Major F.V. Longstaff, *Esquimalt Naval Base: A History of Its Work and Its Defences* (Victoria: Victoria Book and Stationery Ltd., 1941), 24–25.

14. She drew more than 22 feet, the depth over the sill at the Mare Island dock.

15. Rear-Admiral G.F. Hastings to secretary of the Admiralty, December 3, 1868, Adm. 1/6056.

16. "Copy of a Report of a Committee of the Honourable the Executive Council, approved . . . 11th day of June, 1877"; copy in Adm. 116/744, fols. 241–43.

17. de Horsey to secretary of the Admiralty, October 9, 1877, fols. 171–78. His proposals reached the British ministry. See "Memorandum Respecting the Canadian Pacific Railway and the Esquimalt Graving Dock," printed for the Cabinet, August 1878, CO 880/8, Vol. 98.

18. 28 and 29 Vic., c. 56: "to secure Accommodation for Vessels of the Royal Navy in British Possessions abroad."

19. "The Cofferdam: The Ceremony of Giving Possession," *Daily British Colonist*, March 22, 1876.

20. This type of dock is usually excavated and made of concrete, masonry lined. After the gates are closed, water is pumped out, leaving the ship dry and on blocks.

21. Longstaff, *Esquimalt Naval Base*, 37n7. The Admiralty report *Graving Docks, Floating Docks and Patent Slips in the British Empire, 1922* (London: HMSO, 1923), 91, describes the length of the dock to be 450 feet, 8 inches. Presumably at some time the dock had been extended from its original length in order to hold the ships of the Canadian Pacific Railway's Empress service. Full descriptions of this and other docks in British Columbia in 1922 are given in ibid., 91, 103, 111.

22. Rear-Admiral M. Culme-Seymour to secretary of the Admiralty, November 9, 1887, Adm. 116/744, fol. 62.

23. Arthur H. Ives, "First Graving Dock" (typescript, n.d.), MMBC.

24. "Memorandum by Colonel Sir W.F.D. Jervois . . . [on] the defenceless condition of our Coaling Stations and Naval Establishments Abroad," January 7, 1875, confidential, Carnarvon Papers, PRO 30/6/122, pp. 44–46.

25. Ibid.

26. C.H. Nugent, "Memorandum on the Relative Importance of Coaling Stations," April 1, 1877, confidential, ibid., pp. 19–21. The bases were ranked as follows: Cape of Good Hope, Hong Kong, Singapore, Jamaica, King George's Sound, Mauritius, Esquimalt, St. Lucia, Falkland Islands, Ascension and Fiji.

27. de Horsey to secretary of the Admiralty, May 13, 1877, Adm. 1/6416.

28. See A.T. Mahan, *The Influence of Sea Power upon History, 1660–1783* (London: Sampson Low and Co., 1890), 14.

29. See Admiral G.A. Ballard, "British Frigates of 1875: The 'Shah,'" *Mariner's Mirror*, 20 (1936): 305–15.

30. de Horsey to the Admiralty, March 17, 1877, Adm. 1/6414; Harris to de Horsey, May 10, 1877, encl. in de Horsey to secretary of the Admiralty, June 25, 1877, ibid.

31. See Captain J.C.R. Colomb, "Russian Development and Our Naval and Military Position in the North Pacific," *Journal of the Royal United Service Institution*, 21 (1877): 659–80, and discussion, 680–707. Also Reginald H. Roy, "The Early Militia and Defence of British Columbia, 1871–1885," *British Columbia Historical Society Quarterly*, 18 (1954): 13.

32. *Victoria Colonist*, February 9, 1878.

33. Not until 1893 were Russian and British warships in the Pacific instructed to give previous notice before visiting a port of the other power. E. MacGregor to Rear-Admiral Hotham, March 13, 1893, RG 8 IIIB, Vol. I, fols. 86–88, LAC.

34. From report of Captain F.C.B. Robinson, HMS *Opal*, at Esquimalt, February 20, 1878, described in de Horsey to secretary of the Admiralty, April 4, 1878, Adm. 1/6454.

35. See Roy, "Early Militia," 13–19.

36. de Horsey to secretary of the Admiralty, June 28, 1878, confidential, Adm. 1/6460.

37. Ibid.

38. Admiralty to under-secretary of state for war, June 1, 1878, confidential, ibid.

39. By Lieutenant-Colonel J.W. Lovell, RE; Lieutenant-Colonel T.B. Strange, RA; and Colonel Crossman, RE. See Roy, "Early Militia," 19–22; Richard A. Preston, *Canada and "Imperial Defense"* (Durham, NC: Duke University Press, 1967), 130–31, 164–65; and Schurman, "Esquimalt," 62–64.

40. Culme-Seymour to secretary of the Admiralty, September 8, 1885, Adm. 1/6762.

41. Rear-Admiral J.K.E. Baird to secretary of the Admiralty, June 25, 1885, and enclosures, Y121, Adm. 1/6762.

42. Report of CDC, encl. in Admiral Sir Alexander Milne to CO, April 1, 1878, Adm. 1/6460. The Admiralty strongly supported this report and advised the Colonial Office that the general duties of the Pacific station "make it often impossible to keep H.M.

Ships in Ports, and local batteries are therefore indispensable." Hall to under-secretary of state for the colonies, April 20, 1878, ibid. Lieutenant-Colonel D.T. Irwin, Inspector of Artillery, was sent to British Columbia to supervise the erection of the coastal batteries.

43. "Third and Final Report of the Royal Commission appointed to inquire into the Defence of British Possessions Abroad . . . 1882," Carnarvon Papers, PRO 30/6/126. A summary of the Commission's findings as they relate to Esquimalt is in Preston, *Canada and "Imperial Defence*," 131–33. For their relation to the Empire as a whole, see Donald C. Gordon, *The Dominion Partnership in Imperial Defense, 1870–1914* (Baltimore: Johns Hopkins University Press, 1965), 63–71.

44. "Defence of Vancouver Island," by H. Jekyll, secretary of CDC, May 1, 1885, printed for the Cabinet, Cab. 11/27, 2M, p. 2.

45. Report of the Committee on Colonial Garrisons, 1886, confidential, CO 323/366, No. 23204, p. 11.

46. Roy, "Early Militia," 28.

47. The colonial secretary, Sir Henry Holland, for example, considered that the route from Esquimalt across the Pacific would develop so that a British coaling station at Hawaii would become "a necessity." J. Bramston (CO) to secretary of state, FO, June 11, 1887, confidential, Adm. 1/6865. A short review of British opposition to the "cession" is given in Merze Tate, *Hawaii: Reciprocity or Annexation* (East Lansing: Michigan State University Press, 1968), 200–210.

48. Culme-Seymour to secretary of the Admiralty, July 20, 1886, Adm. 1/6813.

49. J. Pauncefote (FO) to under-secretary of state, CO, December 10, 1887, confidential, Adm. 1/6865.

50. See Merze Tate, "Hawaii: A Symbol of Anglo-American Rapprochement," *Political Science Quarterly*, 79 (December 1964): 574. On the naval ramifications see A.T. Mahan and Lord Charles Beresford, "Possibilities of an Anglo-American Reunion," *North American Review*, 159 (1894): 551–73.

51. Rear-Admiral F.H. Stirling to Adm., June 24, 1881, confidential, Adm. 1/6581; and Rear-Admiral A.M. Lyons to Adm., February 7, 1883, confidential, Adm. 1/6666.

52. C. Bridge (Director of Naval Intelligence) and Sir A. Hoskins (a Lord of the Admiralty), April 10, 1893, on Rear-Admiral C.F. Hotham to Adm., February 20, 1893, Adm. 1/7142.

53. "Coaling Station off Central America," 1898. Cab. 11/27, 135M.

54. Minute of Sir Frederick Richards, December 7, 1897, Adm. 1/7334B.

55. Lyons to secretary of the Admiralty, May 13, 1882, Adm. 1/6617.

56. Pacific Station Standing Orders, 1888, p. 52; in Y65, Adm. 1/6914.

57. See Rear-Admiral L.A. Beaumont to Adm., March 27, 1900, Y144, Adm. 1/7374. Esquimalt again developed into the headquarters of the station, but, strangely, was never officially declared as such.

58. Observations on *Warspite* are drawn from British Colonist reports of the age; see James K. Nesbitt, "New Flagship Brings Gaiety," *Daily Colonist*, July 9, 1972, 13.

59. Information from Rear-Admiral P.W. Brock to author. Heneage's relief was C.F. Hotham.

60. Robert E. Johnson, *Thence Round Cape Horn: The Story of United States Naval Forces on Pacific Station, 1818–1923* (Annapolis, MD: United States Naval Institute, 1963), 152.

61. Minute of Major H. Pilkington, Director of Works, February 2, 1891, Adm. 116/820, fol. 150. Admirals Bedford, Fairfax and Bridge supported Rear-Admiral Hotham in the view that Esquimalt should be retained. See ibid., fols. 54, 124–28b.

62. Minute of E.A. B[arlett, M.P.], February 26, 1892, ibid., fols. 128–28b.

63. *Memorandum on the Standard of Defence at Esquimalt; Printed for the Committee on Imperial Defence*, May 1903, Cab. 5/1/2c, p. 3. See discussion of "C" Battery, Royal Canadian Artillery, 1887–1893, in the previous section of this chapter.

64. Parks Canada pamphlet "Fort Rodd Hill and Fisgard Lighthouse," n.d.

65. Preston, *Canada and "Imperial Defense*," 198.

66. Rear-Admiral A.K. Bickford to secretary of the Admiralty, September 17, 1901, confidential; Minute of R.N. Custance (Director of Naval Intelligence), October 11, 1901, Adm. 1/7513; and B. MacGregor to Commander-in-Chief, Pacific, October 17, 1901, RG 8, IIIB, Vol. 15, fol. 134, LAC.

67. Minute of Admiral Walter T. Kerr, October 14, 1901, Adm. 1/7513.

68. Bickford to secretary of the Admiralty, September 17, 1901, ibid.

69. WO to CO, October 27, 1897, in *Memorandum on the Standard of Defence at Esquimalt; Printed for the Committee on Imperial Defence*, May 1903, Cab. 5/1/2c, p. 4. The estimate for adequate defence was a garrison of 4,000 men costing £250,000 per annum. On the American naval implications of territorial expansion in the Pacific, see Harold and Margaret Sprout, *The Rise of American Naval Power, 1776–1918* (Princeton, NJ: Princeton University Press, 1939), 241–45.

70. Heneage to Adm., June 9, 1888, and other correspondence, Adm. 1/6914; Rear-Admiral Hotham to Adm., June 21, 1890, Adm. 1/7023.

71. Information from R.W. Sandilands, 2015. See Stanley Filmore and R. Sandilands, *The Chartmakers: The History of Nautical Surveying in Canada* (Toronto: NC Press, 1983).

72. Adm. to CO, March 8, 1898, in *Memorandum on the Standard of Defence at Esquimalt . . . 1903*, Cab. 571/2c, p. 5.

73. Ibid.

74. Ibid.

75. Ibid. This was approved valid to 1909.

76. Admiral Kerr, Minute of October 14, 1901, on Bickford to Admiralty, September 17, 1901, Adm. 1/7513.

77. See Samuel F. Wells, Jr., "British Strategic Withdrawal from the Western Hemisphere, 1904–1906," *Canadian Historical Review*, 49 (December 1968): 335–56; noteworthy in this article is the description of Admiral Fisher's success in overcoming much opposition to the withdrawal of nearly all British naval forces from Canada and the West Indies.

78. See Arthur J. Marder, *British Naval Policy, 1880–1905: The Anatomy of British Sea Power* (London: Putnam and Co., 1940), chapter 21, especially 432n10, on the naval strengths of the great powers.

79. See Ian H. Nish, *The Anglo-Japanese Alliance: The Diplomacy of Two Island Empires, 1894–1907* (London: Athlone Press, 1966).

80. Charles J. Woodsworth, *Canada and the Orient: A Study in International Relations* (Toronto: Macmillan, 1941), 102–3, 168–70; P.C. Lowe, "The British Empire and the Anglo-Japanese Alliance, 1911–1915," *History*, 54 (June 1969): 212–25; and Geoffrey Bennett, *Coronel and Falklands* (London: Pan Books, 1967), 53–55, 57, 86–87.

81. This policy was made public in the celebrated memorandum of the Earl of Selborne, the First Lord of the Admiralty, December 6, 1905: "Distribution and Mobilization of the Fleet," *Parliamentary Papers*, 1905, 68 (Cmd. 2335).

82. Arthur J. Marder, *From the Dreadnought to Scapa Flow: The Royal Navy in the Fisher Era, 1904–1919*, Vol. 1, *The Road to War, 1904–1914* (London: Oxford University Press, 1961), 40–43.

83. "Financial Effects of Fleet Re-Organization," confidential, Selborne Papers, 1904–1905, pp. 2–3, N.L.

84. J. Goodrich to secretary of the Admiralty, March 1, 1905, Adm. 1/7806.

85. "Naval Necessities," Selborne Papers, pp. 10–11, N.L.; and P.K. Kemp, ed., *The Papers of Admiral Sir John Fisher*, Vol. 1 (London: Navy Records Society, 1960), 100, 130, 161, 193.

86. See Gilbert N. Tucker, *The Naval Service of Canada: Its Official History* (Ottawa: King's Printer, 1952), 1:104–211.

87. Gordon, *Dominion Partnership*, 287; see also his "The Admiralty and Dominion Navies, 1902–1914," *Journal of Modern History*, 33 (1961): 407–22.

88. Gilbert N. Tucker, "The Career of H.M.C.S. 'Rainbow,'" *British Columbia Historical Quarterly*, 7 (January 1943): 1–30.

89. For a fascinating account of these ships, see Gilbert N. Tucker, "Canada's First Submarines, CC1 and CC2: An Episode of the Naval War in the Pacific," ibid., 147–70. A Canadian commission investigated the purchase, consumed a lot of time and paper, and exonerated the premier of any misdoing in the contracts. See Patricia E. Roy, *Boundless Optimism: Richard McBride's British Columbia* (Vancouver: UBC Press, 2012).

90. For conditions of transfer, see Adm. to CO, October 1907, CO 42/914. See also Gordon, *Dominion Partnership*, 185–86; and C.S. MacKinnon, "The Imperial Fortresses in Canada: Halifax and Esquimalt, 1871–1906," 2 vols. (Ph.D. thesis. University of Toronto, 1965).

91. "Canadian Naval Establishments (Esquimalt Dockyard) Order, 1911," Adm. 116/993, 246ff. For the imperial withdrawal from Esquimalt, 1905–1910, see C.P. Stacey, *The Military Problems of Canada: A Survey of Defence Policies and Strategic Conditions Past and Present* (Toronto: Ryerson Press, 1940), 69–70.

92. *British Naval Expenditure in Aid of the Dominion of Canada during the Nineteenth Century (secret), printed at the Foreign Office, October 26, 1912, copy in Borden papers, MG 26H 1(a), LAC.*

93. Admiral John Moresby, *Two Admirals* (1st ed. London: John Murray, 1909; revised ed. London: Methuen and Co., 1913), 114.

94. Admiral Sir Cyprian Bridge, *Some Recollections*, 2nd ed. (London: John Murray, 1919), 119–23.

$\mathcal{B}$IBLIOGRAPHY

ARCHIVAL RECORDS

I. THE NATIONAL ARCHIVES, KEW, SURREY, UK

A. Official Correspondence and Records
Adm. 1. (In-letters from Admirals, Captains and Departments).
Adm. 2. Continued as Adm. 13 (Out-letters).
Adm. 3. Rough Minutes.
Adm. 7. Miscellaneous; various reports on foreign navies.
Adm. 12. [IND 4761]. List of Admirals' dispatches, 1813–1847.
Adm. 50. Admirals' Journals, 1855–.
Adm. 53. Ships' Logs.
Adm. 116. Various reports on Esquimalt.
Adm. 128. Naval Stores.
Adm. 155/1. [IND 24473]. Index to first 22 volumes of Pacific Station Records in Ottawa.
Adm. 172/1-4. Pacific Station Records, 1843–1853.
BT 1/470/2506. Draft of Vancouver Island Grant, 1848–1849.
Cab. 5 and 11. Various reports on Esquimalt and Halifax.
FO 5. America.
FO 50. Mexico.
FO 58. Pacific Islands.
CO 6. Boundaries between British North America and the United States.
CO 42. Original Correspondence, Canada.
CO 60. Original Correspondence, British Columbia.
CO 62. Sessional Papers, British Columbia.
CO 63. Government Gazettes, British Columbia.
CO 64. Blue Books, British Columbia.
CO 338. Register of Correspondence, British Columbia.
CO 305. Original Correspondence, Vancouver Island.
CO 323/366 No. 23204. Report of the Committee on Colonial Garrisons, 1886.
CO 880/9, 10. Strategic uses of the CPR.
WO 1/552-3. Warre and Vavasour's reports.
WO 32, 33. Various reports on Warre and Vavasour, defences of Esquimalt, telegraphic communication, military uses of CPR.
B. "private" papers
PRO 30/6 Carnarvon Papers.
PRO 30/9 Colchester Papers.
PRO 30/12 Ellenborough Papers.

II. BRITISH LIBRARY, LONDON, UK

Aberdeen Papers.
Barrow Bequest.
Byam Martin Papers.

Gladstone Papers.
Halifax Papers.
Peel Papers.
Lt. George Peard, Journal of HMS *Blossom*, 1825–1828. Add. MSS. 35, 141.

III. NATIONAL MARITIME MUSEUM, GREENWICH, UK

BAY/- Baynes Papers.
BED/- Bedford Papers.
HAM/- Hamond Papers.
JON/- Jenkin Jones Papers.
PHI/- Phipps Hornby Papers.
JOD/21. John Cunningham, "Voyage to the Pacific, 1823–5."
JOD/42. Thomas Dawes, "Journal of H.M.S. 'America.'"
LOG/N/P/1. Journal of A.V. Maccall, 1854–1856.

IV. HUDSON'S BAY COMPANY ARCHIVES, MANITOBA ARCHIVES, WINNIPEG, MB

A. 8/6-9, 14, 17-20. Correspondence with Adm., FO, CO, Ordnance.
A. 11/61-3. Correspondence, Sandwich Islands.
A. 11/64. Correspondence, San Francisco.
B. 191/- Correspondence, Accounts, Sandwich Islands.
B. 223/6/35-42. Letters, Fort Vancouver.
B. 226/6/1-20. Letters, Fort Victoria.
G. 1, 3. Maps and Views.

V. NAVAL LIBRARY, MINISTRY OF DEFENCE, LONDON, UK

Selborne Papers.
Photo albums of Esquimalt.

VI. LIBRARY AND ARCHIVES CANADA, OTTAWA, ON

RG8, IIIB. Pacific Station Records, 39 vols.
RG9. Various reports on the defences of Esquimalt and British Columbia.
RG24, F71. Henry J. Warre Papers, including Warre's "Travel and Sport in North America, 1839–1846."

VII. ARCHIVES OF BRITSH COLUMBIA, VICTORIA, BC

F series; Ships' Letters.
"Admiralty Correspondence," 6 vols.
Journal of R.C. Mayne, 1859–60.

TYPESCRIPTS

Anderson, Alexander Caulfield. "History of the Northwest Coast," 1878. Original in Academy of Pacific Coast History, University of California, Berkeley.
Farrington, Lt.-Cdr. L. "The Versatile Beaver: Her Majesty's Ship Beaver Charts the Seas, 1863–1870," 1958.
Finlayson, Roderick. "History of Vancouver Island and the Northwest Coast," n.d.

VIII. MARITIME MUSEUM OF BRITISH COLUMBIA, VICTORIA, BC

Esquimalt Naval Establishment Records, 3 vols.

Brock, P.W. Dossiers of Royal Navy warships and BC, including *President* and *Racoon.*

Ives, Arthur. "First Graving Dock." Typescript, n.d.

IX. OTHER ARCHIVAL MATERIAL

North West Company Documents including William McGillivray [?]. "Some Account of the Trade Carried on by the North-West Company." [1809]. Royal Commonwealth Society Collection, University of Cambridge Library

Quine, Radcliffe. Letters. In Letters of Emigrants to America. British Library of Political and Economic Science, London School of Economics

Ross, F. "Journal and Water Color Sketches . . . of H.M.S. *Tagus* . . . 1813 . . . 1814." New York Public Library, Manuscripts Division.

Seymour of Ragley Collection, 20 vols. (papers of Admiral Sir George Seymour). CR 114A. Warwickshire Record Office, Warwick

X. PRINTED SOURCES

Parliamentary Papers, Hansard and the *Navy List* (set of the latter in MMBC).

The following volumes of *Parliamentary Papers* are of particular value:

"Correspondence Relative to the Negotiation of the Question of the Disputed Right to the Oregon Territory, 9 Aug. 1842," 1846, 52 (Cmd. 695).

"Treaty between Her Majesty and the United States . . . Oregon Boundary . . . 1846," 1846, 52 (722).

"Labuan Papers," 1847–1848, 62 (460).

"Correspondence between the Hudson's Bay Company and the Secretary of State for the Colonies relative to the Colonization of Vancouver's Island," 1847–1848, 42 (619).

"Papers relative to the Grant of Vancouver's Island to the Hudson's Bay Company," 1849, 35 (H. of C. 103).

"Papers relative to the Discovery of Gold on Fraser's River," 1859 (cmd. 2398, 1st ser.).

"Papers relative to the Affairs of British Columbia," 1859–60, Part 1, 17 (Cmd. 2476); Part 2, session 2 (Cmd. 2578); Part 3, 44 (Cmd. 2724); Part 4, 36 (Cmd. 2952).

"Report from the Select Committee on Colonial Military Expenditure," 1861, 13 (H. of C. 423).

"Papers re: Union of British Columbia and Vancouver Island," 1866, 49 (3667, 3694).

"Further Papers re: Union of British Columbia and Vancouver Island," 1867, 48 (3852).

"Return showing the number of Her Majesty's ships and vessels on the different stations on the 1st day of March of each year from 1847–1867 . . . ," 1867–68, 45 (H. of C. 167).

"Proceedings of the Colonial Conference," 1887, 56 (Cmd. 5091).

"Distribution and Mobilization of the Fleet," and "Arrangements Consequent on the Redistribution of the Fleet, 1905, 68 (Cmd. 2335 and 2430).

BOOKS, ARTICLES, THESES

Adamov, E.A. "Russia and the United States at the Time of the Civil War." *Journal of Modern History*, 2 (1930): 586–602.

Adams, Ephraim D. "English Interest in the Annexation of California." *American Historical Review*, 14 (July 1909): 744–63.

———. *Great Britain and the American Civil War*. 2 vols. London: Longmans, Green, and Co., 1925; reprint, London: Peter Smith, 1957.

Admiralty. *Graving Docks, Floating Docks and Patent Slips in the British Empire, 1922*. London: HMSO, 1923.

Akrigg, G.P.V., and Helen B. Akrigg, *H.M.S. Virago in the Pacific 1851–1855: To the Queen Charlottes and Beyond*. Victoria, BC: Sono Nis Press, 1992.

Albion, Robert G. *Forests and Sea Power: The Timber Problem of the Royal Navy, 1852–1862*. Cambridge, MA: Harvard University Press, 1926.

Allen, H.C. *Great Britain and the United States: A History of Anglo-American Relations (1783–1952)*. New York: St. Martin's Press, 1955.

Anderson, Bern. *Surveyor of the Sea: The Life and Voyages of Captain George Vancouver*. Toronto: University of Toronto Press, 1960.

"Appeal of the North West Company to the British Government to Forestall John Jacob Astor's Columbian Enterprise." *Canadian Historical Review*, 17 (September 1936): 304–11.

Audain, James. *From Coalmine to Castle: The Story of the Dunsmuirs of Vancouver Island*, New York: Pageant Press, 1955.

Aylmer, Captain Fenton, ed. *A Cruise in the Pacific: From the Log of a Naval Officer*. 2 vols. London: Hurst and Blackett, 1860.

Bach, John. "The Maintenance of Royal Navy Vessels in the Pacific Ocean, 1825–1875." *Mariner's Mirror*, 56 (August 1970): 259–273.

———. "The Royal Navy in the South Pacific, 1826–1876." Ph.D. thesis, University of New South Wales, 1964.

Bailey, Thomas A. "The North Pacific Sealing Convention of 1911." *Pacific Historical Review*, 4 (1935): 1–14.

Ballard, Admiral G.A. "British Frigates of 1875; The 'Shah.'" *Mariner's Mirror*, 20 (July 1936): 305–15.

———. "The Fighting Ship from 1860–1890." *Mariner's Mirror*, 38 (February 1952): 23–33.

Bancroft, Hubert H. *British Columbia, 1792–1887*. Vol. 27 in *History of the Pacific States of North America*. San Francisco: History Company, 1887.

———. *History of Alaska, 1730–1885*. Vol. 33. San Francisco: A.L. Bancroft and Co., 1886.

———. *The Northwest Coast*. Vols. 22 and 23 in *History of the Pacific States of North America*. 2 vols. San Francisco: A.L. Bancroft and Co., 1884.

Barrow, Sir John. *Autobiographical Memoir*. London: John Murray, 1847.

———. *Voyages of Discovery and Research within the Arctic Regions, from the Year 1818 to the Present Time*. London: John Murray, 1846.

Barry, J. Neilson, ed. "Broughton's Log of a Reconnaissance of the San Juan Islands in 1792." *Washington Historical Quarterly*, 21 (1930): 55–60.

———. "San Juan Island in the Civil War." *Washington Historical Quarterly*, 20 (April 1929): 134–36.

Bartlett, C.J. *Great Britain and Sea Power, 1815–1853*. Oxford: Clarendon Press, 1963.

———. "The Mid-Victorian Reappraisal of Naval Policy." In K. Bourne and D.C. Watt, eds., *Studies in International History: Essays Presented to W. Norton Medlicott* (London: Longmans, Green and Co., 1967), 189–208.

Baxter, James P. *The Introduction of the Ironclad Warship.* Cambridge, MA: Harvard University Press, 1933.

Beaglehole, J.C., ed. *The Journals of Captain Cook on His Voyages of Discovery: The Voyage of the "Resolution" and "Discovery," 1776–1780.* 2 parts. Cambridge: Hakluyt Society, 1967.

Bedford, F.G.H. *The Life and Letters of Admiral Sir Frederick George Denham Bedford, G.C.B., G.C.M.G.* Newcastle upon Tyne: printed privately, [1960].

Beechey, Frederick W. *Narrative of a Voyage to the Pacific and Beering's Strait to Co-operate with the Polar Expeditions, 1825–28.* 2 vols. London: Colburn and Bentley, 1831.

Belcher, Captain Sir Edward. *Narrative of a Voyage round the World, Performed in Her Majesty's Ship "Sulphur," during the Years 1836–1842.* 2 vols. London: Henry Colburn, 1843.

Belyea, Barbara. "The 'Columbian Enterprise' and A.S. Morton: A Historical Exemplum." *BC Studies,* 86 (Summer 1990): 3–27.

Bennett, Geoffrey. *Coronel and Falklands.* London: Pan Books, 1967.

Blue, George Vern. "The Policy of France toward the Hawaiian Islands from the Earliest Times to the Treaty of 1846." In *The Hawaiian Islands,* Publication of the Archives of Hawaii No. 5 (Honolulu: Archives of Hawaii, 1930), 51–93.

Bonner-Smith, D., ed. *Russian War, 1855, Baltic: Official Correspondence.* Vol. 84. London: Navy Records Society, 1944.

Bonner-Smith, D., and Captain A.C. Dewar, eds. *Russian War, 1854, Baltic and Black Sea: Official Correspondence.* Vol. 83. London: Navy Records Society, 1943.

Bourne, Kenneth. *Britain and the Balance of Power in North America, 1815–1908.* London: Longmans, Green and Co., 1967.

Boutilier, James A., ed. *RCN in Retrospect 1910–1968.* Vancouver: UBC Press, 1982.

Bowsfield, Hartwell, ed. *Fort Victoria Letters, 1846–1851.* Winnipeg: Hudson's Bay Record Society, 1979.

Bradley, Harold W. *The American Frontier in Hawaii, 1789–1843.* Palo Alto, CA: Stanford University Press, 1942.

———. "Hawaii and the American Penetration of the Northeastern Pacific, 1800–1845." *Pacific Historical Review,* 12 (September 1943): 277–86.

Bridge, Admiral Sir Cyprian. *Sea-Power and Other Studies.* London: Smith, Elder and Co., 1910.

———. *Some Recollections.* 2nd ed. London: John Murray, 1919.

Briggs, Sir John Henry. *Naval Administrations, 1827 to 1892.* London: Sampson Low and Co., 1897.

British Columbia Archives. *Report of the Provincial Archives Department of the Province of British Columbia for the Year ended December 31st, 1913.* Victoria, BC, 1914.

Brodie, Bernard. *Sea Power in the Machine Age.* Princeton, NJ: Princeton University Press, 1941.

Brookes, Jean I. *International Rivalry in the Pacific Islands, 1800–1875.* Berkeley and Los Angeles: University of California Press, 1941.

Brown, Robert. *On the Geographical Distribution and Physical Characteristics of the Coal-Fields of the North Pacific.* Edinburgh: Neill and Co., 1867.

Bruce, Captain H.W. "A Winter Passage round Cape Horn." *Nautical Magazine,* 7 (1838): 577–87.

Bulloch, James D. *The Secret Service of the Confederate States in Europe or How the Confederate Cruisers Were Equipped.* 2 vols. London: R. Bentley and Son, 1883; reprint, New York and London: T. Yoseloff, 1959.

Burns, Flora Hamilton. "The Exploits of Lieut. Mayne." *The Beaver,* Outfit 289 (Autumn 1958): 12–17.

———. "H.M.S. *Herald* in Search of Franklin." *The Beaver*, Outfit 294 (Autumn 1963): 3–13.

Burpee, L.J. *Sandford Fleming, Empire Builder*. London: H. Milford, 1915.

Burt, A.L. *The United States, Great Britain and British North America, from the Revolution to the Establishment of Peace after the War of 1812*. New Haven, CT: Yale University Press, 1940.

Byron, Lord G.A. *Voyage of the "Blonde" to the Sandwich Islands, 1824–25*. London: John Murray, 1826.

Campbell, Charles S. Jr. *Anglo-American Understanding, 1898–1903*. Baltimore: Johns Hopkins University Press, 1957.

———. "The Bering Sea Settlements of 1892." *Pacific Historical Review*, 32 (1963): 347–38.

[Carnarvon, Earl of]. *Royal Commission to Enquire into the Defence of British Possessions and Provinces Abroad*. 3 vols. London: War Office, 1880–1883.

Caswell, John E. "The Sponsors of Canadian Arctic Exploration, Part III—1800 to 1839." *The Beaver*, Outfit 300 (Autumn 1969): 25–33.

Chevigny, Hector. *Russian America: The Great Alaskan Venture, 1741–1867*. New York: Viking Press, 1965.

Clark, R.C. *History of the Willamette Valley, Oregon*. 2 vols. Chicago: S.J. Clarke, 1927.

Clayton, Daniel W. *Islands of Truth: The Imperial Fashioning of Vancouver Island*. Vancouver: UBC Press, 2000.

Clowes, William Laird et al. *The Royal Navy: A History from the Earliest Times to the Present*. 7 vols. London: Sampson Low, Marston and Co., 1897–1903.

Colomb, Captain J.C.R. "Russian Development and Our Naval and Military Position in the North Pacific." *Journal of the Royal United Service Institution*, 21 (1877): 659–707.

Corney, Peter. *Voyages in the North Pacific*. Honolulu: Thorn. G. Thrum, 1896.

Coues, Elliot, ed. *New Light on the Early History of the Greater Northwest: The Manuscript Journals of Alexander Henry . . . and of David Thompson*. 3 vols. London: Suckling and Co., 1897.

Coughlin, Sister Magdalen. "California Ports: A Key to Diplomacy for the West Coast, 1820–1845." *Journal of the West*, 5 (April 1966): 153–71.

Cox, Ross. *Adventures on the Columbia River, including the Narrative of a Residence of Six Years on the Western Side of the Rocky Mountains*. 2 vols. London: H. Colburn and R. Bentley, 1831.

Crowe, George. *The Commission of H.M.S. "Terrible," 1898–1902*. London: George Newnes, 1903.

Davidson, Donald C. "Relations of the Hudson's Bay Company with the Russian American Company on the Northwest Coast, 1829–1867." *British Columbia Historical Quarterly*, 5 (January 1941): 33–51.

———. "The War Scare of 1854: The Pacific Coast and the Crimean War." *British Columbia Historical Quarterly*, 5 (October 1941): 243–54.

Davidson, G.C. *The North West Company*. Berkeley: University of California Press, 1918.

Dawson, Commander L.S., comp. *Memoirs of Hydrography . . . 1750–1885*. 2 vols. Eastbourne, UK: Henry W. Keay, 1885.

Day, Vice-Admiral Sir Archibald. *The Admiralty Hydrographic Service, 1795–1919*. London: HMSO, 1967.

de Thierry, C. "Naval Bases of the Empire: Esquimalt and Halifax." *Windsor Magazine*, 1907, 593–600.

Denman, Rear-Admiral, and others. *The Bombardment of Valparaiso*. Liverpool, 1866.

Dewar, Captain A.C., ed. *Russian War, 1855, Black Sea: Official Correspondence.* Vol. 85. London: Navy Records Society, 1945.

Dorricott, Linda, and Deidre Cullon, eds. *The Private Journal of Captain G.H. Richards: The Vancouver Island Survey (1860–1862).* Vancouver: Ronsdale Press, 2012.

Douglas, George M., ed. "Royal Navy Ships on the Columbia River in 1839." *The Beaver,* Outfit 285 (Autumn 1954): 38–41.

Dudley, William, and Michael Crawford, eds. *Naval War of 1812: A Documentary History.* 3 vols. Washington, DC: Naval Historical Center, 1985–2002.

Duff, Wilson. *The Indian History of British Columbia.* Vol. 1, *The Impact of the White Man.* Victoria, BC: Provincial Museum, 1964.

Dyer, Brainerd. "Confederate Naval and Privateering Activities in the Pacific." *Pacific Historical Review,* 3 (1934): 433–43.

Eardley-Wilmot, Lieutenant S. *Our Journal in the Pacific by the Officers of H.M.S. Zealous.* London: Longmans, Green and Co., 1873.

Egerton, Mrs. Fred (Mary Augusta). *Admiral of the Fleet Sir Geoffrey Phipps Hornby, G.C.B., A Biography.* Edinburgh: Wm. Blackwood and Sons, 1896.

Epstein, Katherine. *Torpedo: Inventing the Military-Industrial Complex in the United States and Great Britain.* Cambridge, MA: Harvard University Press, 2014.

Evans, Robley D. *A Sailor's Log: Recollections of Forty Years of Naval Life.* New York: D. Appleton and Co., 1901.

Fawcett, Edgar. *Some Reminiscences of Old Victoria.* Toronto: William Briggs, 1912.

Filmore, Stanley, and R. Sandilands. *The Chartmakers: The History of Nautical Surveying in Canada.* Toronto: NC Press, 1983.

Findlay, A.G. *Directory for Navigation of the Pacific.* 2 pts. London: R.H. Laurie, 1851.

[Finlayson, Roderick]. *Biography* [of Roderick Finlayson]. Victoria, BC: [1891].

FitzRoy, Robert. *Narrative of the Surveying Voyages of Her Majesty's Ships "Adventure" and "Beagle" Between the Years 1826 and 1836.* 3 vols. London: Henry Colburn, 1839.

Fleming, R. Harvey, ed. *Minutes of Council of the Northern Department of Rupert Land 1821–31.* Vol. 3. London: Hudson's Bay Record Society, 1940.

Fleming, Sandford. *Memorandum in Reference to a Scheme for Completing a Great Inter-Colonial and Inter-Continental Telegraph System by Establishing an Electric Cable across the Pacific* by Sandford Fleming, 20 November 1882. London, 1882.

———. *A Railway to the Pacific Through British Territory.* Port Hope, ON: 1858.

Forbes, Alexander. *California: A History of Upper and Lower California.* London: Smith, Elder and Co., 1839.

Forbes, Charles. *Vancouver Island, Its Resources and Capabilities, as a Colony.* Victoria, BC: Colonial Government, 1862.

Fox, Grace. *British Admirals and Chinese Pirates, 1832–1869.* London: Regan Paul, Trench, Trubner and Co., 1940.

Fremantle, Admiral Sir E.R. *The Navy as I Have Known It, 1849–99.* London: 1904.

Galbraith, John S. "Fitzgerald versus the Hudson's Bay Company: The Founding of Vancouver Island." *British Columbia Historical Quarterly,* 16 (1952): 191–207.

———. *The Hudson's Bay Company as an Imperial Factor, 1821–1869.* Berkeley and Los Angeles: University of California Press, 1957.

———. "Perry McDonough Collins at the Colonial Office." *British Columbia Historical Quarterly,* 17 (1953): 207–14.

Gibson, James R. *Sea Otter Skins, Boston Ships, and China Goods: The Maritime Fur Trade of the Northwest Coast, 1785–1941.* Montreal and Kingston: McGill-Queen's University Press, 1992.

387

Gilbert, Benjamin F. "Rumours of Confederate Privateers Operating in Victoria, Vancouver Island." *British Columbia Historical Quarterly*, 18 (1954): 239–55.

"A Glance at Vancouver and Queen Charlotte Islands—By the Officers of H.M.S. "Virago"—in the Summer of 1853." *Nautical Magazine*, 23 (March 1854): 113–23.

Glazebrook, G.P. DeT., ed. *The Hargrave Correspondence, 1821–1842*. Vol. 24. Toronto: Champlain Society, 1938.

Glover, Richard, ed. *David Thompson's Narrative, 1784–1812*. Vol. 40. Toronto: Champlain Society, 1962.

Gluek, Alvin C. Jr. *Minnesota and the Manifest Destiny of the Canadian Northwest: A Study in Canadian-American Relations*. Toronto: University of Toronto Press, 1965.

Golder, Frank A. *Russian Expansion in the Pacific, 1641–1850*. Cleveland: Arthur H. Clark Co., 1914.

———. "The Russian Fleet and the Civil War." *American Historical Review*, 20 (July 1915): 801–14.

Gordon, Donald C. "The Admiralty and Dominion Navies, 1902–1914." *Journal of Modern History*, 33 (1961): 407–22.

———. *The Dominion Partnership in Imperial Defense, 1870–1914*. Baltimore: Johns Hopkins University Press, 1965.

Gough, Barry M. "Crown, Company, and Charter: Founding Vancouver Island Colony—A Chapter in Victorian Empire Making." *BC Studies*, 176 (Winter 2012/13): 9–54.

———. *Fortune's a River: The Collision of Empires in Northwest America*. Madeira Park, BC: Harbour Publishing, 2007.

———. "From British Columbia to Pax Britannica and Return." *British Columbia History*, 48, no. 2 (Summer 2015): 13–20.

———. *Gunboat Frontier: British Maritime Authority and Northwest Coast Indians, 1846–1890*. Vancouver: UBC Press, 1984.

———. "H.M.S. *America* on the North Pacific Coast." *Oregon Historical Quarterly*, 70 (December 1969): 292–311.

———, ed. *The Journal of Alexander Henry the Younger, 1799–1814*. 2 vols. Toronto: Champlain Society, 1988, 1992.

———. *Pax Britannica: Ruling the Waves and Keeping the Peace before Armageddon*. Basingstoke, UK: Palgrave Macmillan, 2014.

———. "Pioneer Missionaries to the Nishga: The Crosscurrents of Demon Rum and British Gunboats, 1860–1871." *Journal of the Canadian Church Historical Society*, 26, no. 2 (October 1984): 81–97.

———. "Records of the Royal Navy's Pacific Station." *Journal of Pacific History*, 4 (1969): 146–53.

———. "Sea Power and South America: The 'Brasils' or South Station of the Royal Navy 1808–1837." *The American Neptune*, 50, no. 1 (1990): 26–34.

Graebner, Norman A. *Empire on the Pacific, a Study in American Continental Expansion*. New York: Ronald, 1955.

———. "Maritime Factors in the Oregon Compromise." *Pacific Historical Review*, 20 (November 1951): 331–46.

Graham, Gerald S. *Empire of the North Atlantic: The Maritime Struggle for North America*. 2nd ed. Toronto: University of Toronto Press, 1958.

———. *Great Britain in the Indian Ocean: A Study of Maritime Enterprise, 1810–1850*. Oxford: Clarendon Press, 1967.

———. *The Politics of Naval Supremacy: Studies in British Maritime Ascendancy*. Cambridge: Cambridge University Press, 1965.

——. "The Transition from Paddle-Wheel to Screw Propeller." *Mariner's Mirror*, 44 (1958): 35–48.

Graham, Gerald S., and R.A. Humphreys, eds. *The Navy and South America, 1807–1823: Correspondence of the Commanders-in-Chief on the South American Station*. Vol. 104. London: Navy Records Society, 1962.

Grant, W.C. "Description of Vancouver Island." *Journal of the Royal Geographical Society*, 27 (1857): 268–320.

Greenhow, Robert. *The History of Oregon and California*. London: John Murray, 1844.

——. *Memoir, Historical and Political, on the North West Coast of North America*. Washington: Blair and Rives, 1840.

Grey, Earl. *The Colonial Policy of Lord John Russell's Administration*. 2 vols. London: R. Bentley, 1853.

Gunns, G.H. *The Log of H.M.S. "Sutlej," Pacific and China Stations, 1904–1906*. London: Westminster Press, 1906.

Hacking, Norman. "Early Maritime History of British Columbia." Master's thesis, University of British Columbia, 1934.

——. "Paddlewheels and British Oak on the North Pacific." *The Beaver*, Outfit 265 (March 1935): 25–28.

Hall, Basil. *Extracts from a Journal, written on the Coasts of Chili, Peru, and Mexico, in the Years 1820, 1821, 1822*. 2 vols. 2nd ed. Edinburgh: Archibald Constable and Co., 1824.

Hamilton, Admiral Sir R. Vesey, ed. *Journals and Letters of Admiral of the Fleet Sir Thom. Byam Martin*. Vol. 1. London: Navy Records Society, 1903.

Hathaway, R.W. *The Logs of H.M.S. "Arethusa" 1899–1903*. London: Westminster Press, 1903.

Hawgood, John A., ed. *First and Last Consul: Thomas Oliver Larkin and the Americanization of California—a Selection of Letters*. San Marino, CA: Huntington Library, 1962.

Haynes, William. *My Log: A Journal of the Proceedings of the Flying Squadron*. Devonport, UK: Clarke and Son, 1871.

Hazlitt, William C. *British Columbia and Vancouver Island*. London: G. Routledge and Co., 1858.

Historical Manuscripts Commission. *Report on the Manuscripts of Earl Bathurst, at Cirencester Park*. London: HMSO, 1923.

"H.M.C.S. 'Rainbow.'" *British Columbia Magazine*, 6 (November 1910): 1005–10.

"HMS *Modeste* on the Pacific Coast 1843–47: Log and Letters." *Oregon Historical Quarterly*, 61 (December 1960): 408–36.

Howay, F.W., ed. *The Early History of the Fraser River Mines*. British Columbia Archives Memoir No. 3. Victoria, BC: BCA, 1926.

——. "An Outline Sketch of the Maritime Fur Trade." In *Canadian Historical Association Annual Report, 1932*. Ottawa: CHA, 1932.

——. *The Work of the Royal Engineers in British Columbia 1858 to 1863*. Victoria, BC: Printed by Richard Wolfenden, 1910.

Howay, F.W., and others, eds. "Angus McDonald: A Few Items of the West." *Washington Historical Quarterly*, 8 (July 1917): 188–229.

Howay, F.W., W.N. Sage and H.F. Angus. *British Columbia and the United States*. New Haven, CT: Yale University Press, 1942.

Howay, F.W., and E.O.S. Scholefield. *British Columbia, from the Earliest Times to the Present*. 4 vols. Vancouver: S.J. Clarke, 1914.

Howison, Neil M. "Report of Lieutenant Neil M. Howison on Oregon, 1846." *Oregon Historical Quarterly*, 14 (March 1913): 1–60.

Hussey, John A. *The History of Fort Vancouver*. Tacoma: Washington State Historical Society, 1957.

——, ed. *The Voyage of the "Racoon": A "Secret" Journal of a Visit to Oregon, California and Hawaii, 1813–1814* [by Francis Phillips]. San Francisco: Book Club of California, 1958.

Imlah, Albert H. *Economic Elements in the "Pax Britannica."* Cambridge, MA: Harvard University Press, 1958.

——. *Lord Ellenborough: A Biography*. Harvard Historical Studies, vol. 43. Cambridge, MA: Harvard University Press, 1939.

Innis, Harold A. *The Fur Trade in Canada*. Revised edition. New Haven, CT: Yale University Press, 1962.

Ireland, Willard E. "The Appointment of Governor Blanshard." *British Columbia Historical Quarterly*, 8 (July 1944): 213–26.

——. "The Evolution of the Boundaries of British Columbia." *British Columbia Historical Quarterly*, 3 (October 1939): 263–82.

——, ed. "James Douglas and the Russian American Company, 1840." *British Columbia Historical Quarterly*, 5 (January 1941): 53–66.

——. "Pre-Confederation Defence Problems of the Pacific Colonies." In *Canadian Historical Association Annual Report, 1941*, 41–54. Toronto: CHA, 1941.

Irving, Washington. *Astoria*. 3 vols. London: R. Bentley, 1836.

Irwin, Leonard B. *Pacific Railways and Nationalism in the Canadian-American Northwest, 1845–73*. New York: Greenwood Press, 1968.

John Bate. *The Cruise Round the World of the Flying Squadron, 1869–1870, under the Command of Rear-Admiral G.T. Phipps Hornby*. London: J.D. Potter, 1871.

Jackson, C. Ian. "The Stikine Territory Lease and Its Relevance to the Alaska Purchase." *Pacific Historical Review*, 36 (August 1967): 289–306.

——. "A Territory of Little Value: The Wind of Change on the Northwest Coast, 1861–67." *The Beaver*, Outfit 298 (Summer 1967): 40–45.

James, William. *Naval Occurrences of the War of 1812*. London: Conway Maritime, 2004.

Jevons, W.S. *The Coal Question*. 3rd ed., revised. London: Macmillan and Co., 1906.

Johnson, Robert E. *Thence Round Cape Horn: The Story of United States Naval Forces on Pacific Station, 1818–1923*. Annapolis, MD: United States Naval Institute, 1963.

Johnston, W. Ross. *Sovereignty and Protection: A Study of British Jurisdictionalism in the Late Nineteenth Century*. Durham, NC: Duke University Press, 1973.

Jones, J. Michael. "The Railroad Healed the Breach." *Canadian Geographical Journal*, 73 (September 1966): 98–101.

Jones, Robert F. *Astorian Adventure: The Journal of Alfred Seton, 1811–1815*. New York: Fordham University Press, 1993.

Jones, Wilbur D., and J. Chal Vinson. "British Preparedness and the Oregon Settlement." *Pacific Historical Review*, 22 (November 1953): 353–64.

Journal of the Journey of His Excellency the Governor-General of Canada [Lord Dufferin] *from Government House, Ottawa, to British Columbia and Back*. London: Webster and Larkin, 1877.

Judson, Katherine B. "The British Side of the Restoration of Fort Astoria." *Oregon Historical Quarterly*, 20 (1919): 243–60 and 305–30.

Kaufman, Scott. *The Pig War: The United States, Britain, and the Balance of Power in the Pacific Northwest, 1846–72*. Lanham, MD: Lexington Books, 2003.

Kemble, John H. "Coal from the Northwest Coast, 1848–1850." *British Columbia Historical Quarterly*, 2 (April 1938): 123–30.

Kemp, P.K. ed. *The Papers of Admiral Sir John Fisher*, Vol. 1. London: Navy Records Society, 1960.

Kennedy, Captain W.R., RN. *Sporting Adventures in the Pacific, whilst in command of the "Reindeer."* London: Sampson Low, Marston, Searle and Rivington, 1876.

Knaplund, Paul. "James Stephen on Granting Vancouver Island to the Hudson's Bay Company, 1846–1848." *British Columbia Historical Quarterly*, 9 (October 1945): 259–71.

———. "Letters from James Edward Fitzgerald to W.E. Gladstone Concerning Vancouver Island and the Hudson's Bay Company, 1848–1850." *British Columbia Historical Quarterly*, 13 (January 1949): 1–21.

Knox, B.A. "Colonial Influence on Imperial Policy, 1858–1866: Victoria and the Colonial Defence Act, 1865." *Historical Studies: Australia and New Zealand*, 11 (November 1963): 61–79.

Kuykendall, Ralph S. *The Hawaiian Kingdom, 1778–1854*. Honolulu: University of Hawaii Press, 1938.

Laing, Lionel H. "An Unauthorized Admiralty Court in British Columbia." *Washington Historical Quarterly*, 26 (1935): 10–15.

Lamb, W. Kaye, ed. "Correspondence Relating to the Establishment of a Naval Base at Esquimalt, 1851–57." *British Columbia Historical Quarterly*, 6 (October 1942): 277–94.

———. "Early Lumbering on Vancouver Island." *British Columbia Historical Quarterly*, 2 (January 1938): 31–53 and 95–121.

———. "The Founding of Fort Victoria." *British Columbia Historical Quarterly*, 7 (April 1943): 71–92.

———, ed. "Four Letters Relating to the Cruise of the 'Thetis,' 1852–53." *British Columbia Historical Quarterly*, 6 (July 1942): 189–206.

———. "The Governorship of Richard Blanshard." *British Columbia Historical Quarterly*, 14 (April 1950): 1–40.

———, ed. *Journal of a Voyage to the North West Coast of North America during the Years 1811, 1812, 1813 and 1814*, by Gabriel Franchère. Vol. 45. Toronto: Champlain Society, 1969.

———. "Introduction." In E.E. Rich, ed., *The Letters of John McLoughlin from Fort Vancouver to the Governor and Committee; First Series, 1825–38*. London: Hudson's Bay Record Society, 1941.

Lambert, Andrew. *The Challenge: Britain against America in the Naval War of 1812*. London: Faber and Faber, 2012.

———. *Trincomalee: The Last of Nelson's Frigates*. London: Chatham, 2002.

Lansdowne, Marquis of. *Canadian North-West and British Columbia: Two Speeches by His Excellency the Marquis of Lansdowne*. Ottawa: Department of Agriculture, 1886.

Laurie, Maj.-Gen. J.W. "The Protection of our Naval Base in the North Pacific." *Journal of the Royal United Service Institution*, 28 (1883): 357–81.

Lewis, Michael. "An Eye-Witness at Petropaulovski, 1854." *Mariner's Mirror*, 49 (November 1963): 265–72.

———. *The Navy in Transition, 1814–1864: A Social History*. London: Hodder and Stoughton, 1965.

Lincoln, A. "The Beechey Expedition Visits San Francisco." *Pacific Discovery*, 22 (1969): 1–8.

Longstaff, F.V. "The Centenary of the Pacific Station, 1837–1937." *British Columbia Historical Quarterly*, 3 (1939): 221–23.

———. *Esquimalt Naval Base: A History of Its Work and Its Defences*. Victoria, BC: Victoria Book and Stationery Co., 1941.

———. *H.M.C.S. Naden Naval Barracks, A History of Its Work, Senior Officers, and Ships*. 2nd ed., Victoria, BC: Published by the Author, 1957.

———. "H.M.S. Ganges, 1821 to 1929." *Canadian Defence Quarterly* (July 1929): 487–92.

———. "Notes on the Early History of the Pacific Station and the Inception of the Esquimalt Royal Naval Establishment." *Canadian Defence Quarterly*, 3 (April 1926): 309–18.

———. "Notes on the History of the Pacific Station from the Colonial Period and the Early Period of Confederation until the Regular Service Across Canada of the C.P.R. in 1887." *Canadian Defence Quarterly*, 4 (April 1927): 292–309.

Longstaff, F.V., and W. Kaye Lamb. "The Royal Navy on the Northwest Coast, 1813–1850, Part I." *British Columbia Historical Quarterly*, 9 (January 1945): 1–24.

———. "The Royal Navy on the Northwest Coast, 1813–1850, Part II." *British Columbia Historical Quarterly*, 9 (April 1945): 113–28.

Lowe, P.C. "The British Empire and the Anglo-Japanese Alliance, 1911–1915." *History*, 54 (June 1969): 212–25.

MacDonald, Duncan G.F. *British Columbia and Vancouver's Island: Their History, Resources, and Prospects*. London: Longman, Green, Longman, Roberts and Green, 1862.

Macdonald, John, of Garth. "Journal from England to the Columbia River, North West Coast of America." In B.C. Payette, ed., *The Oregon Country under the Union Jack*. Montreal: privately printed, 1961.

Macfie, Matthew. *Vancouver Island and British Columbia: Their History, Resources, and Prospects*. London: Longman, Green, Longman, Roberts and Green, 1865.

Mackie, Richard. *Trade beyond the Mountains: The British Fur Trade on the Pacific, 1793–1843*. Vancouver: UBC Press, 1997.

Mackinder, Sir Halford J. *Democratic Ideas and Reality*. London: Constable and Co., 1919.

Mackinnon, C.S. "The Imperial Fortresses in Canada: Halifax and Esquimalt, 1871–1906." 2 vols. Ph.D. thesis, University of Toronto, 1965.

Mahan, A.T. *The Influence of Sea Power upon History, 1660–1783*. London: Sampson Low and Co., 1890.

———. *Sea Power in Its Relations to the War of 1812*. 2 vols. Boston: Little, Brown and Co., 1905.

Mahan, A.T., and Lord Charles Beresford. "Possibilities of an Anglo-American Reunion." *North American Review*, 159 (1894): 551–73.

Marder, Arthur J. *British Naval Policy, 1880–1905: The Anatomy of British Sea Power*. London: Putnam and Co., 1940.

———. *From the Dreadnought to Scapa Flow: The Royal Navy in the Fisher Era, 1904–1919*. Vol. 1, *The Road to War, 1904–1914*. London: Oxford University Press, 1961.

Markham, Admiral Sir Albert H. *The Life of Sir Clements R. Markham*. London: John Murray, 1917.

Martin, Robert M. *The Hudson's Bay Territories and Vancouver's Island with an Exposition of the Chartered Rights, Conduct, and Policy of the Honourable Hudson's Bay Corporation*. London: T. Brettell, 1849.

Mayne, Richard C. *Four Years in British Columbia and Vancouver Island: An Account of Their Forests, Rivers, Coasts, Gold Fields, and Resources for Colonization.* London: John Murray, 1862.

——. "Report on a Journey in British Columbia in the Districts Bordering on the Thompson, Fraser and Harrison Rivers." *Journal of the Royal Geographical Society,* 31 (1861): 213–23. (Text of a report to the Admiralty, July 7, 1859.)

McCabe, James O. *The San Juan Water Boundary Question.* Toronto: University of Toronto Press, 1964.

McKay, Corday. *Queen Charlotte Islands.* Victoria, BC: Province of British Columbia, Department of Education, 1953.

McKelvie, B.A. "The Founding of Nanaimo." *British Columbia Historical Quarterly,* 8 (July 1944): 169–88.

——. "Sir James Douglas: A New Portrait." *British Columbia Historical Quarterly,* 7 (April 1943): 93–101.

Meany, Edmond S., ed. *Vancouver's Discovery of Puget Sound.* Portland, OR: Binfords-Mort, 1942.

Meares, John. *Voyages Made in the Years 1788 and 1789, from China to the North West Coast of America.* London, 1790.

Mellor, G.R. *British Imperial Trusteeship 1783–1850.* London: Faber and Faber, 1951.

Melrose, Robert. "Royal Emigrant's Almanack concerning Five Years Servitude under the Hudson's Bay Company on Vancouver's Island." *British Columbia Historical Quarterly,* 7, nos. 2, 3 and 4 (1943).

Merk, Frederick, ed. *Fur Trade and Empire: George Simpson's Journal.* Revised edition. Cambridge, MA: Belknap Press, 1968.

——. "The Genesis of the Oregon Question." *Mississippi Valley Historical Review,* 36 (March 1950): 583–612.

——. *The Oregon Question: Essays in Anglo-American Diplomacy and Politics.* Cambridge, MA: Belknap Press, 1967.

Miller, Hunter. *San Juan Archipelago: Study of the Joint Occupation of San Juan Island.* Bellows Falls, VT: Printed at the Wyndham Press, 1943.

——, ed. *Treaties and Other International Acts of the United States of America.* 8 vols. Washington, DC: US Government Printing Office, 1931–1948.

Milton, Viscount. *History of the San Juan Boundary Question.* London: Cassell, Petter, and Galpin, 1869.

Milton, Viscount, and W.B. Cheadle. *The North-west Passage by Land . . . An Expedition from the Atlantic to the Pacific, Undertaken with the View of Exploring a Route across the Continent through British Territory, by One of the Northern Passes in the Rocky Mountains.* London: Cassell, Petter, and Galpin, 1865.

Minutes of the Council of Vancouver Island, 1851–1861. British Columbia Archives Memoir No. 2. Victoria, BC: BC Archives, 1918.

Moresby, Admiral John. *Two Admirals.* London: John Murray, 1909; revised edition London: Methuen and Co., 1913.

Morley, Lord John. *The Life of William Ewart Gladstone.* 3 vols. London: Macmillan, 1903.

Morrell, W.P. *Britain in the Pacific Islands.* Oxford: Clarendon Press, 1960.

——. *British Colonial Policy in the Age of Peel and Russell.* Oxford: Clarendon Press, 1930.

Morris, James. *Heaven's Command, An Imperial Progress.* New York: Harcourt Brace Jovanovich, 1971.

Morton, A.S. *A History of the Canadian West to 1870–71.* 2nd ed. Toronto: University of Toronto Press, 1973.

——. "The North West Company's Columbian Venture and David Thompson." *Canadian Historical Review,* 17 (1936): 284–88.

Morton, W.L. *The Critical Years: The Union of British North America, 1857–1873.* Toronto: McClelland and Stewart, 1964.

Murray, Keith A. *The Pig War.* Tacoma: Washington State Historical Society, 1968.

Nasatir, A.P. "International Rivalry for California and the Establishment of the British Consulate." *California Historical Society Quarterly,* 46 (March 1967): 53–70.

Nichols, Irby C. Jr. "The Russian Ukase and the Monroe Doctrine: A Re-evaluation." *Pacific Historical Review,* 36 (February 1967): 13–26.

Nicholson, George. *Vancouver Island's West Coast, 1762–1962.* Victoria, BC: Morriss Printing Company, 1962.

Nish, Ian H. *The Anglo-Japanese Alliance: The Diplomacy of Two Island Empires, 1894–1907.* London: Athlone Press, 1966.

Noble, Dennis. *The Coast Guard in the Pacific Northwest.* Washington, DC: US Coast Guard, 1988.

Norman, Francis Martin. "Martello Tower." In *China and the Pacific in H.M.S. "Tribune," 1856–60,* 246–90. London: George Allen, 1902.

"Notes on Vancouver Island." *Nautical Magazine,* 18 (June 1849): 299–302.

O'Byrne, William. *A Naval Biographical Dictionary.* London: J. Murray, 1849.

Okun, S.B. *The Russian-American Company.* Trans. C. Ginsburg. Cambridge, MA: Harvard University Press, 1951.

Oliver, E.H., ed. *The Canadian North-West: Early Development and Legislative Records.* Publication No. 9 of the Public Archives of Canada. 2 vols. Ottawa: Government Printing Bureau, 1914–1915.

Ollivier, Maurice, ed. *The Colonial and Imperial Conferences from 1887 to 1937.* 3 vols. Ottawa: Queen's Printer, 1954.

O'Neil, Marion. "The Maritime Activities of the North West Company, 1813–1821." *Washington Historical Quarterly,* 21 (October 1930): 243–67.

"Oregon and Vancouver Island." *Nautical Magazine,* 17 (October 1848): 517–23.

Ormsby, Margaret A. *British Columbia: A History.* Toronto: Macmillan, 1958.

Osborne, Lt. Sherard. "Notes Made on a Passage to the Ports of San Blas and Mazatlan, on the Coast of America." *Nautical Magazine,* 18 (March 1849): 139–45.

Palmer, William H. *Pages from a Seaman's Log: Being the First Eighteen Months of the Cruise of H.M.S. Warspite in the Pacific.* Victoria, BC: Munroe Miller, 1891.

Parizeau, Henri D. *The Development of Hydrography on the Coast of Canada since the Earliest Discoveries.* Toronto: University of Toronto Press, 1934. Reprint from Pacific Science Association, *Proceedings of the Fifth Science Congress,* vol. 2.

Parry, John Franklin. "Sketch of the History of the Naval Establishments at Esquimalt from Their Commencement until the Abolition of the Pacific Squadron in 1905 and Miscellaneous Matters Connecting British Columbia with His Majesty's Navy." Typescript of a paper read before the Natural History Society of BC, February 19, 1906; from *Victoria Daily Times,* February 20 and 21, 1906.

Patterson, E. Palmer, II. *Mission on the Nass: The Evangelization of the Nishga, 1860–1890.* Waterloo, ON: Eulachon Press, 1982.

Payette, B.C., ed. *The Oregon Country Under the Union Jack.* Montreal: Privately printed, 1961.

Pemberton, J.D. *Facts and Figures Relating to Vancouver Island and British Columbia.* London: Longman, Green, Longman and Roberts, 1860.

Penn, Geoffrey. *"Up Funnel, Down Screw!" The Story of the Naval Engineer.* London: Hollis and Carter, 1955.

Perkins, Dexter. *The Monroe Doctrine, 1823–1826.* Cambridge, MA: Harvard University Press, 1932.

Phillips, Lawrie. *Pembroke Dockyard and the Old Navy: A Bicentennial History.* Stroud, UK: History Press, 2014.

Pierce, Richard E., and John H. Winslow, eds. *H.M.S.* Sulphur *on the Northwest and California Coasts, 1837 and 1839.* Kingston, ON: Limehouse Press, 1979.

Pomeroy, Earl S. *The Pacific Slope.* New York: Knopf, 1966.

Porter, David. *Journal of a Cruise Made to the Pacific Ocean . . . in the United States Frigate "Essex" . . . 1812, 1813, and 1814.* 2 vols. Philadelphia, 1815.

Porter, Kenneth W. "The Cruise of the *Forester.*" *Washington Historical Quarterly,* 23 (1932): 262–69.

———. *John Jacob Astor, Business Man.* 2 vols. Cambridge, MA: Harvard University Press, 1931.

Pratt, Julius W. "James K. Polk and John Bull." *Canadian Historical Review,* 24 (1943): 346.

Preston, Richard A. *Canada and "Imperial Defense."* Durham, NC: Duke University Press, 1967.

Pritchard, Allan. "What's in a Name? Captain Courtenay and Vancouver Island Exploration." *British Columbia Historical News,* 37, no. 4 (Winter 2004): 3–7.

"Proceedings of H.M.S. *Sulphur* in the Pacific Ocean." *Nautical Magazine,* 7 (1838): 611–22.

Ramm, Agatha. "The Crimean War." In J.P.T. Bury, ed., *The Zenith of European Power, 1830–1870,* vol. 10 of *The New Cambridge Modern History,* 468–92. Cambridge: Cambridge University Press, 1967.

Rath, Andrew C. *The Crimean War in Imperial Context, 1854–1856.* New York: Palgrave Macmillan, 2015.

Rattray, Alex. *Vancouver Island and British Columbia: Where They Are, What They Are, and What They May Become.* London: Smith, Elder and Co., 1862.

Ravenstein, Ernest G. *The Russians on the Amur: Its Discovery, Conquest and Colonization.* London: Trubner and Co., 1861.

Rich, E.E. *The Fur Trade and the Northwest to 1857.* Toronto: McClelland and Stewart, 1967.

———. *The History of the Hudson's Bay Company, 1670–1870.* 2 vols. London: Hudson's Bay Record Society, 1958–1959.

———, ed. *The Letters of John McLoughlin from Fort Vancouver to the Governor and Committee; Third Series, 1844–46.* London: Hudson's Bay Record Society, 1944.

Richards, Captain George Henry, RN. *Vancouver Island Pilot: Sailing Directions for the Coasts of Vancouver Island and British Columbia.* London: Hydrographic Office, Admiralty, 1861.

Ritchie, George S. *The Admiralty Chart: British Naval Hydrography in the Nineteenth Century.* New ed. Edinburgh: Pentland Press, 1995.

Roberts, Joseph. "The Origins of the Esquimalt and Nanaimo Railway: A Problem in British Columbia Politics." Master's thesis, University of British Columbia, 1937.

Robinson, Leigh Burpee. *Esquimalt: "Place of Shoaling Waters."* Victoria, BC: Quality Press, 1947.

Roche, A.R. *A View of Russian America in Connection with the Present War.* Montreal, 1885.

Ronda, James P. *Astoria and Empire.* Lincoln: University of Nebraska Press, 1990.

Roosevelt, Theodore. *The Naval War of 1812.* New edition. Annapolis, MD: Naval Institute Press, 1987.

Rose, J. Holland. "Sea Power and the Winning of British Columbia." *Mariner's Mirror,* 7 (March 1921): 74–79.

Roskill, Captain S.W. *The Strategy of Sea Power: Its Development and Application.* London: Collins, 1962.

Ross, Frank E. "The Retreat of the Hudson's Bay Company in the Pacific Northwest." *Canadian Historical Review,* 18 (September 1937): 262–80.

Roy, Patricia E. *Boundless Optimism: Richard McBride's British Columbia.* Vancouver: UBC Press, 2012.

Roy, Reginald H. "The Early Militia and Defence of British Columbia, 1871–1885." *British Columbia Historical Quarterly,* 18 (1954): 1–28.

Royle, Stephen. *Company, Crown and Colony: The Hudson's Bay Company and Territorial Endeavour in Western Canada.* London: I.B. Tauris, 2011.

Russell, E.C. "The Royal Navy on the North-West Coast of America, 1837–1860." Bachelor's thesis, University of British Columbia, 1951.

Rydell, Raymond A. *Cape Horn to the Pacific, the Rise and Decline of an Ocean Highway.* Berkeley and Los Angeles: University of California Press, 1952.

Sage, Walter N. *Sir James Douglas and British Columbia.* Toronto: University of Toronto Press, 1930.

Sarty, Roger. "Canadian Maritime Defence, 1892–1914." *Canadian Historical Review,* 71 (1990): 462–90.

———. "'There Will Be Trouble in the North Pacific': The Defence of British Columbia in the Early Twentieth Century." *BC Studies,* 61 (Spring 1984): 3–29.

Schafer, Joseph, ed. "Documents Relative to Warre and Vavasour's Military Reconnoissance [*sic*] in Oregon, 1845–6." *Quarterly of the Oregon Historical Society,* 10 (March 1909): 1–99, with maps of defences attached.

———, ed. "Letters of Sir George Simpson, 1841–1843." *American Historical Review,* 14 (October 1908): 70–94.

Schefer, Christian. "La monarchie de Juilliet et l'expansion coloniale." *Revue des Deux Mondes,* 6e série, 11 (1912): 152–84.

Scholefield, Guy H. *The Pacific: Its Past and Future and the Policy of the Great Powers from the 18th Century.* London: John Murray, 1919.

Schurman, Donald M. "Esquimalt: Defence Problem, 1865–1887." *British Columbia Historical Quarterly,* 19 (1955): 57–69.

Schuyler, Robert L. "The Recall of the Legions: A Phase in the Decentralization of the British Empire." *American Historical Review,* 26 (October 1920): 18–36.

Scott, Andrew. *Encyclopedia of Raincoast Place Names: A Complete Reference to Coastal British Columbia.* Madeira Park, BC: Harbour, 2009

Seattle Historical Society. *The H.W. McCurdy Marine History of the Pacific Northwest.* Seattle, 1966.

"Secret Mission of Warre and Vavasour." *Washington Historical Quarterly,* 3 (April 1912): 131–53. [Reports of Warre and Vavasour from FO 5/440, 442, 457.]

Seemann, Berthold C. *Narrative of the Voyage of H.M.S. "Herald," 1845–51.* 2 vols. London: Reeve and Co., 1853.

Shelton, W. George, ed. *British Columbia and Confederation.* Victoria, BC: Morriss Printing for the University of Victoria, 1967.

Shiels, Archie W. *San Juan Islands: The Cronstadt of the Pacific.* Juneau, AK: Empire Printing Company, 1938.

Simpson, Sir George. *Narrative of a Journey round the World During the Years 1841 and 1842.* 2 vols. London: H. Colburn, 1847.

Slacum, William A. "Report on Oregon, 1836–7." *Oregon Historical Quarterly,* 13 (1912): 175–224.

Smith, Dorothy Blakey, ed. "The Journal of Arthur Thomas Bushby, 1858–1859." *British Columbia Historical Quarterly,* 21 (January–October 1957–1958): 83–198.

Smith, Goldwin. "Notes on the Problems of San Juan." *Pacific Northwest Quarterly,* 31 (1940): 185.

Smith, Robin Percival. *Captain McNeill and His Wife the Nishga Chief.* Surrey, BC: Hancock House, 2001.

Smith, T.T. Vernon. "Pacific Railway." *Nautical Magazine,* 31 (1861): 133–40, 201–8, 245–253.

Sprout, Harold and Margaret. *The Rise of American Naval Power, 1776–1918.* Princeton, NJ: Princeton University Press, 1939.

Stacey, C.P. *Canada and the British Army, 1846–1871.* Revised edition. Toronto: University of Toronto Press, 1963.

——. "The Hudson's Bay Company and Anglo-American Military Rivalries during the Oregon Dispute." *Canadian Historical Review,* 18 (September 1937): 281–300.

——. *The Military Problems of Canada: A Survey of Defence Policies and Strategic Conditions Past and Present.* Toronto: Ryerson Press, 1940.

——. "The Myth of the Unguarded Frontier, 1815–1871." *American Historical Review,* 56 (October 1950): 1–18.

Stanton, William. *The United States Great Exploring Expedition of 1838–1942.* Berkeley and Los Angeles: University of California Press, 1975.

Stapleton, Edward J., ed. *Some Official Correspondence of George Canning.* 2 vols. London: Longmans, Green and Co., 1887.

Stewart, Alice R. "Sir John A. Macdonald and the Imperial Defence Commission of 1879." *Canadian Historical Review,* 35 (June 1954): 119–39.

Story, D.A. "H.M. Naval Yard, Halifax in the Early Sixties." *Collections of the Nova Scotia Historical Society,* 22 (1933): 43–71.

Synge, Captain M.F. "Proposal for a Rapid Communication with the Pacific and the East, via British North America." *Journal of the Royal Geographical Society,* 22 (1852): 174–200.

Tanner, J.R., ed. *Samuel Pepys's Naval Minutes.* London: Navy Records Society, 1926.

Tansill, Charles C. *Canadian-American Relations, 1875–1911.* New Haven, CT: Yale University Press, 1943.

Tate, Merze. "British Opposition to the Cession of Pearl Harbor." *Pacific Historical Review,* 29 (November 1960): 380–94.

——. *Hawaii: Reciprocity or Annexation.* East Lansing: Michigan State University Press, 1968.

——. "Hawaii: A Symbol of Anglo-American Rapprochement." *Political Science Quarterly,* 79 (December 1964): 555–75.

——. "Twisting the Lion's Tail over Hawaii." *Pacific Historical Review,* 36 (February 1967): 27–46.

Tate, Vernon D., ed. "Spanish Documents Relating to the Voyage of the *Racoon* to Astoria and San Francisco." *Hispanic American Historical Review,* 18 (May 1938): 183–91.

Temperley, Harold W.V. *The Foreign Policy of Canning, 1822–1827.* London, 1925.

Thom, Adam. *The Claims to the Oregon Territory Considered.* London: Smith, Elder and Co., 1844.

"The Transfer of Esquimalt." *British Columbia Magazine,* 6 (November 1910): 1011–14.

Tronson, J.M. *Personal Narrative of a Voyage . . . in H.M.S. Barracouta.* London: Smith, Elder and Co., 1859.

Tucker, Gilbert N. "Canada's First Submarines, CC1 and CC2: An Episode of the Naval War in the Pacific." *British Columbia Historical Quarterly,* 7 (January 1943): 147–70.

———. "The Career of H.M.C.S. 'Rainbow.'" *British Columbia Historical Quarterly,* 7 (January 1943): 1–30.

———. *The Naval Service of Canada: Its Official History.* 2 vols. Ottawa: King's Printer, 1952.

Tunstall, W.C.B. "Imperial Defence, 1815–1870." In *Cambridge History of the British Empire* (Cambridge: Cambridge University Press, 1961), 2:807–41.

Twiss, Travers. *The Oregon Question Examined in Respect to Facts and the Law of Nations.* London: Longman, Brown, Green and Longmans, 1846.

United States. *Alaskan Boundary Tribunal Proceedings.* Senate Documents, 58th Congress, Second Session. 7 vols. Washington, DC: 1904.

———. *American State Papers, Foreign Relations.* 6 vols. Washington, DC: Gales and Seaton, 1833–1859.

———. *Official Records of the Union and Confederate Navies in the War of the Rebellion.* 30 vols. Washington, DC: Government Printing Office, 1894–1922.

Van Alstyne, Richard W., ed. "Anglo-American Relations, 1853–57." *American Historical Review,* 42 (April 1937): 491–500.

———. "Great Britain, the United States, and Hawaiian Independence, 1850–1855." *Pacific Historical Review,* 4 (1935): 15–24.

———. "International Rivalries in the Pacific Northwest." *Oregon Historical Quarterly,* 46 (1945): 185–218.

———. *The Rising American Empire.* Oxford: Basil Blackwell, 1960.

Vevier, Charles. "American Continentalism: An Idea of Expansion, 1845–1910." *American Historical Review,* 65 (January 1960): 323–35.

Vouri, Mike. *Outpost of Empire: The Royal Marines and the Joint Occupation of San Juan Island.* Seattle: Northwest Interpretive Association, 2004.

———. *The Pig War: Standoff at Griffin Bay.* Friday Harbor, WA: Griffin Bay Bookstore, 1999.

Walbran, Captain John T. *British Columbia Coast Names, 1592–1906.* Ottawa: Government Printing Bureau, 1909. (Various imprints since 1971).

Waite, P.B. *The Life and Times of Confederation, 1864–1867.* Toronto: University of Toronto Press, 1962.

Walpole, Lieut. Frederick. *Four Years in the Pacific in Her Majesty's Ship "Collingwood" from 1844 to 1848.* 2 vols. London: R. Bentley, 1849.

Ward, John M. *British Policy in the South Pacific, 1783–1893: A Study in British Policy towards the South Pacific Islands prior to the Establishment of Governments by Great Powers.* Sydney: Australasian Publishing Co., 1948.

Watson, G.C. *The Commission of H.M.S. "Amphion," Pacific Station, 1900–1904.* London: Westminster Press, 1904.

Watt, James, E.J. Freeman and W.F. Bynum, eds. *Starving Sailors: The Influence of Nutrition upon Naval and Maritime History.* Greenwich, UK: National Maritime Musem, 1981.

Watters, Reginald Eyre, ed. *British Columbia: A Centennial Anthology.* Toronto: McClelland and Stewart, 1958.

Webster, Sir Charles K. *The Foreign Policy of Castlereagh, 1812–1815.* London: G. Bell and Sons, 1931.

Wells, Samuel F. Jr. "British Strategic Withdrawal from the Western Hemisphere, 1904–1906." *Canadian Historical Review,* 49 (December 1968): 335–56.

Whittingham, Paul Bernard. *Notes on the Late Expedition against the Russian Settlements in Eastern Siberia; and of a Visit to Japan and the Shores of Tartary, and of the Sea of Okhotsk.* London: Longman, Brown, Green and Longmans, 1856.

Wilkes, Charles. *Narrative of the United States Exploring Expedition during the Years 1838, 1839, 1840, 1841, 1842.* Philadelphia: Lea and Blanchard, 1845.

——. "Report on the Territory of Oregon by Charles Wilkes, Commander of the United States Exploring Expedition, 1838–1842." *Quarterly of the Oregon Historical Society,* 12 (1911): 269–99.

Wilson, George T. *The Log of H.M.S. "Phaeton," 1900–1903.* London: Westminster Press, 1903.

Wilson, H.W. *Ironclads in Action.* London: Sampson Low and Co., 1896.

Winks, Robin W. *Canada and the United States: The Civil War Years.* Baltimore: Johns Hopkins University Press, 1960.

Wolfenden, Madge. "Esquimalt Dockyard's First Buildings." *British Columbia Historical Quarterly,* 10 (July 1946): 235–40.

Wood, Commander James. "Vancouver Island, British Columbia." *Nautical Magazine,* 27 (December 1858): 663–66.

Woodsworth, Charles J. *Canada and the Orient: A Study in International Relations.* Toronto: Macmillan, 1941.

Wright, E.W., ed. *Lewis and Dryden's Marine History of the Pacific North-West.* Portland, OR: Lewis and Dryden Printing Company, 1895.

Yonge, C.D. *The History of the British Navy.* 3 vols. London: R. Bentley, 1866.

INDEX

Also by
Barry Gough

Pax Britannica:
Ruling the Waves and Keeping the Peace before Armageddon

From Classroom to Battlefield:
Victoria High School and the First World War

The Elusive Mr. Pond:
The Soldier, Fur Trader and Explorer Who Opened the Northwest

Juan de Fuca's Strait:
Voyages in the Waterway of Forgotten Dreams

Historical Dreadnoughts:
Arthur Marder, Stephen Roskill and Battles for Naval History

Fortune's a River:
The Collision of Empires in Northwest America

Fighting Sail on Lake Huron and Georgian Bay:
The War of 1812 and its Aftermath

HMCS Haida:
Battle Ensign Flying

Gunboat Frontier:
British Maritime Authority and Northwest Coast Indians, 1846–1890

The Northwest Coast:
British Navigation, Trade, and Discoveries to 1812

The Royal Navy and the Northwest Coast of North America, 1810–1914:
A Study of British Maritime Ascendancy